Race and representation

To the memory of my uncle, Braham Dev Saggar (1932–89)

Race and representation

Electoral politics and ethnic pluralism in Britain

Shamit Saggar

MANCHESTER UNIVERSITY PRESS

MANCHESTER AND NEW YORK

Copyright © Shamit Saggar 2000

The right of Shamit Saggar to be identified as the author of this work has been asserted by him in accordance with the Copyright, Designs and Patents Act 1988.

Published by Manchester University Press
Oxford Road, Manchester M13 9NR, UK
and Room 400, 175 Fifth Avenue, New York, NY 10010, USA
www.manchesteruniversitypress.co.uk

Distributed exclusively in the USA by
Palgrave, 175 Fifth Avenue, New York NY 10010, USA

Distributed exclusively in Canada by
UBC Press, University of British Columbia, 2029 West Mall,
Vancouver, BC, Canada V6T 1Z2

British Library Cataloguing-in-Publication Data
A catalogue record for this book is available from the British Library

Library of Congress Cataloging-in-Publication Data
A catalog record for this book is available from the Library of Congress

ISBN 13: 978 0 7190 80395

First published in hardback 2000 by Manchester University Press
This paperback edition first published 2009

Printed by Lightning Source

Contents

List of tables	*page*	vi
Convention on terminology		viii
Foreword by Baroness Prashar of Runnymede		ix
Preface		xi
Acknowledgements		xv
1	Introduction	1
2	Framing conceptual and theoretical questions	26
3	Ethnic minorities as a political constituency	59
4	Electoral engagement	89
5	Party choice and partisanship	120
6	Issues and attitudes	148
7	Race card politics	175
8	Candidates and representatives	203
9	British racial and electoral politics in transformation	221
Methodological appendix		242
References		249
Index		262

List of tables

2.1	Most significant issue among Asian voters, 1991	*page* 31
2.2	Most important issues (of two) by ethnic group, 1987 general election	33
2.3	Levels of Labour and Conservative support among ethnic minorities, 1974, 1979, 1983, 1987, 1992, 1997	42
2.4	Voting intention by social class, 1979 and 1992	49
2.5	Treatment of non-whites by authorities, 1991	52
3.1	Voting likelihood among ethnic minorities registered to vote, 1983	68
3.2	Attitudes towards Asian and black parliamentary candidates, 1991	73
3.3	Trust and Asian interests, 1997	78
4.1	Breakdown of ethnic origin of UK resident population, 1991	94
4.2	Citizenship by ethnic group, 1997	97
4.3	Electoral registration by ethnic group, 1997	100
4.4	Turn out by ethnic group, 1997	103
4.5	Verified electoral registration by age group and ethnic group, 1997	107
4.6	Turn out by age group and ethnic group, 1997	107
4.7	Reasons for voting abstention by ethnic group, 1997	109
4.8	Reasons for voting by ethnic group, 1997	110
4.9	Political impotence sentiment by ethnic group, 1997	111
4.10	Turn out among men and women by ethnic group, 1997	112
4.11	Registration by class and ethnic group, 1997	114
4.12	Turn out by class and ethnic group, 1997	115
5.1	Labour and Conservative support among ethnic minority voters, 1974–97	122
5.2	Asian and black voting choice, 1997	125
5.3	Asian and black (intended) voting choice (MORI surveys 1996–97)	126
5.4	Vote distribution by ethnic group, 1997	129
5.5	Ethnic minority group source of parties' vote, 1997	132
5.6	Ethnicity, social class and Labour vote, 1997	135
5.7	Voting intentions among different ethnic groups by class, 1979	136

5.8	Logistic multilevel model of Labour voting, 1997	142
6.1	Ethnic minority attitudes and aspects of ethnic pluralism (extent of racial prejudice), 1997	162
6.2	Ethnic minority attitudes and aspects of ethnic pluralism (efficacy of anti-discrimination law), 1997	163
6.3	Ethnic minority attitudes and aspects of ethnic pluralism (tolerance of separate dress codes), 1997	163
6.4	Value of non-white immigration, 1997	168
6.5	Attitudes toward customs and traditions of immigrants, 1997	169
6.6	Positive discrimination in employment, 1997	170
6.7	Government spending to tackle poverty, 1997	171
6.8	Criminal sentencing policy, 1997	172
6.9	Equal opportunities for women, 1997	173
7.1	Public anti-immigrant sentiment within the EU, 1997	184
7.2	Political parties' perceived concern for blacks and Asians, 1997	187
7.3	Value of immigration among whites by generation, 1997	194
7.4	Britain learning from other countries, 1997	197
7.5	Extent of racial prejudice, blacks and Asians, 1997	200
7.6	Views of the Conservative and Labour Parties' positions on equal opportunities, blacks and Asians, 1997	201
7.7	Perceptions of party campaigns to attract racially prejudiced voters, blacks and Asians, 1997	202
8.1	Attitudes toward increased ethnic minority parliamentary representation, 1997	213
8.2	Attitudes toward a separate political party, 1997	216
	Response rates attained in different stages of the ethnic minority booster sample, BES cross-section survey, 1997	247

Convention on terminology

The term 'ethnic minority' is used throughout this book to denote people of South Asian, African and Caribbean origin. It is used more or less interchangeably with the term 'minority' and the common expression 'black and Asian'. On occasion, this convention involves reference to 'Afro-Caribbean' people, a term in wide circulation in research until quite recently, though now superseded by black African and black Caribbean. Use of these key terms as broad, umbrella labels is deliberate in order to capture the wide diversity found among black and Asian ethnic groups in contemporary Britain. Departures from this convention are clearly signalled where greater precision is required in individual chapters and sub-sections to focus upon particular component groups.

The study's principal focus was geared to five main components of the ethnic minority population: Indians; Pakistanis; Bangladeshis; black Africans; and black Caribbeans. These groups represent the largest and most recognisable ethnic minority sub-groups in Britain. Consequently, there was a deliberate attempt not to tap the political behaviour or attitudes of other minority ethnic groups, such as those of the south east Asian, Chinese and the Irish communities. The research methodology also included a sixth non-white category, described as 'Miscellaneous' throughout the book. It is likely that some of these groups fell into this category alongside some respondents of Mediterranean and Middle Eastern origin. The lack of agreed standardisation as to which minorities fall into this category and which do not, means that it cannot be treated as reliable for research interpretation purposes. Although the BES research did not formally extend to these less prominent groups, Chapter 8, on parliamentary candidacies in 1997, includes reference to Chinese and Indo-Chinese origin candidates. Inclusion of some or all of these additional minority groups must rank as an important area for future research in this field.

There is, inevitably, considerable debate and disagreement on the question of race and ethnicity and nomenclature. This book seeks to offer some fresh empirical insights into this debate, not least in terms of drawing attention to lines of inter-ethnic and intra-ethnic difference and commonality. That said, readers are reminded that no specific political or sociological inference should be drawn from the use made in this book of the above convention on terminology.

Disclaimer: The views and interpretations expressed in this book are those of the author and not necessarily those of the sponsors, the Economic and Social Research Council and the Commission for Racial Equality.

Foreword

Engagement and participation by ethnic minorities in the political process is perceived as an important activity by all concerned. Ethnic minorities see involvement and participation as a way of influencing those areas of actvity which impact upon their lives, such as housing, employment, discrimination, etc. Political parties see it as a way of increasing their support and gaining political leverage, particularly in those constituencies where there is a large concentration of ehtnic minorities. Those concerned with 'promoting good race relations' and involved with public policy see it as a way of ensuring that ethnic minorities are an integral part of society, articulating their aspirations though legitimate democratic processes. Consequently, the involvement of ethnic minorities in the political system has attracted much attention over the last four decades.

However, the main focus of the debate has been about levels of participation, the electoral muscle of ethnic minorities, that is, 'voting power' and 'ethnic marginals'. Various initiatives which have been developed by political parties to engage ethnic minorities into the political process have been characterised by ambivalence. Ethnic minority participation has either been overlooked where it did not matter or embraced on the basis of self-interest or for tactical considerations.

Similarly the academic and the research community have concentrated on evaluating levels of participation, political leverage and the degree to which ethnicity shapes political participation and action. Moreover, most of the research to date has assumed that ethnicity is one of the main factors in political engagement. While concentration on these areas is understandable, the consequence of this has been that the complex and subtle interplay of different factors, such as class, geographical location, ethnicity, socio-economic considerations and comparison with the participation of white counterparts have been overlooked.

Often simplistic and narrow views are taken and everything is seen in terms of race and ethnicity. There has been paucity of broader analysis. Consequently, there is lack of understanding and knowledge of all the factors at play and the ensuing debate has been limited.

Race and representation has sought to provide fresh insight into the involvement of ethnic minirities in the political process. Its analysis is about unpacking the claim that ethnicity has created or is at least associated with a political cleavage in British electoral behaviour and political attitudes. Unlike other studies it has compared the voting behaviour of ethnic minorities with their white counterparts. It has gone beyond some of the earlier studies and examined the levels of ethnic minority participation and attitudes of ethnic minorities towards the democratic process and how far those attitudes correlate with their participation. It has established how ethnic minorities differ from each other and the white population taking into account their socio-economic profiles. It has highlighted the complex interplay of race and class.

It also throws light on the degree to which ethnic minorities are influenced in their political attitudes and behaviour by considerations that distinguish them from their white counterparts, that is, political difference, its consequences and causes, and how ehtnicity impacts on political outlook and action.

It all, this study should improve considerably our understanding of the political attitudes of ethnic minorities and their electoral behaviour within a broader context. Furthermore, analysis in this study should facilitate a more meaningful and mature debate about ethnic pluralism and not just ethnicity.

In the final chapter, Dr Saggar has discussed some of the broader challenges, opportunities and dilemmas which this study has raised. He states, 'Ethnicity, therefore, counts though without any serious suggestion that it does so in any fundamental way. The real point of debate, then, is the question of how far political initiatives respond to this picture by attempting to aggregate and then articulate the political interests of ethnic minorities'. What is evident from this study is the fact that simple targeting of ethnic minorities is not the answer if we are serious about ethnic pluralism and social inclusion.

The complexity and the subtlety of voting patterns and electoral behaviour revealed by this study will, I hope, lead to an informed debate *and* to more sophisticated practical action by political institutions.

Electoral behaviour is an important indicator of engagement or otherwise of ethnic minorities in society. It is an indication of how they use the electoral system to influence, to register dissent or alienation. This study has highlighted some important issues and its findings should be widely disseminated and discussed because these findings are not just important in relation to political participation, they are equally pertinent for discussion in the area of public policy where similar dilemmas and challenges exist. Social research of this nature, in my view, would be equally revealing in public policy debates where there are tensions between race and ethnicity, on the one hand, and ethnic pluralism and diversity, on the other. In all this book should be widely welcomed for helping to unpack a much broader set of issues and enabling a more meaningful debate.

Baroness (Usha) Prashar of Runnymede

Preface

The integration of Britain's black and Asian ethnic minorities into the mainstream democratic process is the subject of a large amount of legitimate interest. It is a theme that has regularly punctuated the system of party competition and, on occasion, has even be described in terms of the underlying stability and credibility of the country's political institutions. For a long time, academics, politicians, journalists and other commentators have observed what appear to be unusual electoral allegiances between ethnic minority voters, on the one hand, and the major parties, on the other. However, beneath this headline story there can be discerned another concern, namely to ask whether these ethnic minority electors are affected to the same degree by the factors that are associated with and appear to drive political differences among the white electorate. Without doubt, ethnicity appears at first glance to be the central factor that separates the political behaviour and attitudes of voters in Britain. What has been less easy to judge has been how far ethnicity represents a major, stand-alone type of cleavage in British electoral politics. It is the central puzzle that is the intellectual agenda for this book.

The theme of this book has undoubtedly risen in prominence since the 1970s both within and beyond academia. Formal academic research on the political participation of Britain's ethnic minorities began in earnest in the mid-1970s with the launch of the Community Relations Commission survey-based inquiry based on the autumn 1974 general election. Prior to that a few partial snapshots had been gathered on the general theme, though empirical accounts that were generally based on local participation. Indeed, the author's doctoral supervisor recounts the tale of the early exit poll-type studies conducted outside damp, miserable polling stations in Bradford in the early 1960s. The initial breakthrough for such analyses presumably came in the aftermath of the first CRC report. In particular, the unusual climate produced by a wafer-thin parliamentary majority following the October 1974 general election, coupled with an unexpected national result in February 1974, contributed to the rapid development of a coherent political agenda devoted to evaluating racial politics. Party strategists, press commentators and others were briefed on this situation in readiness for arguments that began to formalise the question of to what degree, if any, an 'ethnic vote' existed in British electoral politics. An important subsidiary interest lay clearly in the ways in which such an ethnic group vote could be identified and hopefully mobilised. The upshot, in other words, was that interest in black and Asian voters originally stemmed from a greater willingness by political parties to appeal to this newly discovered electorate.

The rest should not be seen in simplistic or superficial terms, but a lot of subsequent research in this area has tended to follow a predictable path. It is apparent that this initial development was an important turning point for researchers interested in ethnic minority politics. In its wake the research volume of empirical research on the topic grew rapidly, many elements of which are reported in the substantive part of this study. However, the biggest intellectual lacuna created by this growth industry of research and comment has been the systematic failure to tackle the question of how far, and in what ways, ethnic minority voting patterns and political involvement can be understood through the prism of collective identity – to say nothing of the more complex notion of collective interest. Scholars have disagreed fundamentally on these core questions. Indeed, the underlying conceptual issue has been about the notion of corporate interests attached to a discrete group of voters. This, in turn, has tended to define the heart of the theoretical debate over the politics of race and ethnicity in Britain. Many of the patterns uncovered by researchers have pointed in the general direction of ethnic collectivity as the basis of common political behaviour and attitudes. The difficulty that this has spawned is not in being so linked to such a pattern, but rather the issue of how far circumstantial factors, unrelated to ethnic group, have driven distinctive patterns of political participation, to say nothing of political thinking. The challenge has been to put real flesh on the bones of an ethnically-related theory of political behaviour and thought. It is this task that characterises the long-term target of the book.

The challenge is one that is tackled from a range of approaches that are designed to lock together. To begin with, it was vital to bring forward research evidence that genuinely examines ethnic minority political participation alongside that of their white counterparts. This in turn, propelled the study in a particular methodological direction, and these mainly were addressed using a framework that both borrowed from earlier social research experience and also contained some fresh departures. Additionally, the empirical side of the study is one that is painted on a theoretical canvass that sets out the possibilities for thinking conceptually about ethnic minority political distinctiveness. A wide range of theoretical perspectives can be identified and it is important that understanding of fresh research data – whether advanced in this study or another – should be subjected to the rigorous tests thrown up by this discussion. Some of the early chapters are particularly aimed at prosecuting this demand and also designed to have a resonance in further research by others on this theme. The research also makes efforts to throw light on those areas in which ethnic group membership either fails to divide or else does so along lines that are not fully appreciated in political circles. Thus, it is clear that divisions of attitude and behaviour are found within the ethnic minority groups examined in the study. These are important to reflect on for the signals they contain about the influence of ethnicity alongside other social factors in shaping political outlook and action. The upshot is that the study not only presents new findings on aspects of difference across ethnic groups but also tries to relate this knowledge to understanding of intra-ethnic group politics. This is a subtle and seemingly complex relationship that often raises as many questions as it resolves. Finally, as mentioned previously, the study's unifying theme is the thesis of the political integration of black and Asian Britons.

Developing a research strategy based on such an approach is far more difficult than might at first appear to be the case. For one thing, there is an immediate need for greater clarification of the kind of formal indicators that are to be used to gauge political integration. The study adopts a multi-pronged approach, whereby evidence is gathered from areas such as electoral involvement, party support and affiliation, the influence of social class upon party vote, and, of course, characterisation of political attitudes on putatively 'ethnic' and 'non-ethnic' concerns. Added together, the study is able to put forward the argument that signs of such political integration are unmistakable in certain crucial areas, but that a large gap persists in attempts to generalise across ethnic minorities as a whole. This twin message is useful, not least because it points to the influence among ethnic minorities of the sources of political similarity and difference found among white voters. However, as these sources appear to have a much greater impact among some minority groups than others, and in respect to certain issues and propositions than others, it is apparent that a single, unifying thesis remains beyond reach. Indeed, the study indicates elements of growing convergence alongside greater divergence, and it is this type of pattern that is the subject of generalisation. How systematic and reinforcing such patterns are is obviously difficult to know, especially in relation to the realm of democratic politics in which inter-ethnic comparative research has been limited.

One further purpose of the study was to stimulate fresh research and debate on the subject of the political participation of ethnic minorities. The call of other researchers and commentators for new and innovative empirical data was heard clearly, and hopefully the study has managed to cover some ground towards this goal. However, the wider debate over democratic inclusion remains the principal target of the empirical leg of the research and its deployment within the discipline. This debate has tended to remain curiously constrained in Britain, with most attention falling on the superficially large difference in voting patterns between ethnic minorities and whites. Little has been asked systematically about the causal relationships underpinning this picture and certainly electoral research has been disturbingly silent on this point. It has long been hinted at that circumstantial factors linked to social background have played a part in the picture as it appears. However, even here, British political science debate has concluded, almost by default, that race and ethnicity has trumped class in accounting for, among other things, voting preference. How far this slogan can be said to be credible is a moot point, and one that this study seeks open up to wider investigation. If the findings and interpretations of this study can help to clarify this debate, or provide tangible answers to some of the questions raised, then the author will consider it a job well done.

Acknowledgements

This book has inevitably benefited from the efforts of a large number of people. Before they can be thanked individually, it is necessary to acknowledge the financial support given to the research from the Economic and Social Research Council (grant number R-000-222-123) and the Commission for Racial Equality. Both of these bodies provided the financial backing to carry out the Ethnic Minority Election Study project as an integral part of the 1997 British Election Study.

I owe a large debt to Pippa Norris for her encouragement in getting the ethnic minority booster project off the ground. Our discussion on this idea first began in 1993 and a year later we had hatched a tentative plan to pursue the idea through to a formal proposal. Her input was again timely during 1996 when the research grant application was prepared. Pippa's comments on a number of publications of mine around the 1997 general election were especially useful in fine-tuning some of the arguments pursued in this book. The initial research strategy also benefited from the timely input of John Curtice and Roger Jowell (both senior members of the Centre for Social and Electoral Trends consortium). However, the biggest intellectual debt that I owe is to Anthony Heath for his extensive collaboration throughout this project. Anthony became quickly convinced of the breakthrough that could be achieved through our strategy of working within and adopting, the 1997 BES format and he was most helpful in trying to identify the major debating points upon which our work needed to concentrate. Furthermore, Anthony and I plainly shared a number of instincts regarding the questions that our research could best answer and how we might approach these debates through published research. Chapter 5 of this book has benefited in particular from our collaboration on a related publication. He has been a fine colleague to work with and I hope that our scholarship will hit some of the markers that we had in sight at the start.

In addition, the research upon which this book is based has been refined by the comments, both formal and informal, of a number of others: David Sanders, Tony Messina, Zig Layton-Henry, Andrew Geddes, John Crowley, Marco Martiniello, Joni Lovenduski, Richard Wyn Jones, David Butler, Usha Prashar, Peter Kellner, Satnam Virdee, Khozem Merchant, Simon Woolley and Colin Hann. I am indebted to them all for the time and thought they have given to my work. A special word of gratitude goes to Katarina Thomson (of the National Centre for Social Research) for her assistance in fieldwork methodological queries and in turning the BES cross-section data into a usable form. She also assisted in drafting the contents of the methodological appendix of this book. The early input of Alison Park and Lindsay Brook at NCSR is also acknowledged. Back at base, I am grateful for the support and encouragement given by colleagues in the Department of Politics at Queen Mary and Westfield College, and especially Ken Young, Wayne Parsons and Anne Kershen. Jasmin

Salucideen, as ever, proved instrumental in filtering my numerous commitments both within and beyond College to a manageable level.

I would also like to thank Nicola Viinikka, Pippa Kenyon, Tony Mason and Rachel Armstrong at Manchester University Press for their support and understanding in getting the book out into the market.

I am grateful to Taylor and Francis Publishers for allowing me to use parts of an earlier UCL Press publication as the basis for Chapter 2 of this book.

I am also grateful to Baroness (Peta) Buscombe for allowing me to cite some informal comments made by her at a private engagement held at the London Business School in autumn 1999.

All of my academic work serves not only as a formal record of achievement, but also embodies the quite considerable moral support provided by my family. My greatest thanks goes, as ever, to my father, Krishan D. Saggar, who has consistently given me an emotional backing that has allowed me to achieve many of my ambitions. In addition, his younger brother and my uncle, Devinder K. Saggar, has despite the large physical distance between us been a steady source of inspiration to my work. A special and affectionate thank you is owed to my wife, Rita Alfred, not merely for her enduring patience but also for her ability to halt my many obsessive intellectual tendencies in their tracks. This is no mean achievement. Finally, there are our two beautiful daughters, Shelley and Shaan (five and one, respectively at the time of writing), who have been the real engines of fun, laughter and love in our home. With their regular distractions, this book has been much delayed; however, it has been a delay that has been more than worth it and has reminded me of the constant need to keep matters in perspective.

As the old saying goes, the rest is through my efforts and failings. I have personally spent a decade and a half thinking, researching and writing about racial and ethnic politics in our country. As regular readers of my work will recognise, I have long believed that some of the most critical debates within this theme have remained poorly developed in formal scholarship. The need to integrate our understanding of racial and ethnic politics with knowledge about the British democratic tradition has been a particular concern of mine. If this book can nudge academic and real world interest in these directions, I will consider my work immensely worthwhile and personally successful.

Shamit Saggar
London

1

Introduction

Opening remarks

The involvement of three million ethnic minority[1] people in Britain's political system has been the subject of recurring and extensive debate. Starting from a sluggish base in the 1950s and 1960s, ethnic minority political participation has quickly gained momentum. Early stabs at researching empirically the extent of participation in national and local elections revealed a determination by many minority groups to try to use the potential of democratic politics in order to gain influence and tackle discriminatory barriers in jobs, housing and elsewhere. Furthermore, the realm of democratic politics has frequently been held up by political leaders and insiders as a legitimate and symbolic outlet for ethnic minority aspirations to be involved in the mainstream of British society. Of course, it is a moot point at to whether this vision has been the tacit basis for the emergence of racial politics in an institutional sense. Critics of Britain's emphasis on the politics of race have frequently argued that the unintended outcome has been to codify ethnic group membership as the basic building blocks of democratic action. This result may be exaggerated, but is anyway to be regretted because of the tendency to overlook the possibility of shared political characteristics across white and ethnic minority voters. Whatever the truth of this, Britain nevertheless exhibits levels and forms of ethnic minority political mobilisation that are largely unheard of across continental Europe. In some eyes, the British example is seen as reminiscent of US thinking and practice by which racial categories not only matter in politics but to a great degree appear to define the political process.

The British picture, at first glance, tends to stand out within the European context, for two main reasons. First, the widespread assumption of full political rights by post-war immigrants, at the point of entry or shortly thereafter, has served to guide minority political participation debates in a particular direction (Layton-Henry, 1992: 100). To be sure, Britain has not been characterised by any overt political disputes concerning the granting or extension (or possible removal) of political rights in the same way as France or Germany (Gouldbourne, 1998a: 61). This background has meant that, among other things, academic and non-academic interest has quickly focused on the question of the representativeness and responsiveness of the electoral process and the party system (a point amply summarised by Messina, 1998). Secondly, in Britain there has been an established tradition among political actors, academic researchers and other commentators of measuring ethnic minority political participation in order to gauge both political and non-political forms of integration. Indeed, political participation debates have not been viewed as especially unusual or detached from a number of broader questions relating to social integration and ethnic pluralism (Prashar, 1999). Managing the politics of ethnic diversity has necessarily involved both the use and evaluation of the democratic process of which electoral politics has been a prominent feature. The centrality of the electoral dimension on the canvass of democratic participation has been the subject of debate and divergent viewpoints (Shukra, 1998b: 10–26). That said, political participation has led to many associated dilemmas in an emergent multicultural society such as Britain. In many ways, the political participation of ethnic minorities has been both the tool and the subject of analysis.

The task of measuring mainstream political participation has been anything but straightforward, principally because of an unsatisfactory division of labour among researchers, who have often been involved in studying different aspects of minority politics. Framing such measurement correctly (and, hopefully, increasing precision as well) involves at least three inter-related questions. First, studies have been devoted to important methodological and conceptual matters to do with how, and how not, to study minority political participation (see, for instance, Studlar, 1983; FitzGerald, 1985b, for two earlier attempts to frame these concerns). This continues to be a vexed question despite almost three decades of national surveys on the topic, and this book addresses these points by outlining the rationale for its own development of survey and measurement techniques and the evidence produced therein.

Secondly, scholars have debated extensively the question of how best to interpret the broad structural characteristics of ethnic minority political participation. One recurring theme has been the relationship between mainstream electoral and other channels of participation (see, for instance, Werbner and Anwar, 1991; Josephedes, 1990; Small, 1994). This theme is considered more extensively within this book, but at this point it is sufficient to recall that perhaps inevitably the lion's share of attention has been devoted to electoral questions. Ballot box politics has contained an attraction for scholars – and others – who have collectively addressed themselves to several underlying sub-themes. The most prominent of these, as this book goes on to explore, has been to assess why minority patterns of participation and partisanship look as they do. A number of quite striking patterns have been discernible from earlier evidence and are examined in considerable detail – through comparison with the current data featured in this book. The task in this regard often seems to revolve around the question of whether notions of ethnic-based association, identity and interest can account sufficiently for distinctive lines of political thinking and behaviour. In short, academic research and commentary has, often unwittingly, been focused on the degree to which ethnicity fundamentally shapes political outlook and action. While behavioural patterns that are found among ethnic minority groups appear to vary considerably from those that are found among their white counterparts, it is not clear whether these differences are attributable to circumstantial factors to do with the social, economic, generational and geographical location of minorities in Britain. If, as is widely suggested, ethnicity counts in mainstream British politics, two interlinked questions remain: in what sense, and to what extent, does it matter?

Thirdly, it is fairly obvious that the driving force behind interest in minority political participation has been an attempt to evaluate the political leverage of ethnic minorities. One clear example of this approach has been the ethnic bloc vote argument, so familiar in British election campaigns. This viewpoint is sometimes articulated in relation to specific minority communities but more usually in respect to ethnic minorities as a whole (Anwar, 1994). Different indices of political leverage have been put forward over the years, but the most visible – though not necessarily the most important – have developed a calculus of the electoral muscle of minorities, most commonly based at the constituency level (an early attempt at which was made by Crewe, 1983). The evidence supporting and detracting from these arguments is dealt with in this book. At this point, however, it is useful to our purpose to stop and examine just how influential this literature has been in shaping the broad agenda of electoral-based research on minority participation.

Conventional views and counter perspectives

Within the extant literature on ethnic minority electoral participation it is reasonably easy to spot something of a conventional view of minority electoral strength. This school, although increasingly dated, holds that ethnic minorities in Britain have been relatively weak, isolated and divided on the country's electoral landscape (Crewe, 1983; Studlar, 1986; McAllister and Studlar, 1984; Studlar and Layton-Henry, 1990). Not surprisingly, this has been a challenging and sometimes unpopular assessment, frequently made in the face of growing political ambition on the part of new waves of minority political leadership (Anwar, 1998; Gouldbourne, 1998b; Azim, 1996). However, this perspective has been rooted in consideration of a number of fundamental features of the British electoral context. The long running resilience of these fundamental features within British thinking towards democratic representation remains rather less certain. Catt (1999), for instance, has recently suggested that the so-called politics of presence can be associated with a much wider range of representative outputs than has been usually assumed by commentators.

At the top of the list of such fundamentals has been the issue of numbers. In the mid-1980s it was said that there were too few to matter, given the obvious constraining influence of electoral power as a function of sheer numbers of voters in a single-member, first-past-the-post electoral system (Curtice, 1983). Added together, black and Asian ethnic minority numbers then were estimated to be below 3 per cent of the electorate, rising to around 4 per cent at century's end (Crewe, 1983). Current calculations based on rather different enumeration conventions suggest that these totals have been and remain, for the moment, not far wrong.[2] Deeper exploration of the calculus behind the electoral muscle thesis is reserved for later in the book. In the meantime, it is not difficult to see the basic point: comparable debates over electoral strength in the US take place in a sharply different demographic context, whereby black, African-Americans alone constitute greater than one-tenth (and comparative newcomers such as Asian-Americans make up 4 per cent) of the electorate (see Marable, 1995: 55–72; Perry, 1992; Espiritu and Omi, 2000; Ong, 2000). British claims about ethno-electoral muscle are necessarily curbed as a consequence of this numeric reality.[3] Not surprisingly, a second line of interest has focused on the geographic clustering of minority residential patterns. However, adherents to the conventional viewpoint have pointed out that these concentrations, though potentially valuable in principle, tend to be in already safely-held seats (usually Labour) and are thus far removed from the geographic heart of party strategy in marginal seats.

A further building block of this school of thought has tried, with some success, to make capital out of minority voters' strong bias towards the Labour Party (Saggar, 1999). Far from endearing the party to the interests of its ethnic minority supporters, however perceived, this relationship, has according to critics proven to be a turbulent one characterised by on-going mutual distrust and recrimination. Labour, the argument goes, has neglected this constituency of voters, partly because it has felt that it can risk doing so (the actual evidence of risk being quite small), and partly because of the failure by minorities to follow an alternative electoral path (few have tried at all). A picture of contemptuous marginalisation has resulted, reinforcing the poverty of the electoral muscle argument. Not all commentators have endorsed this critical position, however, and some have stressed that Labour's reputation needs to be viewed in a more realistic light with few, if any, viable alternatives on offer: 'The interests and influence of ethnic minorities as a collective political constituency are to an unprecedented degree now structurally embedded in the Labour Party and its policies' (Messina, 1998: 66).

Finally, the conventional view has dwelt on figures that indicate that significant problems continue to exist in the registration and turn out rates of some groups of would-be ethnic minority electors. These gaps only served to weaken further the potential for electoral leverage, not least because doubts persisted as to whether such deficiencies were fully explicable in socio-economic circumstantial terms (Saggar and Heath, 1999). Coming on top of demographic evidence showing the younger age profile of minorities (thus rendering many too young to vote), the upshot of the argument was clear: a participation deficit would need to be closed before any plausible assertions could be made about the wielding and targeting of hypothetical electoral power. The conclusion drawn by the conventional school was that the chances of substantial electoral influence were discounted in a political system that contained precious few prizes (Crewe, 1983). This in turn had obvious gloomy implications for the politics of patronage and the distribution of electoral spoils where the potential electoral muscle of minorities was thought to count minimally.

The main response to this argument has been a counter perspective that for our purposes can be described as the 'ethnicity counts' school of thought. It should be noted at the outset that a large slice of this perspective is not strictly involved in taking the opposite position to that of the conventional school on questions of the structural features of the electoral process and the minority electorate. Instead, its champions have been interested primarily in advancing the case for collective, common interest among minority communities in Britain. Such a case cannot avoid a normative element. Moreover, this counter school accepts elements of the position taken by the orthodox school, namely the characterisation of ethnic minority interests as marginal to party strategists (Sewell, 1993; Shukra, 1998a; Jacobs, 1986). This is accounted for not so much in terms of rational party strategy but as the result of racial exclusion and hostility from white-dominated political institutions (TUC, 1999). This notion of exclusion and distance is backed up graphically by extensive attitudinal evidence, for instance, that gathered by Whiteley *et al.* (1994) of Conservative Party members. These hostile and exclusionary attitudes must inevitably create enormous barriers to minority participation at all levels within and surrounding the party. However, the reality of historic hostility towards minority participation within all political parties is a point freely conceded by both sides of the 'ethnicity counts' debate. The point that appears to divide these schools is not so much the marginalisation of minority participation and interests but rather the reasons behind party activists' and managers' capacity to deviate from this dictum (Norris *et al.*, 1992).

The 'ethnicity counts' argument hangs centrally on the idea of an ethnically-based way of explaining political thought and action. Thus, ethnic minority voting behaviour is approached in terms of a model of ethnic voting which implies a vast sub-text on uniform ethnic group swing, the influence of so-called 'ethnic issues' and the en bloc mobilisation of voters. The evidence to back up this sub-text is patchy to say the least. However, the model is also couched in the language of the potential behaviour of minority voters and, therefore, attaches great weight to minority group socialisation and capacity-building efforts. For instance, the growth of Asian minority community-based organisations is seen as a sign of an underlying trajectory in the potential for ethnic-based voting to take off (Samad, 1996; Azim, 1996; Lyon and West, 1995; Eade, 1989). Ethnic minorities, it is contended, are beginning to perceive political mobilisation through the lens of ethnic solidarity and, therefore, voting campaigns built around this base are thought to be a natural and fairly imminent possibility. At the local level there have been some solid signs to support this line of argument. For example, in the 1997 general election few are likely to forget quickly the very real impact of such ethnic voting campaigns in constituencies such as Bethnal Green and Bow in London's East End[4] (Saggar, 1997b). However, these cases tend to be fairly rare. The question that matters is whether they symbolise an unfolding pattern that is ascendant in the world of minority electoral participation or merely uncharacteristic blips that can be easily ignored (Geddes, 2000). In any case, the counter school stresses the former, chiefly because these incidents provide clear grounds for theories of ethnically-based electoral mobilisation. The fact that they are sporadic is the inevitable result of a stable yet overbearing party system that accentuates the two-party system as a way of thinking about and behaving politically in the electoral arena.

Ethnically-driven strategies to deliver tangible rewards remain a distinct and potentially powerful option. Political opportunity, it is claimed, requires the presence of additional factors to buttress this option, and the most powerful of these is the dispute over the nature of overtly defined ethnic issues or concerns. These are by no means rare or easily glossed over in the more heated world of local politics where various 'who-get-what' types of questions are often framed in terms of community identities (Ranger et al., 1996). For this reason, the counter school has been most influential in relation to the literature on sub-national politics. It is a thesis that is not necessarily undermined by the seeming lack of evidence at national level. The structural limitations of national party and electoral systems are only impediments to the extent that ethnic identity and loyalty continues to be a fairly odd, or at least unfamiliar, way for researchers to look at the map of voting behaviour.[5] Odd, but not entirely dismissable, one might add because this has led to a general acceptance that social class and related factors cut little ice in explaining the continuing skewed party allegiances of minority voters: 'The political behaviour of blacks is not to be explained by their class situation. They are much more inclined to the Labour Party than white voters in similar class situations, housing, local milieux, and so on. Perception of group interest or processes of group identification are more plausible' (Heath *et al.*, 1991: 113).

The 'ethnicity counts' perspective, therefore, rests on the processes of group membership being linked, perhaps equated, with group identification and interest. This is a central point of dispute between conventional and counter school enthusiasts, not least because it goes somewhat farther than trying to flesh out any distinctive theory of ethnically-linked political participation. In fact, this point leads to the setting for an even larger debate, namely over the long-term political integration of Britain's ethnic minorities. Political integration, as we shall see, is a concept that can be conceptualised narrowly as well as broadly. The next section discusses political integration and its relationship to the debate outlined so far and in connection with the objectives of this study.

Participation and political integration placed in context

Social and political exclusion has emerged as a powerful and widely recognised paradigm through which race relations in Britain are viewed and understood. Taking care not to overdo the degree to which such a concept drives racial politics, it is nevertheless striking that so many commentators and studies have ended up concluding that fairly wide, unaccounted disparities characterise white and ethnic minority political life. In particular, the focus has tended to be on ethnicity as a major new shaping influence in the political thinking and actions of specific minorities. Indeed, several previous studies have begun to ask (and this study returns to consider) the degree to which ethnicity is a permanent, stand-alone cleavage in British politics. Analysis of electoral behaviour is a prime tool with which to address this hypothesis and this study aims to supply a more definitive answer than has been previously researched and published.

However, notions of ethnically-based, or even related, forms of political exclusion require a more rigorous examination of the nature and sources of political difference. Opinion may be divided on the racial exclusion paradigm, but it is necessary to be able to say something about how to judge similarities and dissimilarities in group-level behaviour. For this reason, in assessing such a paradigm, proponents of the argument are obliged to scan the wider picture of electoral participation in order to develop a measure of electoral integration (Blackstone *et al.*, 1998). The intellectual launch point of this book is, therefore, to provide an up to date examination of the degree to which Britain ethnic minorities are integrated into the mainstream electoral process. This does not mean just looking at inclusion (i.e. participation) within voting but also at whether circumstantial or other factors best account for major lines of cross-ethnic dissimilarity. There are several important theoretical and applied debates surrounding the political integration question. Perhaps the most challenging of these has been the discussion over the political arena generally – and the electoral process specifically – in measuring broader social inclusion/exclusion. This book cannot in itself furnish a definitive answer to this debate, but it can put forward a relevant and fresh perspective that allows us to tie wider social patterns to empirical voting data. An additional debate has raged over strategies for ethnic minority political mobilisation and influence. It almost goes without saying that, although this study does not in fact use party competition in its core conceptual framework, it does nevertheless have a lot to offer on this front. Finally, the political integration question acts as a spark to debates over the extent to which convergence or divergence patterns are fed back as independent factors into the political process. This debate often touches on normative argument about political representation strategy. However, this book addresses the so-called 'refeeding' debate by exploring the meaning of recent empirical voting evidence for representation theory and political strategy.

The racial exclusion paradigm continues to retain support and influence mainly because it effectively links an important strand of sociological analysis of racialisation of institutional policies and process with behavioural political science interest in patterns and levels of representation. Indeed, from this interface has emerged one of the key points of concern and dispute, namely over theories of under-representation in political life. Electoral participation is a prime arena in which to evaluate political under-representation claims and counter-claims. This is because it lends itself to three closely aligned arguments about procedural and substantive democracy. First, disaggregated levels of political participation are said to be important as they provide a passing, though useful, comment on the legitimacy and relevance of political institutions (Pattie and Johnston, 1998; Sabucedo and Cramer, 1991). Political parties and the tools of political communication are obvious sources of interest for this type of argument. Secondly, the quality and reputation of the democratic processes, beyond that of specific institutions, is often thought to be at stake when examining so-called democratic system performance questions among different groups within society (Schaffer, 1981). The sentiment of minorities in considering how far the British electoral processes is to be valued, distrusted, conditionally accepted or fully embraced is a recurring feature of academic and political debate (Layton-Henry and Studlar, 1985).[6] Thirdly, certain patterns of under-representation might, it is sometimes claimed, mask considerably deeper forms of political alienation. If large pockets of society – in this case specific minority groups or communities – remain substantially aloof from mainstream participation norms, then it is likely that liberal interpretations of under-representation will be successfully challenged in both academic and practitioner circles (Pryce, 1979; Gilroy, 1987; Keith, 1993).

In any case, concerns about minority representation by no means end at assessing the participation levels of ethnic minorities themselves. Rather, these debates revolve around systemic questions about political institutions, electoral systems, the policy interface and achieving political leverage. In other words, the debate is about the representation of ethnic minority interests as much as ethnic minorities themselves. The obvious lacuna here is the question of precisely what these interests are and, more awkwardly, the degree to which these can be described in coherent terms (see Messina, 1998, and Saggar, 1998a, for two contrasting interpretations on this question). In this respect, it is vital to inform our discussion with a full and candid appreciation of the literature on these themes generally, and on the leverage question in particular. It is this picture that drives better understanding of the place of minority politics and participation on the British political map. Moreover, it also allows us to consider more rigorously the relationship between electoral and non-electoral political participation, a link that is all-too-often swept aside or paid lip-service to in studies of minority voting.

In many ways it is just as worthwhile spending time examining various non-electoral forms of political participation as it is looking at electoral politics. This is because some of the constraining effects of limited numbers, central to the conventional school mentioned previously, have begun to be appreciated within minority groups and at the level of minority leadership in particular (Sia, 1994). Electoral politics offer some possibilities for representation in the political system, but these possibilities have tended to be fairly modest and often driven by the support of sympathetic white liberal politicians (Sooben, 1990; Studlar and Layton-Henry, 1990). Not surprisingly, attention has veered toward other mechanisms for representation and influence over policy. There are essentially two ends of a spectrum of options here. At one end, there has been the relatively closed world of trying to obtain influence over policy-makers. This is the stuff of lobbying, discreet contacts, specialised briefings and follow-up on matters of policy detail. It is by its very nature focused on achieving small changes in public policy; changes that are none the less both valuable and the foundations for potential secondary changes (Nixon, 1982; Young, 1983). At the other end, there is the politics of confrontation, protest and alienation. Much has been made of this type of option, for the most part suggesting that it is linked to something of a 'threat hypothesis', whereby large-scale minority protest is the danger associated with snail-like changes in either policy or electoral representation (Sivanandan, 1983; Studlar, 1985; Abbott and Davis, 1987). As this study goes on to argue, the notion of black electoral abstention has emerged as an important building-block in this perspective.

The links between options within this spectrum, explicit and latent, is a theme taken up more fully in later chapters. What is important here is to emphasise two basic points. First, any discussion of the relationship between electoral and non-electoral politics needs to guard against taking a simplistic view of the substitution possibilities of either strategy. In most cases they amount to complementary strategies based on trying to affect outcomes in very different parts of the political system. There is no strict equivalency at work since each of these strategies, in fact, serves rather different functions in politics. Secondly, having made allowance for non-electoral aspects of political representation, there remains the question of how to factor in debates over minority participation in other aspects of public life. For instance, there are important debates over minority representation in areas such as the media, the professions, the judiciary, academia, public appointments and so on. There is little getting away from the heightened emphasis placed by politicians and commentators on some aspects of such participation, though in areas such as public appointments the recent focus has been solely on recruitment questions (NHS Executive, 1999; Fritchie, 1999). Even mainstream Westminster politics has not escaped the gaze of those who have suspected that under-supply arguments have been overdone and in any case cannot be examined in isolation from other areas of public life (CRE, 1999). We cannot skip easily over these debates since many involve natural and understandable points of comparison with electoral representation. In this sense, it is important to understand that there is a complex connection between political–electoral and non-political, non-electoral forms of representation (BSC, 1999). This connection can be exploited for our purposes since few debates about the latter venture farther than the overtly political realm. But, once again, it is vital to ensure against over-simplification as so much of the connection hangs on overt lines of comparison. The underlying theme is that of minority involvement in the mainstream of British society, of which electoral politics is one part only, albeit an important aspect.

Theories of ethnic minority electoral participation and representation

The idea of the representation of ethnic minorities and ethnic minority interests on the one hand, and the representation by ethnic minorities on the other, is one of the most powerful distinctions to draw in debates over minority political participation. This distinction is not merely about different aspects of common political strategies. Rather, it is rooted in contrasting ways of thinking about first, the role of representation in an ethnically diverse society, and secondly, the adaptation of British traditions of party-based politics and government to changing circumstances and new challenges.

Above all, British approaches to electoral behaviour research have tended to be built on a familiar understanding of the importance of party-based mechanisms for political representation. Much of this is certainly understandable given the prominence attached over the years to the theory of responsible party government. This view held that it was the combination of disciplined, programmatic parties and the accountability of majority party governments to both parliament and the electorate, that has enabled political parties to be placed and remain at the heart of British representation thought (Hofferbert and Budge, 1994). The importance of this contextualising feature cannot be dismissed, although in recent times evidence has crept in of some erosion in the confidence in the doctrine of responsible party government (Heywood, 1994; Curtice and Jowell, 1997). However, at the same time, most approaches to minority political participation have avoided emphasis on party-based channels of representation and have instead been built on sharply contrasting understandings of the purpose of representation. In part, the story of these two views and how they have been entangled reveals a great deal about the introduction of new social relationships into a political system not previously particularly oriented to rival, perhaps culturally-driven, perspectives of electoral and social representation. Additionally, as Phillips (1995) has contended, analysts are still likely to stumble on questions of how far sources of socio-cultural and socio-psychological diversity are successfully reflected in the representative process. Catt (1999), echoing this standpoint, has argued that such processes may not themselves be properly suited to absorbing and communicating a 'politics of presence', thereby further revising the parameters of normative representative theory.

Ethnic minority political participation debates have meanwhile, tended to operate around a set of assumptions that accentuate the social dimension of representation. By this is meant that the democratic viability and health of a political system is assessed in terms of the degree to which the presence of distinctive social groups reflect the social composition of that society in identifiable arenas. Such arenas might typically include political representation as well as a variety of bodies and institutions subject to some form of public accountability. It should be noted this is not restricted in scope to just public bodies and may often include private organisations such as political parties themselves. Party membership, as well as party office-holders, has been a common point of reference of such thinking in recent years (Pinto-Duschinsky, 1997).

These social groups will perhaps be quite numerous and vary from one part of the country to another. Even quite modest inter-constituency variations are likely to be pored over by those keen to get the representative formulae right. The relative importance of specific groups can be expected to vary over time and, indeed, this variance itself may be reflective of underlying changes in social and cultural values. However, in modern Britain it is fairly clear that the social composition – which includes a range of descriptive identities ranging from gender, sexual orientation, generational and so on – of the general population tends to generate considerable exposure and attention. For instance, most social representation arguments are centred on the social class, gender, generational or regional composition of the electorate. Issues of ethnic group composition also receive attention, as do often related questions about linguistic and religious group composition. It is hard to draw any wide generalisations about the relative importance of specific notions of social representation in the British political system. What is clear is that social representation claims and counter-claims have become pretty vocal at the beginning of the twenty-first century in a way that would have been impossible to imagine, let alone predict, a couple of generations earlier. Additionally, this emphasis has led to a strong counter-reaction among those who argue that social or descriptive representation can be taken to absurd lengths. For instance, a recent correspondent in *The Times* colourfully lambasted the Tories for entering the spirit of representation-by-social-microcosm with misplaced enthusiasm: 'The idea that women are better represented by women, blacks by blacks and gays by gays is a modern fallacy. Last week ... a candidate announced that as the only openly gay candidate he had a special responsibility to homosexual voters. How is this different from a racist candidate declaring a special responsibility to "whites"?' (Rankin, 1999: 24).

Part of the new social representation politics is the product of social and demographic change alone. By the 1970s the ethnic minority population was fairly small by current standards, even though it had experienced substantial growth as a result of immigration during the 1950s and 1960s. At local level there were barely a handful of parliamentary constituencies in which this population constituted much more than one-fifth of the entire population, though several local government wards easily passed this level of concentration. By the late 1990s this traditional picture had changed dramatically. The national figures reveal that the current ethnic minority numbers of one in twenty of the poulation are steadily increasing toward a one in ten level within a couple of generations (Runnymede Trust, 1997: 5). However, locally there are numerous local authorities, parliamentary constituencies and even whole cities where very sizeable minority groups have gathered (Le Lohé, 1998). Against this backdrop, commentators have begun to speak of the politics of parity whereby proportionate strength in the wider population is equated with aspirations for pro rata political representation and, for that matter, a share in local spending decisions and other policy benefits. The politics of parity is one commonsense way to describe this trend (Kellner, 1999). A second factor underpinning this new politics has been the doctrine of 'equal shares' or 'fair shares' in managing racial policy and politics. The historic roots of this doctrine lie in large part in the affirmative action movement within US race relations and it is interesting that key aspects of the debate have had transatlantic appeal. In many British cities today it has become commonplace to observe a local political culture that is geared towards addressing these basic parity questions in terms of a political logic that is linked to ideas of equality in racial and ethnic affairs (Marable, 1995: ch. 6).

Of course, such equality is highly procedural and nominal, and arguably has little to do with substantive equality either in theoretical or practical terms. This then leads to a third feature of social representation, namely its overwhelming concern with descriptive or symbolic forms of representation, presumably even at the expense of substantive representation of political interests. According to one veteran commentator of ethnic politics in Britain, so far had the parity school travelled that it was possible, even desirable, to make assessments of group-level participation at national level based wholly on parity measures:

> Parity between the proportions of the population and the proportions of the [local government] councillors may now exist in many places, particularly for Asians. In 1978 ... there were 35 ethnic minority councillors in the London boroughs. In 1990 it was reported that there were 179. Enquiries following the 1994 borough elections raised this figure to 213. Asians increased from 21 in 1978, to 35 in 1982, to 69 in 1990, and to 145 in 1994. It does now seem that Asian people participate fully in British politics both as voters and as councillors and progress towards parity in the House of Commons is to be expected. (Le Lohé, 1998: 94)

This argument is itself centred on the doctrine – as it has almost become – of the under-representation of ethnic minorities. Noting the point made by the conventional school, observers have indeed confirmed the slow pace with which the British electoral process has delivered representative rewards to ethnic minorities in terms of group presence in legislative or local authority chambers. In these circumstances, the remarkably upbeat tone of Le Lohé's remarks and prediction should not be missed. Electoral prizes have been secured, according to this view, very rapidly indeed.

However, the larger point is the understanding of representation by social group based entirely on parity indicators. The implication of this that, even where large-scale breakthroughs can be secured in numeric and proportionate minority representation, this is distinct from any discussion of the representation of the distinctive interests of a political or social group. The idea that ethnic minorities have such distinctive and collective interests in politics has been debated regularly in Britain and is further considered, along with some detailed evidence on this question, in Chapter 6 of this book. However, it is clear that such a claim hangs on a view of the group as a sufficiently distinctive and self-identifying category to justify the cause of a political interest or set of interests (Werbner, 1991b). In the case of ethnic minorities two views have emerged on the nature and causes of such supposed distinctiveness. One of these holds that common ethnic origins and cultural ties are the long-term basis for the political interest, while another view contends that it has been the common experience of migration and race relations that has, somewhat circumstantially, built the basis of a particular political interest. There is obviously something much more temporary and conditional about the latter perspective than the former. Nevertheless both accounts see the prize as mobilisation through politics to realise common and distinctive minority interests. In other words, it is substantive representation of these interests that are valued and not, significantly, representative positions held by minorities alone. This is a potentially powerful divide within social theories of representation and one that this study shall return to on different occasions in this volume (Pitkin, 1967). It is arguably the relationship between these potentially rival views that really matters, perhaps because of the implicit suggestion of a tension, even a trade-off, in the practical world of ethnic minority political mobilisation. If so, a number of questions arise about the symbolic character of putative representative institutions as well as the ability of ethnic groups to call to account both institutions and individuals. It is these questions, taken up in the empirical sections of this book, which will help us to tackle the basic political integration question outlined previously.

Theories of social representation, however, tend to compete with other more traditional ways of conceptualising representation. As already mentioned, party-centred notions of representation have been prominent in British politics, although social representation links have always been somewhat important within this tradition (Beer, 1982). The organised working-class movement, for instance, has commonly looked toward the Labour Party in order to reflect and articulate the interests of this social group (Smith and Spear, 1992). The fact that such an expectation has occasionally been vexed in Labour Party circles reinforces the point that social representation is often problematic when applied to British political institutions. The difficulty appears to lie in the extent to which wider social movements and groups have succeeded in aggregating and incorporating their interests and perspectives into formal mass political parties (Perrigo, 1996). As we shall see, this is a recurring point of tension in the case of ethnic groups and the transmission of collective interests into the prevailing system of party competition.

In the meantime, some immediate dilemmas are apparent in trying to graft social representation views on to party-oriented systems of representative democracy. The first of these is the question of whether all, indeed even most, members of a social group who participate in elective politics – either as voters or party workers or candidates – actually identify with the collective interests of that particular social group. The conventional view on this question has been that any cross-group identification was likely to be fairly limited and of minimal passing consequence. This was primarily because of the dominance of essentially non-ethnic-based political parties in attracting and retaining the identification of political participants. In addition, it was thought that social group identification came into the limelight only in the private realm or at least far removed from the domain of public affairs. In any case, conditional identification with the social group was felt to be a long way from social representation in its full-blown form. The latter required considerable organisational and mobilisation input, much of which could be supplied and, therefore, displaced by political parties. An alternative viewpoint, however, has suggested that the social characteristics of participants do, in fact, matter, at least to the extent that this creates potentially powerful forms of allegiance and representative muscle within parties themselves (Norris and Lovenduski, 1995). This school is important because it not only acknowledges the difficulties associated with the interface between social and other notions of representation, but also through its appreciation of the internal management of these social identities by mainstream political institutions. It is, arguably, the politics of this interface and the management questions that it raises that is potentially so interesting in studying representative theories in action in modern liberal democracies.

A second related dilemma stems from the expectation mentioned previously that political institutions – legislatures most notably but also extending to the executive and possibly even parts of the career administration – need to reflect the social composition of the populations they serve. A similar line of expectation can be, and recently has been, extended to the realm of public appointments more generally (Manzoor, 1999). The attractiveness of this argument has grown in recent years and strengthened in quality as well. Indeed, the whole political under-representation argument is explicitly couched in these terms, equating parliamentary representation with a social microcosm normative understanding of the role of public institutions. However, even as these arguments have gained greater prominence, it is striking to note that political parties have continued to hold the whip-hand in transmitting pressure for microcosm politics into elective politics. At the very least they have performed a useful role in limiting the scope of social representation theory to party-based channels. Beneath this lies a fundamental dilemma: how far should members of a common social group show loyalty to that group beyond loyalty to party? The hidden assumption, whether mistaken or not, is that members of the group are more likely to be associated with a particular set of political interests (a point made amply in relation to the political interests of women by Hewitt and Mattinson, 1987). In fact, the evidence suggests that many are, while many others are not. Therefore, the tension is caused by the need to make assessments of this kind of likelihood, and, it must be said, this probability may be all that remains to fall back on. The calculus can be virtually impenetrable because both motives and action are regularly clouded by a veiled, often self-contradicting rationale. What is more reliable is to try to examine how far members of different social groups appear to be willing to push the group loyalty perspective. In a number of cases, the claim seems to stretch a considerable distance so long as the countervailing costs are restricted or perhaps even displaced. But the chances of completely off-loading these costs tapers off in other situations where group members are forced to make uncomfortable choices between evenly matched though fundamentally different options. The case of voting for same ethnicity candidates in local and national elections is a prime illustration of this dilemma in action (Le Lohé, 1989; Bald, 1989). In some circumstances this example might even extend to cases in which powerful social and ideological loyalties are placed in a position of zero-sum confrontation. This book examines this dilemma with the use of empirical survey evidence and reveals that the institutional-circumstantial aspects of social representation are often crucial to understanding causal relationships. What is certain at a general level is that comparatively few members of such social groups will normally count upon high levels of group loyalty to the extent found in mandate theories of representation. This 'normal' assumption is reliable under equally 'normal' conditions but is subject to extensive and rapid revision following departures from convention. In a sense the test is to map out the parameters of 'normality', and to assess this position in the context of a mature and developed ideological tradition as found in British politics.

Towards a theory of ethnically-related political behaviour

Ethnically-related theories of political behaviour involve two related spheres: questions of political thought and outlook – political orientation one might say – and questions of political involvement and participation – basically political action as well as inaction. When added together, these perspectives amount to attempts to theorise and model several central questions. First, precisely what, if anything, can be said about ethnic relationships as a force that shapes political behaviour? Secondly, to what degree do different ethnic groups have to deviate, both from one another and from dominant 'norms', for their political behaviour to be thought of as sufficiently distinctive and thus worthy of comment? Finally, how well do ethnically-related theories of political behaviour cope with examples of non-ethnically-related political behaviour or, more pertinently, evidence of mixed and interwoven causal influence that touch upon ethnicity spasmodically? The last of the questions is the most disputed area of all because it requires otherwise simplistic theories to tackle complex terrain and also because it deals with the notion of partial or indirect causal relationships.

It should be recalled that the above questions all overlook an additional way in which to think about the potential of ethnicity to shape political behaviour. When Deakin (1965) published his landmark study of the 1964 general election it was fairly obvious that the main focus of academic and practitioner thought was on the ways in which the white electorate had responded to the immigration issue. Thus, the influence of ethnicity was thought of entirely in terms of the effects of ethno-cultural diversity and change – the blunt everyday impact of non-white immigration – upon a largely white group of voters. There is nothing in itself to stop us trying to carry out similar analytical exercises today. Nothing, that is, other than to note that first, that the ethnic composition of society and thus the electorate has changed, and secondly, that the reactive stimuli (the immigration issue and the form of social change it embodied) is plainly much less salient today than it was in 1965. However, the effects of ethnicity are still being measured in the sense that it is primarily an independent variable. Ethnically-related theories of political behaviour, therefore, must take care to ensure that applicability to white (or overwhelmingly white) ethnic groups is not disregarded in the rush to account for ethnic minority behaviour. A fourth, related question, then, might be to ask how far ethnicity serves as a contextual feature of mainstream participatory politics. In this sense we can also try to account for voters' and others' responses to issues, events and other stimuli that are perhaps thought to be about affecting the ethnic character of society at large. Whether empirical measurement is focused around one ethnic group or another hardly matters as the analysis is about unlocking the simultaneous dependent and independent aspects of ethnicity at one and the same time.

Political science theory can conceptualise the role of ethnicity in a number of ways. The most prominent aspect of this has been to look at the question of an ethnic minority political agenda, sometimes referred to as a race agenda or perspective (Messina, 1998; Amin and Richardson, 1998; Marable, 1995: ch. 2). The evidence surrounding this debate has been hotly contested over the years and it is still unclear in its main conclusions. At an empirical level, the debate has revolved around the degree to which ethnic minorities have been stimulated and motivated by exclusively racial or ethnic considerations in their political behaviour. As already noted, at one end of the debate there has been something of an essentialist viewpoint that has stressed the importance of a powerful and discrete set of common values and priorities among members of minority groups. At the other end, so-called sceptics have poured scorn on this claim, suggesting that any major inter-ethnic variations are either fully explicable through circumstantial factors or else the ever-declining product of transitional change. In addition, the debate has featured lively and pointed dispute over the role of alternative or supplementary forms of ethnic minority community-based organisation (Ali, 1992; Hall, 1996; Kalka, 1991). Participation organised around specific cultural, religious or similar ties has plainly played an important part among some minority communities, most notably certain south Asian groups, at the local level. The task has been to map these forms of quasi- or alternative politics. Are they merely significant in *ad hoc*, single issue terms? Or, more robustly, can it be said that they are genuinely autonomous and possibly rivals to orthodox political institutions such as political parties? The traditional view held that they amounted to potentially important learning zones in which newcomer groups could absorb the customs and mores of the British party-based system (Hill and Issacharoff, 1971; Katznelson, 1973). Though dated, this view still holds sway in some quarters despite its occasionally patronising undertones. However, more recent views have dwelt on the usually latent capacity of such ethnically-based organisations to feed strong lines of political difference among minorities in relation to their white counterparts. Of course, the major criticism of these recent claims has been the stress placed on latency and capacity, both of which regularly strayed into the troubled and fractious realm of normative argument.

In examining such powerful organised instances of ethnic identity and group loyalty it is vital to observe two basic tests. The first is to ensure that the evidence is not excessively contaminated by signs of non-political, leisure or culturally-led activity among minorities that might distort assessments of political difference. Such a trap can be slipped into quite casually and unknowingly, leading to some quite preposterous and immeasurable claims about the politics of ethnicity (Eade, 1996). This leads to a second check: how far is ethnicity, both overtly in the political realm and elsewhere, the source of a permanent, stand-alone cleavage in British politics? The latter question, in fact, forms the basis of several chapters in the middle part of the book. In essence, it is a question that arises from the original political integration theme highlighted at the start of this chapter. It is stated in terms that neatly and subtly draw together the twin concerns with the social basis of voting, on the one hand, and the characterisation of party competition in Britain on the other.

Previous research: ethnicity, elections, data and appraisal

Hitherto research into the voting behaviour of ethnic minorities in Britain has focused on two relatively narrow issues. First, it has asked how far both the level of electoral participation and the direction of partisan choice among ethnic minorities differs from what would be expected given their socio-economic background. Secondly, it has asked how much voting power the ethnic minorities might have by identifying constituencies where the number of ethnic minority voters is greater than incumbent majorities. This previous research has given us some understanding of ethnic minority voting behaviour but the conclusions from this work remain tentative at best. For instance, it would appear that Asians are more likely to vote than their white counterparts, while blacks are generally less likely to do so. Meanwhile, when they do vote, members of the ethnic minorities are substantially more likely to vote Labour than are whites (Layton-Henry and Studlar, 1985; Anwar, 1986). There are intriguing hints in the literature that Asians may have a lesser propensity to support Labour than do black voters, while socio-economic differences (explored in more detail in Chapter 4) do not appear, on the face of it, to create the same divisions within ethnic minority communities that they do within the white population. In other words, ethnicity may trump class, with middle-class blacks and Asians voting more on the basis of their ethnic identity than according to their class interests. None of these conclusions are, however, firmly established as yet and in any event it is not clear that all the findings of the earlier literature, based primarily on the first generation of ethnic minorities who migrated to Britain, will still hold true today.

The limited nature of our understanding of ethnic minority voting behaviour is a result of several crucial weaknesses in the research designs that have been commonly employed in the past. Three difficulties have stood out. First, the voting behaviour of the ethnic minorities has often been studied in isolation from that of the larger, mainly white electorate (CRE, 1984). This problem of reliance on stand-alone data sets cannot be underestimated for our purposes in terms of exploring and understanding political integration among minorities. Secondly, the data derived from quota samples with possible (but essentially unknown) biases in their coverage. This methodological drawback has inevitably meant that constraints have had to be placed on accompanying generalisations about messages contained in the data. Thirdly, there has been little detailed work on differences within and between the various ethnic minorities. It has often been assumed that, politically, ethnic minorities can be treated as a homogeneous bloc. Research on other aspects of ethnic minorities, such as their patterns of geographic segregation, intermarriage, gender relations, educational and occupational participation indicate that there are sometimes very large differences between blacks and Asians, as well as within these two composite groups.

The first significant survey-based research into ethnic minority voting behaviour was pioneered by the then Community Relations Commission. The CRC published a landmark report after the October 1974 general election (CRC, 1975). Its main focus was the claim that ethnic minorities had played a pivotal role in determining the election outcome. The Labour Party secured an overall parliamentary majority of only three seats in autumn 1974. Meanwhile, it was noted that there were far more than three constituencies where Labour's majority was less than the number of ethnic minority voters. Although this superficially powerful thesis was relatively easy to refute methodologically and substantively, the report was nevertheless treated seriously by the major political parties who each increased their efforts to recruit and/or retain ethnic minority voters. In particular, the Labour Race Action Group, working principally at constituency level, played a large role in keeping the theme at the fore of Labour's re-election discussions in the late 1970s (LPRAG, 1979). On the Conservative side, a number of important institutional reforms resulted from the raised awareness that accompanied the CRC report. In 1976 the party established a dedicated unit in its Central Office bureaucracy to spearhead its campaign to bring ethnic minorities to the Tory cause and into its membership base.

A similar approach was taken by the CRC's successor, the Commission for Racial Equality. In 1980 the CRE published the findings of its study of the May 1979 general election (CRE, 1980). Another attempt was made to advance what by now had become known as the 'ethnic marginals' thesis, but with only limited impact on this occasion. This survey, together with the CRE's studies of the general elections of 1983, 1987 and 1992, all retained the characteristics of examining ethnic minority political participation in isolation from the electorate as a whole (CRE, 1994; Ali and Percival, 1993). Such an approach might have been defensible in the 1970s when comparatively little was known about ethnic minority voting behaviour, but by the 1980s this framework was becoming a serious limitation.

A further resource for empirical knowledge has stemmed from various press-sponsored surveys of ethnic minority voters. For instance, NOP began some limited work on this topic for various national newspapers in the 1970s (NOP, 1978), and was also associated with a number of other polls on the subject over the years. In 1983, London Weekend Television commissioned a valuable poll carried out by Harris Research which contained some of the first detailed questions on issues and underlying attitudes (Harris Research Centre, 1983). Later, in 1987, Harris Research followed this up by carrying out a similar type of poll for Hansib, a major ethnic minority publisher (Harris Research Centre, 1987). In the early 1990s Harris Research executed a special mid-term survey of ethnic minorities (both as citizens and as voters) sponsored by the *Independent*, a national newspaper, and the Runnymede Trust, a race relations charity (Amin and Richardson, 1992). Finally, Harris Research was also involved in a small survey of Asian voters in 1991, commissioned by BBC Pebble Mill (Harris Research Centre, 1991). This last survey also contained some useful new questions that sought to probe Asian opinion in a range of areas where minority attitudes have frequently been taken for granted (e.g. issues of law and order, educational selection and immigration policy).

In addition, a handful of other sources exist which serve to complement the existing rather dated literature. For instance, a useful survey of attitudes and outlook of London's ethnic minorities was carried out by the Greater London Council in 1984–85 (FitzGerald, 1985a; 1987). The GLC report may have had a number of deficiencies on matters of methodology, but it nevertheless provided a very rich seam of empirical material on attitudes towards a variety of social and public concerns. More recently, the Institute of Public Policy Research, a left-leaning think-tank, commissioned and published a comparative survey that focused on white and non-white attitudes to cross-ethnic perceptions of integration (Alibhai-Brown, 1999).

While valuable, these surveys have typically relied on quota samples. Moreover, there have been major limitations in their coverage of ethnic minorities. No genuinely representative probability samples of ethnic minority voters have been obtained, with the exception of those contacted in the course of standard academic surveys such as those in the British Election Study (BES) series. However, these large-scale surveys of the electorate as a whole are also inadequate: members of ethnic minorities constitute no more than 5 per cent of the adult population and they tend to be under-represented in sample surveys. For instance, they constituted little more than 3 per cent of all respondents in the 1992 BES, perhaps partly due to problems of under registration. As a result, the BES has until now contained too few ethnic minority respondents to permit any detailed comparison of their behaviour with that of the white electorate. Thus, in their discussion of ethnicity using the 1987 BES, Heath *et al.* (1991) were forced to group together all ethnic minorities, a practice that has been shown to be seriously flawed in parallel studies of ethnic minority educational and occupational attainment (Cheng and Heath, 1993; Heath and McMahon, 1997).

The 1997 general election: building the empirical research agenda

The main empirical objective of this study is to compare the voting behaviour of ethnic minorities with that of the electorate as a whole.

Thus, the research design deliberately steered away from administering a specially designed questionnaire exclusively to members of the ethnic minorities. Instead, the research design was based on administering a general purpose questionnaire to both the ethnic minority and white communities. This tactic would ensure that the BES contained sufficient ethnic minority respondents to enable meaningful comparisons to be made of their attitudes, values and behaviour with those of the white majority. This, then, lay at the heart of the strategy to push forward empirical analysis of the main political integration thesis.

This strategy additionally opened up a wide range of intellectual opportunities. First, as already noted, the study was interested in the extent to which ethnic minorities were integrated into mainstream electoral process. It was important to try to go beyond earlier studies of levels of ethnic minority participation and to examine the attitudes of ethnic minorities towards the democratic process and to establish how far these attitudes are correlated with their participation. In particular, interest focused on trying to demonstrate whether electoral abstention among ethnic minorities is primarily circumstantial – as existing research suggests it is among the white population (Swaddle and Heath, 1989) – or whether it reflects alienation from the political system.

Secondly, the research based on the 1997 BES sought to establish how far the main ethnic minorities differ from each other and from the white population in their electoral choice, taking account of their diverse socioeconomic profiles. Crucially, with a mountain of impressionistic evidence from earlier elections implying that ethnicity effectively trumped class in shaping voting behaviour, it is fairly vital to be able to throw new light on this central theme. One derivative of this theme is the possibility that grand generalisations that unify all ethnic minority groups would prove to be to difficult, and that ethnicity is associated with a powerful effect on voting in the case of some ethnic minorities and not others (or that the effects were more powerful among certain groups than others). Furthermore, the research was keen to discover how far the ethnic minorities can be treated as internally homogeneous communities in their political orientations. An increasingly prominent possibility is that they display the same kind of internal differentiation that is found in the white population. It is at least credible to suggest that some, though perhaps not all, of these similarities across white and non-white ethnic groups might be found in the research findings.

Thirdly, the research was committed to substantially improving the understanding of the political attitudes of the ethnic minorities underscoring their electoral behaviour. The BES is particularly apposite for this purpose as it contains a much wider range of measures of such attitudes than other comparable surveys. The aim was to explore the attitudes of ethnic minorities towards both 'racial' issues and issues that are not overtly 'racial', and further to examine their main lines of difference from that of the white population. Central concerns within this theme were to capture those issues on which the different ethnic minorities shared similar views, and by contrast, those issues where their cultural histories and experiences of migration led to, or were at least closely linked to, divergence. As previously noted, research on other aspects of ethnic minority experience in Britain has suggested that it is essential to differentiate blacks, Indians, Pakistanis and Bangladeshis at the very least. By controlling for qualifications, gender, age and year of arrival, for example, it is apparent that major differences in rates of unemployment among ethnic minorities persist (Heath and McMahon, 1997). In short, the research asked whether these differences are reflected in attitudes towards the political system and the role and reputation of political parties.

Finally, the research also sought fresh insight into on whether ethnic minority support patterns were guided by the same processes that operate within the white population. For instance, it might be that towards some issues – unemployment and inflation, for example – ethnic minorities adopt exactly the same attitudes as the population as a whole, although their uncharacteristic risk of unemployment may lead them to distinctive political behaviour. Or it could be that their political attitudes and voting behaviour are influenced by somewhat different issues and concerns, such as those of race and immigration which typically have played only a small part in white voting behaviour (Studlar, 1978; Miller, 1980; Heath *et al.*, 1991). Alternatively, it might be that different kinds of process are involved. Notions of community and community norms may be more important among ethnic minorities and, therefore, a collectivist model of voting is more appropriate for the ethnic minorities than the increasingly individualistic, issue-oriented models that are usually applied to the white population.

Added together, these elements of the research will enable an analysis that can identify the extent to which the different ethnic minorities are integrated into or excluded from British political society. The analysis is ultimately interested in unpacking the claim that ethnicity has created, or is at least associated with, a significant political cleavage in British electoral behaviour and political attitudes. Testing this claim is important because, more than anything, empirical research must point to whether members of the ethnic minorities are fully integrated into similar sources of political difference that characterise the white population. The political cleavage of ethnicity must first be rigorously modelled before it is examined empirically and assessed for its likely meaning in modern British politics.

Notes

1 The term 'ethnic minority' is used in this volume to denote people of south Asian, African and Caribbean origin. It is used interchangeably with the term 'minority'. Deployment of these terms as broad, umbrella labels is deliberate in order to signify the wide variety of non-white ethnic groups resident in contemporary Britain. Where greater precision is required in particular chapters, as with reference to specific component groups, allowance and departures from this convention are clearly signalled.

   The reader's attention in drawn in particular to the book's use of original data from the 1997 British Election Study and in particular the delineation of the ethnic minority population into five principal categories: (Asian) Indian; (Asian) Pakistani; (Asian) Bangladeshi; Black-African; and Black-Caribbean. These five groups were isolated in the original research design of the BES to represent the significant elements within the ethnic minority population. A further miscellaneous category was included, which allows the analysis to include ethnic minority respondents who did not fall easily into the previous scheme (though this will necessarily amount to a very heterogeneous group). The research did not extend directly to southeast Asian, ethnic Chinese and Indo-Chinese groups, though some of these groups might have been picked up under 'Asian other' categories (and therefore included under the miscellaneous heading). Naturally the author is aware of the sensitivities of debates over race, ethnicity and nomenclature in British politics (as well as somewhat doubtful about the actual merits of such arguments for the purposes of precision in empirical research). Indeed, as one prominent commentator has recently observed, the on-going effects of cross-ethnic marriage, cohabitation and child-bearing are likely to make redundant, at least partially, many of our presently cherished terms and labels of description (Parekh, 1999a). These developments are impacting as genuine constraints upon debate and empirical research rather quicker than many commentators have previously supposed or are willing to acknowledge. There is probably a case for taking a circumspect approach to the long-term value of some of the positions taken within the race and nomenclature debate. There is equally a strong case for pragmatic responsiveness when facing the task of researching empirical patterns and relationships, the fruits of which can realistically be turned back to the sources of the debate itself. No particular political or sociological inference should be drawn from the use of this convention on terminology.

2 Census-based data from the early 1990s indicates that the total ethnic minority population stood at around 5.5 per cent of the population. However, this figure perhaps underestimates the true picture and successive Labour Force Surveys during the 1990s indicated that considerable growth continued in this population generally and among certain elements within it in particular. Substantially higher birth rates among ethnic minorities than among whites accounts for the biggest factor behind on-going growth, and recent estimates suggest that real inter-ethnic convergence is perhaps 30 to 50 years away. In the meantime, the younger age profile of the minority groups at present means that they are not fully reflected in the population of eligible voters (over two-thirds were under 35 years of age in the mid-1990s compared with around one-half of their white counterparts). The corollary of this fact is that very large numbers will come of electoral age in the near future, thereby swelling their numbers within the potential electorate. Repeating a rule-of-thumb used in describing the 1997 general election, perhaps around one-third of the

minority population are presently ineligible to register to vote on age grounds (Saggar, 1997a). This figure suggests that the estimate put up in the early 1980s – 4 per cent of the electorate – continues to be reasonably reliable, although arguably not for very much longer (Crewe, 1983). In aggregate terms, the barrier of 5 per cent of the electorate is likely to be crossed at some point between the first and second parliaments of the twenty-first century (Norris, 1997b).

3   With the obvious caveat that such numeric limitations are subject to longer term migratory trends involving settlers and displaced peoples from Asian, African and Caribbean sources. For a provocative counter-perspective that tries (on the basis of technological and communications evidence) to challenge the need or case for such migration see: <www.labs.bt.com/people/pearsonid>.

4   A similar turn of events took place in May 1997 in Bradford West in which an Asian Sikh candidate for the Labour Party was elected but with a significant reduction in the share of the vote.

5   With the partial exception, of course, of recent studies of the Scottish electorate and, in particular, the influence of 'Scottishness' not only on vote but also on attitudes towards party identification and constitutional questions. For instance, see: Brown *et al.* (1998) and Surridge *et al.* (1999).

6   In their unrelated work on ethnic minority local councillor attitudes, Adolino (1998) and Purdham (1998) both make the wise point that forms of political involvement can and should be measured across a range of indicators relating to political interest, political knowledge and *ad hoc* participation in public affairs or events.

2

Framing conceptual and theoretical questions

Introduction

It is commonplace to hear suggestions that ethnic minority political participation, whatever the advances of recent years, still lags behind the standards expected of a mature industrial democracy.[1] In everyday terms this suggestion is illustrated by a broad cross-party willingness to encourage enhanced ethnic minority voter participation and occupation of elective office. It is further entrenched by a range of party and extra-party efforts to build democratic institutions that are more accurate social microcosms of British society. Against this backdrop, it is also common to witness sharply contrasting claims made by political activists and party managers alike concerning the nature and behaviour of ethnic minorities in the democratic process (Saggar, 1998b; Back and Solomos, 1992; Malik, 1995). Britain is far from being unique in this sense and parallel debates can be seen in several other countries (Swain, 1993). In 1979, some twenty years after the first party-based attempts to capture the so-called 'ethnic vote', conceptual understanding of that term remains substantively as wide open as ever (Messina, 1998). The search is on to discover the essence of ethnic minority political identity.

This chapter explores some of the ways in which the British political tradition has conceptualised ethnic minority political participation. It is primarily interested in the central race-voting nexus and sets the discussion within a wider conceptual framework. The chapter begins by highlighting the kinds of conceptual and conceptually-related difficulties that are thrown up in the study of race and ethnicity as variables in electoral behaviour. It then considers a major recurring controversy in both academic research and practical politics, namely the existence and inherent character of a distinctive ethnic minority political agenda. Moving away from minority voters, the chapter then assesses the ways in which party strategy has developed to take account of ethnicity and ethnic minorities. Lastly, there is a discussion of the need for greater conceptual clarity, in order to offset, at least partly, loose speculation about the motives and interests of ethnic minorities as citizen-participants in British electoral politics.

Conceptual uncertainties

The importance attached to race and ethnicity in shaping voting choice has been the subject of considerable academic, as well as journalistic and practical political, interest. It has, however, been a topic associated with some muddled thinking. A large element of this fascination has been both predictable and, in some senses, understandable. For one thing, significance may be afforded to ethnicity as a variable in the sense that it is associated with, and may even yield, a powerful influence upon party choice. That is to say, ethnicity amounts to an amalgam of contributory factors shaping voting, selectively symbolising and uniting aspects of shared experience and common outlook. Few theorists of electoral behaviour have made much headway in explaining what it is about or what is embodied within the concept of ethnicity that counts in shaping political outlook and action. (Notable early exceptions to this generalisation, based on analysis of the US voter, might include the work of Verba and Nie, 1972: ch.10, and Nie *et al.*, 1976: 104-5.) This central job of mapping out the terms and scope of such an ethnically-related form of thinking and acting politically is something that is considered more fully later in this chapter.

However, it may appear that in itself, ethnicity does not mean very much for the job of predicting voting other than to measure group membership sizes and proportions. Moreover, confusion sets in once ethnicity is described as a variable when, in fact, theoretical inquiries seldom attempt to treat it as something that actually varies. Indeed, sociological research on this front has been quite convincing in suggesting that ethnic identity and its composition does vary, often quite considerably, from one setting to another (Dahya, 1974; Samad, 1993; Nazroo, 2000). Academic voting studies usually go no further than treating it as a nominal variable, typically distinguishing patterns of non-white and white political behaviour. The only variance that does show up in such studies is that which distinguishes, however imperfectly, membership from one group to another (Heath *et al.*, 1991). The familiar argument that a variable must vary is thus especially pertinent here. Furthermore, no appreciable attempt is made in empirical research to link either 'lower' or 'higher' forms (let alone different notions) of ethnicity or ethnic identity with political behaviour. It is not in that sense a particularly useful or adaptable variable for voting studies, or even one that counts greatly or can be measured meaningfully. One reason for this may be that ethnicity tends to work well enough as a variable for the narrow purposes of survey research, while lacking sufficient coherence on content as an analytical concept. This approach to identifying its meaning and use, while radically different from the comments above, nevertheless draws attention to the task of interpreting correctly the relatively limited 'hard' data that exists on race and ethnicity and voting in Britain. Both approaches then add up to largely the same kinds of questions.

These mainly methodological difficulties aside, ethnicity remains a concept that clearly matters for the purposes of moulding electoral choice. What is less clear is whether it is a metaphor for underlying causal relationships or indeed something that has a direct bearing on political orientation and activity.

If ethnicity is to be treated as an analytical category – as it should – it is usually thought of as an explanatory factor that applies to only a small segment of the electorate (Heath *et al.*, 1991: 99). As such, it is the *ethnicity of ethnic minorities* that analysts are concerned with, something that in Britain is, therefore, almost certainly incapable of having a large impact across the electorate as a whole. For that reason, we have become used to thinking that ethnic minorities do not influence overall election outcomes.[2] These voters are too few in number and concentrated away from the seats that matter, so the sceptical argument goes, for them to matter greatly on the wider political landscape (Crewe, 1983). Yet, despite this stark message, there have been numerous claims regarding their great potential in delivering electoral victory (e.g. the much embellished 'ethnic bloc' voting argument), or in avoiding electoral oblivion (e.g. the Labour Party's reliance on 'ethnic safe seats' in its routs of 1983 and 1987).

The complicating twist has been that commentators have been driven by the assumption that for ethnic minority voters ethnicity alone counts. In what sense does it count? Is it something of a coincidental feature of their ethnic identity or is it the product of a distinctive agenda of issue and policy concerns? This problem seems to lie at the heart of most of the conceptual muddle in the literature and is explored in the following section.

Race and ethnicity: a distinctive agenda?

In the period since 1979 the volume of research on ethnic minority political behaviour in Britain has grown at a tremendous pace (Saggar, 1998c; Gouldbourne, 1998a: ch. 3; Shukra, 1998b: ch. 5). However, a feature of this plethora of research interest has been an underlying confusion over the distinctiveness of ethnic minority political outlook and action alike. At one end of the spectrum there have been strong cases made in favour of the idea that ethnic minorities are united under a common banner of shared political interests and persuasions (as an example of this see, Werbner, 1991a). A theoretical variant of this line has been an insistence that an ethnically-related way of thinking and behaving politically is at work. The body of this arguably strong assertion is examined below. At the other end of the spectrum, harsh denials of such claims have been advanced, concluding that the basis of common behaviour has been a response to shared social class and racial discrimination experiences, without any real sense of collective consciousness resulting from this process (see FitzGerald, 1987 and Studlar, 1993, for illustrations).

In considering the empirical evidence of ethnic minority political behaviour a number of different approaches have emerged in the academic and non-academic literature. It is important to emphasise that these approaches themselves are reflections of wider disagreements, usually, though not exclusively, linked to normative discussions about non-white political advancement. To that extent, the task of mapping the political behaviour of ethnic minorities is as much about interpreting the evidence at the heart of disputed conceptual territory as it is about describing positivist models of voting behaviour.

It is perhaps useful to think of relevant behaviour as comprising four inter-related faces. Furthermore, our understanding is probably advanced if we think of ethnic minority political attitudes and behaviour as several overlapping and inter-related phenomena.

A separate 'race agenda'
First, *ethnic minorities collectively may vote in line with a fully separate and discrete set of issues not shared at all by their white counterparts.* For instance, ethnic minority voters may base their discrete agenda on a sense that racial discrimination and exclusion is both widespread and endemic in British society. By constructing a political view of the world that is centred on racialisation (in a negative sense) as a fundamental feature of society, this is probably what is meant by the term 'race dimension'. There is considerable reason to think, for example, that this kind of dimension has been at the heart of radical black political activists' efforts in promoting Black Sections in the Labour Party (Shukra, 1990). Similar lines of blunt differentiation based on ethnic group membership, and the experience that has resulted from racial discrimination processes can be seen in writing that goes beyond party political affairs (Parmar, 1982; Pryce, 1990; Schiele, 1990; Fletcher and Newport, 1992). By the same token, the common experience of racism in British politics and society generally has undoubtedly contributed to the development of something of a 'race dimension' for ethnic minority voters and political elites across all parties (FitzGerald, 1990: 21-6).

What is important for the analyst to assess, however, is the degree to which ethnic minorities' political outlook is based exclusively on racial divisions. Only if the evidence suggests a strong degree of such exclusivity, may this be dubbed a 'race agenda' in the sense that race and race-related issues are the prism through which the world is understood politically.

For the most part empirical evidence tends not to affirm such a position. In a 1991 NOP survey for instance, four in every five black respondents agreed with the proposition that Britain was a 'very or fairly racist society' (Kellner and Cohen, 1991; NOP, 1991). (The comparable figures for whites and Asians in the survey were 67 and 56 per cent, respectively.) This kind and level of feeling might be described as the building-blocks of a wider 'race agenda' world-view. In some instances a strong sense of counter-hostility toward 'white society', combined with reactive ethnic pride, have been highlighted by researchers interested in the so-called 'culture of resistance' of black youth (Miles, 1978; Troyna, 1979). That said, the 1991 NOP survey data – in common with other similar survey findings – had little to say about the depth of feeling over race or racial discrimination and exclusion. These data may, indeed, conceal another hidden face whereby the relevant ethnic minorities' views are highly skewed in one direction but are views that are not held very strongly. Indeed, numerous commentators observing the broad canvas of race relations in Britain make the common assumption that these groups of voters are intensely motivated by racial considerations and that shared assessments about racism in society are the strongest motivators of all (e.g. Mullard, 1985).

The disappointingly limited evidence that is available on this point, in fact, hints at the reverse being closer to the mark. In another 1991 survey of Asians carried out by Harris Research, a sizeable 37 per cent reported that the question of racial attacks was the most important issue they faced (Harris Research Centre, 1991). For this group at least, race and racism were not political issues in any general sense, however much they may have felt themselves to be the victims of racial hostility either individually or collectively. Race and racism for them were priorities in the sense that their ethnic group membership left them especially vulnerable to a particular form of violence and intimidation. It would certainly be safe to infer that this concern amounted to a racialised dimension of issues relating to crime and law and order. It may be less safe to claim that their perception of violence being directed at them on the basis of visible appearance necessarily led them to interpret race and racism in broad, let alone universal, political terms. At another related level, one might ask: does survey data showing that over one-third of a specific group are anxious about 'racial attacks' tell us something about the racial significance of their concerns or something about perceptions about individual and collective security? Table 2.1 tells the story, and cannot firmly discount or confirm one or the other of these interpretations.

Table 2.1 *Most significant issue among Asian voters, 1991 (%)*

Issue	(%)
Education	41
Racial attacks	37
Health service	29
Housing	25
Immigration	17
Poll tax	11
Mother tongue teaching	10
Separate schools	4

Source: Harris Research (1991).

Another common presumption is that ethnic minorities themselves necessarily hold liberal or progressive views on traditional bread-and-butter race relations issues. Again, the limited evidence on this point usually ends up clouding matters and seldom gives much reason to back such a claim conclusively. The same 1991 NOP survey revealed that 12 and 15 per cent of Asians and blacks, respectively, disagreed with the suggestion that immigration had enriched the quality of life in Britain. Furthermore, 5 and 7 per cent of each respective group felt that British laws against racial discrimination were, in fact, too tough (Kellner and Cohen, 1991; NOP, 1991).[3] A 1997 MORI survey reinforced the idea that many Asians held fairly illiberal views on immigration (MORI, 1997). These figures, while fairly modest, would presumably come as a shock to numerous commentators and be treated with a large dose of politically correct denial.

A similar pattern is seen when considering the old chestnut of ethnic minority support for the principle of ethnic minority political representatives. Only a small fraction of Asian voters in 1991 said that they were more likely to vote for a candidate of the same ethnic origin as themselves (Harris Research Centre, 1991). Just 27 per cent of Asians in 1997 thought they were either certain, very or quite likely to change their vote to a candidate of their own ethnic group (MORI, 1997). The same note of ambivalence, possibly even scepticism, is arguably at play when it comes to political leaders taking up positions on issues in order to influence votes along ethnic lines. However, the ethnic background of certain leaders, rather than simplifying so-called 'ethnic issues', may turn out to undermine and blur claims made by such leaders. For example, in the early 1990s, both Keith Vaz's and Max Madden's similar responses to the Rushdie affair were heavily driven by their perceived constituency interests and seemed unaffected by the fact that one of them was an Asian MP and other was a white MP.

More typically perhaps, activists who both have a stake in such a claim and who also hold a normative commitment to such an agenda commonly express suggestions that a race agenda characterises the political orientation of ethnic minorities. Partial support among the ethnic minority electorate for a race agenda will usually mean that these voters at least are undecided as to whether political participation can be understood in exclusively racial terms. More typically, such voters would not particularly want to rule out the existence of, and subscription to, a race agenda but, at one and the same time, would fail to give much more than nominal support to race agenda political activists. In a sense then, critics might argue that these voters want to have things both ways. To be fair, this criticism has some weight since the normally racially subdued texture of everyday British politics ensures that such starkly opposing choices are seldom forced upon minority voters. Even the presence of starker choices as found in American racial politics, does not ensure any greater support for such ethnic enclave political agendas (Rodriguez, 1999: Morris, 1992; Steele, 1990).

The account of the race agenda presented above may serve to put forward a caricature of ethnic minority voters who are motivated on racial grounds alone. This would be simplistic to the point of being naive. What may be taking place is an unusual and specific way of looking at politics. A hard-line perspective based on racial divisions is, of course, one, rather crude, illustration of this phenomenon, but it may not be particularly representative of ethnic minority voters in general. An alternative to this might be the suggestion that ethnic minority cultures create a sufficiently distinct approach to politics and political activity (Field, 1984). At first glance, the cultural link displayed by many Asian, African and Caribbean voters seems to provide plentiful evidence for such an agenda, though it would be only fair to describe this as a cultural rather than racial approach to politics. In any case, however attractive this line of argument may seem (and it is regularly exploited by media commentators and politicians alike), the question remains as to whether this agenda shapes ethnic minority political participation in any exclusive or near-exclusive sense. Whatever the strength of the cultural basis of, say, Asians' political outlook may be, the argument is undermined if this factor is one of several shaping political behaviour (an oversight graphically evident in Eade, 1993). The theme of culture in modelling ethnic minority electoral behaviour will be returned to in the discussion at the end of the chapter.

The key point that counts about 'race agenda' type claims is that, while there is much that ethnic minorities have in common with one another, researchers are hard put to say with confidence that this kind of commonality forms a sufficient basis for a unique and exclusive political outlook. The distinct cultural heritage of south Asians, for example, provides a rich seam for researchers interested in this topic but few have been able to provide generalisable interpretations of the impact of their ethnicity upon politics. The most that can be said reliably is that ethnicity undoubtedly does have an imprecise and varying impact at the collective group level. The evidence for this assessment stems largely from studies of the involvement of ethnic minorities in local politics and focused around the mobilisation of ethnicity for various tangible spoils. One of the most convincing examples can be seen in the documented account of the use of ethnic identity and loyalties as resources against far-right violence in the late 1970s in Southall, a west London suburb (Southall Rights/CARF, 1981). The effective 'spoil' that was the centre of this deliberate rise in ethnic consciousness might have been interpreted as relative freedom from racial intimidation and violence; this is undoubtedly a valuable benefit for many ethnic minorities but one which may be difficult to quantify. The ethnicity of ethnic minorities even here tends to serve as an additional influence on their political behaviour, alongside a range of familiar non-ethnic factors (Rath and Saggar, 1992).

Similar agendas, different priorities
Secondly, *the political outlook and behaviour of ethnic minorities and their white counterparts may be based on the same range of issues and policy concerns but reordered in priority and emphasis.* In very simple terms, what we are interested in is the likelihood of overlap between ethnic minority and white political agendas allowing additionally for differences of emphasis across ethnic boundaries. A fairly typical illustration can be seen in survey data from the 1987 general election which showed wide variations in the importance white, Asian and Afro-Caribbean voters attached to issues such as housing and defence (see Table 2.2,). Broadly speaking, for white voters the latter held greater significance than among black voters; meanwhile, the former issue resonated strongly among one group of ethnic minority voters and not at all among another. More recent data in the run-up to the 1997 election showed quite significant reordering of priorities across different issues among Asians and Afro-Caribbeans (MORI, 1996, 1997).

Table 2.2 *Most important issues (of two) by ethnic group, 1987 general election (%)*

Issues	Asian	Afro-Caribbean	White
Unemployment	65	70	45
Health	34	25	32
Education	17	13	19
Defence	32	18	37
Law and order	11	4	6
Pensions	6	7	9
Housing	0	21	5
Prices	10	15	7
Race	1	0	1

Source: BBC/Gallup (1987).

The crucial point is that ethnic minority and white agendas are both the same and distinct simultaneously. This does not, however, tell us much about *why* priorities may differ across ethnic lines. For this we need to refine our understanding of causal relationships underpinning inter-ethnic variance. One line of argument is that the role of ethnicity is a bit of a red herring since it displaces the key point, namely that ethnic minorities are more likely to be Labour supporters (or identifiers at least) in any case. Identification with Labour, both at a party political level and in terms of general principles and philosophy, means that they are more likely in turn to attach priority to certain types of issues – and possibly values – rather than others. Issues such as housing, health and education are the traditional staple diet of Labour supporters and this is much the same for ethnic minority, Labour-inclined voters. Thus, different priorities are really very little to do with ethnically-related fundamentals.

Another, related line of argument highlights the contribution made by objective socio-economic differences between the white and non-white electorates (Crewe, 1983). For example, the substantially younger age profile of the latter and the heavier middle-class concentration of the former, both serves to give ethnic minority voters a rather different stake in certain issues over others in comparison with their white counterparts. It is not uncommon to observe that the age and class characteristics of any electoral sub-group shape their general orientation to key issues such as housing and taxation. Residential patterns are another example of orientation towards issues and, in turn, votes for political parties (McAllister and Studlar, 1984: 147).

However, while inter-ethnic variance can be traced back in this way, there is always a danger of researchers overdoing things by concentrating excessively on white versus non-white distinctions. In fact, analysis derived from 1980s Labour Force Survey data by Robinson (1990) rightly draws attention to fairly wide variations in the socio-economic profiles of Asian sub-groups, ethnic Indians and Bangladeshis being prime examples at opposite ends of the spectrum. The upshot of this intra-Asian difference is that there are likely to be different underlying orientations toward political issues that may in some cases outstrip differences between white and non-white electors. An additional risk associated with any social demographic-linked explanation is that this still begs the question of how much convergence is probable over time. Ethnic minority voters in that sense are just another illustration of a sectional electorate, which for reasons to do with migration and labour market participation looks rather different from the rest of the electorate. So much is clear. However, patterns of convergence – as well as some tendency toward greater divergence – are the key to understanding why certain issues count for more than others. Rather greater empirical research along these lines is sorely needed if we are to unpick the mystery of issue salience, and in particular its relationship to issue voting among ethnic minorities.

A further line of argument has been that differences of priority are a reflection of some issues being perceived to be linked to race while others are not. That is to say, ethnic minority voters are in the business of examining the full range of political issues and interpreting for themselves which issues comply with a race agenda and which do not. This argument ascribes a rather higher level of sophistication upon ethnic minority voters (in a way not applicable to white voters), suggesting that any race dimension that is at play is both selective and variable as a factor in itself. Thus, for example, the issue of education for ethnic minority voters can have meaning both in familiar terms to do with, say, school budgets and class sizes, as well as in terms of multicultural curricula and anti-discrimination policies. The 1991 Harris survey mentioned previously revealed that education was the most significant issue for 41 per cent of Asians (Harris Research Centre, 1991). This is formidable evidence of strong issue salience, decisively overshadowing the issue of racial attacks into second place. However, what we cannot tell for certain is whether respondents interpreted the general question of education in racial or non-racial terms. The likelihood is that something of both interpretations is encapsulated in the 41 per cent figure, but distinguishing between them is impossible at this level of analysis. To illustrate issue recognition is one thing, but to demonstrate what is meant by such salience is another, more complex matter.

Parallel agendas

Thirdly, and building on the previous remarks regarding voter sophistication, *white and non-white issue agendas may appear much the same as one another but for the latter group all issues embody some linkage with race and ethnicity*. Therefore, ethnic minority voters seem to shadow white voters' concerns and are interested in all the same issues with an equal degree of importance. Such voters are, to a considerable degree, just like white voters and it would be reasonable to claim that the smaller non-white electorate is merely a sectional element of the larger electorate. But the resemblance goes only so far because the similar issue agenda of non-white voters also comprises a parallel, race-related way of looking at the same issues.

These voters treat issues such as education as being about both non-racial and racial choices at one and the same time, though for somewhat different reasons. This kind of description would seem to be getting closer to identifying a theory of an ethnically-related way of thinking and behaving politically, the need for which was outlined and stressed above. What we are saying, in effect, is that everyday political issues concomitantly have racial and non-racial faces. This much is plausible and helps us to understand that there is no easy way to pinpoint what for ethnic minorities is an issue of race. For such an issue can be a reference to either the 'race issue', as commonly dubbed by politicians and the press (e.g. racial discrimination against ethnic minority schoolchildren), or to a race-related aspect of otherwise non-racial policy concerns (e.g. hidden racial bias in the educational curricula, witness debates over the teaching of British national history and the role of imperial history).

A more helpful way of conceptualising the two related levels of issue formation is in terms of the distinction between overt or direct racism on the one hand, and covert or indirect racism on the other. Traditionally, the so-called 'race issue' has, for ethnic minorities at least, been substantially about the effects of identifiable, direct forms of racial discrimination. In that sense, the question of race stands more or less independently within the social and ideological construction of the issue. It is thus about race (in a negative discriminatory way) first and foremost, irrespective of the wider policy context or environment in which the allegation or grievance is set. This, presumably, is how ethnic minorities interpret powerful public examples of overt bias against black and Asian people in areas such as policing and job hiring. The only uncertainty is whether an individual black or Asian person systematically recognises such an example to be of importance and worthy of attention. Clearly, some ethnic minorities have differences with others as to the authenticity of specific examples of alleged racial injustice. But once there is agreement about the significance of a particular example there is no further uncertainty clouding the question. For example therefore, having been recognised immediately as both salient and authentic, the police shooting of Cherry Groce, a black grandmother, in Brixton in 1985 represented for many British blacks a potent reminder of the race issue in traditional and, sadly, familiar form. A similar perception doubtless followed the Stephen Lawrence affair and the subsequent Macpherson inquiry in the late 1990s (Holdaway, 1998).

However, comparatively few issues are crystallised in such crude racial terms as the result of a single incident. Indeed, naturally, and rightly, cautious researchers have been keen to stress that such an example is by no means the sole interpretation of race in issue terms. The issue is equally about a whole host of anxieties over indirect forms of racial discrimination and hostility. A 1995 survey carried out for the *Guardian* newspaper gave credence to the idea that, whatever their sense of optimism or pessimism about race relations, black Afro-Caribbeans cannot afford to forget the high levels of prejudice that all survey respondents – black and white – admit still persists in Britain. The survey showed that 40 per cent of respondents thought that there was 'a lot of prejudice', joined by a further 39 per cent who thought that there was 'a little prejudice' (*Guardian*, 1995).

Ethnic minorities from time to time have anxieties and express doubts about a variety of attitudes, policies and procedures which they feel may be working against their interests. These complaints are essentially about indirect biases and amount to a belief that negative racial considerations are at play in broad aspects of public and private life. It is also a positivist assessment regarding the extent to which race factors do – rather than ought to – have a bearing on what happens in substantive policy areas as diverse as pensions, healthcare, prisons and so on.[4] This, then, is not as close to the traditional interpretation of the race issue, not least because it embodies a range of beliefs about covert attitudes, actions and processes, not all of which are universally present. As conservative commentators frequently remind us, it is very hard to convince the electorate at large about the legitimacy of the race issue at this much broader level, and some critics have sought to ridicule the claim (Johnson, 1991). Moreover, if some critics are to be believed, there are even doubts about the extent to which the ethnic minority electorate share common beliefs about the existence and/or significance of hidden racism.

The important point to stress is that ethnic minority voters accept that many issue areas have a latent race dimension to them, and that a high degree of selectivity is apparent in deciding what additional priority, if any, should be given to otherwise racially-neutral issue concerns. Race is both an issue and a non-issue. The choice between seeing things in racial or non-racial terms is not a haphazard or unpredictable process, but instead closely linked to the extent to which race is conceptualised in narrow as opposed to broad terms. Thus, criticisms about ethnic minority voters having things both ways would be rather unfair and, in any case, would tend to miss the point about how and why race-related factors come to shape ethnic minority political outlook and behaviour. The problem in the realm of political participation arises once very generalised allegations are made about the treatment of ethnic minorities by political institutions. The risk here is not so much of having things both ways but rather just one, fairly rigid way. According to one vocal activist in the run up to the 1997 general election, participation itself was essentially an issue of race over which minorities had little, if any, discretion (Woolley, quoted in the *Evening Standard*, 1997): '[The main political parties] are equally culpable in pursuing policies and practices which entrenched disaffection among young black people. Black people feel the parties do not listen to them and they don"t feel they have enough political muscle to get their voice heard.'

The same agenda, writ small
Finally, *it is frequently suggested that the issue agenda of ethnic minorities amounts to the same as that for the white electorate, but writ small.* The issue agendas of both groups match one another fully, with only small variations of degree being put down to factors such as the legacy of

migration and transitional adjustments associated with resettlement. In truth, this view of ethnic minority voters has received backing from some of the data on ethnic minority issue salience and voting behaviour (see Tables 2.1 and 2.2,). A glance at much of the historic volume of data reveals heavy long-term support for the Labour Party among ethnic minority voters. This distribution is commonly accounted for by the skewed class structure of the ethnic minority population, which in turn causes these voters to hold a closer interest in relevant class and party-led issue concerns. The underlying picture remains one of ethnic minority and white similarity, distorted temporarily by objective class and demographic factors.

In the longer run, so the argument goes, we can expect to see even greater uniformity across the ethnic minority and white electorates as the former's class structure evolves to match the latter's. The argument is one that tends to veer away from current, front-end evidence of voting patterns and instead focuses more on longer-term, underlying trends (Saggar, 1997c). Even then, there are plenty of conservative-inclined commentators and activists who, looking at current patterns, insist that there is little that is ethnic about the votes of ethnic minorities. Indeed, there is no point in chasing the so-called 'ethnic vote' since, it is argued, it has got very little to do with ethnicity as such. These conservative strategists seem to stress that insofar as the ethnic minority electorate is to be targeted and courted, it should be treated in much the same manner as the rest of the electorate, of which it is merely a geographically-clustered and socially-discrete element (Gillan, 1997; Rich, 1998). Similar positions are not impossible to find among some Labour and Liberal Democrat strategists. The extent to which this type of colour-blind strategy is translated into campaigning tactics is a moot point since few candidates of whatever party seem able to resist the temptation of courting ethnic minority votes in an ethnic-specific manner. The question of party strategy and its relationship to ethnicity is a subject taken up later in this chapter.

For the analyst there is little left to explain if ethnic minority and white agendas have converged or are on course do so over time. If their agendas are alike, it should be expected that both groups would share common attitudes towards the issues that they face in common as well as their general political orientation. Ethnic minority voters thus represent little that is in itself distinct from their white counterparts. Tables 2.1 and 2.2 reveal a remarkable degree of similarity between ethnic minority and white voting agendas, save for some limited differences on a handful of issues. However, as noted previously, these data do not preclude black and Asian voters from concomitantly perceiving that there is an additional race dimension to all of the issues listed irrespective of whether pollsters describe them in obviously race-specific terms.

That such a dimension to superficially non-racial issues may exist is not in contention. Indeed, from time to time, there is likely to be good reason to think that selected issues operate at both levels for those ethnic minorities pushing for wider recognition of ethno-racial bias in mainstream areas of public service delivery such as, say, healthcare, welfare and social services. The difficulty is that this level of analysis cannot hope to reveal the full picture of the "racialisation", as it were, of issues facing these minority voters. This is a methodological difficulty that researchers must live with and, moreover, concede will not be massaged away through speculation or conjecture (Alibhai-Brown, 1999). All we can do is first, report the degree of overall similarity that is shown up by survey research, and secondly, draw modest generalisations about whether race-specific issues seem to play a significant part in the priorities of ethnic minority voters.

Race and ethnicity and party strategy

At the heart of contemporary British politics there is an assumption which implies that ethnic minority voters ought to be courted in ethnically-specific ways. The assumption is broadly shared by the three major political parties and generally receives the endorsement of party leaderships keen not to overlook innovative and unconventional approaches to electoral advantage.

Significantly, even the Conservatives who have attempted to project an ostensibly 'colour-blind' self-image – for example the pointed 'Tories say he's British, Labour says he's black' campaign poster of 1983 – have nevertheless made concessions to ethnic politics (Rich, 1998; Saggar, 1997d, 1998d). The party's Anglo-Asian and Anglo-Conservative Societies, although wound up in the mid-1980s, clearly signalled the acceptance by party managers in the Conservative Party to address these groups of voters – and donors! – using mechanisms that accepted these electors' ethnic distinctiveness. While it may be debatable whether ethnicity counts so centrally for ethnic minority voters as a whole, Conservative Party strategy has been moved by the possibility that it may do so. No doubt the landmark CRC report on the 1974 elections played a big part in shifting Tory strategy, appealing as it did to a narrowly-defeated major party that had historically shown no interest in this section of the electorate. Perversely, the acceptance that ethnicity might count for something among this group of voters has largely failed to shape Conservative Party strategy at any significant level. The party has, even following the elevation of a new guard leadership in 1997, strenuously avoided making any commitments on racial or ethnic lines that could spill over into its broad appeal to voters, white and non-white, at large.

Ironically, since 1979 this willingness, possibly insistence, to see such voters through an ethnic prism of sorts seems to go hand in hand with a widely-held desire to leave the race issue on the backburner of party competition. Race and ethnicity in that sense do not seem to command any great significance – arguably since at least early in the 1983 parliament – and yet these concepts count as much as any when it comes to parties' attempts to gather non-white support. This is a fairly remarkable paradox to say the least. Furthermore, there is considerable evidence of confusion and muddle over the nature of the issues that are thought to motivate these voters (as discussed in the previous section on an ethnically-related theory of political behaviour). Nevertheless, party leaders and strategists remain convinced that a specific racial or culturally driven agenda exists and can be exploited for party gain.

In this section of the chapter, we shall look at the origins and reasoning behind this assumption. We shall pause to consider whether parties and ethnic minority voters are well-served or hampered by this central assumption, and whether electoral politics conducted in these terms is capable of delivering beneficial change for ethnic minorities. We shall also consider how far underlying views of ethnic minority electoral motivation and awareness of self-interest influence this assumption.

The background to this assumption can be traced back to the mid to late 1970s, and in particular to the conscious decision by the Labour and Conservative Parties to pay more attention to wooing the non-white electorate. A key element in this strategic calculation was the myth perpetuated following the October 1974 general election suggesting two things. First, that the Conservatives' second defeat was attributable to neglect of ethnic minority voters in crucial seats, and secondly that these voters were an example of a floating vote that could be solicited on ethnic or racial lines (CRC, 1975). Neither assertion was supported by much credible evidence but none the less proved a powerful force behind the parties' discovery of the so-called 'ethnic vote'. On the first claim, the CRC study sought to highlight so-called 'ethnic marginals', where it was believed the size of the non-white electorate exceeded the size of the winning majority. This claim was methodologically flawed by the use of 1971 Census estimates of the size of the New Commonwealth and Pakistani origin population in these constituencies, making no allowance for calculations of age disqualification (i.e. under-18s), registration rates and turn out. On the second charge, the CRC report made no attempt to substantiate its assertion that the support of ethnic minority voters – whether located in marginal seats or not – was dependent on the major parties' policies and attitudes towards race and immigration issues. A final nail in the coffin of the argument was that, despite showing the degree of electoral volatility that had occurred in these marginal seats from the first 1974 election to the second, it could not produce any evidence to show that a non-white differential switch had resulted in seats changing hands. Indeed, it was just as possible to argue the opposite on the basis of the evidence used: that non-white voters had largely stayed put while white voters had changed sides in order to deliver Tory marginals to the Labour Party.

Added to this, an established ethnic minority political leadership received growing media attention from 1976 onwards. By overtly standing for self-described immigrant interests, this development gave parties further reason to think about and do business with ethnic minorities in ethnically-specific ways. The logic of ethnic minority leadership meeting with a mainstream party system with virtually no experience of handling or aggregating ethnicity, meant that fertile ground was cultivated by proponents of the new ethnic politics. None of this, of course, particularly helps explain whether such a strategy has been empirically well-founded or indeed successful.

Are British political parties correct or wise to approach ethnic minority voters in this manner? The answer would seem to suggest that parties do a poor and patchy job by relying on such a strategy. Two arguments spearhead this response, one which examines the historical-structural context, another based on the outlook of ethnic minority and white voters themselves.

To begin with, it should be recalled that British political parties are not in the universal business of trying to attract ethnic minority voters. In truth, some parties have flirted from time to time with the notion of seeking the support of this constituency, while others have been content to let the issue lie undisturbed. The distinction, moreover, is even further underlined when examining the approaches taken by different individual politicians. Intra-party variance on this question reveals that the ethnicity of ethnic minorities can often be shunned and embraced simultaneously.

However, for the most part political parties have worked fully within the understanding that ethnic minority voters are both attitudinally and geographically among the safest constituencies of the Labour Party. As Table 2.3 makes clear, long-term backing for Labour from ethnic minorities remains strong and remarkably stable.[5] To be sure, even the marked dip in Labour's support at the 1987 general election proved to be an embarrassing false dawn by the time of the 1992 contest. In any other context, this group of voters would not be described as a particularly worthwhile opportunity for Labour's rivals. Recognising both Labour's reliance on non-white voters and these voters' strong orientation towards Labour, it has become increasingly apparent that few spoils are on offer to parties competing on this territory. Indeed, Labour's posture toward its ethnic minority supporters has been described in terms of neglect, if not arrogance (FitzGerald, 1988; Shukra, 1998b: ch. 5; Howe, 1988). None of this has particularly discouraged those who continue to be determined to perpetuate still further the all too hollow 'ethnic marginals' thesis (CRE, 1994; Ali and Percival, 1993; BBC, 1995).

Table 2.3 *Levels of Labour and Conservative support among ethnic minorities, 1974, 1979, 1983, 1987, 1992, 1997 (%)*

	1974[a]	1979	1983[b]	1987	1992[b]	1997[a]
Labour	81	86	83	72	81	78
Conservative	9	8	7	18	10	17

Notes: [a]October 1974 general election. [b]Figures represent recalculated average of Asian and black support levels.
Sources: adapted from CRC (1975), CRE (1980), CRE (1984); Harris Research Centre (1987), Ali and Percival (1993) and Saggar (1997a).

In any case, whatever efforts have been made across the political parties to marshal ethnic minority support have been rather unique and unprecedented in the sense that, historically, ethnicity has long counted for little in British party competition. Britain certainly has hardly any tradition of religious definition or determination of party labels and loyalties comparable with many continental European political systems. Equally, the ethno-linguistic character of politics in places such as Belgium, parts of Iberia, and further afield in Canada, appears largely alien in the British system. The extent to which the ethnicity of ethnic minorities receives attention in British politics is thus novel and far-removed from the traditional class basis of modern political mobilisation (a point properly driven home some while ago by FitzGerald, 1985b: 1).

In fact, it is not so much the ethnic identity of ethnic minorities that is the subject of attention but, rather, the presumption of politicians that racism and race relations are what count for black and Asian participants above all else. As we have already seen, this presumption is rather ill-considered since, according to existing, although patchy, survey research, ethnic minorities do not as a rule prioritise a race agenda over other concerns.

The upshot of this is that it has become increasingly difficult for ethnic minorities to participate in local and national politics without reference first, to their ethnic identity, and secondly, to the wider meaning given to their ethnicity in British politics and society. Critics of this state of affairs would claim that ethnicity has thus become institutionalised and been co-opted into mainstream political thinking. This scenario possibly presents several opportunities for ethnic minority political leaders and sympathetic white politicians to push ahead and secure tangible gains on behalf of the black and Asian population. Indeed, much of this kind of advancement had already taken place during the 1980s, especially at local level, enabling Asian and black Britons to achieve important breakthroughs in, for instance, accessing public service delivery processes and decision making (Gyford, 1985; Nanton, 1989).

On the deficit side, however, there has been something of a steady tightening of the ethnicity straitjacket that shapes major party strategic thinking towards ethnic minority participation. This may not necessarily strike all observers as a drawback since it successfully tackles the longer-standing complaint of colour-blindness characterising party thinking. The deficiencies are more apparent when it is asked to what extent ethnic minorities define their interests in solely ethnic-specific terms. Evidently there is some ambiguity here. Much hangs on the reading of the data though, in general, it is reasonably clear that ethnic minorities are not exclusively preoccupied, let alone obsessed, with such an agenda. Whether these voters interpret ethnic-based channels of political action and policy influence as an opportunity or as patronising and burdensome is a debatable question. It is also a question worthy of extended empirical research in the future, and a point that is touched upon in relation to attitudes towards race relations discussed in Chapter 6.

Putting aside this debate for the moment, there are some important conceptual implications that stem from the argument that valuable benefits accrue to ethnic minorities through the current conduct of electoral politics and affiliation with the Labour Party. The most significant of these implications is to ask what kind of benefits proponents of this argument have in mind? The most common response has been to restate the view that ethnic minority interests are best served by policy commitments that target unemployment, educational attainment, housing provision, urban renewal, etc. Many of these policy commitments tend to overlap with traditional Labour and centre-left ideological territory, thereby encouraging the view that the Labour Party specifically is best placed to advance ethnic minority interests. However, once again the complication arises from the distinction between race and race-related policy concerns on the one hand, and various superficially non-racial, mainstream policy concerns on the other. One reading would be to insist that ethnic minorities, by virtue of their socio-economic and geographic location, are likely beneficiaries of a range of public policy commitments that are aimed at improving conditions and opportunities for disadvantaged, less prosperous, urban population groups. Black and Asian people are thus not so much the targets of Labour or centre-left policies but, rather, the indirect and disproportionate 'winners' from such a policy agenda and its inherent priorities. This interpretation, if widely shared and expounded in Labour thinking and self-image, can serve as a powerful rationale for the party to continue presenting its policies towards ethnic minorities in such a generalised, non-targeted way. After all, if it can be argued that Labour's priorities will serve to benefit ethnic minorities indirectly, it becomes increasingly possible to defend a strategy of avoiding making any direct appeals to this group of voters. This defence can in turn appear seductive within a wider electoral landscape that additionally perceives, and thus fears, the power of a white 'backlash'.

Any argument that portrays ethnic minorities as potential beneficiaries of Labour's non-racial policies alone suffers from one overwhelming drawback. Namely, that it is quite misleading to claim that these voters are not courted in ethnically or race-specific terms. Clearly they are courted in such terms both by parties in general, and in particular by Labour's well-rehearsed display of overt policy commitments to further non-whites' collective interests. Labour in particular has come to be regarded by ethnic minority and white electors as the 'ethnic minority-friendly party', though, as we shall note in the discussion of issue voting below, past experience casts severe doubts on the party's right to deserve such a reputation. In any case, Labour's putatively closer association with ethnic minority interests makes it difficult for the party to continue to insist that the non-ethnic bond between party and group is all that matters. In many inner city constituencies, as witnessed in 1997, Labour's long track record of involvement in various internal ethnic minority concerns demonstrates that its appeal for their votes is not solely a question of its indirect appeal on traditional employment, social policy and social welfare issues.

Furthermore, almost as if to ignore Labour's structural head-start, other parties have periodically made efforts to attract ethnic minority voters using strategies that both recognise the ethnicity of this electorate and also make play of various related and unrelated factors. These factors can be said to underscore parties' strategic thinking about the nature of the ethnic minority electorate and are discussed in greater depth below.

Ethnic and racial considerations come into focus even more sharply when we examine the particular appeal that the Labour Party has attempted to project toward ethnic minorities. Despite numerous misgivings within the hierarchy of the national party over any visible association with ethnic minority voters, it is nevertheless clear that the party has amassed a variety of policy commitments aimed at maintaining the loyalty of its non-white supporters. The unambiguous thinking behind this posture presumably must be that race issues matter and matter significantly to this constituency of supporters. For example, the party has gone on record to promise that it would introduce new legislation to promote race equality measures (particularly in public services) and to expand the legal basis of indirect discrimination (by subjecting the police service to existing laws, for example). While Opposition Labour also indicated that it would take on many of the proposals from the Commission for Racial Equality to expand its powers (Layton-Henry, 1992: 119), though there has been a lot of back-pedalling on this issue since taking office. Elsewhere, it also committed itself while in Opposition to scrapping the 1981 British Nationality Act, though this pledge was updated with another to remove the discriminatory aspects of the 1981 law. To a very considerable extent, its future plans for immigration policy remain sensitive to the electoral charge that it is a fundamentally weak party on immigration (Seyd and Whiteley, 1992). Even these plans must be seen in the context of the party's main pledge which has been to remove the discriminatory aspects of the 1981 legislation as a partial prelude to the possibility of wholesale immigration reform. (As an early gesture, in May 1997, Labour's Home Secretary announced the scrapping of the 1983 'primary purpose' immigration rules.) As a party of government few voters, least of all ethnic minority voters, can have much doubt that Labour persists in its long-standing stance of backing non-whites' interests in ways that are universal and focused on general socio-economic change. Labour is at the same time squarely behind these interests using policy pledges that are ethnically and racially-defined and thus of primary concern to ethnic minority voters.

Does this mean that the Labour Party qualifies for the reputation of 'best promoter-designate' of ethnic minority interests? Arguably not, since far too much is taken for granted in terms of conceptual and theoretical understanding of such interests. For one thing, this perspective necessarily reduces the question of race as a political issue to its barest essentials, relying instead on the idea that formal claims to eradicate discrimination are the same as substantive change. In the minds of many ethnic minorities this simplistic equation may command respect but, equally, among others it may not. One reason for a possible disjuncture is that some ethnic minorities may distinguish between rhetoric and reality when it comes to questions of race and politics. They may, indeed, be correct to do so given the experience of vacillation and tough talk over race and immigration politics since the late 1960s.

Another reason, may simply be that they do not think that these kinds of interventionist policies are best suited to addressing British race relations. Instead, by viewing the conflicts thrown up by ethnic and racial pluralism in somewhat different terms, it is not hard to imagine that some ethnic minority voters might have some scepticism about the efficacy of legislative and public policy 'solutions'. These ethnic minority 'doubters' would not necessarily need to be described as neo-conservative opponents to conclude that alternative strategies, perhaps based on emphasising cross-cultural education and compromise, might be the best way forward.

Yet another reason is that Labour's arguably stronger, more activist approach to tackling race relations may be met with indifference and disinterest by yet other ethnic minorities. Thus, what for Labour – and indeed progressives in other parties – may be seen as a priority, may not be accepted as such by elements of the target constituency. In other words, it is increasingly apparent that it is hard, perhaps impossible, to make sweeping generalisations about the stance of ethnic minorities as a whole toward race relations questions. (Indeed, in the following section we shall discuss some of the evidence on ethnic minorities' attitudes to liberal race relations policies.) If this is hard enough, it is even less meaningful to try to draw a strong correlation between Labour's policies on race on the one hand, and opinion on race among ethnic minorities on the other. The biggest hurdle would appear to be that there is only limited evidence to show that ethnic minorities attach special – let alone overwhelming – priority to the kinds of policy concerns upon which Labour's race-specific strategy is based (CRE, 1994).

More generally, as other parties attempt to make overtures to ethnic minority voters, many cannot avoid pitching their appeal in ways that mimic elements of Labour's strategy. Conservative and Liberal-Democrat thinking may remain steadfast in its determination to avoid Labour-style overt racialisation of political discourse, however, it is noticeable that both parties have been prepared to utilise reasonably explicit strategies that assume that ethnic minority voters are chiefly interested in race and race-related issues. Both parties, for instance, begin by making great play of the notion that they are committed to rooting out racial discrimination in their own ranks, and that anti-discrimination laws have a proper and legitimate role in society. Each of them have also been through embarrassing public rows over the persistence of racism among their own party members and in high profile campaigns (e.g. the Conservative's tussle over John Taylor's candidacy in Cheltenham in 1992 and the Liberal-Democrats' racially ambiguous messages in local elections in Tower Hamlets in 1993 and 1994). These episodes both demonstrated that neither party could afford to maintain silence in the face of very serious complaints about racism. A part of their response has, presumably, been shaped by the need to at least recognise that potential ethnic minority supporters hold legitimate worries that are directly related to race. Equally, both have accepted and even made some play of the argument that ethnic minority voters are not the only ones concerned about racial discrimination; indeed, white, liberal sentiment on the theme is arguably of some considerable influence in shaping thinking in both parties.

Elsewhere, the Conservatives have made capital over alleged separatist demands made by Black Sections supporters in the Labour Party. However, with the constitutional blocking of such a proposal within the Labour Party, it is worth remembering that the Conservative's own One Nation Forum existed until 1998 chiefly in order to marshal ethnic minority votes and money by an appeal that was based on both racial and non-racial grounds. Equally, the Liberal-Democrats have been keen to condemn Labour-style codification of race especially in local government. However, they too retain a formal and informal apparatus to rally ethnic minority supporters, chiefly through aggressive self-promotion of the party's longstanding progressive stance on race and immigration.

Having rightly drawn attention to the remarkable degree of shared thinking toward race and electoral campaigning across the major parties, it is of course only fair to acknowledge that there is one area in which

Labour's boast is founded on irrefutable evidence. The opportunities that have been carved out for ethnic minority political candidates since the mid-1980s serve to mark the party out as being especially sensitive to its ethnic minority constituency. Geddes (1993) reported several years ago that a colossal 85 per cent of all ethnic minority local government councillors belonged to Labour's ranks, while Le Lohé (1998) has updated this picture with estimates that show a diminution of Labour's dominance. After 1997, all nine ethnic minority MPs are Labour representatives. The remaining ethnic minority 'also-rans' in 1997 and 1992 contained a much greater number of Labour candidates who were within reach of victory (though the absolute number of Labour candidates roughly matched the Conservative field). Underlying this track record, Labour has undoubtedly built up a much deeper seam of ethnic minority activists, officials and would-be candidates. It is from this seam that future numbers of successful candidates will emerge at both national and local levels, and we can expect the current picture of party imbalance among ethnic minority representatives to perpetuate into the future (Norris and Lovenduski, 1995: 237–48; Saggar and Geddes, 2000).

The Labour Party, then, is in a curious and rather difficult position. It both receives the overwhelming bulk of ethnic minority votes cast and also champions, albeit rather conditionally, the rights and interests of Britain's ethnic minorities. However, this position also means that it is also under an obligation to present the ethnic minority electorate with policy commitments that are designed to benefit this group of voters. The choice of commitments tends to vary but at heart it means that the party has to supplement its broad-based policies aimed at its general constituency of supporters and potential supporters. This in effect means that, however limited and superficial, Labour must offer a race-specific package of commitments that target non-white voters. The irony is that it is unclear whether the party needs to go to any great effort to massage what is, after all, among one of its safest constituencies. Furthermore, Labour's need to show *sensitivity* towards racial and ethnic concerns is founded on very loose evidence that such issues are the key to retaining the support of ethnic minorities.

Such sensitivity is by no means confined to Labour's ranks and, to some degree, is shared by political parties in general. The willingness of parties to operate in these terms is, of course, partly a consequence of features within ethnic minority community-based politics. Nevertheless, British political parties are unlikely to rid themselves entirely of this style of strategic mobilisation and all regard the ethnic minority electorate in some way or another as an important component of electoral competition for the pursuit or retention of office.

Characterising the political interests of ethnic minorities

If ethnic minority voters are to some degree or another perceived by political parties as the common target, what can be said that best characterises the collective interests and mobilisation of this group of voters? Research conclusions on this point tend to be somewhat patchy, not least because few commentators have seen the need to map out available evidence at a conceptual level. In this section of the chapter we shall explore some possibilities and try to assess whether or not political parties base their appeal upon a coherent, and therefore defensible, understanding of ethnic minority political interests and mobilisation.

There are arguably three basic ways in which we can think of ethnic minority voters as being capable of either having or developing a sense of shared common interest. With each of these characterisations we can see wide variations in the conceptual basis for thinking and acting with common cause. Some limited degree of similarity is apparent when interpreting survey data, and much depends on the extent to which we accept that ethnic minorities themselves are aware of, and are influenced by, a race-specific issue agenda.

Social class

First, *the interests and motivations of ethnic minority voters can be described in socio-economic terms based on class membership and accompanying party identification*. This interpretation is itself founded on traditional class-centred analyses of British electoral behaviour, whereby class has been used as a predictor of party choice (Pulzer, 1967; Robertson, 1984; Butler and Stokes, 1974; see also Lipset, 1960). The point about mapping non-white voting behaviour in class-based terms is that this approach takes account of the continuing concentration of ethnic minorities among lower socio-economic groups relative to their white counterparts (Jones, 1993). It is thus not surprising to learn that most ethnic minorities identify themselves with the manual working-class and, in turn, with key institutions related to that class (Layton-Henry, 1992: 66). So much is true and helps us explain ethnic minority working-class political orientation. What is more difficult to fathom is the persistently high level of middle-class ethnic minority support for the Labour Party, with a degree of conviction and loyalty to rival their non-middle class co-supporters. In this respect, it would appear that they are locking onto identification with their 'community' as much as with anything else (such as class). A rival interpretation might highlight the extent to which middle-class ethnic minority support for Labour is the outcome of additional higher education (Price and Sanders, 1993). University education for the electorate as a whole tends to push up the likelihood of supporting Labour and, in the case of ethnic minorities, it may be that increasing

Table 2.4 *Voting intention by social class, 1979 and 1992ᵃ (%)*

	1979 general election								
	White			Asian			Afro-Caribbean		
	ABC1	C2	DE	ABC1	C2	DE	ABC1	C2	DE
Labour	20	35	38	42	50	50	41	49	48
Conservative	57	40	32	25	28	25	17	11	15
Liberal	9	5	5	6	3	0	5	8	3
Other	15	20	25	28	19	25	35	32	35
N	3588	3290	3145	36	32	40	29	37	40

	1992 general election			
	White (N = 1879)		Non-white (N = 857)	
	ABC1	C2DE	ABC1	C2DE
Labour	37	52	54	78
Conservative	47	28	31	8

Notes: ᵃExcludes Liberal-Democrats and others.
Sources: BBC/Gallup (1979), CRE (1994).

levels of participation in higher education are fuelling continuing loyalty to Labour, albeit for a range of non-class-related reasons. Table 2.4 tells the story of class-deviant Labour voting among middle-class ethnic minorities over two typical elections.

A very large element of Labour's support among ethnic minorities can be attributed to the skewed class profile of this group. However, not all of it can be put down to social class. In looking at the strength of Labour support beyond that accounted for by social class, Heath *et al.* (1991: 113) argue that: 'Perceptions of group interests or processes of group identification are plausible explanations'. Therefore, other factors are almost certainly at work, though the impact of race and ethnicity factors may be just as much of a reason against certain examples of party choice as they are for it. For instance, a 1983 Harris Research survey revealed that 76 per cent of Labour voting, Afro-Caribbeans justified their choice by citing that 'they [Labour] support the working class', followed by a crucial 9 per cent who said that they 'did not want the Conservatives in government', and 7 per cent who felt that 'they [Labour] supported blacks and Asians'. The comparable figures for Asians in the same survey were 64, 8 and 31 per cent respectively (Harris Research Centre, 1983). In a 1996 survey, 31 per cent, of blacks who supported Labour explained their choice in terms of class representation, against just 8 per cent who saw Labour as 'best for black people' (MORI, 1996). These data tell us that other factors are serving to build anti-Conservative bonds between some non-white voters and the Labour Party. Though smaller in magnitude than the positive link between them, this point cannot be ignored as a long-term key variable stunting the development of greater Conservative identification and/or voting.

This characterisation sees ethnic minority voters as creatures of their objective socio-economic environment. Thus, working-class membership is not all that counts and is added to the host of other indicators of environment. For example, 1991 Census data showed that elements of the black population occupied a generally weaker social and economic position disproportionate to their numbers; aspects of this position include housing tenure, physical housing conditions, lone parenthood, long-term illnesses, unemployment, types of economic activity, etc. However, on other indicators certain sub-groups within this population were tending to fare rather better than their white counterparts (e.g. in terms of participation in further and higher education, and entry into professional occupations). Analysis based on LFS data by Berthoud in the late 1990s reinforced this picture of pockets of success in educational and employment areas, most notably among young black women (Berthoud, 2000). This picture of differential experience within one group indicates that crude class generalisations should either be avoided or at least seen in their proper context (Owen, 1994).

As voters whose loyalties are shaped by environment, ethnic minorities have been strong Labour identifiers and supporters mainly as a consequence of first, their entry into the labour market following immigration, and secondly, the continuing legacy of manual work among first generation settlers. These two factors have meant that for a long period – and possibly still today – non-white voters have considered themselves to be natural Labour supporters. However, this environment has begun to alter over time, allowing us to gain an insight into changes in labour market participation patterns. Labour identification has so far waned barely at all, despite the fact that tangible evidence exists to show, for example, steady socio-economic upward mobility among some ethnic minorities, and sharp erosion of job opportunities in older manual industries (Virdee, 2000). Significantly, recent research has highlighted the strong concentration of Indians among the former socio-economic pattern, with marked evidence of fairly rapid upward movement seen in some geographically and generationally localised instances (Owen and Green, 1992). Such illustrations of advancement were noticeably missing in the cases of Pakistani, Bengali and Caribbean groups, making the Indian stride seem that much greater. In one way or another, this type of development is likely in turn be linked to new patterns of party identification. The surprising thing is that so far there has been precious little impact upon overall ethnic minority voting patterns. In 1992 Labour's popularity remained as strong as ever at the aggregate level, recovering much of the modest seepage to the right and centre ground that had occurred at the time of the 1987 election (CRE, 1994). By 1997 a slight turnaround among Asians was discernible in contrast to the picture among black voters where Labour support tightened even further (MORI, 1996; 1997;

Saggar and Heath, 1999). Significantly, a 1991 NOP survey showed that levels of Labour support among Pakistani and Bengaladeshi Asian voters were barely higher than among ethnic Indians (64 and 63 per cent as against 56 per cent, respectively). However, despite this, one-fifth of the latter group stated an intention to vote Conservative, a noteworthy minority given the date of the survey against a backdrop of poor Conservative standing in many other national polls (Amin and Richardson, 1992: 29).

Issue voting
Secondly, *ethnic minority party choice can be viewed in strictly rational terms based on accurate knowledge about, and willingness to act on, the issue preferences of non-white voters*. In a sense and for fairly obvious reasons examined below, this interpretation has been one over which commentators have, knowingly or unknowingly, been most preoccupied. Indeed, it was noted earlier that this model has invited both analytical and speculative attempts to unlock the questions of first, what such preferences are, and secondly, whether they are sufficiently important to shape electoral choice. Most such attempts have been rather poorly thought through and consequently are very wide of the mark. By contrast, others have treated the subject with notable distinction. Examples of each speak for themselves and arguably need not be rehearsed here.

The task for successive researchers has been to profile the issue preferences of ethnic minorities. As we saw earlier, it is hard to say for certain that ethnic minorities share a common preoccupation with race-related issues (an argument originally driven home by Studlar, 1986). Indeed, for the most part, they seem to subscribe to an issue agenda that has considerable similarity with their white counterparts, though as we have also noted it is debatable whether or not they perceive there to be a hidden racial dimension to some, most, or possibly all issues. So much for issues in general. A rather different picture begins to emerge when we consider the perceptions of ethnic minorities toward issues touching on the extent of racial discrimination and exclusion in modern British society. Here the evidence is complex and difficult to draw a conclusion from. Data from a 1985 survey of ethnic minorities in Greater London revealed that a slim majority of Asians felt that ethnic minority people in Britain were treated the same as white people. Almost 57 per cent of black respondents by contrast reported unequivocally that black people were treated worse than others (FitzGerald 1985a: 6). Later (1991) data from NOP confirmed aspects of this pattern: over two-thirds of blacks thought that non-whites were treated less well than whites by employers against 42 per cent of Asians and 39 per cent of whites (Amin and Richardson, 1992: 44). Table 2.5 shows a similar pattern opening up across a range of concerns.

Table 2.5 *Treatment of non-whites by authorities, 1991 (%)*

	White	Asian	Black
Employers			
better	9	3	1
worse	39	42	67
same	44	44	22
Police			
better	7	2	0
worse	48	45	75
same	36	40	16
Schools			
better	14	2	1
worse	13	15	38
same	61	74	48
Courts			
better	10	2	1
worse	24	19	57
same	55	53	26

Source: Amin and Richardson (1992).

How is this evidence from a decade ago to be interpreted? To begin with, there is a clear-cut distinction between Asians on the one hand, whose attitude towards societal racism is rather similar to whites, and blacks on the other hand, who seem to take a more critical and perhaps hostile view. Thus, we may surmise that this profile could lead Asians to a more accommodationist position in British society and encourage blacks to adopt greater suspicion and possible positions of confrontation. However, the difficulty lies in first, being certain that these attitudinal differences are real in the sense that ethnic minorities attach weight to such questions in general, and secondly, assessing the degree to which these views, even if strongly held, then shape political thinking and behaviour. It would, of course, be implausible to claim that attitudes towards societal racism were irrelevant in moulding political opinion. Indeed, strongly-held and deeply-critical views on this front are almost certainly responsible for skewing basic political instincts and, very probably, political behaviour as well.

The question is whether causal relationships and levels of cognisance are sufficiently defined to result in beneficiaries and losers among political parties. To put it another way, for what reason should we particularly think that the price of black resentment will be laid only at the door of, say, the Conservative Party? A rough glance at the current political landscape, might suggest this to be the most likely outcome. However, a number of factors disturb the simplicity of this picture. First, these would-be voters may be just as likely to internalise their alienation from society and opt not to participate in the electoral process at all. The cost would then be felt just as much, if not more, by Labour, relying as it does on non-white votes in a number of its urban heartlands. Secondly, such electors may conclude that direct action, such as protest politics, perhaps even violence, is a more suitable alternative outlet for their frustration, thereby circumventing the formal electoral process and consequently shunning parties almost randomly. Thirdly, initial feelings of anger that arguably lie beneath a 'culture of resistance' had faded somewhat by the late-1990s. The result of this could involve a higher level of indifference towards the Conservatives – whether in government or in opposition – than might have been supposed. The Conservative Party in that sense may console itself in concluding that it is paying a smaller cost for such alienation than it may have done 10 or 15 years earlier. At worst, and more worryingly, that this is the single largest reason why its efforts to woo non-white voters have come to so little. Finally, the benefits that might be thought to flow to, say, Labour from the frustration of such would-be voters may be curtailed by the party's sense of ambiguity in presenting itself as the party of the dispossessed 'have-nots'. These potential supporters still need to be rallied to Labour – and away from the non-participation option in particular – if their pessimistic assessment of racism in British society is to count in electoral terms.

A rational choice-based model also implies that foundations exist for selective issue-voting by ethnic minorities over the policy questions they perceive to affect them alone or disproportionately. Therefore, ethnic minority voters are relied upon to distinguish between political rhetoric on the one hand, and policy deeds on the other. If this is a safe assumption to make, a number of surprising outcomes may result. The best illustration can be seen over immigration policy, an area that over the years has received extended attention by political parties and where objectively-defined non-white interests have suffered considerably. For instance, non-white voters are liable to take with a pinch of salt many of Labour's strongly-principled policy promises to undo Tory immigration regimes, remembering that the party reneged twice on clear commitments to repeal Conservative immigration statutes following electoral victory in 1964 and 1974. (This dismissal of Labour's charms on immigration must, of course, be seen in the context of the party only promising to revise these laws and to do away with overtly discriminatory rules, where found.) Ethnic minority voters must themselves discount for false or incredulous promises. By contrast, they may take a more positive view of the Conservative record on immigration which in the past has been shown to be something less than the party's sharp rhetorical bite. The Heath administration's perhaps surprising decision to allow the entry of significant numbers of expelled British Asian refugees from Uganda in 1972 stands out especially. The Wilson government's rather sordid last minute attempts to backtrack on commitments to allow in comparable immigrants from Kenya in 1968 is frequently cited by critics as testimony of Labour's blotted reputation.

By separating promises from deeds, we can perhaps begin to explain how the immigration issue has led to sometimes confusing responses among ethnic minorities. A 1991 Harris survey of Asian political attitudes revealed that a small though remarkable proportion thought that (then) present immigration controls were either 'about right' or 'not tough enough' (Harris Research Centre, 1991). Superficially, it may seem as if this group of voters had adopted a stance out of line with its objective interests. However, other arguments may apply in their case since the Harris survey or other comparable evidence did not demonstrate that strong immigration controls were, by definition, against Asian political interests. Such a claim is meaningful only to the extent that a common bond is shown to exist among Asian voters who recognise the discriminatory impact of such controls on fellow Asians, and non-whites generally, if not themselves. This group of Asians quite patently had distinguished themselves from others who were more likely to be subjected to tougher controls. Consequently, we might reasonably conclude that for this group of Asians the Conservative Party's reputation for toughness on immigration control was not perceived as a barrier to pro-Tory sympathy and support.

This is perhaps a generous interpretation since it portrays Asian Conservative supporters as being fully cognisant with notions of objective and revealed interest. It sees them as knowingly undaunted by the blunt and hostile rhetoric that occasionally characterises immigration debates in Conservative ranks. Neither assumption may be reliable. For one thing, we should remember that these Asian voters, however limited in number and atypical, are just as likely to be bloody-minded and blind to evidence as their white counterparts. After all, the phenomenon of working-class support for Labour in spite of its policies rather than because of them is well documented in the psephological literature (Sarlvik and Crewe, 1983). In addition, these voters may accept that Conservative policies on immigration are hostile to them, but at the same time choose to rationalise their party choice on other, non-race related grounds. The Conservatives, therefore, are thought of as potential beneficiaries of non-white votes in terms that by-pass, and possibly neutralise, immigration questions or indeed any other race-related issues.

By backing parties that promise them benefits and by taking race as a salient concern in a selective way, we can conclude that ethnic minority voters are not the natural constituency of any of the parties. What then drives some commentators to argue that ethnic minority voters naturally veer in one ideological direction or another? This question conveniently leads to a third and final way of conceptualising common interest among ethnic minorities, namely by reference to voting preference as a cultural manifestation.

The cultural thesis

Thirdly, *the central motivation behind ethnic minority political outlook can be reduced to cultural forces, albeit ones that are operating in a wider British political and social landscape.* In making such a suggestion, we should recognise that culturally-based arguments have been among the most speculative attempts to characterise ethnic minority political behaviour. That does not in itself render such an approach worthless, but it does mean that the researcher must tread with care in examining what is often a poorly defined and notoriously ambiguous variable.

Putting this argument into context in the British case it usually takes the form of a characterisation of putative 'community values', which are said to underpin and subtly unite discrete ethnic minority groups. The British Asian population tends to be the largest reference point for this claim, a group which according to 1991 Census findings approaches 1.4 million in number.[6] Ignoring any social, economic or other distinctions that may exist within this population, the argument goes on to claim that Asians are the subjects of, and subscribe to, a community-wide value system that has various precise features. High among these values are said to be, *inter alia*, respect for traditional family structures, deference to authority both in the home and beyond, importance given to education and socio-economic advancement, support for the institutions of law and order, and willingness or even overt determination to socialise future generations in support of similar values. The testimony of intergenerational immigrant succession, most notably among East African Asians, is sometimes singled out in addition (Bhachu, 1985). This set of values forms the nucleus of an outlook that is said to foster a deeply conservative group which is both suspicious of strong government in certain spheres while supportive in others.

With the image of an inherently conservative group already sketched, it is only the smallest of intellectual leaps that enables cultural model enthusiasts to talk of an electoral group that is naturally allied with the Conservative Party (Buscombe, 1999). Whether what is meant by this thesis is that the group has the potential to become allied to the party in such a fashion is a moot point. The key feature of the model is its natural, quasi-deterministic base and its resulting description of an inevitable rediscovery of common interest between group and party. Asian voters, according to the rhetoric, are faced with a choice between a nominal champion of increasingly outdated immigrant rights (Labour), and a natural home for their true yet hitherto suppressed interests (the Conservatives). Put in these fairly stark and superficial terms, commentators and voters alike are encouraged to believe that the passage of time alone will serve to reveal the Conservative Party as a 'true home'. Labour voting is thus explained as structural aberration resulting from an historical legacy based on three sources. First, it acknowledges the group's immigrant past. Secondly, the thesis draws a powerful parallel with earlier left-leaning immigrant cohorts (e.g. Jews). Finally, it observes the Conservatives instinctively, though foolishly, shy away from courting a potentially valuable constituency.

Asians, therefore, are viewed typically as a late, though not lost, opportunity for the Conservatives. In particular, this group is highlighted for its on-going adherence to communal, non-individualised ways of thinking and behaving. This last point is highly significant because much of the characterisation thus far has been linked explicitly with the Conservative Party. However, by making in-roads into implicitly ideological territory regarding the existence and inherent value of 'community', it is not hard to see why both Labour and Liberal-Democrat strategists have seized on aspects of the paradigm. To be sure, the focus on politically-inspired attempts to rekindle 'community values', are close to electoral agendas right across the party system. Therefore, the so-called 'model minority' represented by Asians cannot be absorbed fully into or monopolised by Conservative strategy since elements of the characterisation have a much broader ideological appeal. This factor appears to be especially important to centre-left strategists, aiming to ditch hostages from the past and concentrate on exploiting the Asian example on as level a playing field as possible (Sanders, 1999). Thus, past and, indeed, present Labour identification is interpreted as a sign of a positive bond between party and group, with both occupying similar territory on one reading of the 'community values' argument. There is nothing inevitable about seepage of support to the Conservatives, according to this counter-argument (Saggar, 1998d). Indeed, Tory presentations of the party as a 'natural home' are frequently rebutted as disingenuous ploys to mask covert hostility to non-white participation in Conservative ranks.

In the final analysis the cultural thesis is remarkable because of the dearth of evidence to support its claims. It is certainly more than conjecture since it makes play of forces and patterns that are widely accepted to exist. Yet it falls far short of a coherent explanation, not least because considerable doubts exist as to what type and level of evidence would be needed to bolster the various assertions made in its name.

Perhaps the single biggest piece of circumstantial evidence comes from the much-cited example of earlier Jewish immigrant succession. Here, it was claimed, was a newcomer group that over time abandoned its close association with the left and found a base, if not a home, in supporting the Conservative Party and participating in its affairs (Alderman, 1983). Several generations on, Jews are widely cited for their strong presence in elite Conservative ranks and their electoral support for the party is taken for granted in many areas. The parallel is just too striking and irresistible for proponents of the cultural model.

Since the vast bulk of the model's supporters are Conservative sympa-

Framing conceptual and theoretical questions · 57

thisers, strategists, thinkers or commentators, researchers have to be cautious in interpreting much of the anecdotal evidence that is scattered about. Nevertheless these voices count and cannot be dismissed entirely. One reason is that Conservative strategists have been fairly active – and successful until comparatively recently – in luring the support and funds of Asian business leaders. Their efforts have met with limited success and clearly important markers have been established on both sides. It is commonplace for these strategists to go on record and predict the rightward drift of Asian voters over the medium to long term. Such assessments, while usually littered with embellishment, are not unimportant since they contain within them a measure of the real investment of a party with countless other priorities. It is unlikely that so much would be made of the long-term dividends of this strategy unless those responsible for its implementation were sufficiently convinced of its prospects. Their conviction may, of course, be grossly mistaken but it provides a good guide to where and how future efforts to court ethnic minorities are likely to take shape.

Before then, in conclusion, strategists from all parties must work within the existing electoral landscape. The here and now of ethnic minority voting patterns in the early twenty-first century is clear and remains more or less unshakeable in the short to medium term. A strong bias in favour of Labour, which has persisted throughout successive Tory victories (and one Labour landslide), should not, and arguably cannot, be easily ignored. Perhaps the daunting task facing the right and centre has meant that there is little to be lost by promoting a loosely defined cultural caricature of potential ethnic minority supporters. Whatever the cause – and indeed meaning – of stubborn Labour loyalty, it is fairly certain that the cultural model will continue to find a convenient outlet as the stuff of Sunday supplement feature writing and weekday op-ed thoughts. As the saying goes, 'watch this space' as political caricature is measured against political reality in the remainder of the volume.

Notes

1 An earlier version of this chapter was published in Saggar (1998c). Pre-publication early drafts of this chapter were read to audiences at the 1995 annual meeting of the American Political Science Association (Chicago, September 1995), and at a British Council seminar entitled 'Reflections on two multicultural societies' (Brussels, January 1996). Working drafts were also presented and discussed at departmental seminars at Salford University and QMW (both February, 1995). I am grateful to various individuals present on these occasions for their informal feedback.
2 Counter, that is, to the 'ethnic marginals' orthodoxy that held so much influence in British electoral politics during the 1970s and beyond; see CRC (1975), CRE (1980).
3 These proportions carry only limited statistical weight, but the notion that

58 · *Race and representation*

counter-intuitive views are found among the ethnic minority groups cannot be discounted altogether.

4 A well argued and evidenced example can be seen in a recent study of ethnic minorities in public housing; see Lee and Murie (1998). A similar approach is found in recent work on public libraries to cite one further example; see Roach and Morrison (1998).

5 Table 2.3 makes use of MORI estimates of black and Asian party support in 1997. These are quite considerably at variance with the picture described in Chapter 5 using BES evidence. The former were derived from pre-election, stand-alone surveys based on voting intention and were conducted between 5 and 10 months before polling day. A strong note of caution might therefore be added to the MORI figures.

6 A figure closer to 2 million probably best estimates the size of the Asian origin population prior to the scheduled 2001 Census. For LFS sources of this estimate, see Saggar and Heath (1999) and Berthoud (1999).

3

Ethnic minorities as a political constituency

Introduction

Political difference has a great deal to do with political distinctiveness but the two are conceptually not the same. In the context of the British political system, based chiefly on doctrines of indirect electoral representation, there is a constant clamour for evidence to support and justify the notion of political difference across ethnic groups. Indeed, as we are already aware in some areas of politics there is a good deal of both argument and evidence to back up this focus and, indeed, inter-ethnic variations have been recognised for a long time. However, this kind of political difference is mainly centred on gross disparities in the electoral loyalties of ethnic minorities in comparison with their white counterparts, disparities that are not obviously accounted for in terms that might also be relevant to the white electorate. It is, in itself, little to do with a well-founded basis for political distinctiveness in the sense that ethnic minorities are either less subject to the usual sources of political difference found among whites, or else subject to a hole host of ethnically-related socialisation and mobilisation factors. Thus, difference and distinctiveness are connected to the degree that both are features of the political participation of minorities, but crucially both concepts are in fact measuring very dissimilar processes.

In this chapter we shall explore the grounds for thinking that a social group such as Britain's internally diverse ethnic minorities or, indeed, even specific minority sub-groups constitute a sufficiently distinctive political constituency. As we shall see, testing for this hypothesis makes sense at two levels. The first is based on the notion of political constituency in rather normative terms; that is, an exploration of how various social, cultural and other characteristics might potentially serve as the fuel of ethnically-related political strategy. The latter differs considerably in that it looks primarily at how the extant political landscape, dominated by parties and liberal participation theory, treats most political constituency claims. In short, these two levels of analysis are inter-related as political constituency claims are often varied in their scope and crucially are subject to hard tests of coherence. Political institutions make a lot of difference in this regard because the 'ethnic minorities as a political constituency' claim can face a warm reception in some quarters while being shunned and rejected in others. The chapter is, therefore, geared to providing an overview of these rival arguments and counter-trends. Thus the political constituency question is examined principally because of its basic pertinence to the larger political integration question pursued in this study.

The chapter is divided into four main components. First, the chapter begins by tracking the broad voting patterns of ethnic minorities over the period for which there is usable empirical data. This section amply drives home the point that sharp inter-ethnic differences have existed throughout this period and that, to the extent that we have reliable comparative data, much of these variations cannot be easily explained by social, economic or other circumstantial factors. Secondly, the chapter turns to examine rival and complementary interpretations as to why minority participation patterns, especially in terms of voting choice, have differed from the white 'norm' or base line. Put another way, this section is interested in mapping the possibilities for ethnic minority 'commonness' when facing and responding to mainstream democratic institutions. Thirdly, the chapter highlights some of the essential implications for political parties generally and for the strategy pursued by the Labour Party in particular. This section sets the scene for a more protracted discussion of racial politics and party strategy in two later chapters. Finally, the political constituency question is considered in terms of its relevance to ethnic minority political activists. The role of candidates and elected representatives is singled out principally because of the special pressures – and opportunities – facing them in translating various political constituency-type claims into practical politics.

Taken together, the main purpose of this chapter is to act as a three-way link between the theoretical discussion offered in the previous chapters, examination of core empirical evidence on electoral participation in the following chapters and evaluation of broader implications found in the final chapter. The underlying political integration theme of the book requires that we make important connections between social, cultural and structural determinants of minority electoral participation and its knock-on consequences. Moreover, we need to be mindful of the ways in which peculiarities of the political system, such as the voting systems in different types of election or the predominance of the two party system can in turn influence the political behaviour of ethnic minorities. It should be stressed that this study is concerned with examining minority electoral politics in the context of the British political tradition, a context which certainly has tended to be lacking in so many earlier studies of the electoral politics of race and ethnicity in Britain.

Historic context and appraisal

Seen with an historic detachment, it is quite astounding to observe the extent of ethnic minority voters' loyalty to the Labour Party stretching back to 1974. Minorities have supported Labour with such strength and regularity that some have raised openly the possibility of neglect (at best) and cynical exploitation (at worst). The problems that this picture poses for Labour are examined more systematically later in the chapter as part of a fuller appraisal of dominant, one-party politics and the representation of political interests (FitzGerald, 1988; Shukra, 1998a; Jeffers, 1991; Knowles, 1992; Lentze, 1998). On this basis, it is interesting to note that Conservative and centre party responses have taken one of two forms. On the one hand, some have argued that ethnic minorities represent the most committed of Labour's troops and thus hold little possibility for rival parties seeking to court their support (Messina, 1998). This view has taken the historic record at face value and tried to show that the opportunity costs of appealing to this group of voters has been relatively unattractive in that scarce resources have been needed to target more promising social groups of voters. On the other hand, it is clear that many Tory and centre party strategists have seen the picture through the prism of political opportunity (Saggar, 1998d). This perspective has emphasised the temporary nature of the Labour-minority nexus in voting, and has also suggested that potentially rich dividends exist for parties that play to the growing fluidity in ethnic minority social and political aspirations.

The October 1974 election

Up until the mid-1970s the electoral participation of ethnic minorities had received very little attention within academic research. Instead, 'race politics', a growing field of interest in social research, had been preoccupied with tracking the political consequences of mass non-white immigration (Deakin, 1965; Foot, 1965; Deakin and Bourne, 1970). The initial discovery of race within British psephology was led by the first significant empirical study on the topic by the then Community Relations Commission. As previously noted, this publication went a long way toward setting an agenda for future research in this field, not so much because of its systematic approach or theoretical quality, but rather because of its primary interest in the electoral geography of minority participation (CRC, 1975). It was on this foundation that the notion of an 'ethnic marginal' was built.[1]

Lying beneath the preoccupations of the 1975 CRC report, there was to be found another deeper-seated interest in the trying to assess the importance of the ethnic minority electorate. We have already noted that much the same focus has underscored the bulk of academic, political and press interest in minority electoral participation. The CRC publication departed from the previous conventional wisdom on the topic by suggesting that minority voters were, in fact, increasingly located in non-stereotypical, Labour stronghold constituencies. Instead, the report's authors argued that many were to be found in the marginal seats contested by the two major parties in 1974. This aspect of their argument was fairly free from controversy since it was based ultimately on the reliability of, and interpretation placed on, figures from the 1971 general Census that placed a notional estimate on minority population size at constituency level. Over the years these data have been replaced by more accurate measures of the size of this population and its main component groups, with the key breakthrough coming in the 1991 Census' use of a direct, ethnic origin question (Coleman and Salt, 1996). In any case, leaving disputes of measures aside, the chief driving force behind the electoral calculus of minority voter strength has been the question of residential concentration and rates of internal geographic mobility. Unsurprisingly, most indicators have pointed to a small yet steady degree of geographic drift since the early to mid-1970s, and Britain's minority population as a whole is somewhat less concentrated in inner urban areas than previously (Wrench *et al*, 1993; Bonnet, 1993; Ageyman and Spooner, 1997). Of course, some minority groups have remained relatively exempt from this trend and others have featured heavily in suburbanisation trends (Berthoud, 2000). The core point raised in the CRC report's assessment continues to be a central issue in similar exercises in the mid-to late 1990s.

The more controversial side of the 1975 report was its line of argument concerning a bloc vote based on ethnicity. Oddly, the report's authors were keen to stress that minority voters ought not to be thought of as safe Labour supporters, in spite of the fact that even their own evidence pointed to a firm, vice-like grip by the Labour Party on this group of voters. By taking this approach, the report at least raised the possibility of what might result at both national and constituency level if minorities abandoned their overwhelming Labour partisanship. The floating vote thesis was, therefore, not so much a balanced description of the evidence as a normative perspective on a significant recasting of the empirical evidence (Layton-Henry, 1993). As such, the spin was aimed at parties and party strategists to encourage something of a new spirit of political thinking and debate about the strength and potential application of the minority electorate. The logic was that parties in general might start to respond more positively to minorities, who in turn could be expected to reward and punish in a more dispassionate and sophisticated manner. The approach, in other words, was unmistakably built on the foundations of a rational choice, sub-consumerist view of voters and parties. Such foundations signalled an important attempt to question, possibly weaken, existing sociological-led theories of the role of identity, and ethnicity in particular, in shaping voting outlook and behaviour (see Norris, 1997a, ch. 6, for a general discussion on this point).

All told, the landmark 1975 report hit many important buttons in academic and non-academic understanding of race and politics in Britain. In particular, it seems that it touched two particularly vital and sensitive chords beyond the research community. First, by basing its general analysis on the 1971 Census, the report revealed a marked and somewhat unexpected surge in the size of the minority population. The full implications of these increased numbers had been far from being fully appreciated until that point, and certainly the obvious knock-on implications for the political process had barely been debated by leading politicians. The report thus served to shape the agenda of minority political participation by highlighting that the numbers involved were considerably greater than negligible and were projected to rise yet further. Secondly, the report's conclusion, although not fully grounded in convincing evidence or sound methodology, none the less encapsulated an emerging mood in British party competition theory and practice. It appeared to argue successfully that parties could no longer afford to casually neglect key social groups within the electorate merely on the basis of historic precedent (luke-warm relations and/or interest), or lack of past success (few already backed them). Instead, as social and historic ties between voting groups and political parties waned it was expected that this process would result in a more even playing field on which voters could be courted by parties. Of course, the main sub-text for this fresh intellectual mood, stemming from the late 1960s onwards, was the question of the continuing influence of social class upon political loyalties. The issue of ethnicity merely emerged as another illustration of this wider trend in conceptualising the social fabric that lay behind voting choice. The report thus captured a significant window of opportunity by addressing party strategists in terms with which they were already familiar (Saggar, 1999). Moreover, it might be argued that the CRC report crystallised not just a new agenda on race and voting but rolled out an even larger agenda containing the core ingredients of social identity and party strategy.

The report is also just as well known for its spirited pursuit of the ethnic marginals thesis, partly in order to give a measure to the argument about the strength of the minority electorate, but also to reinforce the concept of an ethnic minority bloc vote. The method relied on a comparison of majorities of sitting MPs and the size of the constituency's minority electorate, with cases in which the latter exceeded the former being focused on by the report. Some 85 seats made the cut in the report (no less than 1 in 8). This figure fell to 59 seats that were said to be potential 'ethnic marginals' in both 1974 elections, 13 of which were also among Labour's 17 net direct gains from the Tories between both polls.

On this logic the report contended that minorities had played a pivotal role in determining the general election outcome. Moreover, it is possible to see a third reason why the report was so warmly received. By stressing the importance of a tiny handful of seats, the authors merely repeated one of the main psephological stories of the 1974 elections, namely that government could easily change hands on even the slenderest of shifts in public opinion and that orthodox seat–vote ratios could no longer be counted upon in times of minority administrations (Norris, 1997a: 35–42 and 108–14). The lesson that the report sought to preach was that a narrow Conservative defeat – in seats rather than votes – might have been averted if a more sensitive approach had been taken toward ethnic minority voters. Of course, there were several lines of spurious logic in this so-called lesson but these tended to melt away in the eyes of Tory strategists who became convinced that a needless defeat had been incurred.

It has already been noted that the CRC report contained the first reasonably reliable indicator of minority voting patterns. Despite the spin put on its conclusions, the figures paint a fairly clear picture of Labour strength. Indeed, the survey upon which it was based recorded a 4 in 5 ratio of Labour support against support for Labour's rivals. In the decades since this has often been known as the 'iron law' of British ethnic minority party choice, and its stability or otherwise has preoccupied almost two generations of scholars. The question of this Labour partisanship and the sources of ideological bias (if that is what it represents) are considered more fully later in the chapter.

The 1979 election
The 1975 report was followed in 1980 by another, published by the Commission for Racial Equality (the CRC's successor) on the May 1979 general election (CRE, 1980). The broad thrust of this analysis followed the pattern set in the earlier work and in particular persisted with the argument that Labour's opponents had missed a vital opportunity in ignoring the interests of the minority electorate. A key section of the report highlighted a small handful of seats that had been included in both the 1974 and 1979 analyses: it was claimed that evidence had been found to show a clear Asian swing from Labour to the Conservatives in five of these seven cases. The underlying point was rather more crucial, namely that the advancement of minority support for the Conservatives might be accelerated among certain ethnic groups more than others. The report thus put the spotlight on differential swing among Asians and blacks for the first time. This claim, surely, ranks as one of the most pressing for further investigation and is something that is taken up within the limits of the data in Chapter 4 below.

The difficulty lay in the hazards of over-generalisation on the basis of such a small number of constituencies. This posed a real problem for the report and its political supporters. Plainly, the inference that a pro-Conservative swing among elements of the minority electorate was one that increasingly commanded a political lobby that could not be easily ignored (Crewe, 1979; Lawler, 1984). For one thing, the Conservative's own Department of Community Affairs, launched in 1976, had worked assiduously to promote the party's image among middle-class Asian voters at this sensitive time. In winning a return to office in the late 1970s, it was at least hoped that a similar swing could be recorded among the party's newest target group of voters. On the other hand, the report undoubtedly jumped the gun in proclaiming sufficient evidence to back this central claim. Certainly a limited Asian swing had been measured in a tiny number of seats and it was not unreasonable for the report to highlight the fruits of Tory campaigning. However, the wider issue remained how far it was possible to describe Asian voters as characteristic of a slowly emerging, floating electorate. The acid test then, and in 1997, was the nature of the Labour minority electorate nexus. In this the report was unusually silent. However, in an analyses of minority participation in general elections in the 1980s it is evident that there is a growing need to address this core theoretical question, and to debate with some vigour the sources of the Labour Party's quite astonishing success in attracting the support of these voters (Messina, 1998). It is to this debate that attention is focused in the following section of the chapter.

This weakness aside, the 1979 study was greatly strengthened by its determination to shed fresh light on the earlier conundrums over minority registration and turn out. There had been previously been doubts as to whether minority registration and turn out rates could be equated unquestioningly with those of white voters. One principal doubt surrounded the idea that relatively new immigrants would possess sufficient political, cultural and other knowledge to allow them to participate fully in British democratic politics. This point had already been picked up and later amplified by those who had been concerned about the effectiveness of political 'buffers' such as community relations councils (Jacobs, 1982). Another doubt surrounded the relatively accessibility and responsiveness of electoral registration agencies and political parties in promoting full registration and turn out among the minority groups. Furthermore, there were half expressed doubts about the interest in mainstream electoral politics shown by small segments of the minority population. The younger male members of the black and Asian population, especially those concentrated among the poorly educated and skilled with fragile employment prospects, were singled out for special concern as most likely to shun the orthodox electoral process. Significantly, a full generation on, similar 'underclass'-type doubts are attached to debates about minority political participation (see, for instance, the *Guardian*, 1995, 1996a).

The report contained some revealing data on these points. For instance, it reported that black registration rates stood at an impressive 81 per cent, having leaped from a sluggish 63 per cent in the previous election. Asian rates meanwhile had barely changed from the mid-70s range. However, in showing a white registration rate of 94 per cent, it was clear that any analytical or other assumption that ignored differential registration continued to be deeply mistaken. On turn out, the report reiterated an earlier finding which had shown tremendous strength in the Asian propensity to cast votes, outstripping both white and Afro-Caribbean rates by a clear margin. These Asian turn out rates typically rose above 90 per cent and were doubly significant because of the way in which they bucked the pattern associated with electoral turn out in inner city constituencies. This finding in particular prompted a suggestion that previously poorly understood social and cultural factors might lie behind Asian participation habits. The report concluded that Asian willingness to be involved in the political process was important to the extent that, when combined with enduring Labour loyalty, this had contributed to the Labour Party holding on to some of its marginal seats in the face of a strong Tory national advance. Beneath this lay the question of how far Asian participation could be characterised as following a different path from that of black Britons. This is a question that has obvious importance because of its party strategy and electoral campaigning implication. Evidence to illustrate the question is raised in Chapter 4 together with a wider discussion of debates about electoral versus other forms of participation.

The 1983 election

The June 1983 election became the subject of an explosion of interest, academic and otherwise, in minority electoral participation. The two earlier CRC and CRE studies had served to establish a base line interest in many of the underlying issues of democratic theory and practice. The 1983 case in contrast appeared to shift attention more decisively towards matters of party competition. The chief driving force behind this slight reorientation stemmed from the task of measuring minority participation in a radically altered political climate. While 1974 and 1979 served as backdrops for relatively close competition and slim margins of success and defeat, by 1983 the political atmosphere had changed to assessing minority electoral behaviour in the context of Labour's historic rout. This context undoubtedly served to add a new twist to trying to map out first the strength of the minority electorate (an existing debate), and the degree of Labour indebtedness to minority supporters (a new and potentially exciting debate).

The CRE was one of several teams that produced analyses on the 1983 case (CRE, 1984). Others included academic analyses by Layton-Henry and Studlar (1985) and Saggar (1984) utilising a much richer data set

Ethnic minorities as a political constituency · 67

assembled by a polling organisation for a television programme (Harris Research Centre, 1983). The upshot was that the 1983 election yielded two major data sets that allowed a limited degree of comparison between minority groups, and across white and non-whites for a single election. The CRE data featured just over 2000 respondents in a sample that took in just 25 seats containing high ethnic minority concentrations. The Harris data meanwhile used a sampling frame that relied heavily on such constituencies. In both cases, while understandable logistical and financial reasons drove the sampling strategy, there were some worries that minorities that resided in less concentrated places might have been under-represented in the samples produced. Finally, pooled pre-election survey data from Gallup collected for the BBC yielded a third data set though containing too few ethnic minority cases for detailed analysis. The Harris data in particular permitted the most extensive examination of minority political attitudes and behaviour, and in particular threw new light on to the old disagreements concerning minorities as floating voters. Placed together, the Harris Research and CRE surveys revealed that Asian and Afro-Caribbean support for Labour had endured the national decline in the party's fortunes. In short, the anticipated surge in Tory performance, most notably among Asian voters, had failed to materialise despite the spectacular nature of the party's landslide victory.

On registration and turn out, both data sets pointed to continuing improvements in minority participation. Asian registration was reported to be 94 per cent, fully in line with earlier studies, while black rates now stood at 82 per cent signifying a major leap from previous elections (Harris Research Centre, 1983). The CRE data showed rates of 79 and 76 per cent, respectively but took in rather fewer seats located in inner cities alone (CRE, 1984). However, as Table 3.1 shows, the Harris data revealed a major disparity between Asian and black disposition to turn out to vote. The participation deficit unsurprisingly became the subject of widespread comment among the media and politicians. Significantly, Chapter 4 notes that a similar disquiet underscored debates about possible black abstention in the 1997 election.

By disaggregating the likely black abstainers in the Harris survey, it was apparent that the rate of non-participation among young 18–24 year olds was as high as 3 in 4. Even among blacks who reported a clear identification with the Labour Party, the likely turn-out rate was just 44 per cent; that is, over half of Labour's troops among the black registered electorate failed to endorse the party where and when it mattered. In comparison, young Asian abstention, while high at 1 in 2, was effectively half that of young blacks, and some 62 per cent of Labour identifiers, it was reported, actually delivered their votes on polling day.

Thus, by 1983 it was apparent that serious question marks were raised about long-term black willingness to participate fully within the electoral

Table 3.1 *Voting likelihood among ethnic minorities registered to vote, 1983*

Voting intention	Asian (%)	Black (%)
Absolutely certain to/certain to/probably will vote	94	72
Probably/certainly will not vote	6	28

Source: Harris Research Centre (1983).

process. Reservations about ballot box democracy were also held by their Asian counterparts, but not on the same worrying scale. Furthermore, the difficulty for analysts and commentators alike was in not being able to measure and assess this deficit satisfactorily alongside patterns found within the white population. The degree to which non-participation could be linked to circumstantial factors to do with social class, education or geography was presumed to be a relevant aspect of this assessment, though it was doubly discomforting that this contextual feature could not be adequately assessed. Nevertheless, the debate over black electoral abstention had firmly taken root within the academic and non-academic communities.

The 1987 election

In many ways the analysis of the 1987 election tended to follow on seamlessly from 1983. This was partly the result of the commissioning of Harris to conduct new surveys of Asian and black participation, thereby producing a data set that allowed some considerable comparison over a pair of elections (Harris Research Centre, 1987). Minority support for Labour continued to be very strong, though, in one notable departure from this pattern, it was noted that Asian levels of support for the Conservatives had broken through an important psychological ceiling (23 per cent in 1987 as compared with just 6 per cent among black voters). Added to the Liberal-SDP alliance share of the Asian vote, it appeared that almost one-third of Asians had abandoned their traditional Labour moorings. The possibility of widespread Asian seepage to the centre, chiefly on issue-voting grounds, had been heavily trailed in the 1983–87 parliament (the Liberal-SDP Party leader, David Owen in 1985, for instance, placed commitment to positive action measures at the heart of the two-party alliance's strategy toward urban policy) (see Owen, 1985). The sampling frame in the Harris survey took in both areas of high and low minority concentration, although again a bias existed in drawing respondents from the former rather than the latter. Significantly, among minority voters as a whole, support for the Conservatives rose dramatically from 15 per cent in high concentration areas to a staggering 39 per cent in low concentration areas. These rates suggested that a profound change was at work among the minority electorate even without allowance being made for the usual effects of constituency-level factors.

In addition, it had long been assumed that significant advances in support for the Conservatives were most likely to be achieved against the backdrop of Tory national electoral hegemony. The 1983 election had proven a disappointment in this regard. The data in 1987, however, revealed that strong national polling was an essential prior ingredient for a breakthrough among Asian electors.[2] Further evidence was produced on the on-going question of the willingness of minorities to participate in the electoral process. The Harris data, collected days before polling days, reported that three-quarters of Asians were 'absolutely certain' to cast a ballot as against a half of black respondents.

An important question over constituency or environmental factors was raised in the 1987 Harris data set. Clearly minority voters behaved differently in different types of constituency. Moreover, if it could be demonstrated that environmental factors linked to constituency characteristics were an important part of the calculus of minority voting behaviour (as with white voters), then future attention would switch to examining rates and patterns of minority group resettlement in non-traditional areas. This was obviously a crucial dimension for future analysis. Several explanations were put forward to account for these differences. Most commonly, it was supposed that the actual local level of minority concentration was a determining factor in the sense that more ethnically plural areas were more likely to be associated with Labour support and ideological sympathy. That is, levels of minority settlement, once above a minimum threshold, have an important reinforcing influence upon the minority voters who already have the pre-disposition to back the Labour Party. This process has immediate relevance in terms of party strategy to counter the forces of long-term minority defection from Labour. The counter perspective to this approach, however, contends that ethnicity, in fact, has little or nothing to do with variations in minority voting behaviour in different types of constituency. Instead the explanation is centred on the surrounding socio-economic characteristics of different constituency types. Areas of high concentration are very often also areas of moderate to severe economic deprivation, typically in inner-city areas. These types of constituency, irrespective of whether they contain sizable numbers of minorities, are precisely those that are traditionally linked to a strong and habitual Labour identification. The arrival and settlement of new immigrants from Asian, African and Caribbean sources merely extends and reinforces this traditional link between Labour and its heartlands.

The relationship between age and voting behaviour also resurfaced in the 1987 Harris data. For some time it had been thought that variations in Labour identification and support among minorities was relatively insulated from generational factors. The data bore this supposition out by showing that 73 per cent of younger minority voters (18–24 years) and 68 per cent of slightly older minority voters (25–44 years) had backed Labour (the figures for the 45–64 and 65 years plus cohorts were 78 and 86 per cent, respectively). The real story, however, lay in the detail. This generational contrast, while modest by general standards, had grown considerably from the patterns revealed in earlier analyses. In 1983 for instance, just 11 percentage points separated the lowest (25–34 years) and highest (65 years plus) categories. This finding, therefore, signalled another key line of future inquiry. If generational factors were at play in shaping long-term minority political outlook and behaviour, it was vital to get to grips with precisely how this process worked and with what consequences.

Three lines of explanation needed to be explored more rigorously. First, the usual political effects of ageing that were apparent in the electorate as a whole could be expected to be at work among minorities, with sympathy for the left structurally more prevalent among the young than the old. A life-cycle effect, if there was one, needed to be sustained by more extensive evidence. Secondly, it was important in the case of minorities to look for specific evidence of 'period' effects, not merely in their voting behaviour but just as crucially in aspects of their political attitudes and orientation. Specific generational effects were rather more likely to have relevance for minority voters precisely because of the comparatively recent experience of migration and settlement. Thus, the focus was on trying to spot key differences at play among second and third generation ethnic minorities whose collective, one-off experiences would have, by definition, differed from their immigrant parents and grandparents. Finally, another approach might seek to examine the relationship between life-cycle and period effects. This would mean trying to assess to what degree younger and older groups of minority voters differed fundamentally from one another in both socio-cultural and political terms (Peach, 1984). A common view in the sociology of race in Britain had suggested that a form of racialisation of public and political domains would serve to undermine and deflect such inter-generational differences (Shaw, 1994). Racialised divisions would in other words take precedence. The interesting question would be to explore the evidence in support of this perspective. In particular, in the 1990s attention had been trained on the degree to which younger generations of Asians and blacks perceived racial issues to be central to their political outlook. Evidence on issue salience and issue-voting, taken up in Chapter 6, will be of importance in trying to map out the role of generation.

The 1992 election

By the time the CRE commissioned a new survey of minority voting behaviour in the 1992 general election, the volume of secondary research on this topic had grown quite significantly. Several scholarly studies had made extensive use of the various data sets (see Layton-Henry, 1992; Messina, 1989). In addition, an important research-based pamphlet was published by the Runnymede Trust just prior to the 1992 election containing evidence from a separately commissioned survey undertaken in 1991. Added to this, in 1991 a small but useful survey of Asian voting behaviour was commissioned by the BBC for use in a special programme devoted to the impending general election. The CRE survey of the 1992 election revealed a great deal of continuity in the broad picture of minority participation and partisanship. To start with, Tory support among Asians, the overt target group since 1987, had fallen back to just 11 per cent by 1992 (as compared with 23 per cent estimated by the Harris data and 15 per cent by the CRE in 1987). This represented a major setback for the Conservatives, many of whom had believed that 1987 heralded the start of a new trend. Furthermore, at 77 per cent, Asian support for Labour now stood within reach of the 85 per cent level recorded among black voters. The key contextual issue surrounding Labour's reassertion of dominance among minorities at this time was, of course Labour's, parallel, modestly improving fortunes in the country as a whole. The real opportunity for Tory advancement during the landslide victory years of the 1980s had effectively come and gone.

The CRE report on the 1992 contest was mainly concerned with two related questions: namely, the nature of ethnic minority public opinion on election-sensitive and other issues; and the rising spectacle of attempts by Asian and black candidates to win election to office. The striking conclusion offered in relation to the former was that the issue of race, as traditionally and narrowly defined, was of primary concern to hardly any respondents in the survey. By drawing in white respondents to the survey, it was possible to reinforce this core message: just 4 per cent of whites thought that 'race' was an important issues as compared with 13 per cent of minorities. Instead, a range of issues that were familiar and of broad concern to their white counterparts, chiefly drove the issue agenda of minorities. The issue of crime, for instance, stood out as the second or third ranked issue of importance for all three groups surveyed. Elsewhere, there was very little to separate the issue saliency profile of the three groups. On the matter of candidate selection and performance, the report was fairly coy in drawing firm conclusions about underlying patterns and trajectories. Its main offering, however, was to signal that the voter survey showed barely any support for candidates on particular ethnic lines. Indeed, it was suggested that same ethnicity preferences – or prejudices – had been so negligible as to have not affected the performance of such well-known minority candidates as Keith Vaz in Leicester East or Diane Abbott in Hackney North and Stoke Newington. The inference was that the impact of such factors had been peculiarly restricted to John Taylor's (unsuccessful) bid in Cheltenham and Piara Khabra's (successful) candidacy in Southall. Despite expressing doubts about the same ethnicity thesis, the report nevertheless conceded that in two seats featured in the survey (Brentford and Isleworth in west London, and Birmingham Small Heath), Asian Tory candidates had managed to attract levels of minority support far in excess of the prevailing Tory share of the minority vote in other seats examined (10 per cent). However, in failing to observe the party's performance in neighbouring and comparable seats, the report was unconvincing in making claims about the relative strength of these two Asian hopefuls. Allowing for the slightly unusual nature of these contests, it was evident that a powerful distinction needed to be drawn between the same ethnicity preferences expressed by voters, on the one hand and the record of same or similar ethnicity voting on the other.

A similar point was picked up in the 1991 survey carried out by NOP for the Runnymede Trust (Amin and Richardson, 1992). As Table 3.2 shows, despite obvious slight inter-group variations, there was a flat rejection of the same or similar ethnicity proposition across Asian, black and white communities (strikingly, an 8 or 9 in 10 level of opposition). Closer analysis of the Runnymede report on class and age revealed some interesting small variations. For example, whereas younger blacks were rather more likely to endorse black candidates than their older counterparts, younger Asians were less likely than their older counterparts to support black candidates. How far this reflected a form of imputed discrimination or hostility within the generational groups of the minority communities is a moot point. On Asian candidates, little separated younger and older opinion among all three groups, though older blacks were markedly wary of this option, with 13 per cent content to admit their reluctance to give support. Social class, meanwhile, appeared to have little impact on attitudes towards candidates.

Finally, the Runnymede report returned to the question of electoral non-participation. The data it presented here showed that the likelihood of blacks to vote (taking in the 'certain', 'very likely' and 'fairly likely' categories) stood at 67 per cent; among Asians, this figure reached 83 per cent and just 76 per cent for whites. Once again, clear evidence could be cited to show significant levels of probable abstention among black potential voters. Further examination of this phenomenon was now badly required, as was a systematic attempt to place black abstention rates in the context of social class and other circumstantial factors.

The Labour Party and the ethnic minorities: a special case?

The relationship between the Labour Party and the ethnic minority electorate has long since been the subject of extended academic analysis and

Table 3.2 *Attitudes towards Asian and black parliamentary candidates, 1991*

Attitude toward black candidates	Black (%)	Asian (%)	White (%)
More likely to vote for them	16	9	2
Less likely to vote for them	1	1	6
Makes no difference	81	87	91
DK	2	0	0
Attitude toward Asian candidates	Black (%)	Asian (%)	White (%)
More likely to vote for them	8	15	2
Less likely to vote for them	7	1	11
Makes no difference	80	80	84
DK	3	3	1

Source: Adapted from Amin and Richardson (1992: 19).

comment. FitzGerald (1988) argued that Labour's continuing triumph was chiefly the product of the lack of a viable alternative, with the Tories having effectively ceded this electoral territory partly by default and partly by design over many years. Messina (1989) made a similar point in trying to show how ethnic minorities had little choice but to stick with the Labour Party for fear of being completely disenfranchised, an argument he has updated and expanded upon more recently (Messina, 1998). Finally, the work of Shukra (1990, 1998a), while broadly critical of Labour's record through the 1980s and 1990s on issues of equalities, none the less recognised that the party remains the core arena in which debates over minority political influence would be determined in the medium term.

However, this picture of dominance by a single party has become so exceptional in modern British electoral history that it is necessary to go behind the headline levels of support for the party. In particular, it is necessary to examine the major schools of thought that have been advanced to account for this position and also to assess what, if any, evidence exists for underlying changes in the party–group nexus. There are four main schools to consider.

Labour's historic legacy
First, there is the argument that suggests that strong support for Labour is the usual pattern of partisanship expected of immigrants, refugees and

newcomers. In entering British society at lower points on the social and economic ladder, the newcomers quickly adjust to the reality of the political landscape in which political history has shown one of the two main parties to be more closely identified with these groups and their collective interests. Labour sympathy and identification is, therefore, a process that is learnt rapidly following arrival and resettlement. It appears to apply to most immigrant groups, irrespective of their social status prior to migration. The key to this line of argument is that Labour's historic success at marshalling minority voters is not treated too seriously, especially by those involved in shaping the long-term strategy of its opponents. These strategists are keen to point out that the blanket advantage enjoyed by Labour is essentially a one-off, generation factor that has coloured the political outlook of those caught up in the major waves of Caribbean and south Asian (and East African) migration between the 1950s and early 1980s. This is not seen as a period effect since it influenced blacks and Asians across the board throughout this era of dramatic change and was thought to be a factor that many carried with them in the years and decades after settlement (Werbner, 1991b). Moreover, it was a process that touched many different age groups, though the bulk were drawn from those in the peak migration cohorts of between 18 and 44 years at the time of entry to Britain.

An added dimension to this historic legacy school has been the special role of the Labour Party in the eyes of Asian and black migrants in the early post-war era. In particular, Labour's historic role in delivering Independence to India and Pakistan in 1947, setting in motion a tide of post-war de-colonisation, is often cited to illustrate the 'special relationship' that grew between Asian minorities and the party (Dean, 1987). It has to be said that, however central the events of 1947 might have been, the 'special relationship' perspective is rather clouded by the extended involvement of post-war Conservative administrations in the end of Empire and de-colonisation. Another feature in Labour's history that is thought to have been important was the party's sponsorship of the first anti-discrimination laws in the mid-1960s, a process extended under two further pieces of legislation in the late 1960s and mid-1970s (Jenkins, 1967). Labour, it was said, stood squarely behind the racial equality cause at this early and crucial time, and for this contribution the party has occupied a special place in the collective identity and sympathies of ethnic minority voters. Against this, it must be said, is the fact that Labour's 'caring' reputation was probably harmed by its tough line on immigration after 1968 generally and its sponsorship of the Commonwealth Immigrants Bill of that year in particular. Moreover, growing bipartisan support for race relations laws in the 1960s and 1970s perhaps further diluted the party's claim to stand alone for minority interests.

The Labour Party, according to this school of thought, has made the running in the past in taking on ethnic minority interests and causes that other parties have been slow or unwilling to adopt. The evidence surrounding such an argument is rather mixed, but it is clear that it has been Labour which has been most active and ambitious in exploiting the obvious campaign messages that have gone with this self-identity. Certainly, it has been an especially easy case to prosecute at times, given the Conservative Party's regular tendency to give an audience to its hard-line, anti-immigration populist wing. With the Tories often irretrievably prepared to engage in tough rhetoric on immigration and race issues, the challenge for Labour has often been merely to portray itself to ethnic minorities as being on the progressive side of the Conservatives (Saggar, 2000c). It is not hard to see the ease with which Labour has managed this task, to say nothing of the considerable political mileage it has accrued among the minority electorate. That said, the argument is essentially founded on a transition perspective that sees this state of affairs as non-permanent. For the Labour Party, therefore, the going has been relatively easy, with the Tories often leading the right-wing race and immigration agenda. Such an advantageous position, according to this school of thought, is unlikely to endure indefinitely. Practical Tory action to counter Labour's historic legacy has, of course, been widely predicted as well as exaggerated on many occasions in past. The dilemma, therefore, arises that an historic bias that has been to Labour's advantage has been so sufficiently long term that it begins to have the look and feel of a permanent cleavage, sub-ideological in character. This *de facto* divide cannot avoid driving ethnic minority perceptions of the two major parties. An historic legacy must presumably begin to diminish over time, with post-war British politics appearing to give a sufficiently long spell in which this change has been established. In fact, it has not and history's legacy is Labour's bias. The basic question in Tory circles has been how far the party remains willing to accept this skewed electoral terrain, the dismantling of which is likely to be a long-term goal for the party (Pinto-Duschinsky, 1997; *The Times*, 1997c; 1998; *Guardian*, 1998).

Social class, social justice and inequality
A second school of thought has argued that Labour's lead is the result of its class credentials coupled with the unusual social class profile of the minority electorate. As a party that has historically been concerned with social justice and inequality, it has been relatively easy for Labour to its extend its appeal to the minority communities, many of whom have experienced aspects of racial disadvantage and exclusion from mainstream employment, housing and even education. The party has thus built on its past reputation as a champion for the 'have nots' and taken on the crusade of racial equality in this spirit.

It is interesting to note the kind of reasons cited by minority voters to support their links with Labour. In a number of polls over the years, factors relating to the class membership and Labour as the party best suited to represent the interests of their class membership have frequently been at or near the top of the list of responses. In classic party identification theory, this axis is resemblant of the positive bonding between the wider working-class community and the party traditionally said to speak for the working-class, although such overt bonds are thought to have been rather muted in recent elections (Weakliem and Heath, 1999). In this case, the linkage runs through the ethnic group to the social class and through to the party of that social class. In any case, the voting patterns of the minority electorate are chiefly the result of their class composition.

The controversial aspect of this, however, has been that the argument that advances the idea of class consistent voting has occurred at precisely the period in which class deviant voting has been thought to be growing in the electorate as a whole. Many minority voters, in other words, have bucked the trend, either at the level of political identification with their socio-economic class and/or in terms of support in the polling booths for the party consistent with their class membership and identity. The puzzle is further reinforced when we take into account the fact that the Labour Party has been involved in a medium-term project to downgrade its traditional class links and self-identity. The modernisation project, launched by the party after its 1987 defeat, has often been described as leading directly or indirectly to a dilution of the traditional class-based image of the party seen in the early and mid-twentieth century. The danger inherent in this process of modernisation has been that it might unintentionally alienate Labour's working-class constituency, and in particular the party's working-class ethnic minority supporters. Equally, a class or inequality-based way of looking at the ethnic minority-Labour nexus would mean that as and when social mobility touched larger numbers of ethnic minorities it is likely that their class-based identities and association with Labour would also diminish. Labour's dilemma, therefore, can be seen to lie in the longer-term political consequences of pursuing social and other policies that both aim and achieve greater material prosperity and less inequality for its ethnic minority supporters. It is precisely because of this curious dilemma that critics have charged that something of a traditional Labour mind-set has existed, which has unknowingly perceived minorities and minority interests as subjects of, rather than participants in, the Labour movement. This criticism is one that touches directly on the question of what kind of political constituency ethnic minorities make up within and beyond Labour circles, and is a matter returned to in the next part of the chapter.

Labour: the ethnic minority-friendly party?
Thirdly, Labour's links with and instincts towards minorities are frequently described in terms of the party's claim to a stronger and more principled track record in articulating and defending the interests of ethnic minorities. This is an important claim, not least because of the way in it touches the common thinking and political attitudes of political activists and elites on the centre and left. Additionally, it represents a pretty robust claim that must stand up to the evidence in order to sustain itself. If it is the case that Labour is the party of and for ethnic minorities, in what sense and with what consequences does such an assumption operate?

To start with, it might be that ethnic minorities perceive the Labour Party to be a more effective vehicle for the representation of their collective interests. For instance, as long ago as 1983 a Harris poll found that a substantial proportion of Asian voters (31 per cent) rationalised their intended support for Labour on the grounds that 'they [Labour] best supported blacks and Asians'. In contrast, just 7 per cent of blacks in the survey took the same stance (Harris Research Centre, 1983). This suggests that some aspect of Labour's past record or its prospective promise was valued among one group, if not the other, on the basis of a fairly overt identification with these communities by the party. Given that Labour and its opponents are regularly accused of shunning and neglecting these communities, it is perhaps quite an achievement that such a large number of Asians were prepared to credit the party in this manner. More recently, MORI poll of Asians carried out just prior to the 1997 general election sought to test how far each of the main parties were perceived as either 'most trusted' or 'least trusted' to 'look after the interests of Asian people' (MORI, 1997). Not surprisingly, this inquiry revealed a clear Labour lead, with 51 per cent citing the Labour Party as most trusted as against just 15 per cent citing the Tories. This appears safe ground for explaining Labour's huge lead among Asians on voting (80 per cent against 10 per cent for the Conservatives according to the 1997 BES). However, what is striking is the disparity between attitudes towards political trust and political action. Rather fewer Asians seemed to trust Labour than were prepared to vote for it. Such a puzzle might be explained by Labour support enduring in minority communities on a habitual, self-fulfilling basis despite and not because of Labour's reputation for trust on so-called minority affairs. Table 3.3 describes the picture.

Another way to look at the assumption about Labour's sympathetic stance might to be to think of this as a more hard-headed assessment made by ethnic minorities as to the benefits of Labour in office. Such an assessment need not involve the preoccupation with so-called Asian and black interests. Indeed, as we go on to explore in Chapter 6, it is increasingly difficult to know for sure the nature or scope of so-called ethnic minority issues. Thus, minority voter assessments are likely to be made

Table 3.3 *Trust and Asian interests, 1997*

Which party do you trust most [least] to look after the interests of Asian people in this country?

	Most (%)	Least (%)
Conservative	15	32
Labour	51	9
Lib-Dem	2	9
Other	1	9
None of them	21	21
DK	14	23

Source: MORI, 1997.

on the basis of an appreciation of both mainstream political concerns, associated with high degrees of issue saliency (education, health, and employment in the 1990s for instance), and selective reference to the more exclusive concerns of minority groups (racial inequality, racial violence, etc.) (CRE, 1998: 5). The key point is that Labour's reputation is built on a range of factors, most of which are dominated by fleshing out basic propositions as to 'who wins' and 'who wins disproportionately more' under one administration as opposed to another. We may dub this approach as the 'ethnic minorities as disproportionate winners' argument which sees the social and economic programmes associated with Labour's intentions as being of greater direct value to minorities in schools, hospitals and jobs (Saggar, 1998a). The interesting part of such a perspective is that it allows us to account for Labour's striking lead among minority voters without having to link this to any special targeting of policy pledges by party to group. Indeed, Labour can remain largely silent on special treatment or targeting questions – as many felt it did deliberately in 1997 – and still hope to prosper on the basis of its broader, non-group-specific policies and commitments.

Needless to say, there are a number of far-reaching implications that arise from the claim that valuable and tangible spoils accrue to ethnic minorities through affiliation with Labour. As argued elsewhere (Saggar: 1998a: 28–32), the most important question that arises is to ask what kind of benefits or spoils result from this bond according to supporters of this claim. This claim has been associated with the work of commentators such as Messina (1989, 1998), who has suggested that minority interests are best served by public policy pledges that, *inter alia*, prioritises tackling unemployment (especially of the structural, long-term variety linked with sections of the young, under-educated minority communities), raising educational attainment (notably among minorities who are operating at the margins or have fallen out of the mainstream system of schooling), and promoting urban renewal (where geography dictates that minorities will gain from a physical and economic improvement in their environment). Suffice it to say, many of these policy commitments naturally and easily overlap with traditional British centre-left territory. For this reason, it is argued that Labour is specifically best placed to advance ethnic minority collective, yet indirect, interests. The social, economic and geographic location of ethnic minorities in British society ensure that they are the likely beneficiaries of a wide range of public policies that Labour can be expected to defend and possibly advance. In this sense, Messina's claim is that ethnic minorities are not so much the deliberate 'targets' of Labour or centre-left policies but, rather, merely the indirect 'winners' from such a policy agenda. It should be added that this interpretation is widely shared by senior politicians and strategists within the Labour Party. To be sure, it can serve as a powerful springboard from which the party can freely choose to continue to pursue its broad strategy towards ethnic minorities. This posture, of course, is often derided and condemned for its lack of commitment and even complacency. However, it can be defended on two grounds within senior circles of the party. First, it can be described as far from inactive and, in fact, seeks considerable change and advancement for disadvantaged groups, within which ethnic minorities are amply represented. Secondly, and perhaps more importantly, this strategy leaves the party the chance of not alienating those white voters who are sceptical and hostile towards ethnic minorities (or at least sceptical of the need to promote minority interests in an overt fashion). By side-stepping this potential backlash, Labour figures might reasonably contend that their aim is to build a resilient political consensus through which ethnic minorities and their interests can be sympathetically handled. This is no doubt a powerful argument within Labour's strategic discussions, not least because of the overriding need since the mid-1990s to pursue campaign themes that avoid open divisions or question Labour's managerial competence (Saggar, 1998e). The question of issue voting and public attitudes is one that is taken up in greater depth in Chapter 6.

Having said that Labour has pursued a non-targetted stance, and has a lot to gain from doing so, it should not forgotten that aspects of specific policy targeting continue to influence its policy pledges as well as its deeds in office. For example, as early as the end of May 1997, Labour's newly-installed Home Secretary scrapped the 'primary purpose' immigration rules that dated from a Conservative predecessor in 1983. In doing so, he fulfilled a long-standing pledge and also confirmed that in this limited respect there was an important difference that Labour specifically could make. The degree to which such a difference was acknowledged or valued by minority voters is hard to gauge, especially as the underlying saliency of the immigration issue has fallen so dramatically since the mid-1980s. Labour, it should be noted, remains committed to policies to update and expand the role of the Commission for Racial Equality (albeit in fairly vague terms), overhauling the 1981 Nationality Act by removing its racially discriminatory provisions, rolling out fresh non-discrimination requirements for the civil service and police services, and giving priority to policing and criminal justice programmes that tackle racial violence. Since its 1997 general election victory the Labour government has also taken on the cause of expanding ethnic minority recruitment to the senior ranks of the civil service, backing the case for improved ethnic monitoring in both the public and private sectors, and fresh attempts to define potential racial exclusion in areas such as health, financial services and social housing. These initiatives appear to demonstrate a level of activism that would be difficult to sideline and are commonly packed within an agenda of social and institutional modernisation (Mowlam, 2000). In all cases, it is possible see some degree of additional pressure or emphasis brought to bear by a Labour administration, though it might be rather hard to argue that this specific role had led to large-scale, tangible results in the short term.

Tory default: the ghost of Powell

Labour's historic command of the minority electorate is arguably associated most closely with the reputation of its principal rival as a hotbed of anti-immigrant and anti-minority feeling. This school of thought lays stress on the default position adopted by the Tories, whose overt and covert actions have tended to at best keep potential minority supporters at arm's length, and at worse squander those few opportunities it has enjoyed to build a new constituency of supporters. There have been a number of factors that have underpinned this relationship of mutual distrust, hostility and even ill-will. At the top of this list has been the party's continued association with the thoughts and grassroots backers of Enoch Powell whose actions in the late 1960s crystallised divisions on race within and beyond the party (Behrens and Edmonds, 1981). This original fissure effectively served to establish a long-term source of division within Tory ranks in particular, and also ensured that the party's affairs have been regularly punctuated by fairly explicit 'race rows'. Labour, oddly, has contained similar seeds of discord but crucially has lacked any Powellite equivalent tendency around which the party's right-wing, anti-immigrant activists could rally.

The indifference and/or hostility of the Conservative Party to the political interests of ethnic minorities have been well documented in existing research and scholarship (FitzGerald, 1987: 19–29; Gordon, 1990: 175–90; Messina: 1989: 125–49). This much has not been in doubt. However, there has remained a fairly substantial degree of dispute among commentators on the question of how far, and in what sense, such attitudes have driven the behaviour of different tiers within the party. In particular, there is a considerable lack of consensus on the point of the Tories' campaign strategies in appealing to anti-minority political sentiment on the one hand while courting minority voters on the other (Rich, 1986, 1998). Messina's (1998) recent work on this subject has emphasised the continuing importance of underlying essentials, namely the persistence of hostile attitudes at various levels within the party from the 1960s to the present. For instance, it is noted that a major survey of Conservative Party members in 1992 showed that a robust majority (70 per cent) continued to endorse the repatriation of immigrants as a legitimate option for a Conservative administration (Whiteley et al., 1994: 253). A survey of elite opinion featuring Tory MPs (undertaken by Messina in the early 1980s but not published until 1989) had shown just under one-half stood behind a voluntary repatriation position (quoted in Messina, 1989: 129). The point to stress was that a much older survey of Conservative MPs in the late 1960s had revealed an almost identical picture (Frasure, 1971: 206). That is to say, the party's core elite stance had not changed much over this long period and, more significantly by the 1990s was clearly backed up by the majority of mass Tory opinion. If the Conservatives were to be castigated for holding on to Powellite ideas, with their obvious negative impact upon campaigns to attract minority supporters, then this criticism of the party, concluded Messina, was based on sound and unequivocal evidence. The Conservatives were and remained the party of anti-black and Asian sentiment to a degree that could not be dismissed easily by party elites and party leaders. It is precisely this link between grassroots feeling and leadership priorities that has been the real subject of discussion and disagreement since the picture of tough, uncompromising membership attitudes has been clear for all to see and appreciate.

Where, then, has this picture left the Conservative Party's leadership in first, trying to balance rival party interests, and secondly, tackling the basis of its damaged reputation among minorities? A couple of distinctions need to be added in order to clarify and answer this central question. First, it is fairly clear that there has been quite a sharp distinction between the party's rhetoric and the party's deeds on race and immigration matters generally. For instance, despite showing public sympathy for moves to tighten immigration regimes over the years, the Conservatives were famously the party that defied public opinion in granting entry to Ugandan Asian political refugees in 1972. This move risked stimulating the wrath of not just those on the party's right wing but also a fair proportion of moderates who felt that the concession undermined the delicate balance in immigration policy that had been built up between the parties. A further example of this distinction can be seen in the Tories' parliamentary support, albeit a little grudgingly, for successive race relations legislation sponsored by Labour governments in the 1960s and 1970s. In 1976, the willingness of the Thatcher-led party to grant tacit support for the Race Relations Bill came as a surprise to many of its high-ranking members and mass supporters, not least because this move went against the grain of a new onslaught on immigration policy being pursued concurrently by the Tory Shadow Home Secretary. Secondly, a distinction needs to be drawn between political communications used to attract anti-immigrant sentiment against a backdrop of high issue saliency (the 1960s and 1970s), and the modern era in which the issue has effectively dropped off the political agenda (mid-1980s onwards). The upshot has been that claims that the Tories have 'played the race card' in recent elections have often missed the point. Thus, efforts to marshal ethnic minority voters in recent times have been conducted against a potentially more attractive background. The party has had little need to pursue high profile campaigns on the immigration issue as this question has gradually ceased to matter in macro electoral terms. Thus, the party's leaders, irrespective of individual background or personality factors, have had less and less reason to emphasise anti-immigration themes and this in turn has meant that the crude Powellite images of the past have waned in prominence. Efforts to appeal to immigrants or the children of immigrants have become – or ought to have appeared – easier as a consequence.

However, this line of argument overlooks two basic facts. The first is that the party's leadership and senior figures have plainly continued to probe anti-immigrant and anti-minority themes from time to time. However, it is noticeable that the locus of this attention has shifted from immigration and towards several racial equality dilemmas. Many interventions have focused on the terms of racial and ethnic integration, suggesting that cultural diversity efforts have gone much further than either envisaged or supported by public opinion. Thus, the Conservatives continue to be the party of 'race rows', to borrow from the journalistic portrayal of such debates, simply because of the persistence of core disagreements within and beyond party politics about the nature of ethnic pluralism and the role of government. Secondly, we cannot overlook the point raised in Messina's 1998 essay that highlighted the endurance of fairly tough right-wing views on immigration among the party's membership. In other words, we should remember that parties make and retain policy for a whole host of reasons. Responsiveness to public opinion of general issue saliency is an important determinant in this process but by no means the only factor that is responsible. In addition, parties pursue policies and stances because of the significance of internal party opinion and lobbies. Membership views on immigration are such a constituency within the modern Conservative Party that cannot easily be ignored. For this reason, the party continues to be projected as a vehicle for controlled scepticism and hostility toward ethnic diversity chiefly because this is a line of opinion that is well represented in the party at grassroots level. Party image and broad policy stance, therefore, not surprisingly follow a similar trajectory.

Finally, a further factor is worth noting that reconciles the earlier rational party competition picture with the reality of the constraints upon the Conservative Party. The structure of minority opinion is a variable that can be added to the equation. In traditional terms, such opinion has perceived the Conservatives as an unattractive agency representing anti-minority attitudes. For instance, in 1983 a small but important minority of Asian and black Labour voters justified their decision in terms of a negative racial image of the Tories (Harris Research Centre, 1983). The Powellite legacy stood foremost in their minds and no doubt was a feature behind many other minority voters' decision to shun the Conservatives. By 1997 elements of this opinion had begun to shift and in ways that meant that the Powellite legacy was only relevant at the outer most margins of minority voting behaviour. Take the 'old' battleground of opinion on immigration itself. It is striking that a 1997 MORI survey found that Asian views on immigration contained sizeable elements that had drifted to the centre or centre-right, a position almost unimaginable a decade previously (MORI, 1997). Indeed, as early as 1991 an NOP poll revealed similar findings, suggesting that blanket disapproval of the Conservatives' immigration policies could no longer be thought of as a major impediment to Tory support among Asian voters (NOP, 1991). The point that is being made is that the default position of Tory election strategies to court minority support probably does not operate in the same way as it did in the past. At the very least, the Conservatives suffer some considerable loss of potential support because of the open pursuit of controversial racial debates concerning racial integration by party heavyweights. Moreover, the growth in support for either existing or tougher immigration policies among some Asian voters means that on rational issue voting grounds, the party cannot abandon its traditional policy stance entirely. This certainly has left the party in a puzzling and sometimes unenviable position. That said, the party is now required to manage and fine-tune the consequences of its Powellite historic past in a way that would have not been known in the past.

One of the principal hypotheses that, therefore, needs to be tested using updated empirical evidence is how the Conservative Party's cultural and ideological legacy impacts upon current voting outlooks and behaviour. The traditional view of this legacy was that it served as a virtual veto on the party's underlying chances of attracting minority supporters. Not only did segments of the minority electorate cite this as a central factor preventing them from moving closer to the party, it also served as a self-fulfilling argument on its own that prevented many within the party taking risks with radical policies or stances on the broad issue. A lot depended on the contest between various ideological forces within Conservative ranks that saw a variety of responses to the party's declared aim of promoting itself among minority voters. While some factions have pursued an open campaign to court these groups using colourful 'ethnic campaigns', other elements in the party have held that the promotion of black and Asian interests is best achieved without any specificity in policy, campaign or communications. This has obviously been a live and tense debate within the party, and arguably only segments of it have been appreciated among the minority electorate as a whole. In their eyes it has been possible, though not always desirable, to evaluate the Conservatives' profile across a wide criteria. The party's immediate attitudes and actions towards ethnic minority groups have been a prime component in this assessment process. The process has also involved a bundling of other concerns, some relating to attitudes to race and ethnicity alongside others that are far removed from this agenda. The hypothesis thus remains as before, namely to assess how far different ethnic groups have perceived the Conservative Party as especially well or poorly equipped to represent ethnic minorities as a political constituency, however loosely defined. This theme is further discussed in Chapters 5 and 6 and allows us to comment directly on evidence examining group opinion and attitudes on this front. This evidence reveals that much has changed in the contextual framework that surrounds the old default hypothesis. As already mentioned, old inter-group contrasts in opinion no longer necessarily hold true, and the interpretation of the evidence needs to take account of this important development. Rather more importantly, however, the hypothesis needs to be explored in a way that fully allows for wide discrepancies in the notion of representation of political constituency. It is to this debate that we now turn in the final part of this chapter.

A coherent political constituency?

If ethnicity is thought to be an important explanatory factor behind the political participation of ethnic minorities, it is vital to recognise that this analytical category really applies only to ethnic minorities. Its impact has been measured only in relation to a small part of the electorate and this study also follows this approach. Thus, it is the ethnicity of ethnic minorities that we are focused upon and, as such, the possibility that ethnicity is capable of having a large impact among the electorate is summarily ruled out (Heath et al., 1991: 99). As a result, we do not easily accept claims that ethnic minorities influence election outcomes – chiefly for reasons to do with demographic size and political geography – though the much-embellished 'ethnic marginals' controversy lives on (see Chapters 4, 5 and 8, below). That said, the capacity of ethnic-based bloc voting turning results or coming close to doing so, especially at local constituency level, cannot be easily dismissed. In 1997 alone, two prime examples of such a process could be identified with ease: Bethnal Green and Bow and Bradford West. (In both cases, local Conservative candidates were from the 'right' ethnic background, but the 'wrong' party, succeeded in causing severe haemorrhaging of the local Asian vote for the Labour Party. This case is discussed along with others in Chapter 8.) Additionally, the recent history of the Labour Party's wilderness years from 1979 to 1997 is heavily embroidered with references to the importance of ethnic minority supporters. Indeed, the party's considerable reliance on its 'ethnic safe seats', especially during the 1980s, is thought by many in the party – with some basis in evidence – to have played a major part in avoiding electoral oblivion.

With this background of mixed assessments in mind, it is necessary to home in on the question of how far, and in what sense, ethnicity matters on the British electoral landscape. By this is meant three related conceptual questions. First, has the assumption that for ethnic minority voters ethnicity alone counts been overdone? We can see the rationale for thinking that analysis of the impact of ethnicity should be limited to testing its affect on ethnic minorities. However, this assumption is rather different and goes much further by almost removing minority voters from the wider social and economic context. We must ask, therefore, how far and in what manner ethnicity shapes the political outlook and action of ethnic minorities? For instance, can it be attributed to being something of an unrelated aspect of ethnic group membership or possibly to passive forms of ethnic identity? Alternatively, is the role of ethnicity accounted for in terms of a distinctive issue or policy agenda? Going even further, as some have suggested, is the relationship in fact the product of a distinctively ethnically-related way of looking at and acting within the political world? The range of answers is explored empirically in Chapter 6. Secondly, how far are the elements of distinctiveness among ethnic minorities effectively channelled into effective forms of political organisation and influence? It may be the case that a strong, distinctive character in the former is not necessarily linked to let alone the cause of strength in the latter. Indeed, we need to explore the extent to which forms of political articulation and aggregation of interests operate across the party political spectrum, and to test how effectively these interests are served in the institutional context of specific party arrangements. We consider these points in greater detail citing empirical evidence from 1997 in Chapter 5, below. Thirdly, how far is it reasonable and safe to think of ethnic minorities as a political constituency either in its own right or in conjunction with others that is readily identified as an established, long-term feature of British electoral politics? This question is essentially interpretative in its construction and is certainly the subject of widespread dispute among academic and press commentators, activists, officials and others. However, it is a question that requires some precision in its response since it provides us with the central framework within which to assess empirical evidence from the 1997 general election.

The notion of political constituency is in essence shorthand for several inter-related aspects of political participation and policy influence. To begin with, some fresh perspective needs to be thrown on the debate that has emerged since the mid-1980s on the political representation of ethnic minorities in British society. The terms of this debate are useful for helping to unpack the concept of minorities seeking representation on a group basis. One side of this debate has contended that there is little in the way of solid evidence to back the claim that ethnic minorities subscribe to a separate and specific agenda of policy concerns. This contention has been most closely associated with the work of Studlar and Layton-Henry (1990). It notes that Asian and blacks have a sufficiently diverse set of policy priorities so as to render any claims of group cohesiveness virtually meaningless. Moreover, these groups share policy priorities with their white counterparts to a very considerable extent. The hypothesis to be tested, therefore, is to evaluate how far these claims are borne out in up to date empirical evidence; additionally, we need to assess whether inter-group differences are accountable in circumstantial terms to do with variations in social background. In any case, this school of thought has argued that the collective representation of ethnic minorities in the political realm is fraught with impossibly high odds since the political strategy to which it aspires is based on shaky foundations. Collective, shared interests virtually do not exist, and where they do they are insufficiently crystallised into a strong sense of cross-group political cohesion. No amount of political strategy, however sophisticated, can remedy this basic shortfall. At the other end of this debate, in contrast, there is a counter-perspective that argues that an ethnic minority political agenda is, if not fully developed, on the road to such a goal. It cites the growing mountain of evidence from the world of local politics that shows the extensive use made by parties and politicians of ethnic and kinship ties in marshalling support for Labour in particular. The work of Werbner and Anwar (1991) stands out within the 'ethnicity counts' school of thought. As one commentator (Messina, 1998: 49) notes, the linchpin of their argument is to focus on Asians and blacks as political communities, chiefly because this is the way in which they are defined by mainstream political institutions in Britain.

Being a member of one of these principal minority groups, therefore, translates to occupying a distinctive and ideologically specific position on the wider political landscape. This position principally involves minorities taking a recipient role in relation to formal political institutions and the policy process. Public policy programmes, procedures and mechanism are established, the purpose of which is (or at least historically has been) to incorporate the political interests of these minority groups. As 'objects' in the political system broadly, 'non-whites necessarily share a common political and policy orientation that transcends whatever specific issues may divide them. They are a distinct political constituency regardless of whether they cohere around a specific set of explicit political or policy goals.' (Messina: 1998: 49).

The idea of political constituency, therefore, might be operationalised on the basis of the political-ideological context surrounding the presence of upwards of three million ethnic minorities in Britain. It is this context which has, according to this perspective, delivered the 'object' or constrained participant status attached to the political representation of ethnic minorities as a discrete political constituency. In other words, the degree of conformity to a single ethnic minority political agenda among minorities themselves is almost a secondary matter. What matters even more is the agenda setting process associated with ethnic minority political representation. Moreover, it cannot be ignored that ethnic minorities have been and continue to be mobilised in political terms on the basis of common group links and identity. This group-based form of politics is not entirely alien in the British system but certainly it is not easily reconciled with the dominant social class tradition of group-based politics seen in Britain. This has meant that in voting loyally for Labour over many elections ethnic minorities have exhibited many of the features usually associated with group-based mobilisation for Labour, except that in the case of minorities the role of class and related forms of social stratification appear to have played a minimal role. They have, in short, behaved in a way that strongly implies but does not demonstrate a high degree of shared interest solely on the basis of ethnic group membership. For Labour, and indeed any party facing this enviable position, ethnic minorities are easily and understandably perceived to be a single, common political interest.

In order to address the debate over the 'ethnicity matters' assumption, we must take care to note the importance of these kinds of contextual-institutional factors. This chapter has explored various aspects of this assumption but, above all, has sought to describe the ways in which party competition and party-based mobilisation have served to shape the operation of this assumption. Plainly, it does not operate in a vacuum in which the empirical evidence can be read at face value. A more useful approach is to read the data at more than one level and, crucially, examine the relationship that presumably exists linking the two somewhat polarised schools of thought discussed previously. The presumption at this stage is deliberately held that the rival perspectives share more in common than might be appreciated at first sight. Later chapters in this study are devoted to a more systematic empirical exploration of these rival schools. The following chapters also involve an attempt to explain how the introduction of false distinctions in this debate has perhaps proven to be regretfully short-sighted in providing a convincing and enduring analysis of ethnic minorities as a political constituency. This is a dynamic concept subject to institutional and contextual variance as this chapter has argued. Moreover, it is arguably the central conceptual idea around which most of the key debates about the political representation of ethnic minorities and their capacity for electoral-based political leverage revolve. For this reason we need to harness this core concept fully and in a wide variety of ways if we are to describe and assess successfully the broad picture of ethnic minority electoral participation in contemporary Britain.

Notes

1 The CRC study contained several conceptual and theoretical confusions, and overstated the size and importance of the ethnic minority electorate on four counts. First, the 1971 Census figures were taken at face value with no allowance being made in the calculations for those below 18 years and therefore not eligible to vote. Secondly, no estimates, let alone adjustments, were made for possible under-registration by minorities as compared with whites. Thirdly, the question of differential turn-out rates between whites and minorities was overlooked, thereby compounding the failure to describe the latter's probable effect in actual terms. Finally, the report came close to being conceptually flawed by not substantiating the idea that minorities were an internal part of the floating vote. Indeed, the CRC report's own data showed the opposite to be the case with very high levels of Labour support coupled with no evidence to suggest differential inter-ethnic swing between the two 1974 elections. For a fuller discussion of these criticisms see Layton-Henry (1983).

2 Some allowance needs to be made for the Labour Party's headstart in attracting these voters. Le Lohé (1998: 94) has questioned in a recent essay the earlier assumption that national electoral dominance is necessarily and always beneficial. Taking the example of the 1964–70 Labour administration, he has argued that the backdrop of an unpopular Labour government in office at Westminster is the most likely route to raised support for the Conservatives among ethnic minorities in local and national elections. This line of thinking marks a major departure for extant perspectives on the influence of national party fortunes upon support among the minority electorate.

4

Electoral engagement

Introduction

The electoral engagement of ethnic minorities is a central question for the reputation and performance of British democratic politics for three reasons. First, participating in the electoral process is widely taken to be a metaphor for the level and style of involvement in mainstream society. Indeed, in judging the wider parameters of group social inclusion and exclusion, it fairly commonplace for political institutions and leaders to turn to the democratic process itself as a useful and convenient marker. Political parties and others have become accustomed to trying to link the picture of political participation to other aspects of social change. If it is good enough for society as a whole, so the conventional wisdom goes, then it must be good enough to be reflected in the narrower world of politics. A form of 'microcosm politics' has emerged as a recognisable and rather revered principle upon which political institutions are expected to base their actions (KPMG/LWT, 1998). The consequences of this familiar argument are clear to see. For one thing, it is widely assumed that if certain ethnic groups shun or are prevented from participation in mainstream employment, schooling, housing, etc., we often surmise that a similar pattern is likely to follow in their electoral participation. Indeed, according to this argument the former and latter are causally inter-related. In the words of a recent CRE publication on democratic politics speaking to a wide and sympathetic audience: 'All citizens, whatever their background, should have the right and the confidence to be involved and represented fully in the democratic process, as voters, candidates and party activists. The 1997 General Election was an important test of the principles upon which our democracy is built' (CRE: 1998: 1).

Failure to accept that these are legitimate goals is implied to be a major indictment of modern British democracy, at least in the sense that a series of inter-related social and political opportunities are cordoned off for minorities with a resultant diminution in wider social inclusiveness. However, the fact that abject failure has been the norm until quite recently especially in aspects of candidate representation and interest articulation does not prevent this argument seeking and normally receiving a wide and supportive audience.

Secondly, the underlying reputation of liberal democracy is often thought to be at stake when measuring and interpreting the electoral involvement of different ethnic groups. This is chiefly a normative argument that suggests that the democratic process itself is likely to be harmed over the longer term if sizeable pockets of non-participation or possibly even indifferent participation persists in ethnically-concentrated groups (Kellner, 1999). These groups may contain members who remain aloof from participative norms associated with liberal democracy not merely because of a generalised sense of disinterest or apathy, but additionally because of a marked scepticism about the responsiveness of liberal democratic institutions. This line of argument has, to be sure, become closely associated with debates over threatened black electoral abstention and also emerged as one of the more prominent themes taken up by commentators in the run-up to the 1997 election. One common theme was for commentators, especially those linked with prominent minority religious lobbies, to issue warnings that specific policies targeted at ethnic minorities were required in order to capture and hold the interest of minority electors who may otherwise shun participation (Race for the Election, 1997; UKACIA, 1997).

Moreover, the subject of ethnic minority political participation and its impact upon the 'quality of democracy' has been dogged by controversy with sharply different readings of the available data. One of the principal vehicles for this debate and controversy has been the suggestion that sluggish participation levels among specific groups might be attributable to the attitudes and behaviour of political parties (CRE, 1999). An interesting variation on this theme of self-criticism is reflected in the choice of words of the Conservative Party's own newly installed (post-1997) vice-chairman with responsibility for promoting the party cause among women and ethnic minorities:

> The Conservative Party is starting to address the issue of equality by becoming a genuinely inclusive party. We believe it is not acceptable to anyone to treat ethnic groups with kid gloves. We need to actively work to create an environment in which all who want to take part can do whether it is as elected officials within party structures or public appointments. (Baroness Peta Buscombe, quoted in KPMG/LWT, 1998: 22)

If these democratic institutions are at fault, the argument goes, there remain wider unanswered doubts about the commitment of the democratic system as a whole to extending the involvement of ethnic minorities. Worries persist, for instance, about the conspicuous poor and/or patchy representation of ethnic minorities in elected office, party structures and public appointments. As a result, there is considerable and growing agreement that at the very minimum parties, politicians and others cannot make unfettered claims about the representative and responsive qualities of the democratic system unless this image is adequately grounded in measurable reality (Saggar and Geddes, 2000). These claims, where they persist, are thus often fiercely resisted by more radically and critically minded interest and lobby groups said to represent and be in touch with grassroots opinion among the ethnic minorities. Elsewhere, there is a broad determination to ensure that such claims are empirically rather than rhetorically driven.

To these arguments we can reasonably add a third which has both grown in prominence in recent elections and, oddly, often been overlooked in many debates concerning electoral participation. This argument holds that strong and reliable rates of minority electoral participation are a necessary prerequisite for the exertion of electoral leverage for and on behalf of ethnic minorities. There is, of course, a fundamental truth to this point, namely that electoral muscle is largely a determinant of sheer numbers in the (traditional) British single-member, winner takes all parliamentary electoral system (Crewe, 1983; Le Lohé, 1998). By concentrating on mobilising numbers of voters from specific ethnic backgrounds, there is a premium placed on ensuring that the maximum possible number of these voters are both eligible to vote and then do so. Ironically, many of the claims made over the years regarding the exertion of electoral clout by ethnic minorities in order to command enhanced influence over elected policy-makers have tended to be based on confusing signals about group mobilisation. On the one hand, commentators, pressure groups and others have lamented the fact that registration and turn out rates among certain minority groups have (been thought to) lag behind those of others, with all the resultant fears that this implied an under-utilisation of political resources (see, for instance, the *Guardian*, 1996b: 7; KPMG/LWT, 1998: 21). On the other hand, however, confident boasts have been expressed about the possibility of unseating named candidates, and electing others, as part of the so-called 'ethnic marginals' argument (for a classical statement of this see CRE, 1980). This thesis has relied on the selective marshalling of minority voters at the polls, having previously assumed that they were at least as fully registered and likely to turn out as their counterparts among the white population. Plainly, this has not always been a safe assumption to make and the result has been that slightly contradictory claims have been advanced as to the mechanism behind and potential impact of ethnic bloc voting. If these assertions are to be granted credence – and many assume that they already are – then it is more or less taken as read that they are firmly anchored in empirically verifiable knowledge of full and robust minority participation rates. Moreover, where inter-group variations are shown to exist, it is only reasonable to expect that these contrasts will then be reflected in accurate and more realistic debates about group electoral muscle. For instance, the Indian community has been associated over many elections with strikingly high rates of overall electoral engagement, signifying to some that a special bond or commitment to the democratic process exists among members of this particular group. And yet, it is not this group but rather the Pakistani community (and Bangladeshis to a lesser degree) that has stood out in many of the grassroots examples of ethnic bloc voting that have been documented by researchers (see, for instance, Le Lohé, 1975, 1990 and 1998; Anwar, 1990 and 1998). It is important to know that the evidence on numbers does in fact back up this pattern. The alternative explanation might be that rhetorical and actual bloc voting are both conceptually and factually distinct to a degree not immediately apparent when scanning such debates. This possibility would be a source of alarm for those genuinely committed to arriving at reliable evidence on participation rates.

This chapter is devoted to fleshing out the empirical basis for the claims and counter-claims found within debates about ethnic minority electoral participation. It is divided into four principal themes. First, it looks at the nature and function of electorally-based routes to political participation and influence in relation to some of the main alternatives facing minority communities. It notes that, while various options undoubtedly exist on the broad canvass it is important to remember that electoral politics serves some fairly specific and unique functions. Other routes are, therefore, sometimes complementary and possibly ones that might be pursued in parallel, but they are rarely precise or full alternatives to ballot box politics. Secondly, the chapter turns to examine evidence from 1997 on electoral registration and eligibility. This section deals mainly with the issue of differential registration rates and the question of how far designated pressure group campaigns can and should intervene to narrow these variations. Thirdly, the chapter considers evidence on electoral turn out, noting not merely the evidence from the 1997 election but also the large volume of more locally-based empirical research carried out over many years on this theme. Basic distinctions are drawn between the various forms of non-voting identified from one specific group to the next in order to assess how far group-specific factors prevail over circumstantial explanations. Finally, the chapter also contains an extended discussion of the alienation hypothesis that has featured so prominently in debates over minority participation. In particular, this section draws on the findings of more detailed BES items and, additionally, asks whether fundamental racial exclusion can account for the most overt pockets of abstention. The task is to identify the degree to which minority non-participation is driven by racial considerations (as is so often said and repeated) or whether there are circumstantial factors at work that account for inter-group disparities (not commonly thought and perhaps less fashionable in its rhetorical value).

Electoral-based political participation

Demographic influences
The long-term significance of ethnic minority voters has, of course, depended on the demographic characteristics of the larger minority population. Factors relating to the size and composition of the ethnic minority population and its chief sub-groups will shape electoral strength. Indeed, in Britain's constituency-based voting system, electoral power largely hangs on numbers. While this dowdy truth was frequently downplayed by ethnic minority activists and others in the past, by the mid-1990s there appeared to be an open acknowledgement that Britain's minorities both constituted more than a demographic blip and had in places grown to become substantial local communities. The drawback with this kind of acknowledgement was that it often permitted vested interests to exaggerate the influence of minority voters. In a remarkable bid to talk up this case in 1997, an Asian satellite television station, *Zee TV*, released in mid campaign a list of 36 so-called 'Asian marginals' calculated on the basis of raw numbers of Asians at constituency level without accounting for age, registration or likely turn out (quoted in *The Times*, 1997a: 14). This episode was merely part of a general pattern of embellishment, bordering at times on distortion.

The 1991 Census showed that some three million people reported themselves to belong to an ethnic group other than white. At 5.5 per cent of the population, though unevenly distributed, this was up sharply from the notional figure found in the earlier 1981 Census of 2.2 million (or 4 per cent). A leap of around a quarter in a decade seemed more remarkable at a time when the bulk of primary and even most secondary immigration had tapered off. The 1991 figures showed the largest single group to be Indians, whose numbers had reached the psychologically important one million mark (just over 1 in 4 of the minority population taken together). Table 4.1 tells the wider story.

Of course the size of the minority groups needs to be examined in the context of age structure. Not all of the 1.5 million Asians, for instance, are eligible to vote since a large slice of this population comprises those below the age of eligibility (Bangladeshis and Pakistanis in particular). Data from the Labour Force Survey during the mid-1990s showed that around two-thirds of the ethnic minority population was below 35 years of age (compared with around a half of their white counterparts). Over the longer run this disproportionately young population will begin to feed into a growing adult population able in principle to cast a ballot. Estimates suggest that the minority population is likely to stabilise at around 9 or 10 per cent of the total population once birth and mortality rates have converged substantially (Ballard and Khalra, 1994: 15).

In any case, allowance has to be made for the large numbers of ethnic

Table 4.1 *Breakdown of ethnic origin of UK resident population, 1991*

Ethnic group	Number (000s)	Total population (%)	Non-white population (%)
All	54,889	100.0	–
White	51,874	94.5	–
All others	3,015	5.5	100.0
Black Caribbean	500	0.9	16.6
Black African	212	0.4	7.0
Black other	178	0.3	5.9
[Black total	891	1.6	29.5]
Indian	840	1.5	27.9
Pakistani	477	0.9	15.8
Bangladeshi	163	0.3	5.4
[South Asian total	1,480	2.7	49.1]
Chinese	157	0.3	5.2
Other Asian	198	0.4	6.6
Other non-Asian	290	0.5	9.6

Source: 1991 General Census.

minority children who, in proportional terms, had not by 1997 fed through into the potential minority electorate. Furthermore, the 1991 Census figures were of decreasing accuracy in measuring the size of minority electorate by 1997. One estimate suggested that this electorate might have grown by as much as 12 per cent between 1991 and 1996, to be followed by a further projected 20 per cent expansion between 1996 and 2001. Meanwhile, the comparable rise across these periods in the white electorate was estimated at 1 and 2 per cent.[1] A small, yet generally tightly packed minority electorate continued to grow, even without any further fresh primary migration or family reunification being taken into account.

Citizenship

Electoral participation carries with it a lot of issues about motives and consequences held at the group level. Discussion of these dimensions follows later in the chapter. It is necessary to begin with some basic qualifications, however. The most important of these is to specify the extent to which ethnic minorities enjoyment of political rights – including voting rights – is affected by legal citizenship. We should not overlook the fact that, in the wake of large-scale post-war immigration from the Caribbean and the Indian sub-continent, the United Kingdom tended to extend and acknowledge voting rights on more generous terms than was the case in several comparable European nations also subject to significant immigration during this era (Layton-Henry, 1990). These rights were ordinarily recognised at the point of entry into the United Kingdom on the basis of some form of New Commonwealth citizenship. Where such rights were not automatically granted, it was commonplace for Asian and black newcomers to acquire them following normalisation of nationality status, typically involving citizenship through registration and naturalisation shortly after resettlement. The upshot of this legacy has meant that measuring rates of ethnic minority electoral participation does not normally involve any prior need to make awkward (and perhaps dubious) assumptions about citizenship and the political rights attached to citizenship. The vast bulk of these groups of immigrants and their children are not impeded by citizenship from playing a part in the electoral process of the United Kingdom.[2] This is by no means an insignificant assumption since powerful and vexed debates about the extension of voting rights to immigrants and their descendants continue to be a major source of friction in countries such as Germany, Italy and Spain (Hargreaves and Leaman, 1995; Weil, 1996). France, though adopting a more rigorous approach to immigrant integration through the vehicle of citizenship, has not managed to circumvent political controversy over voting rights altogether (Crowley, 1993). In Britain, such debates would appear perverse on any measure of the contemporary political landscape.[3]

A further qualification needs to be added. Not all of the black and Asian ethnic minorities that are the principal subjects of this study comprise those who were linked, directly or indirectly, to post-war New Commonwealth immigration. A proportion of these minorities are more recent entrants, many of whom have not or cannot normalise their citizenship status; some others are currently short-term refugees or asylum-seekers who are obviously prevented from enjoying voting rights; and yet others who are not easily quantified and are in fact undocumented illegals who necessarily fall outside citizenship and voting norms. It is possible that elements of all three sub-groups could have been picked up in the survey (which has tapped Asian and black respondents on grounds of self-declared ethnic group membership and not on citizenship criteria), though it has to be said that no more than a trace presence is likely to have been picked up. In the case of the latter two sub-groups, there will have been fairly obvious reasons behind their self-imposed unwillingness to participate in electoral research or any other type of survey. In any case, it has been noted that even 'regularised' immigrant groups may retain resistance to participating fully in the electoral register because of latent fears of 'fishing expeditions' by the immigration authorities (Anwar, 1990). The essential point is that citizenship and voting rights are only of relevance to an analysis such as this if these questions are contested and the subject of political disagreement. For the most part, they are not in Britain, although it has to be added that controversy of this kind continues to be a hallmark characteristic of extreme right groups who oppose in essence the political-legal settlement surrounding post-war immigration (BNP, 1997).

Added to this we need to take account of the fact that these different ethnic groups have travelled to and established homes in Britain for a variety of reasons (Spencer, 1997, especially ch. 5). These factors range from classical economic labour migrants who made up the bulk of those originally recruited, either explicitly or more casually in the 1950s and early 1960s, to others who held short-term motives for entry to Britain such as students, trainees and temporary workers, and others still whose arrival was attributable to involuntary political or religious reasons. The main point is that crude citizenship figures do not necessarily reveal the full picture of why certain groups have settled quickly, permanently and seemingly successfully in Britain, while others have exhibited greater sluggishness or indecision in their long-term citizenship patterns (thus perhaps mirroring doubts over future homeland identity).

The evidence on comparative rates of British citizenship is summarised in Table 4.2. It shows a fairly striking picture of inter-group variance that has some important, though limited, implications for electoral participation. To begin with, black Africans clearly exhibit the highest rates of non-British citizenship. This group tends to comprise significant numbers of students, graduate trainees and other mainly temporary residents. Moreover, given this socio-economic background, few of them would wish to relinquish voluntarily the citizenship of their country of origin for obvious reasons to do with future resettlement, family and career arrangements. Where actual and permanent immigration has been involved (as opposed to temporary residency), it might be expected that considerably higher rates of British citizenship would follow. Thereafter, Indians and black Caribbeans have similar high levels of British citizenship, approaching and clearly exceeding the 9 in 10 level in the former and latter cases, respectively. Pakistani respondents trail a fraction behind at around the 8 in 10 level. All three of these groups principally have their origins in mass labour migration (and some element of political refuge) dating between the early 1950s and mid-1970s. These two Asian groups, though Indians in particular, also contain sizeable minorities whose origins stem from political crises in East Africa in the late 1960s and 1970s, thereby further contributing to the one-way nature of their settlement and citizenship trajectories from that era (for a more detailed numeric breakdown see Vertovec, 1996: 78). In contrast, Bangladeshis appear to stand out among Asians: around three-quarters hold British citizenship, a notable fact that reflects both their most recent immigration history (much of it from the 1980s onwards), and also the realities of a naturalisation logjam associated with the newest of immigrant groups.

Finally, a word or two needs to be inserted about holders of dual citizenship where some interesting variations are found in the data. This appears to be a reasonably significant option for most minority groups except Indians. If we assume that cases of dual citizenship in fact repre-

Table 4.2 *Citizenship by ethnic group, 1997*

	Ethnic group (%)						
	White	Indian	Pakistani	Bangladeshi	Black African	Black Caribbean	Miscellaneous
Are you a British citizen?							
Yes, British citizen	97.1	85.9	82.6	77.0	50.0	92.0	80.9
No, citizen of another country	2.3	13.7	14.0	14.8	42.9	5.0	18.1
Both countries	0.6	0.4	3.3	8.2	7.1	3.0	1.1
Total N	2481	284	121	61	70	100	94 [3211]
Total %	100.0	100.0	100.0	100.0	100.0	100.0	100.0

Notes: Excludes Scotland. Includes respondents not on the Electoral Register.
Source: BES 1997, merged file (weighted data).

sent social, cultural and familial links between British citizenship, on the one hand and the citizenship of a group's particular national country of origin on the other, then some additional light can be shed on the Indian exception. This group comprises individuals whose ethnic origins are linked with and/or belong in the modern Indian nation. As such, it is impossible for them to also hold a legal tie with the state of India because of the long-standing prohibition on dual citizenship by the Indian government. This fact must presumably serve to raise, somewhat artificially, rates of British citizenship among this group, a quirk that we might surmise does not necessarily imply on its own any greater bond between Britain and members of this group. Moreover, other causes unrelated to dual citizenship rules may also be at work. Very low rates of dual citizenship might also be linked to Indians' much earlier immigrant history, thus resulting in many among this group appearing relatively distant, both chronologically and possibly culturally and emotionally from their (or their parents') Indian national origins. (Both of these propositions, it should be added, can be explored a little further through survey data designed to elicit groups' attitudes towards British identity – these are taken up later in Chapter 6.) Furthermore, we might assume that rapidly reduced rates of dual citizenship are associated with higher and more stable economic progress, educational attainment and underlying confidence in material and non-material prosperity. In all these respects, evidence exists to show considerable Indian socio-economic advancement in recent years (Robinson, 1990), and the question in future will turn to examining how far similar progress affects citizenship patterns among other minority groups.

For the moment, however, it is the black Caribbean group that appears to be anomalous in this regard, a community whose rates of British citizenship exceed all other minorities coupled with relatively low rates of dual citizenship. Socio-economic progress and material prosperity arguments do not often feature especially in relation to this group (in the same way as among Indians for instance), so it appears that this group's citizenship 'anchorage' in modern Britain is likely to be underpinned by other, unrelated factors. In any case, what is important is that this group more than any other does not face any obvious legal impediments to electoral participation (the relevant rates are pretty close to convergence with those of the white community). Most other minority groups share this characteristic. To a lesser degree, and at the same time, it is not a political opportunity enjoyed by one in every two among the smaller black African community.

Registration
Citizenship is not the only qualification required to vote: entry on the electoral roll is also necessary. The accuracy of the electoral register, which is updated annually is subject to variation.[4] For instance, it can be undermined by higher than usual levels of residential mobility, inability or unwillingness to report changes after the annual update, high levels of shared occupancy, difficulties involved in comprehension of an official form and administrative delays and inaccuracies. Further, among some minority groups additional factors might conceivably play a part in eroding accuracy. One example that has been mentioned frequently in previous small-scale studies of registration has been linguistic barriers, though use of publicity material in languages other than English has become more commonplace over the years (Anwar, 1991).

It has also been suggested that general alienation with the political process, possibly underpinned by broader social alienation and exclusion, has been another important factor that has impacted upon certain minority communities (Anwar, 1998: 2). Some of this may be driven by citizen disinterest in the electoral process, in which case appropriate responses are likely to be initiated by political institutions such as parties. However, it is also linked with underlying disillusionment with mainstream public institutions, of which parties and electoral procedures are just two small aspects. Accounts of social alienation based on racial exclusion have been prominent in modern British society in particular with regard to minority group participation in a range of institutions and activities. The state school system and police-community relations are two obvious faces of this debate where black Caribbean as well as Pakistani and Bangladeshi participation have been cited as proxy measures of confidence in the integration strategy of public policy more generally (Berthoud, 1999).

The black community as a whole is frequently cited in this regard, though specific attention has focused on black Caribbeans and especially those from younger age cohorts (MORI, 1996). However, aspects of the alienation hypothesis also extend to members of Pakistani and Bangladeshi youth and, to a lesser extent, young Indians. This thesis is explored more systematically in a later section of the chapter, but for the time being we have merely to keep in mind that some of the explanations that have been attached to minority non-registration specifically aim to highlight barriers that cannot or are unlikely to impact upon white non-registration. A further example has already been mentioned in relation to citizenship, namely that minorities may keep their distance from official registers – either of citizenship or voting entitlement – on the grounds of suspicions about their ultimate use. Residual beliefs about the practices of immigration officials are therefore bound to have some effect on registration accuracy, though this would be virtually impossible to quantify. The thought that electoral registration officers are in the clandestine business of carrying out 'fishing trips' for immigration officers continues to be a genuine worry in some parts of the minority population. Though difficult to gauge for the purposes of electoral analysis, it would be extremely unwise to take all registration figures at face value. That said, given that citizenship drives voting eligibility, it is by no means clear whether the registration figures should be necessarily adjusted upwards for certain groups that are thought to be affected by immigration detection worries. This is because Commonwealth citizenship can also deliver voting eligibility. It is not at all clear to what degree avoidance of registration to vote is a tactical ploy to evade detection for immigration purposes alone. There may after all be other motives involved, ranging from domestic factors to fiscal responsibilities, for which it is virtually impossible to codify let alone make reliable adjustments.

Table 4.3 sets out the evidence on registration among different ethnic groups. Earlier studies have suggested that ethnic minorities are generally less likely to be registered to vote than whites, though the deficit has varied quite considerably from three to 24 points – (CRE, 1984; Anwar, 1990). In another more recent survey by Anwar (1998), based on inner city respondents alone, it was reported that blacks (26 per cent) and Asians (19 per cent) failed to register to a greater degree than whites (18 per cent). Significantly, the claim was made in this study (using data from 1997 and 1998), that 'they were, therefore, excluded from the electoral process', seems somewhat under evidenced and thus unconvincing in relation to Asians at least (Anwar, 1988: 2).

A similar finding, pointing to genuine inter-group variance, is largely confirmed in Table 4.3 in 1997, though, again the nature of the variance is quite significant. Taking all Asian groups together, we can see that registration rates are fairly buoyant, with Indian rates at or about the same level as that of their white counterparts. But even Pakistani and Bangladeshi registration rates are remarkably high. Bluntly, there is scarce evidence for any Asian group dipping much below the 9 in 10 level, with only Indians coming close to parity with the rates for whites. This picture of very high registration for Indians is not new and has been

Table 4.3 *Electoral registration by ethnic group, 1997*

	Ethnic group (%)							
	White	Indian	Pakistani	Bangladeshi	Black African	Black Caribbean	Miscellaneous	
Is your name on the electoral register?[a]								
Yes[b]	97.0	96.5	88.4	91.7	86.1	95.0	90.6	
No	2.7	2.5	11.7	8.3	12.5	4.0	5.3	
Don't know	0.2	1.1	0.0	0.0	1.4	1.0	4.2	
Total N	2480	284	120	60	72	100	95	[3211]
Total %	100.0	100.0	100.0	100.0	100.0	100.0	100.0	

Notes: see Table 4.2, p. 97. [a]Verified electoral registration. [b]At this address/at another address/at this and another address.
Source: see Table 4.2, p. 97.

recorded in earlier studies of participation at local level (Le Lohé, 1998). Such a pattern has often been attributed to a strong interest in politics and public affairs, not shared to the same extent among other minority groups. This claim is easy to exaggerate and it is wise to remember that non-Indian Asian rates are also very strong, suggesting no major fall-off in political interest. This 'interest in politics' proposition is tested in the next section. Furthermore, the data show that black rates are really not considerably lower than Asian rates as a whole, with the black Caribbean group, in fact, virtually matching the average rate for all groups of voters (95 per cent).[5] Where a registration gap exists, if there is one, it appears to be among black Africans, fully 10 per cent below the highest minority group rates revealed in this study. The upshot of these data is that they call into question various pre-election claims about minority non-participation and place these worries in a new and unexpected light (*Guardian*, 1996b). In particular, specific claims made by members of the black press and others that black Caribbeans were substantially under-registered were, it seems, rather wide of the mark and also the subject of some considerable dispute.[6] Furthermore, these data call into serious question the validity of on-going assertions implying that a major problem of electoral registration among ethnic minorities confronts decision makers. For instance, Anwar (1998: 4) recommends that: 'Appropriate measures must be taken by central government and local authorities to improve the registration levels of ethnic minorities and thus provide them with an opportunity to participate in the political process. In this context local authorities should introduce ethnic monitoring of electoral registration.'

On the basis of the evidence shown below, the wisdom of such a course of action in relation to most, though not all, minority groups must be in doubt. Plainly, most minorities are not substantially under-registered in comparison with their white counterparts and public policy measures designed to address a large non-existent problem are likely to be benign and patronising (at best) or possibly inflammatory and counter-productive (at worst). Certainly, registration deficiencies are apparent among specific groups but this is a rather different kind of problem requiring a different less catch-all response in policy and, it must be said, rhetoric.

In sum, it would be fair to say that the evidence shows a picture of tolerably high levels of electoral engagement at the level of registration, together with fleeting signs of slight under- and over-participation following earlier expected patterns. Turn-out data needs to be added to this basic picture in order to help clarify where, if any, real pockets of political abstention (and possible alienation) are concentrated.

Turn out

It is important to find out to what degree those who have registered to vote then cast their ballots on polling day. This information will reveal just how far there are genuine problems of non-participation in the processes that shape the decision to take part in the election among those for whom it is an option to begin with. In addition, turn-out data also helps us to distinguish between casual abstainers, citing various *ad hoc* reasons for not voting, and others who are best described as serial or hardcore abstainers who either have no real interest in an election and/or have rarely, if ever, participated in the electoral process. As far as political parties are concerned, the main focus tends to be on the former group who lie at the margins of participation and hold varying doubts – sometimes unknowingly – about turning out to vote in practice. In terms of minority would-be electors, parties can face some fairly large challenges in mobilising members of this category who often hold underlying, negative assumptions about the value of their participation. However, the real problem stems from addressing the latter categories where these assumptions can often multiply immensely. Democratic institutions are often dealing with reinforced prejudices and scepticism about the importance attached to minority communities in the electoral process and/or wider debates about the representation of 'community interests'. Of course, we should not overlook the fact that individual abstainers at any one election may occupy the margins between these categories (and are hard to identify in terms of their specific grounds for abstention accordingly). In addition, individuals may move between these abstention categories over time taking in different general elections, as well as over the short term taking in the crucial period leading up to the election itself.

Of course, the motives of some in both categories do not necessarily have to be driven by scepticism about engaging the democratic process. Among some groups of ethnic minorities it is possible that language difficulties can create obstacles of their own. This barrier is one that is not easy to overcome on an individual basis (at least in the short run).

Perhaps for this reason, it may easily lend itself to the kind of community-based campaigning methods that have been publicly associated with Asian political participation (Saggar and Geddes, 2000; see also: Khamis, 1992; Eade, 1989; and Le Lohé, 1990). Abstention, therefore, may sometimes be a matter that is not fully explicable in *ad hoc* or in serial terms, and may also tell us something about the supplementary forms of political engagement that are found among certain ethnic groups and not others.[7]

A familiar inter-group pattern is highlighted once more in Table 4.4. The story of highly involved Indians is reflected in the fact that their turn-out rate clearly exceeded the white norm and also the average for all groups (78 per cent). The margin is also hardly negligible making the Indian community, already registered at about the same level as whites, the most participative group of all in the 1997 general election. To earn such a mantle against the backdrop of serious and persistent worries about minority participation elsewhere is arguably not to be understated. Furthermore, the ramifications of this level of involvement are even more significant once account is taken of the size of this ethnic minority group within the minority population (to say nothing of its degree of geographic clustering). The rest of the story contained in the table follows familiar patterns. First, Pakistani and Bangladeshi rates are pegged at around the same level and not far below the level for whites. These are impressive turn-out levels, though possibly ones that have been subjected to some considerable group-level mobilisation efforts. We can reasonably conclude that these groups are not experiencing any serious turn-out deficits and indeed broadly resemble their highly involved Indian colleagues with whom they are so (mistakenly) contrasted. Secondly, a genuine contrast is apparent from even a casual glance at the figures for registered black electors. In both cases, turn-out rates fell below all of the other groups studied and considerably below the rate for Asians. This problem was rather more acute in the case of black Africans, among whom less than two in three actually cast a ballot. A little under a third of all blacks failed to use ballots for which they had registered, suggesting a fairly high wastage rate (closer to a fifth or a quarter for other groups).

The poor black turn-out rates echo the findings of earlier studies (for instance: Anwar, 1990; NOP, 1991; Anwar, 1998). It is also worth returning to the point that serious worries were expressed about possible black abstention in the months leading up to the 1997 election. Earlier it was mentioned that some of these expressions of concern had become muddled in taking elements of polling data a little too literally, and had failed to distinguish between underlying registration and turn out problems. These data now show clearly that future debates about potential minority electoral leverage might be better informed by concentrating on

Table 4.4 *Turn out by ethnic group, 1997*

	Ethnic group (%)						
	White	Indian	Pakistani	Bangladeshi	Black African	Black Caribbean	Miscellaneous
Did you manage to vote in the general election?							
Yes	78.7	82.7	75.0	73.8	64.8	70.4	64.9
No	21.3	17.3	25.0	26.2	35.2	29.6	35.1
Total *N*	2480	283	120	61	71	98	94 [3207]
Total %	100.0	100.0	100.0	100.0	100.0	100.0	100.0

Notes: see Table 4.2, p. 97. Excludes 'don't knows'.
Source: see Table 4.2, p. 97.

genuine areas of difficulty. The task of persuading sufficient numbers of black Caribbean would-be voters to turn-out in May 1997 is clearly such an area. By contrast, the need to target turn out rates among Indians is not. A taxing issue for democratic participation is undoubtedly bound up in these figures but an issue which requires a great deal of fine-tuning of both analysis of available data as well as contextual interpretation.

It is hard to avoid the conclusion that a fairly serious mobilisation problem exists and it will be important to assess whether this is circumstantial and linked to social background or not. In the meantime, these data confirm many existing suspicions that some serious problems and challenges for democratic participation exist in British politics. Such suspicions have often focused heavily on simple Asian–black distinctions, while the data presented here have demonstrated that this division is somewhat exaggerated. The participation deficits are, in fact, found to varying degrees among most minority groups, while for Indians talk of deficits is entirely misplaced. Ultimately, the real significance of these figures lies in their cumulative effect upon participation once registration (and legal eligibility) is taken into account. Earlier in the chapter we learnt that electoral registration varied from one ethnic group to another, with Indians in particular standing closest to the rate found among whites. As already mentioned, it is not hard to see the cumulative impact of both sets of findings for this particular group. However, the paltry turn-out figures found among black Caribbeans were not reflected in this group's registration rate which ranked extremely close to the 'highly-registered' Indians and whites. The conclusion appears to be that black Caribbean participation patterns exhibit deficiency at some point after registration. Electoral mobilisation is thus a task that centres on why it is that this group has such large numbers of abstainers from among those who hold registered valid votes. In the case of their black African counterparts, genuine deficits are apparent in both realms, suggesting that mobilisation problems are rather more general and enduring as opposed to focused and specific. Finally, among Pakistanis and Bangladeshis it appears that mobilisation problems do exist and are similarly two-pronged in character. The latter of these two groups, however, could be reasonably described in terms similar to black Caribbeans, whereby strong and impressive registration rates are generally not capitalised upon in actual turn out.

Taken together, these data show that important variations exist in the extent to which different groups get involved in the electoral process. However, the interpretation lies in knowing whether these differences amount to major grounds for concern. With some pre-election press headlines describing a presumed majority of blacks not intending to vote, it is clear that the real variations uncovered here are rather less or possibly just different than some had imagined. Yet these variations will be described by others, entirely fairly, as rather greater than tolerable in a mature liberal democracy aspiring to political inclusivity.

Standing back a little further, it might be asked how far these figures affect the calculus of electoral leverage. Much will depend on electoral geography, local mobilisation influences and the marginality of the seats in question (something that is taken up more fully in a later chapter). However, for the time being we can say that the sluggish black turn-out rates are, of course, based on a numerically much smaller population than that for Asians. In other words the obvious weakness that goes with small numbers of potentially eligible voters is exacerbated by poor turn out. The message for party strategists might therefore be that Asian voters 'count for more' for these two reasons, and that black voters' worries about political marginalisation are likely to become self-fulfilling on the basis of the turn-out evidence shown here. Furthermore, future debates about under-participation need to take into account this demographic reality and not merely dwell on the sometimes superficial messages of pollsters concerned with hypothetical turn out. Evaluations based on these variations might conceivably suggest that the worst performing groups only vary at the margin compared with the best performing. This view would be to stretch the evidence presented in this chapter rather too far and, in any case, might miss the underlying point concerning absolute group size. Raw numbers of adult individuals from each of the minority groups continues to be the main driving force behind calculations of electoral strength, and this is a basic lesson that we go on to discuss more extensively in the final chapter of this study. A more contextually-based evaluation using a combination of group numbers, demographic characteristics and participation rates is therefore required to make a meaningful contribution to the long-term debate.

The alienation hypothesis

We have seen so far that variations exist in the participation patterns of different ethnic minority groups. At first glance, it is not entirely clear what should be made of these comparisons. To begin with, by looking at specific minority groups there is a temptation to read a lot into the topline differences reported in the data. At the same time, there appears to be an underlying participation 'norm' from which most, though not all, groups do not deviate substantially. However, by limiting the analysis to group level there is an inherent risk of overlooking questions about the degree to which various sub-groups (on generational lines in particular) within named minority communities differ from the underlying 'norm'. That is to say, while most groups exhibit patterns that are reasonably close to one another, can we be certain that any of these groups do not contain substantial numbers who are not? Equally, the extent of variance at sub-ethnic group level is potentially significant because any evidence of sharp contrasts in participation rates will indicate that inter-group-level analysis is less than sufficient in grasping the picture. In other words, the analyses need to look at the real sources of variance, irrespective of whether these are at the inter-group-level or not.

Having recognised that there may be more to the picture than that revealed in an initial glance, we need to be mindful of the debates over electoral abstention. The broad terms of this debate have already been rehearsed earlier in the chapter, and the need here is to try provide some evidence to show how far examples of minority abstention can be accounted for in circumstantial as opposed to fundamental terms. The ways in which the former explanatory categories can be interpreted can be fairly wide in that the underlying factors linked to non-participation often relate to several areas of limited or poor participation in mainstream society. Aspects of education, housing and, most crucially, the employment market are commonly used by political sociologists to build a broad picture of those groups or communities that lie within, beyond and at the margins of mainstream participative norms. Above all, in a study geared to unpacking ethnic minority political participation we are interested to see how far minority patterns follow those that are common among their white counterparts, whatever the comparison between high, normal or low participation cohorts.

There is a school of thought about minority political abstention that argues that a more fundamental constraint exists and is sustained among elements of the minority population that is not found among others. This barrier, so to speak, is said to be a reflection of apathy and alienation among ethnic minorities in respect of the allegedly white-dominated and inaccessible political process. Politics, in turn, is thought to be a microcosm of wider ethnic minority alienation in society in which expectations and evidence persists that certain minority groups are unlikely take full part in various mainstream social process and institutions. Evidence of black and Asian abstention is fundamental, therefore, in the sense that it is not easily comparable with parallel examples of abstention among whites of a similar social, economic and educational background. In particular, the emphasis within this perspective is to draw out inter-ethnic group contrasts among younger would-be voters (and males especially), and those who possess poor or modest education qualifications and/or lower socio-economic class status.

Generational influences

The evidence in Tables 4.5 and 4.6 tackles the issue of youth as the driving factor behind electoral abstention. The story that these tables convey could not be more explicit, although limited sub-sample sizes mean that care must be taken not to read too much into the registration rates for any single age cohort among the smaller minority groups in particular. On electoral registration to begin with, we can immediately see that there is a clear, though quite modest, propensity to not be on the register among young groups of voters as compared with older ones. This pattern appears to apply to all groups. However, the degree of non-registration found among specific groups tends to vary enormously. At the top of the list of young, unregistered members are the black Caribbean group: rather more than a quarter of those between 18 and 24 years were verified as not on the electoral register at the 1997 election. This figure compares with quite high rates among young Pakistanis and Bangladeshis (both 16.7 per cent). (Some caution needs to be exercised in the conclusions drawn here as the base numbers of young Pakistanis and Bangladeshis are quite small.) Meanwhile, a quite different story is told when examining registration rates among young Indians: here just 6.8 per cent of those between 18 and 24 years were unregistered. Significantly, this rate outstrips that of their white counterparts by a significant margin (10.7 per cent). At the same time, the black African 18–24-year group exhibit a very low rates of non-registration of just 5.9 per cent, though we might be cautious of taking this figure at face value given that a colossal one-fifth of the slightly older 25–34-year group were not on the register. The upshot of these data is plain. There is a clear and fairly wide gap in the registration rates of most young minorities in comparison with young whites, and this gap is more profound among young black Caribbeans. Furthermore, it simply does not exist among young Indians and thus reminds us of a continuing pattern seen earlier on.

The core picture of young non-participation is dramatically reinforced once we turn to consider the question of turn out. As Table 4.6 shows, the two youngest cohorts of registered electors were generally rather less likely to cast a ballot than their older peers among all ethnic groups,

Table 4.5 *Verified electoral registration by age group and ethnic group, 1997*

	Age cohort (%)							
	18–24	25–34	35–44	45–54	55–9	60–4	65+	All
Whites	89.0	94.0	97.2	98.6	100.0	99.6	99.6	97.1
N	272	669	652	575	220	256	815	3459
Indian	88.6	95.5	100.0	100.0	100.0	100.0	100.0	97.0
N	44	66	70	50	11	12	13	266
Pakistani	83.3	83.8	92.1	100.0	100.0	100.0	100.0	89.4
N	30	37	38	18	1	4	4	132
Bangladeshi	83.3	100.0	88.9	100.0	100.0	100.0	100.0	93.1
N	18	17	9	4	4	4	2	58
Black African	88.2	79.5	95.0	92.9	100.0	100.0	100.0	87.4
N	17	44	20	14	6	1	1	103
Black Caribbean	69.2	97.4	100.0	100.0	100.0	94.4	100.0	96.3
N	13	39	49	14	15	18	14	162

Notes: see Table 4.2, p. 97, Excludes 'don't knows'.
Source: see Table 4.2, p. 97.

Table 4.6 *Turn out by age group and ethnic group, 1997*

	Age cohort (%)							
	18–24	25–34	35–44	45–54	55–9	60–4	65+	All
Did you manage to vote in the general election?								
White								
Yes	59.6	68.2	77.8	84.0	88.6	88.3	86.0	78.9
No	40.4	31.8	22.2	16.0	11.4	11.7	13.9	21.0
N	272	669	652	575	220	256	815	3459
Indian								
Yes	63.6	83.3	81.4	96.0	72.7	91.7	100.0	82.7
No	36.4	16.7	18.6	4.0	27.3	8.3	0.0	17.3
N	44	66	70	50	11	12	13	266
Pakistani								
Yes	56.7	70.3	86.8	94.4	0.0	75.0	75.0	75.0
No	43.3	29.7	13.2	5.6	100.0	25.0	25.0	25.0
N	30	37	38	18	1	4	4	132
Bangladeshi								
Yes	66.7	76.5	77.8	100.0	75.0	50.0	100.0	74.1
No	33.3	23.5	22.2	0.0	25.0	50.0	0.0	25.9
N	18	17	9	4	4	4	2	58
Black African								
Yes	64.7	52.3	70.0	85.7	83.3	100.0	100.0	65.0
No	35.3	47.7	30.0	14.3	16.7	0.0	0.0	35.0
N	17	44	20	14	6	1	1	103
Black Caribbean								
Yes	15.4	64.1	81.6	71.4	86.7	83.3	57.1	69.8
No	84.6	35.9	16.3	28.6	13.3	16.7	42.9	29.6
N	13	39	49	14	15	18	14	162

Notes: see Table 4.2, p. 97. Excludes 'don't knows'.
Source: see Table 4.2, p. 97.

108 · *Race and representation*

with the same as before applying about generalisations drawn from small sub-sample base numbers. At one end of the spectrum, the failure rate among younger whites and Indians was typically between three or four times that of older whites and Indians. The latter ethnic group, however, exhibited a sharp rise in turn out when it came to examining the 25–34-years age group (abstainers amounted to 16.7 per cent or less than half the rate for the 18–24 years age group). Whie the abstention rate for very young Bangladeshis was impressive at just one-third, it was accompanied by a rate of more than one-quarter among the 25–34-years cohort (again some caution is required in using these findings because of the small base numbers involved). Elsewhere, both the young Pakistani and black Africans groups exhibited higher non-voting still. However, these distinctions amount to the splitting of hairs once we factor in the evidence for young black Caribbeans. The blunt truth of the evidence is that near enough all of those between 18 and 24 years failed to cast ballots they already held. This was accompanied by a very sharp fall among the next eldest cohort, suggesting that abstention occurred in a very concentrated form. As mentioned previously, a great deal of speculation took place before the election on the question of threatened black non-participation. The effects of both the above tables are to show that this amounted to a major and indelible feature of young black Caribbean participation alone. Elements of this kind of abstention existed among other minority groups but on a considerably smaller scale. Finally, a sharply contrasting picture existed among young Indian voters. Ethnic minority political participation and the nature of electoral abstention within it cannot, therefore, be satisfactorily described in homogeneous terms.

The most important thing to drive home about Table 4.6 is that, despite the problems of dealing with modest base numbers in some cases, there is clear evidence of a relationship between age and turn out among all ethnic groups. However, the extent to which age cohort serves as a predictor of turn out varies considerably from one ethnic group to another. Significantly, among black Caribbeans, while the relationship between these variables is no different than among other groups, the force of the influence is much greater. Indeed, the sharpness of the curve is quite striking because it contrasts the behaviour of young black Caribbeans with their older counterparts (who share more in common with older members of all ethnic groups studied). In other words there is an interesting comparison at work among the young of different ethnic groups as well as among black Caribbeans alone.

Non-participation: causes of and attitudes towards
To add some fine-tuning to these data, it is possible to home in on the kind of reasons non-voting respondents gave to account for their failure

to vote on polling. In this case, we should remember that we are only dealing with the non-voters among those registered to vote. Thus, the base line numbers involved within specific ethnic minority groups are really very small and not reliable as a consequence. In Table 4.7, therefore, the analysis is restricted to looking at white non-voters in comparison with blacks and Asians who similarly abstained. In this way, we can pool together otherwise small numbers of specific minorities and present a result that has some meaning at least. The main point to report is that contrasts between whites and non-whites are few given the small base numbers responding to each of the wide range of answers to this question. However, despite this, it is interesting to note that a much higher proportion of black non-voters than Asians or whites claimed to have deliberately opted not to vote. This sub-group can, therefore, be thought in very different terms to those non-voters from each of the three groups who provided essentially circumstantial reasons for not voting (employment and personal commitments, sickness, etc.). This group of deliberate abstainers is also different from the apathetic ('couldn't be bothered') whose attitudes are not strictly to be interpreted as the result of political alienation. That said, those who were in effect life-long, serial non-voters varied between ethnic group, and it may be that their attitude does have something to do with the habit of not voting as reflecting long-

Table 4.7 *Reasons for voting abstention by ethnic group, 1997*

	Ethnic group (%)		
	White	Asian	Black
Why didn't you vote in 1997?			
Voted in election	78.9	79.5	68.2
Deliberately abstained	1.2	1.1	2.6
Work prevented me	1.6	1.1	2.2
Sickness prevented me	1.3	2.0	3.6
Away on election day	3.3	4.1	2.2
Other commitments, etc.	2.6	3.9	4.4
Couldn't be bothered/not interested	2.7	1.3	2.6
Couldn't decide between parties	1.4	0.9	0.4
Not affected by who won	0.6	0.2	1.1
Religious reasons	0.2	0.2	0.4
Respondent had moved	1.0	1.3	1.5
Polling card/station problem	2.1	2.2	5.8
Never vote/have never voted in my life	0.5	2.0	2.9
Other reason	2.3	0.0	0.4
DK	0.1	0.2	1.5
Not answered	0.1	0.0	0.4
N	3471	458	274
Total %	100.0	100.0	100.0

Notes: see Table 4.2, p. 97.
Source: see Table 4.2, p.97.

standing feelings about the value and efficacy of the democratic process. In all, these figures demonstrate a high degree of inter-ethnic group similarity and it would be unwise to suggest that non-voting among minorities is especially characterised by attitudes and reasons that differ from those found among white abstainers.

If we are determined to uncover attitudinal components to electoral participation it is worth looking at how far different groups hold essentially instrumental or principled reasons for voting. By principled is meant the idea that taking part in an election is basically driven by the doctrine of democratic duty. In Table 4.8 this proposition is tested by juxtaposing the notion of duty with the claim that respondents are concerned with and thus value the outcome of the election. The results are basically far from astounding and cannot be used to support an argument of inter-ethnic difference. Certainly, the pattern of attitudes among Asians lies somewhat closer to that of whites than is the case among black opinion. However, very large and comparable majorities in each group appear willing to sign up to the doctrine of democratic duty. Furthermore, it is far from clear whether these two responses are in fact mutually incompatible. Interest in and concern about electoral outcomes could be considered to be a driving force behind commitment to the democratic process, and with it the instinct to see voting as a civic obligation. In any case, ethnic minorities do not appear to exhibit significantly different values or motives from their white counterparts in their decision to vote.

Finally, by exploring the attitudinal fabric of democratic values a little further it is certainly possible to uncover some evidence of inter-ethnic contrast. This can be seen in Table 4.9. In this case, we are interested in the degree to which whites, blacks and Asians sense that they are small influences in or inconsequential to democratic politics and decision making. Of course these respondents are effectively commenting on their sense of political distance from centres of power and influence, and this in principle may operate right across British society irrespective of ethnic

Table 4.8 *Reasons for voting by ethnic group, 1997*

	Ethnic group (%)		
	White	Asian	Black
Care who wins	19.3	16.8	24.0
Duty to vote	79.5	81.0	74.5
DK	1.2	2.2	0.7
Not answered	0.0	0.0	0.7
Total *N*	3471	458	275
Total %	100.0	100.0	100.0

Notes: see Table 4.2, p. 97.
Source: see Table 4.2, p. 97.

Table 4.9 *Political impotence sentiment by ethnic group, 1997*

	Ethnic group (%)		
	White	Asian	Black
People like me have no say in government actions ...			
Strongly agree/agree	57.3	55.5	57.4
Neither agree/disagree	19.1	23.8	23.9
Strongly disagree/disagree	21.5	16.7	14.2
DK/not answered	2.1	4.2	4.6
Total N	2987	240	176
Total %	100.0	100.0	100.0

Notes: see Table 4.2, p. 97.
Source: see Table 4.2, p. 97.

origin. Indeed, there is no particular reason to believe that those who concur with the view that they have little or no say in government actions are minded to do so on the basis of racial or ethnic factors. Such statements of political exclusion or isolation can additionally be reinforced by feelings about racial or ethnic division, but these are dimensions that presumably have no bearing on whites who take this position. In other words, recognising that modern electoral politics does not always succeed in engaging all segments of society, we are interested in the extent to which this process is underscored by any particular ethnic effect. The results contained in the table are, therefore, quite surprising and emphatic. At first glance, it seems that there is no obvious inter-ethnic group variance worthy of comment. Small majorities of each group perceive themselves to be politically impotent. However, if we examine the disaggregated responses we can detect a rather different picture. Two findings stand out. First, blacks are by far the most likely to agree strongly with the proposition contained in the question (25 per cent), as against just 11 per cent of Asians and 15 per cent of whites. This suggests that feelings among 1 in 4 of this particular group are running quite high and represent a core constituency of political disillusionment. Secondly, this picture is reinforced when account is made for those who mildly reject the view that they have no say in government policies: whereas 20 and 15 per cent of whites and Asians, respectively take this moderate stance, only 11 per cent of blacks do likewise. In short, cross-group similarities exist but only to a degree. Black sentiment concerning this question shows some clear signs of adopting a more extreme, less compromising stance, reflective no doubt of some far-reaching attitudes of political weakness.

Gender influences

It has sometimes been suggested that where a severe non-participation problem may exist it is rather greater among younger men than it is among younger women. This kind of pattern has been particularly in evidence in labour market participation and, to a lesser degree in educational and training take-up and attainment (Berthoud, 2000; Heath and McMahon, 1997). What evidence is there to show that this is indeed the case among young black Caribbeans, the sub-group already identified as scarcely relevant to the 1997 general election? Obviously limitations with base numbers of respondents within minority sub-groups serves to hamper this line of inquiry. However, Table 4.10 focuses on black and Asian groups in comparison with whites and highlights the impact of gender.

The findings from Table 4.10 tell a remarkably straightforward story that contains a powerful conclusion. We can see that gender variations in turn out are more or less non-existent in the cases of whites and Asians. Moreover, the actual levels of turn out among white men and women matched very closely those found among Asian men and women. Such a pattern is conspicuously absent in the case of black men and women. Here it is apparent that a gender influence is at play, effectively separating female turn out from male by just over 7 per cent. This is a wide margin, both in absolute terms as well as by the standards of the minuscule differences found among white and Asian men and women. Bluntly, the electoral turn out of black men registered to vote in 1997 fell to less than 2 in 3, or much lower than the lowest ethnic group as a whole. There is little doubt, therefore, that on the basis of this data that black abstention is far from circumstantial. Non-voting among eligible electors does not follow a gender path found among the majority white group (and noticeably shadowed among Asians). It takes its own trajectory with black men exhibiting very high levels of abstention that are independent of gender influences among other ethnic groups. For this reason, black electoral mobilisation tactics might be well advised to target their message to men to a far greater extent than women. With around 15 per cent fewer black men than Asian men voting in the 1997 general election, the evidence points overwhelmingly to the need to make up a lot of lost territory.

Abstention: circumstantial or fundamental?
At the start of this chapter, we posed the question of how far variations in electoral participation were driven directly by ethnic group membership. The worry was that superficially large differences in registration and turn out between groups might conceivably mask causal relationships that had little or nothing to do with ethnicity as such. Indeed, the relationship between social class and electoral engagement has been identified and commented upon over a number of years. Therefore, the spotlight must fall on the extent to which differences in participation are attributable to social class rather than ethnic group membership. If the evidence points

Table 4.10 *Turn out among men and women by ethnic group, 1997*

	Ethnic group (%)					
	White		Asian		Black	
	Male	Female	Male	Female	Male	Female
Did you manage to vote in the general election?						
Yes	78.1	79.6	79.4	79.4	63.8	71.1
No	21.9	20.4	20.6	20.5	36.2	28.9
Total %	100.0	100.0	100.0	100.0	100.0	100.0
N	1574	1897	248	210	116	159

Notes: see Table 4.2, p. 97.
Source: see Table 4.2, p. 97.

to some degree of social class influence upon electoral participation we can expect to uncover some limited, though important, distinctions within the minority ethnic population as opposed to between minority and white groups. Additionally, evidence of this sort will allow generalisations to be made about the causes of electoral abstention. The issue at stake is the degree to which such abstention, as already highlighted earlier in the chapter, is circumstantial in nature (i.e. related to objective variations in social background) or fundamental (i.e. linked to ethnicity). The latter of these possibilities implies some reason to believe that taking part in the democratic process is closely intertwined with racial politics. Such a scenario would have a number of far-reaching consequences for the way in which race and political participation are conceptualised in British public life.

In Table 4.11 some flesh is put on to the bones of this debate. As before, blacks and Asians are examined as whole groups alongside their white counterparts because of the limitations of working with small subgroup samples (the *N* figure for individual cells are shown for ethnic minorities). This table is concerned with class-based variations in registration across the three ethnic groups. The results shown could not be more categoric. There is no discernible relationship between social class and registration in any of the three ethnic groups. Indeed, the level of verified registration is remarkably flat across class groups, and all that can be said is that the data reveal some element of variance among some classes of blacks. However, there is no class correlation at work. The clear message is that the evidence for ethnic groups shunning or being left off the register is non-existent. Furthermore, where variance does show its face it is decidedly not linked to social class. It would appear that in studying patterns of electoral engagement, the general issue of registration can be thought of as a largely administrative matter by which eligible voters do and do not make it on to the register for a number of essentially bureaucratic reasons (relating to the ease with which formal

Table 4.11 *Registration by class and ethnic group, 1997*

	Ethnic group (%)		
	White	Asian	Black
Verified parliamentary registration			
Salariat	97.2	96.1	97.3
N^a		74	71
Routine white collar	96.2	97.3	89.7
N		73	52
Petit bourgeoise	97.1	95.5	85.0
N		42	17
Skilled manual	96.5	94.8	100.0
N		55	34
Semi/unskilled manual	97.6	98.2	100.0
N		112	57
All	97.2	96.7	95.5
N	3228	356	231

Notes: see Table 4.2, p. 97.
[a]Base *N*s for individual cells shown for blacks and Asians only.
Source: see Table 4.2, p. 97.

registration can be achieved).[8] In essence, these do not concern us that greatly and have only very little bearing on what we understand from these data about the building blocks of electoral participation. In order to generate more analytical light, we must turn to the arena of electoral turn out.

Moving to electoral turn out, Table 4.12 starts to bring out the kind of evidence that could support claims concerning non-circumstantial abstention mentioned previously. Remembering that we are looking only at those who were registered to vote (i.e. largely similar proportions among each ethnic group), the data reveals an interesting degree of class-related variation alongside differences that cannot be attributed to social background. It is this interaction that is potentially most interesting and allows us to home in on unusual and unexpected behaviour among certain social-class groups within specific ethnic groups. (Again, small sub-sample sizes mean that we need to look at blacks and Asians as collective groups, with *N* figures for specific cells among ethnic minorities shown in the table below.)

Three important patterns are evident from the turn-out findings and are worthy of additional comment. The first and most obvious point is that the table reconfirms the fact that levels of black turn out run consistently well below those of whites and Asians. Across all social classes we can see that there is around a 10 per cent deficit among blacks registered to vote in comparison with other ethnic groups. Given that white and Asian rates overall closely match one another, this means that the black turn-out rate really is a stark outlyer. This reduced turn-out rate is, in other

Table 4.12 *Turn out by class and ethnic group, 1997*

	Ethnic group (%)		
	White	Asian	Black
Voted in general election			
Salariat	84.6	81.8	71.2
N^a		63	52
Routine white collar	79.3	73.3	74.1
N		55	43
Petit bourgeoise	76.9	86.4	65.0
N		38	13
Skilled manual	75.3	86.2	64.7
N		50	22
Semi/unskilled manual	76.6	83.3	71.9
N		95	41
All	79.4	81.8	70.7
N	2639	301	171

Notes: see Table 4.2, p. 97.
[a] Base *N*s for individual cells shown for blacks and Asians only.
Source: see Table 4.2, p. 97.

words, the broad canvass upon which we need to try to paint some detail on the underlying causes of abstention.

Secondly, the final column of the table shows that there is a rough, though fairly reliable, relationship between class and turn out among blacks. In short, white-collar blacks from the highest social backgrounds stand in contrast to the groups further down the social class scale. The petit bourgeoise among blacks, although rather scarce in absolute numbers in the survey, appear to be the most puzzling, with turn-out rates well below the ethnic group average. In addition, it is noteworthy that it is this social class that is associated with the highest turn-out rates among their Asian minority counterparts. It may be that the Asian experience is closer to being aberrant given that among whites the petit bourgeoise are not especially associated with above average turn-out rates. In any case, the basic point remains undiminished, namely that blacks from higher social backgrounds exhibit patterns of turn out that differ markedly from all other blacks. In very rough terms, we must conclude that this is reflective of a class-based relationship that drives the propensity to turn out to vote among blacks. In this sense, blacks display a turn-out pattern in common with whites that also comprises strong differences between those at the top and bottom end of the socio-economic ladder. However, in the case of whites, the differences across the social scale are somewhat less sharp and overall it is apparent that turn-out rates decline gradually towards the lower end of the social ladder. Among blacks, the differences are rather starker and involve some sharp distinctions between blacks of differing social classes. Indeed, as far as robust turn out is concerned, blacks from routine white-collar backgrounds are an interesting group chiefly because these voters represent the only example of black turn out exceeding Asian turn out. This is no small matter given that black–Asian differences in turn out within specific social classes are typically between 10 per cent and 20 per cent (i.e. Asian excess over black rates). The upshot is that this group of blacks stands out in comparative isolation among all blacks registered to vote. How far they represent a participatory model for other blacks to follow or amount to an exceptional group going against the grain of black involvement is an open question that requires follow-up research.

Finally, the data once again drive home the point that not only is Asian turn out remarkably buoyant in relation to other ethnic groups, it is also strikingly unaffected by social class. The point about the middle column of the table is the flatness of Asian turn-out rates across social class. With the notable exception of white-collar Asians, we can see that class accounts for differences of around 5 per cent or less. Similarly among whites and blacks, variations across classes were of the order of 10 per cent. Asians, in other words, are characterised almost uniformly by high and non-varying levels of turn out. There is very little to go on in the case of the aberrant routine white-collar group of Asians who appear at first glance not to share fully the pattern shown by Asians of all other social backgrounds. That said, this social group of 'low turn out' Asians in fact exhibit a participation rate that is considerably in excess of blacks from almost all social classes. In this sense, their abstention does not seem quite so great. The point is that abstention matters politically precisely because of its relative nature. When the 'low turn out' sub-group of Asians is compared with Asians from other social classes their participation looks poor; in comparison with blacks generally their behaviour appears impressive.

More importantly, the results suggest that Asians, rather than blacks, are the unusual group of voters. That is to say, according to these data both blacks and whites display some form of recognisable relationship between social class and turn out. The relationship is not a perfect one but none the less we can conclude that social background does matter in shaping the relative propensity of registered voters to turn out to vote on polling day. Of course there are stark differences in the overall levels at which blacks and whites of different social classes are turning out to vote. What matters, however, is not so much these levels but rather the fact that both groups exhibit some degree of class-related variations in turn out. For Asians, this kind of generalisation is far from valid. In their case, while small inter-class variations in turn out are evident, the central fact remains that class broadly fails to determine differences in rates of turn out. It is in that sense that we can make the claim that Asians do not fit our underlying model of social class as a key or helpful way to explain turn out variations. Both blacks and whites do conform to this model, or at least do so to an extent that allows us to conclude that the relationship between class and turn out is a valid one. The interesting aspect of this distinction between Asians and others is that the circumstantial reasons suspected to lie behind minority abstention have largely failed to materialise. In particular, there is not enough relative Asian abstention to count let alone allow us to argue that social class accounts for variations in turn out within this ethnic group. In fact, Asian turn out is so flat across different social classes that we can reasonably safely draw the conclusion that the circumstantial factors based around social background that usually explain variations in turn out are not in evidence. Therefore, for Asians at least, the implication appears to be that other collective forms of political calculation and mobilisation lie behind both their overall high levels of turn out as well as the inability of social class to have much bearing on turn out. This appears to spell a relationship between race and political participation which lies essentially outside what we know about the majority white electorate. It also distinguishes Asian from blacks and thus serves to reinforce the idea that collective group-based political identity and engagement strategies underpin the position of Asians in the British democratic process. Furthermore, with precious little evidence to support the claim that black abstention is deliberate or in any way overtly linked to fundamental reasons of race, it is fair to say that circumstantial, class-based factors account for most of the story of turn out variance. The exception remains Asians and it is this group that points the way to fresh perspectives on the social and cultural factors that can be linked to group political involvement.

This kind of thinking, placing group-based notions of ethnic kinship and loyalty at the heart of the analysis is the most significant finding in our examination of the relationship between ethnicity and turn out. It also has important implications for how we might understand the theory of political integration, mainly because of the paradox it poses. On the one hand, Asians stand out among Britain's ethnic minorities for their consistent determination to take part in the democratic process at levels that match and possibly exceed those of the majority white group. This suggests that there are strong signs of political integration based on patterns of behavioural convergence that are at work. On the other hand, once allowance is made for social background, it is clear that it is blacks, not Asians, who follow the basic relationship between class and participation extensively documented among the majority white group. An overriding racial effect may be taking place on the absolute levels of turn out among each social class of blacks. This effect, or some other undocumented cause, certainly serves to suppress black turn out among all social classes quite considerably in comparison with whites. However, beyond that a class effect seems to take hold that accounts for a fair degree of

118 · Race and representation

turn out variance within the black group. This is not dissimilar to that class effect found among whites and singularly not found among Asians. The turn out of blacks, therefore, both follows a shadowing path of potential convergence with whites and also remains characterised by an overarching suppression that cannot be accounted for in conventional terms. Political integration is thus confirmed in some respects and refuted in others. This paradox is important because of what it reveals about the ways in which the theory of political integration needs to be interpreted. At a minimum, it drives home a point raised at the start of this chapter about the importance of drawing up measurements for political integration that are sensitive to actual and contextual patterns and influences. This central point may have the affect of muddying our findings and conclusions in some areas but it retains the virtue of allowing empirical investigation to be conducted using a variety of appropriate yardsticks. Support for a theoretical generalisation in some respects alongside detraction for it in others is a credible conclusion to come to if we can be confident that our questions are well framed. It can also be a useful judgement since, to be sure, there is mounting support for the view that inter-minority group distinctions remain under-researched and poorly understood.

Notes

1 Estimates supplied by Owen (Centre for Research in Ethnic Relations, University of Warwick), as quoted in the Runnymede Trust (1997: 5).
2 The main qualification to this assumption has been the impact of refugees and asylum-seekers, many of whom have emerged particularly in recent years from countries that have had no obvious historical or imperial connection with the United Kingdom (see Gordon, 1989, for an early yet incisive discussion of this post-Commonwealth phase in Britain's immigration policy debate).
3 A suggestion to re-examine these rights was predictably put forward by the British National Party in the 1997 election campaign and, just as predictably, treated as completely irrelevant by the major political parties and by the mass media (BNP, 1997).
4 By polling day, 1 May 1997, the age of the 1997 register was 74 days (or substantially less than the 166 days average age of the register in the ten general elections since 1964.
5 It should be added that the black rates contain sizeable numbers who stated that they were registered at an address other than where they were interviewed and/or at another unknown address (almost one-tenth of black Africans and black Caribbeans). In all cases, Table 4.3 pertains to verified registration that has been cross-checked with the records of the Lord Chancellor's Department (held for a year after polling day).
6 'The campaign will urge black people to use their vote', *Guardian*, (1996b). This story referred to data from a July 1996 MORI poll, 'Black Britain', claiming to show that 86 per cent of black people between 18 and 25 years did not intend to vote. The Director of Research at MORI, Simon Braunholtz, clearly irritated by the use made of the original poll by *The Voice* newspaper,

wrote a short newspaper letter pointing out gross manipulation of this poll: see, the *Guardian*, 1997b. This controversy is difficult to disentangle from wider disputes over the use made by the press of this crucial, though misinterpreted, poll.

7 It is worth pointing out here that the debates over ethnic minority turn out often highlight the paradox of electoral mobilisation facing political leaders, campaign groups and national lobbies in this area. In essence, the idea of political exclusion has been based on data that shows high levels of minority disinterest and apathy in the electoral process. At the same time, the notion of political influence through community-based mobilisation and representation suggests that many of the underlying ingredients of such mobilisation are already largely present. Furthermore, more recent evidence showing the degree to which minority (and Asian in particular) representation has progressed in medium and large cities (chiefly outside London), indicates that the nature of this dilemma is likely to become more rather than less insoluble for many of these groups and their leaders (see in particular Le Lohé, 1998, esp. pp. 86–92).

8 I am grateful to John Curtice (University of Strathclyde) for his verbal comments in reinforcing this point to me.

5

Party choice and partisanship

Introduction

Electoral studies of ethnic minority political participation have been driven by an overwhelming interest in the question of party choice. It is worth noting that the great bulk of empirical surveys have been commissioned by press sponsors, many from among the minority press, whose chief concern has been to map ethnic minority partisan loyalty. Indeed, such has been the direction and extent of partisanship among minority voters that the chief point of departure has tended to be assessments of how far, if at all, Labour's commanding lead has been curbed by younger and more socially mobile groups of minority voters. The evidence overall has suggested that minority voters have backed the Labour Party with exceptionally high strength and regularity. One consequence has been that a perception has grown in some circles that Labour has grown accustomed to its success and has lapsed into viewing such voters with a sense of complacency and neglect. The 'rotten borough' sense of this thinly veiled criticism is hard to underplay and has been prominent in many Conservative and centre party strategic attempts to woo ethnic minority voters. The underlying story of black and Asian party choice, therefore, has been one of mapping and assessing these efforts to lure these Labour voters from their traditional voting patterns. The first substantive section of this chapter is devoted to this question. A secondary, related theme has been the question of how far Labour's historic electoral advantage can be explained by class, in policy or in cultural terms. This debate forms the core of the second section of the chapter. Finally, the electoral integration of ethnic minorities is a question that partially hangs upon testing how far minority partisanship is influenced by or insulated from the sources of political difference that are found in the white electorate. The third section of the chapter is concerned with exploring this question and includes some discussion of evidence of convergence and divergence among and between minority and white voters. Finally, the chapter ends with a discussion of the campaign themes and priorities of the main political parties in appealing to minority voters alongside more broad-based campaign messages aimed at voters at large.

The chapter has an additional, fourth purpose. Having established the degree to which minority and white lines of partisanship differ, both historically and in 1997 it is important to try to tease out any underlying inter-generational factors that may be at work. The really astounding feature of minority partisanship since 1975 has not been its heavily skewed Labour bias but, rather, the minimal degree of defections from the Labour Party. Indeed, some commentators have semi-privately begun talking of an 'iron law' of British electoral behaviour whereby at least four out of five of all voting ethnic minorities have backed the Labour Party in all elections, without exception, since the first studies of minority voting were conducted in the mid-1970s. The upshot has been that such an 'iron law' tends to reinforce the picture of exceptional stability and thus mask the question of inter-generational replenishment. Labour's lead, in other words, needs to be examined more closely in order to find out whether younger groups of Labour-voting ethnic minorities are first, behaving as they are for the same or similar reasons as their older counterparts, and secondly, likely to exhibit new lines of partisanship in the future. Generational politics, therefore, spurred on by social and geographic mobility, is the theme of the fourth section of this chapter.

Party choice in historic context

In order to get a suitable handle on party choice data from the 1997 BES, it is probably worth devoting some space to looking at minority voting patterns across the full range of general elections. Figures relating to party choice over the period since the mid-1970s tend to vary in their disaggregation of ethnic minorities (into Asian and black groups at the very least). In addition, most of these data relate to stand-alone surveys of minorities, most commonly employing quota sampling techniques drawn from sampling points of high ethnic minority concentration. One feature of this traditional approach, as already raised and discussed in earlier chapters, has been that precious few direct points of comparison that have been available between minority voters (either as a whole or disaggregated) and their white counterparts. The major pooled survey data from BBC/Gallup surveys have been one notable exception to this pattern but here the difficulty has been that insufficient numbers of ethnic minority cases have prevented any useful or generalisable conclusions being drawn.

The evidence in Table 5.1 illustrates the extent to which ethnic minority voters have been among the safest constituencies of any political party in modern British politics.[1] Long-term backing for Labour has remained very strong and stable. To be sure, even the blip in the evidence highlighted by the 1987 general election proved to be a false dawn in the sense that by 1992 the familiar 'iron law' of party choice prevailed once

Table 5.1 *Labour and Conservative support among ethnic minority voters, 1974–97 (%)*

	1974[a]	1979	1983[b]	1987	1992	1997
Labour	81	86	83	72	81	85
Conservative	9	8	7	18	10	11

Notes: [a]October 1974 general election. [b]Recalculated (weighted) average of Asian and black party support levels.
Sources: adapted from CRC (1975); CRE (1980); CRE (1984); Harris Research Centre (1987); Ali and Percival (1993); 1997 BES (as Table 4.1).

again. It is worth dwelling on the 1987 case for a moment and postulating that any marked breakthrough in partisanship among Labour's rivals (principally the Conservatives) would according to orthodox thinking in this field be most likely to materialise against the background of high levels of support for the Conservatives across the electorate as a whole. The 1987 election might be thought of as a case in point, whereby the Tory appeal to minorities was built on the foundations of broader cross-group strength. In this respect, any Tory breakthrough would be driven by the fact that Labour's underlying electoral strength had been circumscribed as a national party of government across the electorate as a whole. In short, in the context of the partisan electoral map of the 1980s, any Tory surge would have been fairly closely linked to Labour's broader electoral crisis. The weakness within this orthodox perspective is that it overlooks the very real possibilities for electoral breakthrough among opposition parties under more usual circumstances. In particular, Conservative mid-term surges during Labour administrations, most notably during the 1960s and 1970s, have tended to produce some very tangible results for the Tories.[2] To that end, any suggestion of a Tory breakthrough might be better deferred until the point at which a sitting Labour administration has entered a mid-term period of widespread unpopularity. Unpicking minority voters' attachment to Labour might, therefore, be more realistic against the backdrop of a broader, cross-group sense of alienation and frustration with a sitting government that happens to be a Labour one. Inverting this line of thinking within conventional views about the Conservative's failure to capitalise on 1987 is important. For one thing, this argument does not take anything away from those critics of the Tories' inability to forge a genuine breakthrough, and reminds us that this task can be rather different when viewed from the comparative comfort of opposition politics. Additionally, it also reinforces a point that is often made that suggests that the timeframe for loosening the nexus between minority voters and the Labour Party is likely to be longer than imagined. What is clear is that the surges enjoyed by the Tories in opposition both in the late 1960s and late 1970s were closely intertwined with the party's ability to push successfully into several new social groups where it had previously been poorly supported. A similar trajectory might reasonably lie beneath its hitherto twenty-year record of minimal gain in courting minority voters.

A superficial glance at Table 5.1 might cause the casual observer to wonder whether too much fuss was being created on the back of some fairly unpromising figures for Labour's main rivals. This constituency would not appear to be especially promising for the Conservatives, not least because of the strong resilience shown by minority voters during the Labour Party's wilderness years in opposition. Such loyalty meant that ethnic minorities were often very much of an exception among other social groups that had traditionally been allied with Labour. However, despite the slanted nature of minority political allegiance, it was thought this picture contained tangible opportunities for Labour's opponents as well. For one thing, the increasingly claustrophobic relationship between Labour and its minority supporters was such that questions began to be raised on two related fronts. First, how far had neglect and possibly even arrogance crept into the mind-set of Labour leaders and opinion formers who had been raised on a diet of overwhelming and unprecedented electoral backing from ethnic minorities? Secondly, there were doubts about the precise dividends – either as electoral spoils or as implemented policy pledges – which minorities could reasonably cite in exchange for their support for Labour. To be fair, some commentators, such as Messina (1998), continued to argue that the policy benefits accruing to ethnic minorities from the Labour Party continued to be substantial and not to be dismissed. The impact of both lines of criticism was that from the mid-1980s onwards it was not certain that Labour's emphatic lead could be taken for granted indefinitely. Indeed, one commentator noted that a lack of any viable alternative to Labour was much more of a frame of mind characterising Labour leaders than a realistic strategy upon which to base the party's future prospects (FitzGerald, 1988).

Arguably one of the more enduring by-products of this long and continuing era of Labour strength among minority voters has been the way in which the so-called 'iron law' has consciously and subconsciously fed into dominant party paradigms that have seen minority voting choice as chiefly linked to ethnicity. This framework has often led to a widespread assumption in British electoral politics that perceives the causal factors behind minority participation as driven by the ethnicity of these groups of voters (Saggar and Geddes, 2000). It is notable that this dominant sense of ethnic kinship has tended to have a much more muted impact on assessments of the role of ethnic identity in British politics more generally. Certainly, Scottish and Welsh nationalist identities are commonly perceived by British political parties, whether nationalist or non-nationalist, in rather more contingent terms (Brand *et al.*, 1994; Brown *et al.*,

1998). Such a kinship and sense of identity acts as something of a twist on other more conventional relationships between voters and parties. However, among Asian and black ethnic minorities these subtleties are frequently lost and it is not especially hard to see how this picture might have emerged. One aspect of this assumption must presumably be the role played by issues and policy concerns that touch on race and racism. This is typically reflected in two areas: first, the widespread belief that such concerns count above all else for minority voters (which, arguably, they do not according to empirical evidence on this point); and secondly, that racial issues effectively eclipse any prospect of minorities tracking so-called mainstream issues and policies that are thought to be, in effect, the preserve of their white counterparts. This assumption is a potentially enormous constraining force upon British electoral politics, not least because it works against the appreciation of minority voters as politically aware and sensitive across racial and non-racial boundaries. In particular, the paradigm circumscribes understanding of what and for whom in the end is a racial concern and what is not. This is an aspect of ethnic minority political participation that is picked up and debated more fully in Chapter 9 below.

The question of the incorporation, even institutionalisation, of the 'ethnicity counts' principle into received wisdom about minority voting behaviour necessarily cuts both ways. While this may circumscribe and limit ethnic minority electoral participation in the sorts of ways mentioned above, it is only fair to note that not all activists or commentators would see this as a drawback. For one thing, the perception that ethnic identity and loyalty lies at the heart of minority voting behaviour has certainly disrupted any cosy beliefs about colour-blindness among party leaders and managers. In fact, the notion of colour-blindness has been something of a long-standing complaint held by militant activists within the Labour Party who, in turn, have tended to feed the criticism of asymmetry in the party's relationship with its ethnic minority supporters (Shukra, 1998a). Needless to say, many of these debates within and beyond Labour circles have taken place almost irrespective of the question of and evidence on (Saggar, 2000a) the extent to which ethnic minorities define their political interests in ethnic-specific terms. Thus, arguments that stress ethnic bloc politics as lying behind the so-called 'iron law' continue to be immensely influential in British party competition. The degree to which British parties are justified or indeed prudent in couching their appeal in this way is a much deeper-seated question that was examined in conceptual and theoretical terms previously in Chapter 3. Additionally, it is a central debating point in British party politics that is picked up and explored more thoroughly in Chapters 6 and 9.

Party choice in 1997

The headline evidence from the 1997 general election shows that as expected the integrity of the 'iron law' perspective had held up fully. Indeed, Table 5.1 shows that overall minority support for the Labour Party was safely within the limits of the historic dictum and in many ways had reached virtual saturation point. So much, of course, might be expected against the backdrop of an historically impressive result for Labour and, it might be added, a near collapse in the national standing of the Conservatives. The task facing us in analysing minority support in 1997 is, therefore, less concerned with mapping and confirming the likely overall division in partisanship and more with subtle variations within this picture. In particular, three areas of interest stand out in the data that lies below the aggregate split. First, as always, attention is drawn to the extent of difference found between Asian minority voters and their black counterparts. This interest reflects a much longer-standing suggestion that many previous snapshots of minority voting behaviour based on treatment of ethnic minorities in homogeneous terms have been misleading in underplaying intra-minority variance. Secondly, the 1997 data can be expected to throw light on differences among the Asian and black composite groups themselves. Again, the impetus behind this stems from claims that certain minority sub-groups have been more closely allied to the Labour cause than others, and in particular a continuing focus on the partisan loyalties of some groups of Asian voters (Indians standing out for closest inspection). Thirdly, there continues to be substantial interest shown in auditing the data for signs of any longer-term breakthroughs for the Conservatives and Liberal-Democrats. The 1997 data are of importance not so much for their headline party support levels but rather for their evidence, if any, of underlying movement in partisanship.

Table 5.2 details the differences of Asian party support against that of black voters in 1997. The most striking aspect of these figures is that a genuine difference worth noting occurred in 1997, continuing a pattern seen in previous elections as well as inter-election surveys.

Table 5.2 *Asian and black voting choice, 1997*

	Ethnic group (%)		
	Asian	Black	Total (Asian + black)
Conservative	13.6	3.7	11.3
Labour	81.9	94.5	84.8
Liberal-Democrat	3.7	1.8	3.2
Other	0.8	0.0	0.6
Total N	353	109	462
Total %	100.0	100.0	100.0

Notes: see Table 4.1, p. 94. Excludes 'don't knows'.
Source: see Table 4.1, p. 94.

Table 5.3 *Asian and black (intended) voting choice (MORI surveys 1996–97)*

	Ethnic group (%)[a]		
	Asian	Black	Total (Asian + black)
Conservative	25	8	19
Labour	70	86	75
Liberal-Democrat	4	4	4
Other	1	1	1
Undecided/don't know/refused	22	21	22
Total N	689	703	1392
Total %	100.0	100.0	100.0

Notes: [a]Weighted average (based on numeric size in the electorate). Of those naming a party. Excludes those certain not to vote.
Source: MORI (1996); MORI (1997).

The Asian–black contrast is discernible enough on the basis of these data. However, the relative differences in party allegiances between these two groups of voters should be put into context and are certainly not as great as sometimes alleged (or imagined). Indeed, the immediate pre-election period in 1996–97 witnessed a significant upsurge in claims that Asian Labour allegiances in particular were under heavy strain. Take for instance the deeply misleading survey evidence in Table 5.3 put forward by MORI in two separate polls examining likely voting intentions among blacks and Asians prior to the general election.

The point that is crucial in looking at the MORI evidence is not merely its seeming discrepancy with the BES data but also the impression it gives of a potentially floating electorate. On the key Asian voting group, the MORI picture is one of a group that contains a very sizeable minority (one in four naming a party choice) who are allied to the (then) incumbent Conservatives. This is within reach of the Conservative share of the whole electorate recorded in May 1997 (30.7 per cent), and amazingly paints a remarkable picture of Asian partisanship that very broadly mirrors that of whites. It is, therefore, probably a misleading picture in that it grossly overestimates Tory support among Asians. That said, it is arguably not entirely flawed as a sketch because, as the BES data demonstrate, Asian backing for the Tories in 1997 stood firmly in double figures and contrasted very sharply with the picture of flat rejection of the Conservatives among blacks certain to vote. In other words, the MORI evidence ends up roughly doubling the Tory share of vote among both groups but nevertheless shows that the Asian–black contrast is a feature that cannot be dismissed. This amounts to a full 10 per cent intra-minority gap (13.7 against 3.6 per cent) that is unlikely to be accounted for on incidental or *ad hoc* grounds. It therefore requires explanation in its own terms.

The claims and counter-claims about the propensity of Asians to support the Conservative Party have tended to take on a momentum of their own. Such debates are important often for their normative content. However, the group–party nexus that they describe – or rather exaggerate – are significant in three senses. First, the facts about party allegiances can make a real difference to questions of delivering racially explicit, group-targeted public policy. Certainly, it has been commonplace for many Labour supporting minority political leaders to suggest that overwhelming group backing for Labour means that the party is under an obligation to be at least sympathetic if not overtly responsive to such exclusive policy demands. Whether these expectations are received favourably and with what outcome is arguably a moot point. The Conservative's appeal to Asian voters has not been without some experimentation with similar lines of exclusive group-targeted thinking (Saggar, 2000b). The pitch may sometimes be around aspects of 'homeland' politics or some related cause, and indeed many Conservative candidates have been willing to campaign using a conceptual lens that is most usually associated with their Labour opponents. The main point of difference has been that group expectations have usually been fed by overwhelming group support in the case of the Labour Party, whereas electoral muscle-type claims have tended to sound hollow in Conservative circles.

Secondly, the Tory onslaught (as it has become in several general election campaigns), has been driven by an underlying belief that the 'hidden' ideological preferences of the Asian electorate have been more closely tied with the 'natural' ideological territory occupied by the Conservatives. This viewpoint, essentially equating Asian voter ideological and policy preferences with a cultural value system, has been immensely influential in setting the agenda for Asian community politics (Saggar, 1998f). Indeed, if there is weight in this perspective the striking thing is that it is based on a core understanding of ethnicity and ethnic group membership as the basis for political participation. It is, in other words, a return to an ethnically-related way of thinking and behaving politically, a primary theoretical concern raised in Chapter 2. We shall return to examine the so-called 'cultural thesis' more extensively later in this chapter. In the meantime, it is worth remembering that the Conservative Party–Asian voter interface is unusually flavoured with a need to throw light on the ideological makeup of this arguably diverse group of voters.

Thirdly, any movements in party choice, especially those occurring over long periods of political and social change, are important because of what these changes reveal about underlying developments in the socio-economic position of Asians. It is conventional to think of the causal relationship as the other way around, whereby any socio-economic changes that take place today are presumed to carry the capacity to trigger political and voting changes tomorrow. However, the actual causal links may be rather more complex than this. Moreover, it is important to track signs of convergence and divergence in both the political and non-political domains, not only because of the implications for party choice but also because of the implications for mapping the sources of political difference across different ethnic groups. The Asian–Tory nexus is, therefore, particularly interesting because it is vital to know whether group support for the party is or is not driven by the same sources of difference found among white voters. Equally, any gradual or even abrupt increase in levels of support for the Conservatives might conceivably be associated with very similar or quite different factors among Asians as against both whites as well as non-Asian minorities. In other words, this relationship provides us with a useful opportunity to map a lot more than party choice alone. It provides, additionally, a ready-made table on which to examine the theory of political integration that characterises the approach of this study.

Inter-group comparisons

The BES and MORI data presented above have already established a clear black–Asian contrast in partisanship, albeit of rather different magnitudes. It is worth mentioning that not dissimilar variations were identified in several earlier surveys, both at and between general elections (see, for instance, Amin and Richardson, 1992; NOP, 1991; CRE, 1994). The black community as a whole conforms to the 'iron law' sketched previously but also exceeds this level of partisan support by a significant margin. It is difficult to calculate a direct inter-election swing for this group based on the rather different survey method employed in the 1992 data. However, that this group tightened its allegiance overall to Labour in 1997 is probably not in dispute, although it must be pointed out that the volume of actual supporters this bond delivered against the background of patchy turn out is debatable. It is the Asian community as a whole that matches the 'iron law' in 1997. Furthermore, although it is true that overall Asian support for the Conservatives remained disappointingly small, it was nevertheless some four times the rate shown among black voters. In order get an insight into these headline variations, it is necessary to take the BES cross-section analysis a stage further and examine the partisan loyalties of the main component groups of Asian and black voters.

In Table 5.4 on p. 129 a comparison is drawn between party choices across the main black and Asian sub-groups as well as with white voters in 1997. The detail it reveals is significant because we can see quite clearly that Labour's appeal ebbs and flows from one minority group to another. The range separating the most supportive (Caribbean ethnic origin blacks) from the least supportive (Indians) is just short of 14 per cent, or just a little less than the direct Labour lead over the Tories among white voters.[3]

Furthermore, a similar line of variation is found when examining the

Table 5.4 *Vote distribution by ethnic group, 1997*

	Ethnic group (%)						
	White	Indian	Pakistani	Bangladeshi	Black African	Black Caribbean	Miscellaneous
Conservative	31.0	17.5	7.1	5.1	2.3	4.5	18.6
Labour	47.0	80.3	85.9	84.6	93.2	93.9	72.9
Liberal-Democrat	18.3	2.2	3.5	10.3	4.5	1.5	6.8
Other	3.7	0.0	3.5	0.0	0.0	0.0	1.7
Total *N*	1909	228	85	39	44	66	59 [2430]
Total %	100.0	100.0	100.0	100.0	100.0	100.0	100.0

Notes: see Table 4.1, p. 94. Excludes 'don't knows'.
Source: see Table 4.1, p. 94.

Tories' vote share. Among all minority groups, excepting Indians, it is clear that Conservative support was pitifully low in 1997. However, rate of Indian support for the Conservatives is between two and seven times greater than that among other comparable black and Asian groups. In fact, a hierarchy of levels of support for the Conservative cause can be seen when comparing the main Asian groups with the black groups. Even this pattern disguises the fact that Indian support for the Conservatives stands in a league of its own (more than 1 in 6 voters), while support levels are fairly clustered around the 1 in 20 mark among all others minorities, Asian as well as black. Most significantly, the Indian propensity to vote for the Conservatives in 1997 was a little over half that found among the Tory-weary white electorate. This, surely, amounts to evidence of a limited though important breakthrough of sorts for the Tories. In a generally dismal picture of a collapse in support across the (mainly white) electorate as a whole, at least one ethnic group appeared to have been running against the tide. This type of progress is arguably doubly valuable for the Conservatives. For one thing, it suggests a turnaround in its 20-year history of courting minority voters. For another, it marks a degree of progress among what is, of course, the single largest minority group whose electoral 'presence' based on demographics has been further swelled by comparatively high registration and turn-out levels. The potential to build on this achievement is something that will no doubt be closely monitored in subsequent elections. The Conservative's opportunity presumably lies in not merely holding onto and possibly raising this level of popularity among Asian Indians. The real prize also involves firstly, through the multiplier effect of such popularity, yielding actual voters via buoyant participation rates, and secondly, through the contagion effect of rising popularity (and participation) rates spreading, as it were, to other minority groups.

Ethnic group sources of party support

Whatever is made of the Tory performance among Indian voters, the blunt truth remains that the general record of all of Labour's rivals was very poor in 1997. Perhaps the best that can be said of it is that non-Labour voting among ethnic minorities was no worse in 1997 than in previous general elections (although the methodologies upon which these measures are based varied considerably from one election to the next). The overall distribution of the minority vote in 1997 remained concentrated in one party's hands. It might appear that this is all that needs to be said by way of party winners and losers. However, looking at the ethnic group source of the respective parties' share of the minority vote can extend the analysis considerably. Accepting that the Tories and Liberal-Democrats received very few votes from ethnic minorities, is it possible to say something meaningful about where their votes, however modest, came from? By asking this type of question, we shall see that some additional insight can be added to the analysis that allows our conclusions to be slightly rewritten.

The picture contained in Table 5.5 examines the ethnic group source of all minority votes secured by Labour and the Conservatives in the 1997 election, controlling, in effect, for the variable fortunes of different parties on this front. It highlights an important pattern at work. In terms of the sample design and the results of differential registration and turn out, it is clear that the numerically larger group of Asian voters (i.e. those actually casting votes in 1997) massively outnumbers its black counterpart. This means that all parties, and not just some rather than others, are *de facto* more reliant on Asian voters than on black ones. Indeed, according to the respective sizes of these two groups of voters in the sample of those actually voting we can see that the ratio is around 4:1 between them. Put another way, although it is true that some parties secure many more ethnic minority supporters than others, all parties get the lion's share of their minority votes from Asian sources. This pattern can itself be turned into a message to suggest that on present form Asian voters matter a great deal more to all parties than their black counterparts, though the degree to which this situation effectively translates into actual campaign priorities is a more vexed question. It is mainly the impact of demographics that is behind this picture but the differential mobilisation of different ethnic groups serves to reinforce this outnumbering effect. Any attempts to challenge this fact must, therefore, take a longer-term perspective (over which demographic trends take effect), and also address directly the causes of disappointing registration and/or turn out among sections of the black would-be electorate. It is the latter option that is likely to have more of a short-term timeframe, since some but not all of the causal factors behind poor mobilisation can be tackled, if not remedied, by political interventions.

Such interventions are chiefly based on campaigns to redress the 'thinning down' effects of sluggish black participation: as an already small group (by the standards of the Asian community), it is argued, political parties cannot afford to overlook even modest efforts to bring about small increases in registration and/or turn out. Indeed, the argument is often inverted by suggesting that such small potential increases can have larger proportionate impacts within a small ethnic group. In any case, the phenomenon of 'crowding out' of blacks by their Asian counterparts is something that is driven by two main sources, and the lesson must be that aspects of this are presumably subject to short-term influence. It is precisely in this spirit that the role of campaigning groups such as Operation Black Vote must be assessed: in targeting the targetable the aim is to increase the electoral muscle of a group which, despite size and geography, is firing below par. The difficulty with this approach is that par is largely defined in terms of the registration and turn-out rates of the most mobilised parts of the Asian community. While such a level of participation is undoubtedly attractive as a target, this line of thinking overlooks the question of how far differential participation rates are in fact the result of circumstantial factors related to the socio-economic position of different groups. The most rapid way to close the outnumbering gap is to raise black registration and/or turn out; however, the most direct, if not the quickest, way to do this may well lie in speedy socio-economic advancement among blacks. It is precisely because of the indirect feel of this approach – though it remains as plausible as ever – that campaign and lobby efforts are geared to what appear as (but may not be) direct messages to usually young members of the black community, to become 'involved' in the democratic process. These efforts are not without results and but their logic is predicated more on the availability of such targeted techniques than on any certainty that the signals sent and received have the desired impact.

Once we move the analysis to the party-specific level we can see that the bias effect suddenly becomes even starker than before. Table 5.5 shows that virtually all the Conservative's minority support is drawn from Asian sources, with the black source ranking into insignificance by comparison. The upshot of this picture of severe imbalance is arguably rather more skewed than many observers might imagine. With the Tories collecting a little over one-tenth of the minority vote in 1997, it would appear that this performance was achieved by gathering a modest number of Asian voters and hardly any black ones. This outcome is the product of two processes: first, as already noted, the larger size of the Asian community relative to blacks coupled with a greater participation among the former in comparison with the latter; and secondly, the considerably higher popularity of the party among Asians than among blacks in 1997 (14 per cent against 4 per cent). It is the interaction between these two

Table 5.5 *Ethnic minority group source of parties' vote, 1997*

	(%)				
	Conservative	Labour	Lib-Dem	Other	Total share of ethnic minority vote
Asian	92.3	73.7	86.7	0.0	76.4
Black	7.7	26.3	13.3	0.0	23.6
Total N	52	392	15	3	462
Total %	100.0	100.0	100.0	100.0	100.0

Notes: see Table 4.1, p. 94.
Source: see Table 4.1, p. 94.

processes that results in black Tories counting for barely anything among the party's ethnic minority haul.

With the Labour Party there is another similar bias at play. In this case, the party's Asian reliance is there for all to see (though perhaps running somewhat counter to the perceptions of many activists and commentators), but it is of a much smaller magnitude than the Tory profile mentioned previously. In Labour's case the ratio between Asian and black support roughly follows the proportions of each of these respective groups within the sample of ethnic minority electorate at large. As such, it might seem fair to say that, having allowed for wider imbalance in voting numbers, Labour is not especially reliant on its Asian supporters. However, this sort of claim would be less than the full picture since Labour is in fact a more popular party choice among blacks than among Asians (by about 13 per cent). What is taking place is that Labour is currently a little less reliant on Asian supporters than it might expect to be if it enjoyed more even levels of support across both ethnic groups. Therefore, one of the hidden prices that the party pays for its lower level of success in attracting Asian voters (in comparison with its record among black voters) is that the party's minority supporters are rather more dominated by blacks than would be the case if support levels evened up. Or, put in a completely different way, its relative 'failure' among Asians to match its record among blacks serves to cost the party a much larger proportion of Asian potential voters. There are arguably two possible explanations that could be put on this. On the one hand, it almost amounts to a warning to the Labour Party that its 'true' black reliance might develop into a trend, with the party becoming ever more associated with this particular group within the ethnic minority population. On the other hand, a genuine opportunity might be read into this picture: by prioritising the need to build on its current strength among Asian voters (it captured 82 per cent of the group's votes) will, it would appear, lead to a proportionately larger payoff for Labour. The party is arguably caught on the horns of a dilemma in terms of which of these perspectives to follow. One interpretation risks the party slipping into an ethnic ghetto status unless the current pattern of reliance can be checked and even reversed. The other, meanwhile, carries an attractive dividend for vote maximising strategists but is associated with opening up, and perhaps even diluting, the party's current group-specific appeal.

Standing back for a moment from the group reliance predicaments facing the Labour Party, it is worth noting that the parties in general may have only limited room for manoeuvre in responding to such an analysis. The 'ethnic campaigns' of the parties (discussed more extensively later in Chapter 9) are frequently couched in quite general terms, as if the cutting edge of a party's appeal is aimed at a range of minority groups, perhaps even all minorities, in a particular election campaign. The reality, however, is that all the parties are actually involved in a battle to hold onto and/or attract many more Asian voters than any other minority group of voters. There are clear disadvantages that come with this picture of underlying imbalance. For instance, ever more focused campaigns that target one group such as Asians, or even its numerically large Indian component, risk edging out interest in – and arguably the interests of – other 'less important' groups such as black voters. The rational choice basis for this strategy is hard to dismiss but it may be that there are genuine barriers to any party opting to become so exclusionary in its appeal to minorities. This likelihood is further diminished once account is taken of internal party lobbies and the role of senior party leaders in keeping parties broader rather than narrower in their appeal. A further danger lies in a party that enjoys – or at least experiences – exceptionally heavy Asian reliance. This bias might easily fuel a sense that the party was *de facto* a no go area by other minorities, and this may be a point felt especially by members of the black community. Indeed, there is already a slight risk that the Conservatives suffer from this reputation (Saggar, 1998d). It is fair to point out that the party certainly contains some activists who are prepared to go farther down this road of effective ghettoisation, though the case that they have made thus far has been poorly articulated and/or badly received. A further drawback is one that results from the Labour Party failing to recognise a tendency towards gradual Asian depletion in its ranks of minority supporters. This pattern may go unnoticed in the short to medium term, not least of all because of the party's quite astounding success in capturing the overwhelming bulk of the minority vote at large. The risk may additionally be sidelined by the size and strength of black lobbies within the party who, at least in the short run, might have no objection to or regrets about the party shifting towards greater proportionate reliance on black voters. Ultimately, of course, any shift in the direction of increased black voter reliance would be likely to be masked by the underlying greater supply of Asian voters relative to black voters. The worry might be that short-term complacency in avoiding any attempts to rebalance ethnic group sources of support would be paid for in due course by genuine inability to mobilise minority electors across the board. It is, no doubt, this kind of longer-term trade off that is central to understanding the degree to which Labour will be able to repeat its historic and current performance in elections to come.

Social class influences on partisanship

It has been commonplace for commentators to put forward explanations of British voting behaviour that are centred on traditional social cleavages. These divisions tended to have a significant impact on white voters through much of the twentieth century. Wald's study of voter alignment since the late nineteenth century emphasised that by the immediate post-1918 period, social class had become the central cleavage linked to party support (Wald, 1983). The basis of partisan alignment was largely set thereafter and has continued to be deeply influential in understanding the nature of the relationship between social cleavages and voter alignments (Pulzer, 1967; Butler and Stokes, 1974; Robertson, 1984; Evans et al., 1991). The obvious test, therefore, is to ask how far such a perspective informs and possibly even dictates our understanding of ethnic minority voters.

Before looking at the evidence from 1997 (and earlier surveys), it is worth noting the bare features of the model we are examining. To start with, attention has not been solely devoted to membership of occupationally defined social classes, though this has been important. Additionally, the role of housing tenure has been important in understanding underlying and sometimes cross-cutting social identities and voter outlooks. Specific housing tenures have been said to divide Labour voters from Conservative ones (as well as some Labour supporters from others) and, interestingly, this has sometimes been the case despite surrounding aspects of social identity based on occupation or labour force participation that have suggested traditional class-centred views of partisanship. The influence of participation in higher education has also been linked to higher than expected levels of support for the Liberal-Democrats and earlier centre parties, though this relationship has been rather weaker than those associated with Labour–Conservative divisions in occupational and housing patterns (Elmer and Frazer, forthcoming). The main utility of examining these different but related aspects of social class is that it enables us to ask three core questions. First, how far do these same social factors divide minority voters, bearing in mind the capacity of social class to uncover white partisan division? Secondly, and rather more importantly, if specific aspects of social class are associated with non-Labour voting among white voters (namely those occupying higher social status and associated with entrepreneurship and certain forms of housing), how far is it reasonable to conclude that these factors are likely to deliver a genuine breakthrough for Labour's rivals? Finally, allowing for arguably high levels of Labour support across virtually all social classes of ethnic minority voters, are there any indications of the likely class effects of occupation or housing if Labour's across the board grip waned in the future?

At first glance, the evidence on the influence of social class among minority voters appears pretty uncompromising in its portrayal of minimal class-based differences. Take for instance the picture painted of the general relationship between social class and vote in Table 5.6. This shows the contrasting nature of the basic class–vote relationship if we examine all the white respondents in our sample with the non-white ones. The analysis follows Goldthorpe's stratification of social class and allows us to compare the partisan support of five key social class groupings. This obviously follows a basic social hierarchy, although it is not designed to conform to marketing comparisons between social class groups (see Table 5.7). However, Table 5.6 is particularly interesting because it enables some attention to be given to the arguably pivotal petty bourgeoisie group, a class that has tended to display strong patterns of Conservative voting sympathy among white voters. More importantly, it is precisely this social class that has attracted attention among commentators of ethnic minority affairs because of the over-representation of two groups in its ranks, Asian Indians and the Chinese.[4] Finally, we should be mindful of the constraints caused by the relatively small sample numbers that are involved in Table 5.6. For this reason the analysis is restricted to looking at Labour voting as the actual numbers of blacks and Asians voting for other parties is quite small and cannot be tested separately.

The top line story shown in the table is simple enough, namely that across all social classes (weighted in relation to their presence in the

Table 5.6 *Ethnicity, social class and Labour vote, 1997*

	Voting Labour (%)		
	White	Black + Asian	Net minority–white difference
Salariat	38 (659)	76 (109)	+38
Routine non-manual	44 (409)	86 (99)	+42
Petty bourgeoisie	31 (172)	78 (46)	+47
Foremen and skilled manual	60 (300)	93 (70)	+33
Semi and unskilled manual	63 (402)	91 (125)	+28
All	47 (1942)	85 (449)	+38

Notes: figures in brackets show the base *N*s.
Source: see Table 4.1, p. 94.

Table 5.7 *Voting intentions among different ethnic groups by class, 1979*

	(%)								
	White			Asian			Afro-Caribbean		
	ABC1	C2	DE	ABC1	C2	DE	ABC1	C2	DE
Labour	20	35	38	42	50	50	41	49	48
Conservative	57	40	32	25	28	25	17	11	15
Liberal	9	5	5	6	3	0	5	8	3
Other/non-voter	15	20	25	28	19	25	35	32	35

Source: BBC/Gallup (1979).

sample) the level of Labour support is dramatically greater among minorities than among whites. In fact, as we saw earlier, the incidence is about twice as large when comparing the minority and white groups as a whole. Taking pairs of white and minority social classes together, the sharp imbalance is seen right through all class groups. For all social class groups, the ethnic minority Labour-voting 'lead' amounts to a staggering 38 percentage points. This measure is substantially exceeded among the petty bourgeoisie (approaching an additional 50 percentage points), and substantially undershot among the group comprising semi and unskilled manual workers (28 points). The point that is equally striking is that even in those ethnic minority social class groups where Labour-voting is at its lowest (i.e. 76 per cent), it still stands appreciably above the highest level of support found among white semi and unskilled workers (i.e. 63 per cent). In other words, Labour support among ethnic minorities, at worst, stands at a level that is enviable among even Labour supporters from the party's core constituency of working-class white voters. Once like for like comparisons are used, it is apparent that wide variations in Labour support are found across ethnic groups of the same social class. The problem, however, is that there is little obvious pattern in this, with the widest margins in absolute voting found among members of the second and third classes in our scheme and the narrowest among the first, fourth and fifth classes. Using absolute class-voting differences, therefore, it is hard to see any strong class relationship at work among ethnic minorities. This is chiefly because Labour voting, though subject to variance, is in fact crowded into a small band and stands at a very high level among all classes of ethnic minority voters. The conclusion we may draw then is that the role of ethnicity easily overshadows the role of class. It is a fair conclusion based on absolute measures of class–vote relationships and certainly is not one that is easily dismissed. Furthermore, the figures in Table 5.6 from 1997 are also echoed in earlier evidence looking at this relationship based on absolute class-based voting. Table 5.7 takes evidence from pooled pre-election surveys by Gallup from 1979 (in order to establish a viable number of black and Asian cases). It illustrates again a picture already sketched in relation to 1997.

Party choice and partisanship · 137

Although Table 5.7 cites rather higher levels of general non-Labour support across the ethnic minority class groups in 1979 than the BES data for 1997, the message is a familiar one. Social class (delineated in more familiar market research terms in the Gallup data) appeared to account for very little variation in party support among Asian and black voters but continued to have a strong pull in shaping white party choice. Writing in the early 1990s, using evidence from the 1987 BES, the Heath, Jowell and Curtice team drove home this central message and inferred that additional insight might be gained by looking at different theories of ethnic minority collective political action:

> The political behaviour of blacks [and Asians] is not to be explained by their class situation, however broadly defined. They are much more inclined to the Labour Party than white voters in similar class situations, housing, local milieu, and so on. Individual economic and social factors do not seem to be the answer. Perceptions of group interests or processes of group identification are more plausible explanations. (Heath *et al.*, *1991: 113*)

The conclusion drawn by this set of authors might just as easily apply to the reading of the 1997 BES data reviewed previously. In making such a deduction, two related questions arise. First, with the added capacity to go beyond absolute levels of class-based voting, does this sort of conclusion still hold up? Secondly, does the inference about the potential worth of explanation based on non-class, collective identity and interest rest on solid foundations? The answer to the latter question is pursued a little later in our discussion of ethnically-based theories of political participation. Let us turn initially to pursue the former question.

Placing class influences in context
By looking again at Table 5.6, it can also been seen that in another sense the class voting profile of Asians and blacks broadly follows the pattern established among white voters. That is to say, across white and non-white voters, the actual extent of Labour support tends to be rather lower in the salariat and petty bourgeoisie at the top end of the social ladder while remaining rather higher among members of the upper and lower working class. Of course, the fit of this generalisation is not perfect but it does hold true in separating out the broad influence of class from different ends of the social class spectrum. Indeed, it is only the complication of the somewhat higher than expected levels of Labour support among routine non-manual voters of all ethnic backgrounds that upsets the symmetry of the class-based influence that is detected. To this extent, it is possible to say that the voting behaviour of Asian and black minorities is indeed affected by social class in a way that is similar to but not as profound as the impact seen among their white counterparts.

This rather different conclusion is simply based on comparing the magnitude of absolute class-based differences. In the case of white voters, the role of class results in a substantial degree of dissimilarity between members of different classes. In the case of minorities, though class has an impact, it is equally clear that members of different classes continue to be much more likely not to be divided in their voting choice. For the former, the actual range encompassing highest and lowest Labour support is 32 percentage points (63 per cent against 31 per cent); by sharp contrast, the Asian and black range is just 17 percentage points (93 per cent versus 76 per cent). Therefore, the absolute differences that exist among minority voters are about a half of those pertaining to white voters. The conclusion that can be drawn then is that a smaller absolute range of voting linked to class among minorities than among whites does not amount to sufficient grounds for sidelining, let alone dismissing, the notion that class does indeed have an influence upon ethnic minority voting behaviour. Certainly, the influence does not extend to that seen among white voters but it remains important none the less. At the same time, this conclusion should be qualified by the higher degree of partisan similarity among ethnic minorities from different classes than among whites from the same classes. In other words, the influence of other factors, notably ethnicity in some form, continues to overshadow the modest class effect that can be isolated. The relationship, perhaps even interaction, between these factors is not easy to tackle or measure in social research generally. The task in this piece of electoral research is to firstly, highlight the limits of the roles played by class and ethnicity effects, and secondly, unpack the conceptual and theoretical manner by which these factors may be related to one another.

The potential for class politics
The original point of departure for this section of the chapter was to look at the longer-run potential for class politics in shaping ethnic minority party choice. A great deal has been made about the seeming insularity of ethnic minority voters from the usual dictates of class-based collective politics that have been associated with British electoral behaviour. Indeed, as long ago as the early 1980s, one commentator had stressed that the predominance of ethnic bloc voting on the part of Asian and blacks voters meant that they could not be easily treated as an integral part of the class-centred mobilisation instincts and campaigns of the major political parties (Crewe, 1983: 270–3). Crewe noted, using NOP data from 1978, that the West Indian (black) vote that went to Labour among A, B and C1 voters stood at 90 per cent, among C2 voters support was 94 per cent; and among D and E voters support had reached virtual saturation point at 99 per cent. The figures for these different classes of Asians voters were 86, 93 and 97 per cent, suggesting a very similar

range of variation. The point was that these data showed no signs of the influence of class politics and the inference was that the future potential for traditional class-based political mobilisation was far from encouraging. In terms of political integration, the prognosis was that white and non-white voters held little in common and that few, if any, signs existed that pointed to greater convergence with class-centred influences upon vote.

Therefore, the hypothesis of class potential, as it were, requires us to go beyond looking at the class-based range of variance in Asian and black voting behaviour. Instead, by examining the odds ratios alongside the absolute differences we can explore the influence of class, having allowed for the fact that the data itself shows comparatively little variation in the likelihood of black and Asian non-Labour voting among members of different social classes. In other words, this approach allows us to ignore the cramping of levels of Labour support across the classes. Odds ratios presents us with the ability to control for the floor and ceiling effects. Measuring odds ratios is thus about assessing relative class voting. This is a vital tool in dealing with minority voting patterns given the historic fact that support levels for Labour have been so high as to effectively crowd out any chance of class effects being picked up by measuring absolute differences alone. The upshot of this technique is that it ought to allow us to peer into the question of whether and how far existing minimal class differences in party choice might develop into more substantial voting differences in the context a less monopolistic hold over all minority voters by the Labour Party. If we stand back from the task facing us, it soon becomes clear that the job of evaluating independent class influences upon minority voting behaviour is a rather different one from that of studying the basis of the Labour Party's historic success in marshalling these voters. By using odds ratios we can begin to separate out these tasks and say something about the former while acknowledging the centrality of the latter. That is to say, class-based influences need to be analysed distinctively and ideally away from the contextual influence of strong party performance.

If Labour support were to recede from its present very high levels, we find that the class voting odds ratios for both blacks and Asians are in fact not greatly dissimilar to those of whites. A comparison of Labour support among black and Asian members of salariat with members of the lower working class reveals an odds ratio of 3.2:1. This ratio is just a little higher than that among whites across these two classes (2.8:1). Relative class influences are therefore not quite so easily distinguished from one ethnic group to another and it is rather harder to claim that ethnicity serves to trump class in this sense. This kind of conclusion is drawn from the measurement of class odds ratios and provides us with a markedly different view from the analysis derived from measuring absolute differences. Both approaches are sound and logical ones based on the same evidence as viewed from different vantage points. In sum, we can conclude that absolute class differences in voting choice are fairly small among ethnic minorities as compared with the standards of white voters. These differences, however, are not to be dismissed as unimportant and without relevance to the question of the potential of class to exert a much larger influence upon vote. At present such differences are swallowed up by and are arguably rendered less visible because of the larger picture of dealing with extremely high levels of Labour voting. However, class effects across ethnic boundaries are quite similar in scale once the narrow picture is disentangled from the larger one. This accompanying perspective is even more compelling once we return to tracking absolute differences found among specific ethnic minority groups. For instance, the case of Asian Indians stands out due to the relatively large degree of variation seen in Labour voting between the top and bottom of the social class ladder. The absolute difference separating the Indian salariat from the Indian lower working class stands at 24 percentage points, a figure that is almost identical to the range among whites from these two classes (25 points). Meanwhile, it is the range spanning the black Caribbean salariat and lower working class (just 12 percentage points) that is most striking and so clearly out of line with the white–Indian picture. Here, in other words, is some tentative evidence to show that unexpected class influences have been at work impacting certain sections of the ethnic minority population more than others. It is wise to be cautious about basing too much on these sub-group comparisons as they are inevitably underpinned by fairly small sub-sample sizes. The conclusions, therefore, must remain conditional upon further research that uses enhanced samples of these specific minority groups.

This important caveat aside, it should be remembered that the sorts of inter-class differences (or similarities) that we are detecting might also be related to aspects of underlying labour market participation. For instance, the various different ethnic groups are not located in a typical cross-section of occupations within a particular social class. The distribution of salariat employment in particular is rather different between ethnic groups. Whereas some groups are typically concentrated among the so-called public sector 'helping' professions such as nursing, housing, social work and so on, others tend to be found in private sector managerial and technical jobs such as the legal, medical and accounting professions. We can verify the degree of concentration of white members of the salariat in the latter category. Additionally, there is a tendency among Indians to begin to follow this path, a pattern that only shows signs of further accelerating in the medium to longer term. Meanwhile, the black African and Caribbean presence in the salariat appears to be clustered in the former category with only minimal advancement into the latter. The effect of these contrasting occupational patterns is that the voting behaviour of the salariat of one ethnic group does not always directly compare with that of another group. A mixing up of apples and oranges might be taking place, whereby the partisanship of different types of salariat professionals, who also come from different ethnic groups, is compared without sufficient analytical justification. The need to refresh this line of inquiry with enhanced samples is even more pressing as a consequence if we are to make greater headway in assessing how far inter-class differences are genuinely linked to ethnic group membership or merely driven by a failure to secure meaningful like for like comparison. Class membership and occupational patterns are both separate and linked in different senses. This makes the need for more robust analysis even stronger and, despite the availability of sufficiently large sample sizes, the relationship between class and vote is likely to be coloured by the labour market setting of class membership.

Related social cleavages

If analysis based on absolute and relative class differences can take us only so far with the present data, is it possible to extend our understanding of the influence of social factors? The challenge is to look beyond class membership alone and to examine how far other prominent social cleavages impact on ethnic minority and white voting choice. The following analysis does this by linking the explanatory power of social class membership with firstly housing (measured in types of tenure) and secondly education (gauged by highest level of formal attainment). This technique allows us to conduct a multivariate analysis to evaluate the degree of variance attributable to three independent factors at one and the same time. The method once again relies on Labour voting as our baseline because of the comparatively small numbers who opt for any of the other parties.

A logistical regression model using these three variables is shown in Table 5.8 on p. 142. The parameter estimates it reports are interpreted as fitted log odds ratios. One of the uses of this model is to tackle the question of how far relative class voting may be taking place beneath a picture of only limited absolute class voting. In addition, the technique takes account of the fact that our sample is based on a fairly high degree of geographic clustering by using multilevel modelling. Using census-derived information, the model also introduces a variable that represents the ethnic minority concentration of the sampling point for each respondent. The purpose of this ethnic concentration variable is twofold. First, it has a methodological value because a part of the boosted sample was drawn from areas of comparatively high ethnic minority concentration. This method carries a risk that the sample has been distorted by the effective over-sampling of minorities in these areas, and we need to check

Table 5.8 *Logistic multilevel model of Labour voting, 1997*

	\multicolumn{6}{c}{Parameter estimates}					
	White		Black+Asian		Combined	
Constant	0.40	(0.19)	1.09	(0.78)	0.32	(0.19)
Ethnic concentration (log)	0.023	(0.011)	0.36	(0.20)	0.20	(0.08)
Class						
Salariat	−0.75	(0.17)	−0.70	(0.51)	−0.76	(0.16)
Routine non-manual	−0.52	(0.16)	−0.19	(0.50)	−0.51	(0.16)
Petty bourgeoise	−0.98	(0.22)	−1.02	(0.54)	−0.98	(0.20)
Skilled manual	−0.04	(0.17)	0.25	(0.63)	−0.03	(0.17)
Semi/unskilled manual (reference)	0		0		0	
Housing tenure						
Owner	−0.19	(0.16)	0.71	(0.42)	−0.17	(.16)
Council tenant	0.76	(0.22)	1.05	(0.60)	0.78	(0.20)
Other (reference)	0		0		0	
Highest qualification						
Degree	0.20	(0.19)	−0.97	(0.51)	0.17	(0.19)
Intermediate (GCSE/A level)	−0.29	(0.12)	−0.94	(0.39)	−0.34	(0.11)
None/other (reference)			0		0	
Ethnicity					1.10	(0.34)
Ethnicity* owner					0.74	(0.35)
Ethnicity* degree					−0.82	(0.41)
Level 2 variance	0.57	(0.11)	0.59	(0.36)	0.59	(0.11)
N	1942		448		2390	

Note: Figures in brackets show standard errors.
Source: see Table 4.1, p. 94.

whether any bias has affected the sample. The check against this possibility is to control for the concentration effect and to see what impact this variable has on the results. Any adjustment of the findings that is then required (if at all) is an option that can be exercised in order to preserve the integrity of the data analysis that we are conducting.

Secondly, the variable allows us to investigate how far, if at all, actual support levels for the Labour Party among ethnic minorities are affected by the degree of ethnic minority concentration. In other words, it has been suggested that this factor may have an impact in its own right on Labour voting. There is the continuing suggestion that so-called ethnic neighbourhood effects are important in shaping the voting choice of certain groups of ethnic minorities. If the voting behaviour of ethnic minorities living in largely white neighbourhoods varies substantially from those in largely minority concentrated areas, then this will be of profound relevance to understanding how far political participation is related to wider processes of assimilation. The inclusion of this variable is therefore helpful to be able to test for this potentially important outcome.

The first regression in the above table (shown in the left-hand column) relates to the influence of social class, housing tenure and educational qualifications (alongside ethnic minority concentration) for white respondents in the sample.[5] The second performs an identical analysis for a combined sample of Asians and blacks. Finally, by pooling together ethnic and minority and white respondents, we create a third regression. The first and second regressions allow us to compare informally the impact of these specific social cleavages among whites and ethnic minorities. However, a more formal way of doing this is found in the third regression set that tests specific interactions; this allows us to assess the degree to which the influence of a particular social cleavage for blacks and Asians is the same as its impact among white voters.

The first regression for the white respondents reports a picture that is far from surprising to most observers. To be certain, it shows quite clearly fairly similar relative levels of Labour support among both the upper and lower working class; this support then declines fairly rapidly among the routine non-manual middle class and salariat and, most strikingly, falls off dramatically among white members of the petty bourgeoisie. The evidence on housing tells another familiar story. The position of those renting public housing from local authorities shows expected strong levels of Labour support and this contrasts very sharply with those who are owner-occupiers and private sector tenants. Lastly, the influence of education is interesting because of the way in very low and very high levels of attainment are related to Labour support, displaying a classic U-shaped character. More surprisingly yet, is the role of ethnic minority concentration. This variable reveals that even among white voters the level of minority concentration has a small (though statistically significant) impact on Labour voting. That is to say, those in areas of higher minority concentration are associated with higher level of support for Labour and vice versa. It is imprudent to suggest that this is some sort of ethnicity effect at work, not least because the lines of causation appear to be extremely puzzling. What is more likely is that this variable is something of a surrogate for levels of social disadvantage and deprivation. This suggests that some contextual processes are at work that link areas of minority concentration with socio-economic disadvantage. It is worth trying to investigate further as to whether the remaining neighbourhood effect, having controlled for ethnic minority concentration, is driven by constituency characteristics or by characteristics of the electors found there.

As far as the black and Asian regression is concerned, we can see that this follows a broadly similar profile to that of white voters. For instance, the parameter estimates are virtually identical when comparing ethnic minority and white members of the salariat and petty bourgeoisie classes. Elsewhere, among the other social classes, although the parameter estimates across white and ethnic minority groups show sharp differences, it is also the case that the standard errors suggest that these differences might possibly be within the sampling error. This pattern, however, is not followed when it comes to the impact of the housing and education variables. On the one hand, as expected, we see that black and Asian public housing tenants display the classic hallmark of an appreciably greater relative propensity to vote for Labour. On the other hand, however, it is most striking that the minority owner-occupiers follow an entirely different path to their white counterparts: for this group the parameter estimate is positive and quite strong, while for white voters in a similar housing situation this is negative. This might imply a completely different relationship between private home ownership and vote among ethnic minorities to that which we would expect to be the case (and exists commonly among white voters). However, the drawback in making such a conclusion is that the regression clearly shows some very considerable standard errors and, therefore, it is not possible to know just how far the white and ethnic minority parameter estimates are significantly different from one another.

The third regression will allow us to investigate this difference directly. The parameter estimates for the education explanatory variable show the white and ethnic minorities to be dramatically out of line with each other. Again, the large standard errors complicate the picture because it is possible that these contrasting results are bound up in issues of sampling error. A formal test to compare the two groups is therefore required as well.

The impact of ethnic minority concentration appears to have a rather greater influence on the Labour voting inclinations of blacks and Asians than their white counterparts. (This parameter estimate, however, is a little below the normal standards of statistical significance so our conclusions must be tempered accordingly.) Once again, it implies the likelihood of some genuine contextual factors at work that are potentially of enormous relevance to our line of research inquiry. This question must therefore warrant additional research so as to allow any interim conclusions to be reinforced or else withdrawn.

The third regression features a pooling of our ethnic minority and white samples to create a single, cross-ethnic merged sample. A fresh explanatory term for ethnicity is introduced (whereby 0 is coded for whites and 1 is coded for blacks and Asians). Further, two interaction terms are also introduced in order to test whether the impacts of owner-occupation and degree qualifications, respectively are the same for ethnic minorities as they are for whites. A number of points emerge from our third model. To begin with, ethnicity produces a parameter estimate that is roughly similar in magnitude to those associated with the salariat and the petty bourgeoisie (noted previously). That is to say, in terms of odds ratio measures, the impact of ethnicity upon Labour voting is about the same magnitude as that of social class. This is a fairly powerful finding to say the least.

Moving on, the purpose of the two interaction terms is to throw light on the extent to which both owner-occupation and degree possession parameter estimates differ between whites and ethnic minorities. For owner-occupation the model reveals that the interaction term is 0.74, a value over twice its standard error. This result means that there is a significant difference. Additionally, because the interaction term has a positive value we can conclude that, *ceteris paribus*, the ethnic minority owner-occupiers were more likely to vote for the Labour Party than were white owner-occupiers. This suggests that for ethnic minorities owner-occupation rates and patterns do not have an association with Conservative support that is widespread among white voters. This may appear to be an odd and inexplicable result at first glance, but delving deeper into housing trends may help us to throw some light on this superficial anomaly. Earlier detailed studies have pointed to the unusual housing market that has historically operated among large sections of the ethnic minority population. Rex and Moore (1967) in their classic study of racism reflected in housing opportunities and barriers argued that racial discrimination, both overt and indirect, impacted heavily on the ability of ethnic minorities to participate in and enjoy local public housing. Furthermore, traditional routes into home ownership operated in the case of many ethnic minorities but, crucially, were distorted markedly by the spillover effects of discrimination in the public and private rental sector. Racially-driven constraints on supply were an important determinant of this pattern alongside social and cultural factors that tended to reinforce ethnic minority residential clustering even at the cost of forgone opportunities in property ownership in more attractive residential neighbourhoods. The core of this explanation, however, was that discriminatory processes served to restrict the availability of finance and access to council housing and private renting. Coupled with ethnic preferences for certain neighbourhoods over others, the upshot was that a completely different housing market operated for large numbers of ethnic minorities. The central point was that as owner-occupation patterns arose this form of housing tenure was generally not associated with upward social mobility among ethnic minorities. Nor was home ownership in itself especially linked to abandonment of traditional community-based ties and forms of solidarity. Where minorities moved into their own homes, they did not necessarily 'move up' and nor did they particularly 'move out' of their traditional neighbourhoods. This pattern contrasts with the dilution of working-class neighbourhood ties and identities brought about by white working-class take-up of owner-occupation. This is a subtle finding in the research because it strengthens the argument that it is not owner-occupation in itself or the objective interests of those characterised by this housing tenure that matter for understanding ethnic minority political outlook and behaviour. By contrast, attention needs to be given to the social and cultural processes that are caught up in housing markets and choices. Such an approach can then give meaning to the complex and divergent political implications of housing as a social cleavage among different ethnic groups.

Our final interaction term relates to degree-level educational attainment and aims to show how far parameter estimates for whites and ethnic minorities differ from one another. However, a caveat must be added to its utility since the parameter estimate is twice its standard error (−0.82 and 0.41, respectively), implying an ambiguous level of significance. The relatively small number of black and Asian graduates in the sample is undoubtedly the biggest factor behind this problem of statistical significance and means that strong caution is needed in drawing conclusions based on this result. Furthermore, it is likely that a fairly large proportion of the minority graduate sample comprise respondents holding degrees earned overseas. The degree interaction term has a negative sign, showing that minority graduates were effectively less likely to vote for Labour than their white graduate peers. The influence of the overseas graduates may be of importance here. Its has been suggested that in the particular countries of origin in question (India, Pakistan, Bangladesh and several Caribbean states) there is a much stronger link between social background and participation in higher education than seen in Britain generally. Therefore, possession of an overseas degree among the sample of minority graduates might serve as a proxy for relatively privileged social origins. Such an advantaged social background will often tend to be linked with sympathy and support for the Conservatives, especially if this group of overseas graduates generally perceive themselves as fairly far removed from the social background of the remainder of non-graduate ethnic minorities. In other words, it is the relative social gap between graduates and non-gradates that matters in shaping political outlook and behaviour, and in the cases of blacks and Asians the sample may be picking up a very large social divide of great political importance. In the case of the white sample, higher education may be associated with social background but much less strongly as a reflection of social origins. In Britain, graduates, most of whom are white, are also associated with relatively liberal values and political attitudes. It is not possible to say for certain how far the 'overseas graduate effect', if it can be dubbed as such, is subject to this liberal influence upon attitudes. Again, the privileged social background of these graduates may be so strong and distinctive from other non-graduate ethnic minorities that any liberal influence is minimal at most.

What can be said, however, is that the social, even cultural, meaning afforded to this particular education variable may be very different for ethnic minorities than for whites. Those who were educated to degree-level overseas will be much more likely to be drawn from older rather than younger generational cohorts. It will be interesting to try to observe how far the social context of British higher education has a similar or different influence upon ethnic minority graduates of 'home' universities. This is a point that clearly deserves to be pursued in further research, though our sample is only able to sketch these relationships rather tentatively. Nevertheless, this part of the chapter has served to push home a basic and important lesson, namely that like for like comparison must take account of the possibility that social cleavages based on housing and education are not always characterised by uniform meaning from one ethnic group to another. Such a lesson about differential social and political meaning echoes a theme first visited in Chapters 2 and 3 earlier in the study. It is a theme that has broader application in the next chapter that is devoted to the question of ethnic minority issue preferences as a coherent set of political interests.

Notes

1 See also Chapter 2 (Table 2.3 and fn 5) above which draws attention to varying Asian and black party voting patterns in 1997. Comparison between these two tables reveals rather different findings: MORI data (showing a 78/17 per cent Conservative/Labour split) and BES data (indicating an 85/11 per cent division). The latter results, of course, lie much closer to the long-term, two-party split found among ethnic minority voters.
2 This is a point also made by Le Lohé (1998: 94) when he notes that Labour's mid-term blues at the end of the 1960s delivered to the Conservatives such major northern cities as Liverpool, Newcastle and Sheffield.
3 The BES cross-section final estimates of party vote share among all voters (white and non-white) in the merged file are as follows: Labour (54.8 per cent); Conservatives (27.0 per cent); Liberal Democrats (15.2 per cent); and Others (3.0). This compares with the actual results of the general election as follows: Labour (43.3 per cent); Conservatives (30.7 per cent); Liberal Democrats (16.8 per cent); and Others (9.3 per cent). It is immediately clear that the merged file party vote share figures are heavily influenced by the presence of respondents picked up in the ethnic minority boost (both directly and indirectly). Indeed, the figures for whites only in the merged file are substantially closer to the actual general election results (47.0, 31.0, 18.3 and 3.7 per cent, respectively). The last of the figures in the actual election results (for 'other parties') relates to the UK as a whole and therefore is slightly inflated by the presence of the Scottish and Welsh nationalist parties (combined total of 2.5 per cent of vote share), whereas the figures in Table 5.4 are based on a merged file that excludes Scottish respondents (the ethnic minority booster was limited to England and Wales only).
4 Chinese, along with other southeast and east Asian groups, were not included in ethnic minority booster sample, though it is likely that some of these groups might be contained in the 'other' category shown in previous tables. However, these ethnic groups are included, quite separately, in the analysis of ethnic minority parliamentary candidates found in Chapter 8.
5 Whites respondents in England and Wales only in order to allow direct comparison with the ethnic minority sample (principally comprising the booster sample).

6

Issues and attitudes

Introduction

The role played by so-called racial or ethnic issues in shaping the political outlook and behaviour of ethnic minorities has developed into something of a political caricature in recent years. Throughout many aspects of politics and public life in modern Britain, it has become commonplace to see assumptions and practices that equate ethnic minority politics with a discrete agenda of issues and attitudes. Indeed, it is difficult to understate the extent to which the politics of race in Britain is founded on this kind of assumption, with debate and variation limited to forms and instances of racial and ethnic issues and their impact upon minority political participation. Such an approach is by no means restricted to political participation matters alone and is characteristic of an underlying set of values, norms and protocols that hallmark current attitudes towards and about British multiculturalism.

The task in this chapter is to begin to home in on this debate within minority political participation at the ballot box in order to gauge how far, in evidence, it is true to say that minorities are motivated by a discrete or overlapping issue agenda. The need to tackle this question is a core matter facing empirical political science inquiry on the subject of the underlying political integration of Britain's ethnic minorities. For this reason, we shall take care and space to discuss the interpretations which can be put on existing and new evidence in this field. A second job facing this chapter is to address the question of which kinds of issues and attitudes form the basis of racial and non-racial politics. This question, in other words, is about gaining a handle on the much larger debate concerning public attitudes towards racial pluralism and societal multiculturalism (see, for example, Alibhai-Brown, 1999; Blackstone *et al.*, 1998; Statham, 1999). It is a theme that has been the subject of considerable public debate in recent times, and it is worth devoting our attention to aspects of this debate using attitudinal data that can begin to tie in both ethnic group and cross-group perspectives in an original and novel way. Finally, the chapter is also concerned with making an explicit connection between electoral and non-electoral aspects of the debate over supposedly racial issues. Ethnic minority concerns are said to be such an identifiable and integral part of British multicultural society, that both casual observers and serious commentators frequently overlook the basis for such a claim or its limits. (See, for instance, James, 1997: 75-9 for an illustration of this tendency when discussing the largely failed attempt to initiate government policy during the Salman Rushdie affair.) The evidence presented in this chapter is an appropriate vehicle through which to examine this claim and to do so by aiming to go a little beyond the realms of political participation and party competition. The chapter aims to throw some fresh light on this question by trying to isolate the degree to which racial and non-racial issues and concerns are reflected in evidence both within and beyond mainstream politics. One of the fruits of this discussion, as we shall see in due course, will also be to describe and explain better the scope and credibility of mainstream, electorally-based channels of political involvement against rival or less orthodox routes based on grassroots activism, ethnic kinship or protest movements.

It has to be said at the outset that a very large part of assumption behind a racial issue agenda is driven by the politics of difference and differential experience. That is to say, at a very simplistic, everyday level, it is important not to forget that Britain's various ethnic groups are usually characterised by a lack of uniformity in their social, economic, cultural and other experiences. In this respect, there ought not in principle to be anything very special or significant in uncovering evidence to show that differences between group political outlooks and loyalties are a further reflection of the kinds of variations of experience and perspective found outside the realm of politics. This can be a very persuasive argument in that it reminds us that the sources of political difference from one group to another may lie within politics but are most likely to be related to distinctive features drawn from participation in the labour market, education, housing and so on. Elements of these differences may even be related to external factors to do with 'homeland' political issues (Parekh, 1998; Gouldbourne, 1998b: 25-49; Azim, 1996; Saggar, 2000b). A simple example will suffice to push home this basic yet vital point. A recent Joseph Rowntree investigation into the experience of those on low incomes revealed, fairly unsurprisingly, that groups such as Bangladeshis, Pakistanis and black Caribbeans were dramatically over-represented in this population while their white counterparts were slightly under-represented (Platt and Noble, 1999). However, the report also highlighted a range of other related disparities between the position of white and non-white low income groups: for instance, being on a low income combined with having children was characteristic of well over a half of Bangladeshi cases as against fewer than 1 in 13 in the white population. Using empirical data of this kind, it is not difficult to see how both low income experience and low income family experience can vary enormously across specific ethnic groups. With this in mind, it is immediately clear that a racial or ethnic group twist can be put on not just these kinds of experiences but also on a much broader set of policy and issue concerns surrounding poverty, exclusion and indeed family policy. Once such a racial dimension is a real possibility, it is no great leap to imagine and possibly anticipate that these issues may be debated in racial or quasi-racial terms. This much is easy to understand and make sense of, because it merely represents a following through of differential experience into aspects of group-based ways of thinking about issues and public policy. The more awkward point is the extent to which differential experience is itself explained in racial terms or possibly even linked to a more systematic social theory of group identity and/or political theory of group-based rights. Indeed, this is the essential arena of contestation over race found in British and US politics, a form of disagreement that is awkward at its mildest and more often described as potentially fracturing in its underlying effect on the cohesiveness of these societies. The example cited reflects very well the argument that ethnic group-centred ways of understanding various issues and policies can easily be explained on the back of differences in these groups' position in society. However, such an explanation also highlights the real possibility that this linkage may be far from self-limiting and can spawn a whole way of looking at not just the component issues of politics but rather politics itself. It is this dimension of so-called racial issues, i.e. the capacity to feed and inform politics in racial and quasi-racial terms, that is the striking and moot feature of British multiculturalism. These different features of British politics' undulating concern with racial politics can be seen in areas as diverse as the response and reputation of the police to the Stephen Lawrence affair (Ignatieff, 1999), to the involvement of minorities in shaping monetary policy (*The Times*, 1999), and on-going disagreements about immigration as an electoral issue (Coleman, 1998). It is, therefore, a major concern underpinning the discussion throughout this chapter.

The generic theme of this chapter, therefore, is to explore the dynamics of issue-agenda construction for ethnic minorities and their white counterparts in British electoral politics. As already noted, the single greatest area of debate within this broad theme is the question of how far minorities' political attitudes and potential participation are circumscribed by assumptions about minority politics. To this extent, the chapter is, in fact, concerned with examining another important aspect of the British liberal race relations paradigm. This intellectual framework has provided a rich context through which many policy questions regarding ethnic pluralism have been pursued. Additionally, it provides a way of framing the path of mass political participation by ethnic minorities, whereby emphasis has been placed on first, ethnic group-based voting blocs (a theme taken up in previous chapters), and secondly, the issues and policies thought to be behind minority political involvement (taken up in this chapter). In this study we can put forward fresh evidence to test the continuing influence of this paradigm. However, we can only refer indirectly to data reflecting the extent to which politicians, party managers and other political elites share a common agenda in restricting minority participation to selective issues and concerns. By building on mass participation data to begin with (from the BES as well as other sources), it is possible to construct a basic hypothesis for testing. This hypothesis assesses how far the liberal paradigm holds sway in shaping and possibly dictating the scope of legitimate issues and concerns for ethnic minorities. A tight, constraining effect might suggest that the liberal paradigm continues to be deeply influential in determining what is thought to be an 'ethnic minority interest' and conversely what is not. However, if evidence can be shown describing a looser, less deterministic link, where there are plenty of signs of overlap between supposed racial and non-racial concerns, then this interpretation appears much less compelling. The hypothesis, in other words, asks not merely what are the sources of difference between minority and white political attitudes, but also whether key aspects of such variance are the products of a longer tradition of race relations thinking and practice. The political attitudes of ethnic minorities are most usually studied as an independent variable in existing research concerned with attitudinal influences upon political behaviour. However, attitudinal patterns and structures can also be thought of as a dependent variable in its own right and can be linked with and explained through the context of race relations (Saggar and Geddes, 2000). By pushing the debate in this direction, the chapter aims to extend research understanding of minorities' political interests and attitudes and to begin to integrate this knowledge with wider understanding and interpretations of British ethnic pluralism. Electoral-based research is not solely concerned with behavioural matters, though these are important in comprehending how far political thinking and sentiment is consistent with political action. Electoral research can additionally help to throw new light on underlying debates, both academic and practitioner centred, about the nature of managing Britain's ethnic and racial transformation since 1960. Much has been said and written of the latter, while understanding and insight of the former remains depressingly limited. The aim is to synthesise these concerns to form a single, more rounded analysis of white and ethnic minority responses to liberal values, policy and practice.

Attitudes of ethnic minorities: racial issues and issues of race

The volume of research concerned with ethnic minority political attitudes and behaviour has grown tremendously over the past twenty-five years.

Beginning with Deakin's (1965) pioneering study a continuing feature of a lot of this work has been a sense of imprecision at the very least over the distinctiveness of ethnic minority political attitudes. This question has usually been left on the backburner by a number of researchers and it has been only comparatively recently that a coherent debate between different perspectives has emerged. We have touched on this debate, setting the conventional school of thought against an increasingly vocal counter interpretation at the very start of this study. It is worth restating one or two key elements. One end of the spectrum is occupied by those who have argued the case that the political attitudes and outlook of ethnic minorities can be united under a single banner of shared political interest and persuasion (Werbner, 1991a). The commonality of shared interest is basically driven by ethnic group membership, but it is important to stress that group membership needs to be described in terms of a firm causal relationship with attitude formation and sustenance. In fact, it is clear that researchers and commentators who hold sympathy with this school of thought are commonly found searching for or perhaps merely experimenting with the notion of an ethnically-related theory of thinking and behaving politically that can be said to unite some or all minorities. Such searches and experiments have generally thrown up a mixed bag of results and it is far from clear that a strong or systematic body of theory can be said to underscore on-going research efforts in this direction.[1] That said, the 'ethnicity counts' school, if it can be dubbed as such, is more than a motley collection of incidental pieces of evidence and casual observation. Anwar (1991) in particular has attempted to trace a systematic line through the available evidence in support of this interpretation, while Azim (1996) has made some progress in unpacking the nature of political socialisation that underscores several case study examples of strong Asian collective identity. Werbner (1991b) has also made a similar point in relation to Asian political interests and mobilisation in a northern British city. Mullard's (1973) now dated work makes great play of the idea that a sweeping set of shared values and preferences underscore ethnic minority political participation, both in mainstream institutions and process as well as through fringe activities. Additionally, Purdham's (1999) limited work on Muslim groups and Labour Party participation has made the point that the forces creating collective self-interest may sometimes be external to the core characteristics of the group itself. Finally, Modood (1990) has struck a related note by linking internal and external aspects of the political construction of Muslim identity and political activism surrounding the Salman Rushdie affair. Throughout, different aspects of this literature have shown that even putting aside normative stances there is plenty of reason to view minority political attitudes in ethnically distinctive terms. Collective consciousness based on ethnic kinship is the biggest building block of this argument, but it remains to be seen how far this position itself is contingent on a transformative model of migration and settlement involving second and third generation minorities. Collective identity and political outlook can also be related to the immigrant experience and researchers have to be careful to distinguish the transitory from the universal. As we shall see later in the chapter, a lot of the evidence points to attitudinal differences that are more conditional upon context than appears to be the case at first sight.

A rival school of thought takes a more sceptical line. This group, led by the work of Studlar (1986), FitzGerald (1987) and Messina (1989, 1998), argues that at a minimum claims about a discrete racial agenda have been greatly exaggerated, and that any evidence of common attitudes has been driven by shared class and related experiences. Ethnicity, according to this view, does not count in any fundamental or lasting way, but it may be the cornerstone of political strategy and mobilisation. Whatever the extent of this behaviour, the sceptics have been quick and keen to stress that it is essentially behaviour resulting from circumstantial factors (e.g. education, employment, housing and related conditions of exclusion of which minorities are disproportionately the subjects). The missing link for these commentators is the question of a sense of collective consciousness built on the immediate foundations of ethnicity and ethnic loyalty. Here, it is said, there remain a number of opportunities to found and nurture such ethnic consciousness but in the main these chances have either been missed (at best) or vastly inflated in terms of realistic strategy (at worst). In any case, the political outlook of ethnic minorities is mainly driven by the socio-economic and other circumstances in which they find themselves, and the fact of common circumstances and experiences does not necessarily mean that ethnicity has played an important part. In fact, it probably has not, though the task is to separate out heated rhetoric (of which there is plenty) from sober evidence (of which there is still not a great deal).

A race agenda?
The basic confusion that has emerged in the literature centres on the extent to which it is possible to makes claims for ethnic minorities as a discrete and coherent political interest. As Messina (1998: 48–9) notes, the difficulty has arisen from a failure to answer two questions. First, since 'non-whites and whites share similar policy priorities' (Messina, 1998: 49), it is not at all easy to see how their collective political interests can be said to be sufficiently distinctive from their more numerous white counterparts. In other words, while some minorities adhere to a strongly distinctive platform of interests and concerns, the same is not true of the bulk of ethnic minorities. This creates a major problem in terms of mapping the route and style of minority political representation. Secondly, and perhaps even more awkwardly, there is growing evidence

to show that ethnic minorities are far from an ideologically homogeneous social group within the electorate. Attitudes tend to vary on range of public policy questions and elements of these intra-minority divisions tend to follow ethnic lines, i.e. separating Asian opinion from that of blacks. Indeed, the absence of a single body of opinion among minorities also extends in part to some of the traditional concerns of race relations such as immigration control, policing and even the role of government in integration policy. The upshot is that, once again, the job of articulating a strategy for the representation of these collective interests becomes yet more elusive. Messina (1998: 49) concludes that 'it is far from clear what these shared interests are'. If this is indeed the case, then it is also important to note that quite a lot has been claimed in the name of minority representation that is founded on lines that are distinctive, if not occasionally separate, from the political representation of whites. All this leads to an even bigger question, namely: to what extent are ethnic minorities and their interests satisfactorily integrated into the mainstream political process? In order to address this question it is necessary to do two things. First, we must unpack the confusion over the political concerns and interests of ethnic minorities, and secondly, we need to explore the factors that have led to the belief, however poorly founded in evidence, that these are not well served by political institutions that cater for the representation of political interests.

In its most extreme form, the claim has been made that ethnic minorities are characterised by a separate and discrete set of opinion on issues that are not shared by whites and probably rejected by white opinion as being racially divisive. The most obvious ground for this view has not been any casual sense of collective group consciousness but rather that racial discrimination and on-going racial exclusion persists on a large scale in British society. In sloganeering terms, this amounts to the cry that 'Britain is a racist country' and that specific institutions, notably those of public authority, are guilty of treating minorities in an inferior way to whites. In Britain in recent years there has been little doubt that such a viewpoint continues to hold sway in several quarters. Radical black and Asian leaders have repeated the charge during and beyond the Stephen Lawrence affair, citing that if an institution such as the Metropolitan Police could be described as practising 'institutional racism' then there remained little reason to believe that the fate of minorities would be much better in society at large. Of course, those taking this position from the Lawrence episode were joined by a sympathetic chorus among influential members of the press, and it is exceptionally hard to know in this case whether the label of 'institutional racism' meant anything more than strong or endemic racism.

It has become less common to come across strong claims of this sort. For one thing, it has been hard to sustain a rounded, coherent view of the world that is founded on racial divisions, that is, other than viewpoints found among racial extremists both white and non-white. One prominent illustration of an attempt to build an institutional fabric based on such universalistic racial thinking can be seen in the experience of the Black Sections movement within the Labour Party. Radical minority campaigners in Labour circles from the late 1970s onward pressed for greater recognition of their concerns and increasingly for a form of institutional autonomy within the party's ranks (LPRAG, 1979). The argument that ran through the core of this intra-party movement was that a solid racial dimension to British politics had effectively been frozen out of high level, serious debate over a number of years. The principal reason for this exclusion, so the criticism ran, was that a form of blind, unwitting racism – echoed years later in the Macpherson Report on the Stephen Lawrence affair – had been present throughout in the various ranks of the party. Ultimately, it was felt that the party's own limitations in addressing its internal racial exclusion (of both issues and of candidate-activists) was rather more than a residual irritation faced by radicals within the party. Rather, this problem constituted a major flaw in the party's long-term ability to aggregate and represent the supposedly discrete interests of ethnic minorities. The question of how far the Labour Party has succeeded in tackling this task is a matter that is taken up more extensively later on this chapter. However, the important point to stress here is that this critique of Labour had by the mid-1980s resulted in strong pressure to establish institutional reforms within the party. Many of these pressures were equally resisted by others within the party taking a more moderate line and also taking issue with the core criticism that suggested the party was riddled with racist procedures, practices and values.

The point to draw out of this debate over Black Sections is not so much that radical and moderate voices differed in their assessments of racism within the party but, rather, that the eventual lines of disagreement were also mapped on the basis of ethnic group membership. In other words, Black Sections also involved a basic debate over the relevance and presumed centrality of the common experience of racism. This experience was said to bind together blacks, Asians and other ethnic minorities, and was in essence conceptualised in racially exclusive terms. That is, it was the personal experience of minorities, whether actual or in principle, that counted in determining the calculus of authenticity and conviction in the party's internal debates over race. The role of white liberal opinion was at best viewed with caution and suspicion. Indeed, the prevailing value system that had placed weight on cross-racial campaigns to tackle racism within and beyond politics was taken by many radicals as a target to be assaulted. The position of Roy Hattersley, then one of the most vocal opponents of Black Sections, is particularly remembered as encapsulating the division. His argument, championing the liberal cause, centred on the indictment that Black Sections stood to legitimise racial barriers and exclusion, or 'reverse Apartheid' in the slogan of the times. This, liberals argued, would undermine the party's more general claim to remove racial discrimination in society. However, the counter-criticism launched against Hattersley, more or less personally, was that his argument represented an outdated form of white paternalism that would render ethnic minorities ever more dependent on white political leadership. This attack was rather more personal and heated in reality.

At its heart, the dispute revolved around this basic question of how far, if at all, progressive white opinion could empathise with and internalise the experience of minorities. The question has been put in a number of more complex ways both before and after the height of the Black Sections episode. It highlights very effectively the intellectual and tactical position taken by radicals in their philosophy of black (and minority) autonomy based on authenticity of experience and perspective. Additionally, the Black Sections movement not only reflected but also contributed substantially to the growth in such thinking in British ethnic minority politics. As FitzGerald (1990: 21–6) notes, all parties have subsequently had to address aspects of the fall-out from this original debate. There were many in all the major parties in the 1990s who conceded more readily than before that elements of the Black Sections critique cannot be dismissed out of hand. The leadership of all the parties is clear in its rejection of discrete institutional bodies for ethnic minorities, yet is also willing to accept that a limited degree of autonomy cannot and probably ought not to be resisted. Pragmatic politics, in other words, has meant that contrary to common belief key aspects of the discrete racial agenda advocated by Black Sections supporters and others have been recognised in mainstream British politics. The Black Sections movement may have yielded little by way of genuine sectional autonomy, but its passion and commitment has undoubtedly meant that a 'racial dimension' is taken more seriously in mainstream political circles. As the discussion later in this chapter goes on to observe, the evidence on minority political attitudes shows that the argument might be taken a little too seriously.

The difficulty faced by researchers in this area is to find a way of gauging the extent to which the political attitudes and outlook of ethnic minorities is founded *exclusively* on racial difference. It may be quite easy to show that minorities have some degree of sympathy with the notion that minority group membership sets minorities apart from their white counterparts in terms of their experiences and ability to empathise with minority racial experience. However, this may be a long way short of deep and widespread sympathy (though there is disagreement over how this sentiment might be reliably measured). Additionally, there remains a powerful distinction between underlying support for this position, on the one hand, and willingness to accept racial divisions as informing and influencing political attitudes, on the other. Voting on these kinds of grounds is yet another matter, the evidence for which remains patchy and difficult to interpret. Research that is to be meaningful must, therefore, seek empirical evidence that shows a sustained pattern of political attitudes exclusively or even overwhelmingly based on racial difference and division. It is on this basis that it may be possible to speak meaningfully of a race agenda in British politics. Such an agenda is a powerful interpretative tool for those seeking to explain minority participation in British politics. Sustained supportive evidence of this kind amounts to reliable grounds for an ethnically-related theory of political behaviour described earlier in the chapter. The challenge in theoretical terms is to identify and describe the race and race-related prism through which the world in perceived and understood politically.

In broad terms, it is no secret that empirical evidence to support this position has been extremely limited and is often reliant on unacceptable levels of interpretative stretching. Take for instance the notion that a core race agenda might be based on a collective view held by ethnic minorities which sees Britain in racially hostile and exclusive terms. A survey undertaken by NOP in the early 1990s sought to test this claim and reported that a surprising four-fifths of black respondents accepted that 'Britain was a very or fairly racist society' (Kellner and Cohen, 1991). However, two caveats are attached to this powerful finding. First, the attitudes of blacks' peers among the Asian community, who might have been expected to follow a similar path, were less emphatic: two-thirds agreed with the same proposition, suggesting a level of variance that is not immediately explicable. Some have suggested that such a proposition merely reflects attitudes that commonly follow socio-economic progress among different ethnic groups, but is important to remember that the race agenda thesis is essentially a racial cognitive prism rather than a racial monitor of experience. The two dimensions are undoubtedly inter-linked as experience ordinarily informs frameworks of perception. However, we should be concerned that a large number of Asians dissented from this view in comparison with black respondents. Secondly, the NOP data also reveal that 56 per cent of white respondents also adopted the same view. This finding renders somewhat obsolete the idea that quasi-universal views based on racial difference are the product of actual minority group membership. In fact they are not, and the closeness of the Asian–white findings are significant barriers to the development of any world-view of a race agenda. That said, earlier work from writers such as Miles (1978) and Troyna (1979) has reminded us that attitudes about racial and ethnic distance might be less about white-dominated society and more intertwined with feelings of strong reactive ethnic pride. So-called 'cultures of resistance', as some have put it, draw equally on counter-hostility toward 'white society' and white-dominated institutions, on the one hand, and on group assertiveness and self-promotion, on the other. The point that matters, then, is that talk of a race agenda ought probably to allow for minority attitudes that are not just focused on British society but also sensitive to group consciousness and solidarity. The latter can be a potentially powerful resource for the creation and sustenance of collective political identity and action.

An even more ambitious attempt to identify the basis for a race agenda has been the suggestion that ethnic minorities may be distanced from broad visions of British history and traditions. Some of these visions, it is argued, are at best indirectly hostile to the historic background of minorities and, at worst, might be cynically designed to incite greater inter-racial chauvinism than already exists. In a recent report from the Institute of Public Policy Research, a left-leaning think-tank, the complaint was made that a progressively-minded Labour administration was guilty of using old, out of date visions of British history that could only alienate black and Asian Britons (Alibhai-Brown, 1999). Quoting Tony Blair's 1996 remarks acclaiming 'a thousand years of British history' and boasting of 'the largest empire the world has ever known', the report's author responded with the claim that: 'Black and Asian Britons are unlikely to feel much enthusiasm for this particular British achievement. [Blair's speech is] a case of political leadership attempting to address the aspirations of one section of the population at the expense of the rest.'

The logic of this indictment was that minorities stood on one side of this vision of national history while their white counterparts remained on the other. Indeed, at one level the proposition could hold sufficient weight if tested against the likelihood of different ethnic groups attaching themselves to such a vision. However, looking beyond likelihood measures, there is also a need to consider whether the levels of tacit approval of or even endorsement for such a speech, in fact, contrast between white and non-white groups. Furthermore, there remains the obvious Achilles heel in the IPPR charge: how far does the evidence point directly to white opinion falling on the other side to minority opinion? The claim, in other words, takes as read that white people cannot possibly support an anti-imperialistic line in relation to British history. This surely cannot be defended in the sense that a range of opinion can be found on this vision among whites and, it might be added, even among some ethnic minorities. If quasi-imperialist visions of national history are said to be the kinds of building blocks underpinning a race agenda separating whites from ethnic minorities, the primary difficulty lies in demonstrating in evidence that this fissure both exists and goes beyond differential likelihood. Certainly, the US case often reminds us that Southern Confederate models of national or just even regional history can certainly act as a powerful ideological and cultural cleavage between racial and ethnic groups. In that sense, the IPPR claim must necessarily be taken seriously. However, it requires adequate empirical testing in order to allow useful conclusions to be drawn. Such a rigorous exploration remains wanting for the time being, though some further light is thrown on this question later in the chapter.

The NOP and IPPR examples cited above illustrate a continuing problem. That is, although some survey data can reveal evidence of common feeling and sentiment about race and race-related matters, it is less successful in mapping the depth of such attitudes. Opinion comparing whites and ethnic minorities on a particularly sensitive and reliable indicator might be skewed in one particular direction according to certain data. However, little can be deduced about how strongly such attitudes are held. Indeed, one of the biggest bugbears in the literature is the recurring tendency of researchers and commentators to assume that minority voters are equally motivated by a set of core racial concerns. To compound this basically ill-informed assumption, the analytical distortion is made substantially worse by the accompanying belief that these supposed racial concerns are either the biggest influences upon minorities (at best) or an exclusive causal influence pushing out all other factors (at worst). The latter is a restatement of the analytical approach taken by supporters of the racial agenda school of thought and is certainly a large and questionable assumption to make casually.

In many respects the evidence has over the years pointed to a striking similarity between the political agenda of whites and ethnic minorities in Britain. That is to say, where minorities (or minority sub-groups) highlighted attachment to specific issues that did not fully square with the pattern shown by their white counterparts, this difference was normally easy to explain and thought to be linked to apparently known factors. For instance, a now dated 1991 survey of Asian voters by Harris revealed that a noticeable 37 per cent of respondents felt that racial attacks were the most pressing issue they faced (Harris Research Centre, 1991). The findings of this evidence have been replicated through more recent surveys and also show similar patterns among black and other ethnic minority voters. However, the main point about the 1991 results was that the racial dimension of political issues was conspicuously not interpreted in any generalised, non-specific terms. Quite the contrary was true, namely that race and racism were explicitly linked to hostility and/or violence. This did not imply that these respondents were unconcerned about the effects of racism in other spheres, and indeed one interpretation might be that sentiment about racial attacks was the tip of a much larger iceberg that related to wider feelings of victimhood, both individual and collective, held by Asians. The impact of race appeared to leave more than one-third of Asians feeling especially vulnerable to a particular kind of violence and intimidation. The priority of the issue could possibly be limited to a set of law and order concerns but might equally be a mask for much deeper-seated worries over security. The former spin would allow us to conclude that the race agenda amounted to a racialised aspect of otherwise mainstream issues over law and order. The latter, however, is less easy to force into this type of analytical straightjacket. This account suggests that a form of personal and group vulnerability, leading to the potential for defensive group consciousness, was hidden beneath the superficially narrow racial attacks issue. There is great scope for generalisation about the impact of race seeping into numerous indirectly connected issues and, possibly, shaping the agenda for new political issues altogether, a point made earlier in Chapter 2. We can see, then, that advocates of the racial agenda school of thought also rely on a somewhat broader reading of the evidence. Placing white and minority attitudinal responses against each other does not end by merely reporting overt lines of departure between them. Rather there is an assumed need to account for these differences in a way that is not just circumstantial but also geared to uncovering the cross-cutting and indirect influence of race among political issues as a whole.

Testing basic attitudinal differences

In order to obtain some mileage on the question of how far ethnic minority attitudes differ internally, it is necessary to extend our analytical frame. This question is usually posed because of an underlying belief or assumption that suggests that ethnic minorities are or can be in part treated as a collective political constituency. Much has already been discussed about this proposition in earlier chapters in this study. However, the task is to develop this general proposition into a more substantial hypothesis that can be tested empirically. This may not allow exhaustive treatment of the hypothesis but it should certainly permit a useful attempt to be made at addressing the question of what empirically constitutes a discrete political constituency.

In this section of the chapter different sets of political and social issues are grouped together to form the nucleus of a racial or ethnic political agenda. It has already been noted that the traditional parameters of such an issue agenda tended to be driven by familiar themes such as immigration control and legal equality. In many respects these familiar themes have declined in core salience over the years such that by the early twenty-first century it is fairly meaningless to claim that black and Asian ethnic minorities are solely or even largely motivated politically by the desire to liberalise immigration policies. At one level, such perspectives not only miss the real possibility that minorities might find traditional bread-and-butter issues of greater salience but also run the real risk of failing to capture accurately contemporary minority voter sentiment on issues such as immigration. The findings of the Harris survey of Asian voters in 1991 mentioned previously uncovered the fact that a substantial proportion of respondents from this ethnic group did not, in fact, hold such liberal views on immigration policy as had previously been – and still – thought. Around one-fifth of Asians in the survey reported that the (then) present immigration controls were either 'about right' or 'not tough enough' (Harris Research Centre, 1991). Superficially it may appear that this sub-group had adopted a stance out of line with its objective interests. However, to these respondents other factors may have prevailed in their assessment, and it may even be that other relevant evidence or arguments persuaded them that strong immigration controls were in fact supportive of Asian political interests. Such a claim is meaningful only to the extent that a common bond can be show to exist among Asian voters who are reasonably content to recognise the discriminatory impact of such controls on fellow Asians if not themselves directly. This group, though in the minority among Asians, had clearly distinguished themselves from others who were more likely to be subjected to tougher immigration controls. However, the underlying point that this evidence brings home is that these respondents not only distinguished themselves from what may have been thought of as conventional Asian opinion, but they had also managed to create distance between themselves and the notion of collective Asian political interests based on this kind of traditionally high profile issue. Whether such distance also existed in relation to other familiar 'Asian issues' or 'ethnic minority issues' is not apparent from the 1991 Harris data and is therefore the line of inquiry that is pursued below.

Using questions within the 1997 BES cross-section survey, it is possible to construct a form of proxy agenda for issues of ethnic diversity. These differ somewhat from earlier notions of what comprised 'ethnic minority issues', partly in terms of the changed salience attached to immigration policy but also partly the evolving nature of British debates over ethnic pluralism. Thus, we have chosen to examine three aspects of racial and ethnic relations in contemporary Britain. The first concerns the old chestnut that multiculturalism is about a spirit of open-mindedness in which quite superficial differences (in this case concerning dress codes) are permissible and possibly promoted. This bears on attitudes towards social tolerance and cultural relativism. In addition, one of these questions (on the extent of racial prejudice) is likely to elicit highly subjective responses from among different ethnic groups and is mainly introduced to test whether any large variations exist across different minority groups. Lastly, there is an item seeking assessments of the role of law in curbing discrimination, a rather different matter to prejudice and focused on the proposition that behaviour can and should realistically be influenced by public policy. In all three cases these questions were only administered in the 1997 ethnic minority boost and therefore results are limited to our five principal minority groups studied. These are described in Tables 6.1–6.3 below. These results highlight some interesting points of solidarity and division among Britain's ethnic minorities.

Discrimination and legal remedy

It would appear on the basis of Table 6.1 that there is a discernible hierarchy distinguishing those groups that believe racial prejudice is widespread and endemic from those taking a more relaxed line. Just over one-third of all Asians take the former view, with very little variance among different Asian communities. However, substantially more blacks believe that there is a lot of discrimination in Britain, with close to two-thirds of black Caribbeans holding this perception. The levels for those who felt that 'a little' discrimination existed were roughly inversely correlated with those who felt the problem was much greater. The upshot of this was that more than 4 in 5 of all groups were unable to dismiss the extent of racial discrimination. This suggests that whatever the differences between groups in their assessment of degree virtually all ethnic minorities were united in seeing discrimination as a problem. This does not necessarily mean that views were generally shared as to the causes or consequences of discrimination, let alone questions of responses to it by government and others. Perceptions of societal discrimination represent an often highly subjective view of collective and individual attitudes, and as such concerns something that remains fairly abstract in relation to the political process. It is not even clear whether such an assessment even has anything to do with the political process directly. However, it still amounts to an important background factor in the eyes of ethnic minorities, irrespective of whether or not they or even some among them choose to build elements of political thought or action on the basis of such a consideration.

Table 6.1 *Ethnic minority attitudes and aspects of ethnic pluralism (extent of racial prejudice), 1997*

	Ethnic group (%)					
	Indian	Pakistani	Bangladeshi	Black African	Black Caribbean	Miscellaneous
Do you think that there is racial prejudice against blacks and Asians in GB?						
A lot	38.1	38.8	37.9	48.6	56.4	54.5
A little	54.0	45.5	51.7	44.0	34.9	40.3
Hardly any	6.0	12.7	5.2	3.7	4.8	0.0
DK/not answered	1.9	3.0	5.2	3.7	1.8	5.2
Total N	265	134	58	109	166	77
Total %	100.0	100.0	100.0	100.0	100.0	100.0

Source: see Table 4.1, p. 94.

Table 6.2 *Ethnic minority attitudes and aspects of ethnic pluralism (efficacy of anti-discrimination law), 1997*

	Ethnic group (%)					
	Indian	Pakistani	Bangladeshi	Black African	Black Caribbean	Miscellaneous
Can any law against racial discrimination work?						
Current law effective[a]	46.7	42.5	55.2	37.6	31.9	35.1
Yes	19.6	30.6	8.6	22.0	27.7	18.2
No	17.4	13.4	20.7	29.4	35.5	22.8
DK/not answered	14.4	13.4	15.5	11.0	4.8	13.0
Total N	265	134	58	109	166	77
Total %	100.0	100.0	100.0	100.0	100.0	100.0

Note: [a]those satisfied with current law as effective not asked question.
Source: see Table 4.1, p. 94.

Table 6.3 *Ethnic minority attitudes and aspects of ethnic pluralism (tolerance of separate dress codes), 1997*

	Ethnic group (%)					
	Indian	Pakistani	Bangladeshi	Black African	Black Caribbean	Miscellaneous
Should schools allow traditional dress to be worn by immigrant children?						
Definitely should	18.5	37.3	44.8	22.9	18.7	22.1
Probably should	23.0	32.1	32.8	24.8	32.5	32.5
Probably should not	24.2	13.4	6.9	15.6	19.9	15.6
Definitely should not	30.9	17.2	6.9	33.0	25.9	23.4
DK/not answered	3.4	0.0	8.6	3.7	3.0	6.5
Total N	265	134	58	109	166	77
Total %	100.0	100.0	100.0	100.0	100.0	100.0

Source: see Table 4.1, p. 94.

Not much needs to be added to Table 6.1 by way of narrative. It seems to reveal only the smallest of inter-minority variations in response. The biggest message is that there is a slightly greater intensity behind the opinion of black respondents than Asians who believe that racial discrimination exists in Britain. The general structure of opinion among all groups is fairly similar beyond this distinction about the extent of discrimination. These data confirm suspicions that racial discrimination is perceived to be a feature of British society by quite considerable numbers of ethnic minorities and, as such, remains an issue that cannot be easily dismissed.

We can see that in Table 6.2 there were considerable inter-group differences on the appropriateness and strength of law to tackle racial discrimination. In a key sense, these data take the question of societal discrimination a stage further by bouncing the essentially abstract against the tangible domain of legal remedy. The responses have to be interpreted with a touch of caution because the first row of the table isolates and filters out responses from those who have already (in a previous question) declared that the current legal arrangements were proving effective. For simplicity, we can label these respondents as being contented with the status quo, that is, those who unlike the second row shun the need for extensions to current law. While variations are clear from these two rows, it is not at all clear whether they follow any noticeable pattern. At most, there is something of a tendency among Asians to back the former position to a greater degree than their black counterparts. To that extent, it is possible to speak of an Asian near-majority who would in principle not welcome further extensions of anti-discrimination laws, though it would be stretching things to claim that they were knowingly, let alone actively, opposed to such a measure. (The assumption behind the question is that any new law on this front would involve a significant extension of provision and not merely comprise minor amendment of the extant laws.[2]) In any case, the comparable rate of 'contented' blacks appears rather lower than for Asians and some limited mileage can be gained from this. The bigger point, however, must be that between one-third and a half of all minorities believe that existing laws in this area are working tolerably well. The survey points to some unexpected findings for those respondents who fall outside the 'contented' category. Certainly, both black groups take a markedly more pessimistic view: around 1 in 3 reported that such laws did not work in any case as compared with rather less than one-fifth of Asians. Whether this amounts to a sober reflection of their experiences or whether this should be interpreted as a bucket of cold water for those favouring extended laws is a moot point, however.

Added together, it would seem reasonable to conclude that in terms of measuring active propositions in response to racial discrimination rather less unites ethnic minorities than the previous assessment of the extent of discrimination. In that sense, it would be wise to express a note of caution in trying to build an agenda of common interest around the issue of legal protection and its possible reinforcement through major reform. Indeed, although groups vary from one to another, the findings showed the greatest level of consistent support for the view that laws can be and are effective in dealing with this problem. Therefore, a form of common interest can be said to exist in respect to defending and retaining those legal protections that already exist. This common shield can have relevance in those political debates that involve the possibility of abolition of Britain's race relations laws. Such debates have not, in truth, been widespread since the very early 1980s at which time a new radical Conservative administration raised, and then dropped, this patently symbolic and doubtless inflammatory option. We may conclude then that beyond such extreme circumstances it is difficult to make claims that minority attitudes on anti-discrimination laws are a solid basis for an agenda of common political interest.

Cultural relativism from within

Lastly, our question exploring values of cultural relativism exposes some interesting points. The BES ethnic boost also contains a number of items relating to minority attitudes on issues such as mother-tongue teaching provision, public funding for religious schools and anti-blasphemy laws. However, each of these areas often pose more questions than they answer because they involve some element of government intervention to promote activities that may not or cannot take place of their own accord. Mother tongue education, we should remember, is rather different from the on-going use and practice of mother tongue language. By raising the possibility of its provision through publicly-funded schools suggests that this must be introduced into the schools in an active manner, though, of course, aspects of such mother tongue provision already exists in many cases at classroom level involving those who do not speak English at all. Therefore, the topic of dress codes allows us to get past this initial hurdle because this question tests attitudes in an area that is not only permissible (i.e. children would not be required to dress in one manner or another), but also reflects the acceptance of superficial difference (i.e. dress codes can be thought of as a further extension of visual differences of colour and ethnicity and even 'racial' appearance). In short, we are seeking to explore attitudes among minorities at a fairly basic level that tries, if at all possible, to navigate around more complex dilemmas over the extent to which accepting or even celebrating ethnic diversity is thought of as an end in itself. For our purposes, we are treating dress code as an end as much as possible though, naturally, there are many that have argued that this is a building block of other forms of cultural difference including aspects of the educational curriculum itself.

The differences uncovered in the table that are worthy of mention are essentially matters of degree rather than emphatic contrasts of opinion. Indians along with black Africans and Caribbeans are in support of such a dress code option but rather less equivocally than Pakistanis and Bangladeshis (containing between 37 and 45 per cent who definitely endorse such a position). Equally, it is the Indian group that stands out among the opponents: close to 1 in 2 believed that a different dress code option within schools probably or definitely should not be allowed. Among Bangladeshis, just 14 per cent took this stance and among Pakistanis the comparable figure was twice this rate (31 per cent). It is possible that this line of intra-Asian difference is attributable to internal cultural factors linked to the heavily rural and agrarian background of the latter groups at the point of migration. Indians, especially those with East African origins, have been drawn from a somewhat more urban background in which mixed forms dress has been more common. Additionally, there may also be an influence from the length of residency in Britain, with newer immigrant groups more likely to want to hold on to their traditional dress patterns including and perhaps especially, if possible, for their children within schools. However, while this factor may apply to the Bangladeshi group (with its much more recent immigration history), it is less appropriate as a factor in relation to Pakistanis (roughly as long-standing as Indians).

The cultural explanation can go only so far, however, once we take into account very high levels of opposition among black respondents (in line with the rates for Indians). In other words, the retention of dress codes as a metaphor for cultural relativism and space appears to distinguish Pakistanis and Bangladeshis, on the one hand from the remaining minority groups on the other. This suggests that such attitudes might be linked to other underlying attitudes towards the pace and nature of integration in Britain. Aspects of the dress code question are likely to have an impact among certain minority groups as part and parcel of wider assessments about those issues that matter more than other issues. For black respondents, the issue might simply hold less salience to begin with but, when probed, a fair amount of oppositional sentiment can be detected. Meanwhile, among Indians it may be that a more considered, even tactical, assessment is at work whereby large numbers of Indians would wish to see limits placed on such visible manifestations of cultural pluralism. The issue matters a good deal in their eyes, but for this reason many take a line that is borne of their wider feelings on (and experiences of) integration and assimilation. This wider perspective among Asian respondents allows some (Indians) to arrive at rather different conclusions to others (Pakistanis and Bangladeshis). At one level, we might surmise that wanting to hold onto or promote traditional dress codes is essentially a microcosm for much broader sentiments about the terms and desirability of cross-cultural influences and practices. In other words, it reflects matters that already exist. At another level, opinion among minorities can be thought of in more opportunistic terms whereby taking a relaxed position on this type of issue is possibly seen as compatible with rapid integration or social advancement. It is difficult to say which of these interpretations should be put on the findings but it is reasonable to say that there are no simple cultural or economic explanations. There must, therefore, be reservations about the capacity of this kind of issue to serve as the – or even a – basis for a minority political agenda. With sizeable numbers of some minorities lined up against such an option, it is clear that they are also in conflict with other minorities. Common political interest does not even extend to a base level of tolerance. It is thus reasonable to conclude that visible forms of ethnic difference do matter and probably to a greater degree than is often thought. While so much attention is placed by advocates and critics on other more complex aspects of cultural relativism (e.g. religion in the school curriculum or so-called 'separate' schools), it is wise to remember that basic questions of who wears what and when continue to be powerful everyday dilemmas for ethnic minorities themselves.

Addressing differences and similarities with white opinion
At the beginning of this chapter, stress was placed on the need to examine the extent to which white and ethnic minority Britons were characterised by discrete or overlapping political agendas. This is an important question because it further reinforces our understanding of ethnic minorities as a coherent political constituency based on a solid and identifiable set of collective political interests. In order that this case can be substantiated it is necessary to show that political attitudes and opinions can in fact be predicted, however broadly, on the basis of ethnic group. There are two related levels at which this kind of investigation can be fleshed out. First, we shall look at white and ethnic minority opinion on selected aspects of racial and ethnic concerns. Here we aim to test the structure of opinion on the general sense of value that different groups attach to non-white immigration (in order to gauge the extent to which strongly anti-immigrant and anti-minority sentiment might continue to set whites apart from their black and Asian counterparts). We then look at attitudes toward the nature, pace and underlying desirability of immigrant or newcomer adaptation (checking to see if this traditional bugbear of Britain's older immigration debate any longer distinguishes whites from others). Thereafter, we turn to consider the evidence surrounding a high profile policy principle – positive discrimination – that is frequently mentioned within public race relations debates (an area where it might be thought that white or minority group membership is a firm predictor of opinion). A second level of analysis is taken up later in this section when evidence is reviewed in relation to group attitudes on so-called mainstream issues.

In Table 6.4 it is immediately clear that white ethnic group membership amounts to a rather powerful basis on which to distinguish respondents' attitudes. About 1 in 5 whites endorse the view that such immigration has been beneficial to British society, though, incidentally, this proportion comprised just 2.4 per cent who thought that immigration had been 'very good'. Interestingly, around two-thirds of all minority groups embraced the benefits of immigration. It is hard to tell whether this question was interpreted by minorities as a comment on their own contribution (i.e. it would be inconsistent to think non-white immigrants' contribution and an individual immigrant's contribution were either both positive or negative simultaneously). Furthermore, specific respondents might also have used the question to volunteer opinion about the contribution of their own ethnic group as immigrants as opposed to the value of black and Asian immigration at large. In any case, white and non-white opinion is revealed to be sharply different on this question. This in turn

168 · Race and representation

Table 6.4 *Value of non-white immigration, 1997*

	Ethnic group (%)						
	White	Indian	Pakistani	Bangladeshi	Black African	Black Caribbean	Miscellaneous
Do you believe immigration by blacks and Asians has been good or bad for GB?							
Very/fairly good for GB	19.5	65.8	65.6	67.2	65.2	63.2	55.2
Neither good nor bad	41.1	23.7	17.9	17.2	22.0	21.1	22.9
Fairly/very bad	36.6	6.8	8.9	3.4	5.5	12.0	17.1
DK/not answered	2.9	3.8	3.7	12.1	7.3	3.6	4.8
Total N	3471	266	134	58	109	166	105
Total %	100.0	100.0	100.0	100.0	100.0	100.0	100.0

Notes: Includes 'don't knows'.
Source: See Table 4.1, p. 94.

suggests that a common political interest for ethnic minorities does exist at the level of defending and promoting the basic value, and thus legitimacy, of post-war immigration from south Asia, Africa and the Caribbean. Legitimacy issues are raised in this defence principle since it is arguable that one core element of the politics of race and ethnicity in contemporary British politics is the possibly unresolved matter of the long-term political and social acceptance of this chapter of post-war history. Certainly, anti-immigrant political voices and factions have consistently emphasised this point. In the eyes of those hostile to immigration and immigrants, there is presumably potential in trying to build a common white interest from the raw material of not just the 'sceptics' (37 per cent who saw only immigration's 'bad' side), but also through appealing to the fence-sitters who constitute a further two-fifths of all whites.

If testing opinion on the value of immigration is a necessary first step in building a rounded picture, what can be said of opinion on the integration of immigrants and their offspring now settled in Britain, however much merit is attached to their presence in society? In Table 6.5 respondents were asked to comment on two fairly raw propositions that might presumably underscore basic principles of public policy. Of course, integration policy is rarely a choice between these two options but it is reasonable to think that this type of binary, mutually exclusive framework might broadly govern public attitudes. Indeed, although many respondents might believe that the practice of integration ought to be based around a compromise between these options, it is striking that quite small numbers (from any ethnic group) felt unable to give an answer.[3] The results indicate that important variations exist in opinion both across white and non-white boundaries as well as within ethnic minorities. For instance, the solid 71 per cent of whites who back the proposal that immigrants need to 'blend and adapt into society' is little different from the 66 per cent of black Caribbeans who appear to take a similar line. In fact, in

Table 6.5 *Attitudes toward customs and traditions of immigrants, 1997*

	Ethnic group (%)						
	White	Indian	Pakistani	Bangladeshi	Black African	Black Caribbean	Miscellaneous

Is it better for immigrants to keep customs and traditions or to adapt and blend into society?

	White	Indian	Pakistani	Bangladeshi	Black African	Black Caribbean	Miscellaneous
Keep customs and traditions	22.9	34.6	41.8	60.3	34.9	25.9	29.5
Adapt and blend	71.1	54.1	54.5	29.3	56.0	65.7	61.0
DK/not answered	6.1	11.3	3.7	10.3	9.2	8.4	9.5
Total *N*	3471	266	134	58	109	166	105
Total %	100.0	100.0	100.0	100.0	100.0	100.0	100.0

Notes: Includes 'don't knows'.
Source: See Table 4.1, p. 94.

broad terms clear majorities among all minority groups are prepared to endorse this position with the notable exception of Bangladeshi respondents (where attitudes are more than reversed). It is not immediately clear why this pattern is as it is and there is little obvious reason, other than length of residence, that might separate out the Bangladeshi group.

In general, some degree of common interest can be said to exist across white and most minority groups on this question. This generalisation applies in relation to both sides of the argument on integration policy and it would, therefore, be quite difficult to claim that attitudes across white and non-white groups could not be reconciled. In fact, the evidence from this table seems to imply that several 'adapt and blend' type of trade-offs are already at play among the large majority of Britons, irrespective of the ethnic group to which they belong. To try to build a political agenda of common interest among just ethnic minorities alone would, in short, be to miss the point that such a coalition's most numerous and possibly most prized component are white members of British society.

Finally, it is also worth probing the structure of opinion on an issue that might be expected to be controversial and divisive. Previously we looked at white and non-white opinion on basic strategies shaping the lifestyles and patterns that immigrants ought to follow in a normative sense. However, having noted that a large majority of white and non-white opinion was in favour of 'adaptation and blending', does it follow that this is a good guide to opinion in more concrete policy areas? The answer will tend to depend on the policy proposal itself and in Table 6.6 we focus on the loose but commonly cited doctrine of positive discrimination. The question asked of respondents restricts the parameters of opinion about this doctrine to the area of employment, thus trying to ensure that an otherwise open-ended concept is viewed in a tangible context. Equally it should be added that by focusing on jobs alone, it is always possible that the structure of opinion of positive discrimination

Table 6.6 *Positive discrimination in employment, 1997*

	Ethnic group (%)						
	White	Indian	Pakistani	Bangladeshi	Black African	Black Caribbean	Miscellaneous
Should blacks and Asians be given preference in jobs?							
Should be given priority in jobs	2.0	7.1	18.7	13.8	14.7	6.0	2.9
Should have to compete for jobs	96.7	89.1	75.4	84.5	81.7	91.0	96.2
DK/not answered	1.3	3.8	6.0	1.7	3.7	3.2	1.0
Total N	3471	266	134	58	109	166	105
Total %	100.0	100.0	100.0	100.0	100.0	100.0	100.0

Notes: Includes 'don't knows'.
Source: See Table 4.1, p. 94.

principles might be somewhat different in less pressing or competitive markets (area-based government social and regeneration policy for instance).

The findings, it must be said, are not especially surprising in the case of white respondents. Rather expectedly, just about all whites chose to turn their backs on positive discrimination in employment in favour of blacks and Asians. Such a result must surely be entirely in line with assumptions commonly held by political elites in Britain. However, the area of ethnic minority opinion is a little less straightforward. At one level it is true that overwhelming majorities within all these groups follow the path of their white counterparts on this issue. At another level, however, it is worth noting that this generalisation is a shade less true of some minorities than others. Three groups (Pakistanis, Bangladeshis and black Africans) all contain some notable elements of dissenting opinion, though, to be fair, these numbers never exceed more than one-fifth of a single group. Collectively across all groups, these supporters only make up a very small proportion of the population at large and in political terms they can be all but dismissed. From the perspective of constructing common political agenda, therefore, the most significant thing that can be said about this policy principle is that a substantial inter-ethnic group coalition of opinion exists. Whites, in short, have a lot in common with their black and Asian peers. To attempt to build a discrete ethnic minority agenda on this basis would be to attempt the impossible. That said, there continue to be calls in favour of selective use of this principle in public policy that at least imply that a strength of support from among black and Asian potential beneficiaries. Our evidence indicates that there is really very little basis for such a position.

Exploring mainstream issues and attitudes

Having looked at a small selection of issues that can be said to be closely and overtly linked to race and ethnicity, what of political issues in which there is no obvious association? We will turn now to consider the extent of inter-ethnic group differences or commonality in relation to a selection of such political issues. Drawing from the main BES cross-section, we can easily identify suitable issues for our inquiries that also allow direct comparison across white and non-white groups. Featured below are three further examples that test the structure of opinion in anti-poverty strategy, criminal penalties and equal opportunities for women.

Table 6.7 examines attitudinal differences in relation to the prospect of using increased public spending to tackle poverty. It is an area in which there are probably no obvious reasons to anticipate any substantial opinion variations across ethnic groups other than, of course, to note that a larger proportion of our ethnic minority than white samples will be drawn from lower down the socio-economic ladder and thus notionally closer to the experience of poverty or near poverty. Even then, the differences ought to be modest and it is not readily possible to say why, on the basis of ethnic group membership, respondents might take a different position from one another on this major area of social and economic policy. Indeed, the results tend to confirm our hypothesis in broad terms and the blip shown up by the Bangladeshi case in the table ought not to be interpreted to literally owing too the small number of respondents involved. Our conclusion has to be that this amounts to one major aspect of mainstream politics in which ethnicity holds little sway in shaping attitudes. Political agendas of common interest thus unite ethnic minorities as much as they simultaneously unite whites with ethnic minorities.

Criminal justice is another policy area in which we might be reluctant

Table 6.7 *Government spending to tackle poverty, 1997*

	Ethnic group (%)						
	White	Indian	Pakistani	Bangladeshi	Black African	Black Caribbean	Miscellaneous
Should government spend more money to get rid of poverty?							
Definitely/probably should	88.6	89.4	85.8	72.4	94.5	91.0	90.1
Doesn't matter either way	3.3	3.8	3.7	8.6	1.8	3.6	3.0
Definitely/probably should not	5.1	4.9	4.5	15.5	1.8	5.4	6.0
DK	1.0	1.9	6.0	3.4	1.8	0.0	2.0
Total N	2601	265	134	58	109	166	101
Total %	100.0	100.0	100.0	100.0	100.0	100.0	100.0

Notes: Includes 'don't knows'.
Source: See Table 4.1, p. 94.

to suggest that ethnicity serves as a significant source of division or even distinction in opinion. While aspects of law and order have regularly featured within debates over race relations, this is a far cry from the idea that all aspects of criminal justice are subject to strongly held views that vary from ethnic group to ethnic group. That said, since some groups of ethnic minorities are more likely than others to have criminal charges brought against them and in some cases to receive tougher and/or custodial sentences, we should be mindful that this type of question might conceivably contain a racial twist in its interpretation by some, if not all, respondent groups.

The pattern shown in Table 6.8 indicates that the structure of opinion is far from consistent across different groups. Indians and Pakistanis stand out somewhat as rather stronger supporters of hard-line sentencing than their other ethnic minority counterparts but why this should be the case if far from clear. Interestingly, Bangladeshis are poorly represented among these hard-liners but more than make up for lost territory by joining the ranks of the those who support tougher sentences with less certitude. In all, the proportions that line up on the side of tougher penalties, putting aside the intensity with which they do so, do not particularly vary between ethnic groups. As anticipated, this strongly implies, that there is little or no association between ethnic group membership, on the one hand and political attitudes on the other. Consequently, there is virtually no potential for constructing an agenda of common interest among ethnic minorities in this area. This conclusion might run counter to some political assumptions that hold that 'tough-on-crime' political strategies are always destined to alienate ethnic minorities.

Finally, is there some scope for thinking that attitudes towards the role and rights of women are likely to vary according to ethnic group? This notion would certainly have an intuitive drive behind it because of the wide publicity and coverage given to supposedly conservative attitudes

Table 6.8 *Criminal sentencing policy, 1997*

	Ethnic group (%)						
	White	Indian	Pakistani	Bangladeshi	Black African	Black Caribbean	Miscellaneous
Lawbreakers should get stiffer sentences							
Strongly agree	43.8	51.1	61.2	37.9	35.8	40.4	41.9
Agree	39.9	39.1	34.3	48.3	41.3	39.2	32.4
Disagree	5.0	1.9	0.7	3.4	5.5	7.2	6.7
Strongly disagree	1.0	1.1	0.0	0.0	0.0	0.6	2.9
Not sure/DK	10.4	6.7	3.7	10.3	17.4	12.6	16.2
Total N	3471	266	134	58	109	166	105
Total %	100.0	100.0	100.0	100.0	100.0	100.0	100.0

Notes: Includes 'don't knows'.
Source: See Table 4.1, p. 94.

among sections of the Asian community. While the question does not test directly attitudes on women's roles in areas that are thought to be at the heart of Asian outlook (such as the family centring on women as wives and mothers and their rights in relation to husbands), it does nevertheless border on this general topic. By reflecting attitudes against general society-based assessments, respondents are comparatively free to incorporate family-based concerns alongside others to do with areas such as women in the workplace, in education and even in media roles. Table 6.9 provides some evidence on this question.

The results reveal a picture of quite striking consistency across different ethnic groups. The 'resisters', if the first row can be dubbed in such terms, represent a fairly steady proportion among all groups. However, looking further, the table suggests that those who would like to see equal opportunities to be extended for women are rather more likely to found among the ranks of white and black respondents. These supporters are rather thinner on the ground among Asians in general. This represents a subtle yet powerful endorsement of our original supposition. Parekh (1999b: 8) citing recent data from the Universities Central Admissions System, has noted that there is little evidence to support the notion that Muslim parents are resistant to their daughters pursuing educational qualifications (UCAS, 1998). 'This is a welcome sign', he concludes, 'with obvious implications for the Pakistani and Bangladeshi communities.'

Therefore, Asian conservatism, as it is said to exist on this issue and possibly other related family-centred concerns, is partially borne out through the BES data. What is especially interesting is that such group conservatism appears to have no obvious basis other than a cultural drive; certainly, on this issue, unlike some others previously examined, there is nothing to distinguish Indian opinion from that of Pakistanis and Bangladeshis. Furthermore, the nature of the conservatism may well be

Table 6.9 *Equal opportunities for women, 1997*

	Ethnic group (%)						
	White	Indian	Pakistani	Bangladeshi	Black African	Black Caribbean	Miscellaneous
Equal opportunities for women in Britain							
Have gone much too far/gone too far	9.1	10.2	12.0	13.8	12.9	6.0	6.7
About right	48.8	56.3	50.7	51.7	43.1	36.1	40.0
Not gone far enough/not nearly far enough	40.8	27.9	30.6	27.6	40.4	56.0	49.5
DK/not answered	1.3	6.1	8.9	6.9	6.4	6.0	8.6
Total N	3471	266	134	58	109	166	105
Total %	100.0	100.0	100.0	100.0	100.0	100.0	100.0

Notes: Includes 'don't knows'.
Source: See Table 4.1, p. 94.

culturally value-driven, but it does not manifest itself especially in opinion that sees existing opportunities as having gone too far. Instead, this is reflected in a proportionately smaller chance of wanting to take such opportunities any or much further. Put in these very specific terms, it might be possible to think of an Asian-based political agenda in which the further promotion of women's rights might be seen as a very low priority (at best) or as a possible social reform to be doggedly resisted (at worst).

Notes

1 The main exception being Werbner's (1991a) essay on this theme.
2 The case of a moderate, amending law on racial discrimination is illustrated by the Race Relations (Amendment) Bill introduced by the government in the House of Lords in December 1999. The main purpose of this Bill is to extend coverage of the anti-discrimination provision of the 1976 Race Relations Act to all public bodies without, controversially, inclusion of the doctrine of indirect discrimination.
3 For this reason the 'don't know' group were retained in this and subsequent tables (Tables 6.5–6.7 inclusive) so as to illustrate the clear and widespread views held on these question.

7

Race card politics

Introduction

The notion that anti-immigrant and anti-ethnic minority sentiment underscores mass electoral behaviour has been a familiar and often depressing feature of modern British politics. Indeed, so common has this claim become in the past two generations, it is no exaggeration to say that it has emerged as something of dictum among practitioners and analysts of British politics. The race card doctrine, as this argument has become known, appears to constitute a semi-permanent feature of general elections. This ascendancy is not particularly surprising, given the nature of party competition and strategy over the immigration question in the 1960s and 1970s. The political landscape by the late 1970s appeared to be rooted in an assumption that held that the political interests of ethnic minorities were deeply unpopular among voters at large and, more controversially, that such sentiment was relatively easily turned into electoral spoils for parties wishing to exploit this truth (Crewe, 1983; Studlar, 1974; Miller, 1980). Debates have persisted on the nature and scale of this type of race card dividend but most commentators appear to concur with the view that the factor has been an important influence upon Tory and Labour strategy since the mid-1960s. The idea of a race card, therefore, is a form of political science and journalistic shorthand that refers generally to the structural advantage enjoyed by one major party over its rivals on the electoral issues of race and immigration. More specifically, in the British context the thesis concerns the head start that the Conservative Party has had over Labour on this broad issue, not least within the context of electoral unpopularity on other more mainstream issues (e.g. trade union reform and social welfare provision during the 1970s). The head of steam that had built up in the run-up to the 1997 general election surrounding the Conservative position on the race card cannot be understated. The race card, in essence, was widely thought to amount to a crucial part of a strategy by which electoral survival, possibly victory, might be pulled from the jaws of inevitable electoral defeat.

This chapter is, therefore, concerned with examining the basis for one of the most enduring assumptions about modern British electoral politics.

The assumption spans academic and journalistic commentary and effectively models the position and putative interests of ethnic minorities as a political graveyard for political parties naive enough to embrace this group. Furthermore, it implies that firm distinctions can be drawn between the political interests of ethnic minorities as against white Britons. Lastly, this wide-ranging assumption has been treated in some quarters as an iron law of white antipathy and hostility to non-white immigrants and their offspring. That is to say, this caricature is thought to unite the bulk of white opinion in a near-permanent and unchallengable way. Political parties, therefore, might choose to turn their backs on such skewed public opinion and its associated opportunities; however, traditional rational choice considerations suggest that they adopt such a line at their own peril. There are a pair of implicit suggestions that arise from parties taking the race card as some sort of irresistible force in this way: first, that political parties are both fully cognisant of the structure and character of public opinion (often operating as if they can), and second, that parties are able to alter their position on issues at short notice and with little cost to themselves (an uphill task under any conditions to be sure). The discussion in the latter part of the chapter explores these lines of awareness and flexibility in modern British politics and makes use of the issues of race and ethnicity in order to put forward an assessment of these twin suggestions. The race card in that sense amounts to a case study of wider reputed features of party competition. By testing the limits of the thesis, we might ought to be able to draw some useful conclusions about the extent to which the race card thesis has been developed on likely and plausible understandings of the underlying dynamics of parties, issues and voters.

The chapter comprises three main parts. The chapter's point of departure is a discussion of the historic context in which issues of race, ethnicity and non-white immigration have been debated in post-war British politics. Placing our analysis into this wider historic context is an important task because it reveals not only the genesis of the race card argument but also the conditions under which mass electoral politics were genuinely shaped by these issues. Furthermore, it is important to draw out links, and parallels where necessary, with similar arguments about electoral hostility to immigrants during the early twentieth century (Jewish arrivals from central and eastern Europe during 1930s and 1940s) and, to a lesser degree, the nineteenth century (Holmes, 1988). In this first part, we shall also briefly review the existing evidence relating to issue voting on the question of non-white immigration during the period between the 1960s and early 1990s. Secondly, the chapter turns to look in some detail at the debate during the mid-1990s leading up to and including the 1997 election. The context of the 1992 general election campaign is important in order to understand the context of expectations that had been set for the long campaign culminating in the spring 1997 contest. It is here that some limited yet incisive fresh evidence is presented examining not just the position of the parties but also, most crucially, the reputations that they had earned among the general electorate. At the same time, irrespective of the impact of deliberate race card strategies, it is important to note that lingering scepticism about the motives of parties continues to characterise the outlook of many ethnic minorities. The reasons for this are not hard to locate and our discussion goes on to suggest that some of this evidence can be usefully tied into our understanding of partisanship among minority voters. The reputation of the Conservative Party in the eyes of ethnic minority voters is central in this regard. Race card politics and ethnic minority voting patterns contain an important connection that has often been widely hinted at but rarely described or weighed up analytically. The final section ties up the discussion by revisiting traditional issue voting models and exploring some links across different sets of issues. In brief, this concluding section argues that the real impact of continuing anti-immigrant electoral sentiment is probably no longer felt within the limits of a single issue. Instead, it is suggested, attitudes toward race and ethnicity contain many additional influences to do with the appearance of parties as credible and veracious in the minds of voters. To that extent, the race card maybe an element in a wider picture by which parties gain, retain and forfeit credibility and with it the prospects for electoral success.

The legacy of race card electoral politics

Most of the conventional perspectives on the impact of race issues in post-war British politics have emphasised the competitive electoral advantages thought to result from pandering to anti-immigrant sentiment within the electorate. The most compelling illustration of this school of thought can be seen in the seminal work of Butler and Stokes (1969, 1974) who presented the non-white immigration question as a classic demonstration of issue voting in the 1960s. This view was based on the undoubted experience of mass electoral hostility towards immigrants and immigration at this time and further reflected in substantial academic interest in this phenomenon (see Studlar, 1978; Miller, 1980; Crewe and Sarlvik, 1980; Layton-Henry, 1986; Rich, 1986, 1998; Messina, 1989). Typically, the general elections of 1970 and 1979 are often cited for the decisive though subtle surges in Conservative electoral support on the basis of popular attitudes towards immigration. This kind of thinking has continued to play a background part in explanations of Conservative electoral strength throughout the 1980s, though attention has chiefly remained on issues of economic competence and stewardship. However, the 1992 election represented a further opportunity to revisit and extend the race card thesis (see, for instance, Billig and Golding, 1992; Hardy, 1991). The brief revival of the British National Party in local politics, on the far right of British politics, during 1993–94 has been further cause to re-examine the influence of tough, anti-immigrant sentiment upon mainstream and fringe political parties (Husbands, 1994). In this environment, a Conservative lead on economic-related issues was thought to have been whittled away, and not surprisingly some scholars sought to argue that secondary issues such as immigration, law and order and management of industrial relations had swayed the outcome. The 1992 case, in other words, came close and was presented in terms faintly reminiscent of the Smethwick episode in 1964. Both experiences, it is suggested, demonstrated an in-built attitudinal bias in the electorate's general stance towards not just immigration but additionally a bundle of intersecting race relations questions. In both cases, it took a narrowly fought campaign and a slender election result to highlight the pivotal importance of these issues. In one case, the outcome was the unexpected shock of defeat suffered by the Labour Party's Foreign Secretary-designate (Patrick Gordon-Walker). In the other, the upshot was the equally unexpected victory achieved by a party that had exhausted its ability to argue its case on the basis of core governance issues such as stable management of the economy. The eventual outcomes revealed that a secondary campaign also centred on trust and governance could indeed be waged and play a crucial part in averting what seemed as inevitable defeat.

Both of these controversial cases, and several in the years in between, served to shore up the belief that the Labour Party was subject to a semi-permanent weakness on the issue, whether narrowly or broadly defined. To claim that Labour activists and leaders have felt a sense of self-consciousness on the question is a substantial understatement at the very least. Indeed, Labour's perceived vulnerability on race has clearly become a familiar dictum in British politics. In particular, attention among voters and analysts switched away from the territory of the traditional race card, typically centred on non-white immigration, and toward the party's putative association with ethnic minority interests. A party of special interests may have been one thing, but in this case evidence and anecdote existed to show that the white electorate thought of these groups in highly pejorative and unsympathetic terms. Labour's electoral troubles, in other words, were significantly compounded by this kind of association. Moreover, it was mistakenly thought that the bias it created was a stand-alone feature of public opinion and resultant voting behaviour. This way of understanding the party's weak flank might at least have allowed the leadership of the party to tackle the perceived problem in single-issue, compartmentalised terms. Instead, the issue interlocked with a set of weak flanks. Several of these related to credibility as a potential government and therefore could not be easily isolated. While at first glance this kind of analysis may have appeared rather daunting and even depressing from the perspective of Labour's strategists, in fact, it revealed some grounds for optimism. For one thing, it allowed party policy modernisation thinking to take place in a systematic rather than a fragmented manner (Shukra, 1998a). Furthermore, the analysis indicated that the putative Conservative pivotal edge was rather more conditional and therefore more fragile than previously thought. In fact, by claiming an edge over Labour on race, the Conservatives' strategy remained plausible only so long as it dovetailed with a similar pitch made on a wider and deeper set of issues (Lansley, 1995; Peston, 1994; *The Times*, 1995). The race issue, in other words, was far from a single joker in the pack. It could only be played successfully as part of solid hand in which each card provided strength to and received strength from one another.

The legacy of the 1960s
The Smethwick experience appeared to go a long way toward recasting conventional wisdom concerning racial politics in Britain. It is easy as a consequence to think of the entire period since 1964 as part of a single continuous era in racial politics. This would be an oversimplification and it is worth setting out the basis for thinking that this period divides into three main phases. First, allowance has to be made for an early and fairly long period in which a covert national consensus operated on matters of race and immigration. This spell began very shortly after the Smethwick encounter, was reinforced by the immigration control and racial integration actions of the then Labour administration, spanned the crisis caused by Powell's 1968 interjection, and eventually fell away after Margaret Thatcher's arrival as Conservative Party Leader in 1975. In other words, any capacity to play the race card needed to take account of the extent to which this cross-party consensus managed to dampen down otherwise shrill debates over race at this time. Many commentators have observed that, though fragile at times, such a consensus proved to be remarkably resilient against this often unhelpful backdrop. Moreover, the understanding that operated across the party front benches meant that dissident opinion was often portrayed as not merely extremist but also designed to stoke up crude inter-racial animosities. Finally, account has to be taken of this era's counter-intuitive results. For instance, the Conservative leadership's firm rebuttal of Powell was about as unambiguous as could be imagined, a position that undoubtedly carried a heavy cost to Ted Heath as party leader in terms of rank and file support. Additionally, his government's bold policy gamble in giving entry to Ugandan Asian refugees in 1972 further underlined the party's sharply reduced capability – or willingness possibly – to pander to anti-immigrant opinion at the polls. The era of consensus, it should not be forgotten, also yielded three major Race

Relations Acts (enacted in 1965, 1968 and 1976, respectively), each of which involved assiduous efforts by their Labour sponsors to carry front bench Conservative backing.[1]

A second phase relates to the period following the Tory leadership change in 1975 and extends to the mid-1980s. This period contrasts rather sharply with the earlier consensus era mainly as a consequence of the conscious attempt by the then Conservative Opposition to find ways to appeal to anti-immigrant sentiment in electoral terms. This approach was itself based on a calculus that saw tactical and conditional watering down of the depoliticisation consensus as likely to lead to political gain. However, it is important to stress that this rightward shift on immigration in particular was not pursued as a policy in isolation and nor should it be interpreted a generation later (2000) in discrete terms. By contrast, it was a part of a much broader repositioning of the Conservative Party involving a range of elements of social authoritarianism (law and order, severity and responsiveness of criminal justice) and supplemental issues such as trade union reform, social welfare, individual morality and policies aimed at family cohesion and survival. The point that needs to be made here is that the party's repositioning was largely caught up in and was the product of the decline in the post-war Keynesian consensus, not merely in economic policy but also in many areas of social, industrial and family policy. One view of the Tory approach to immigration would be to see the issue from a classic Downsian perspective. This view emphasises the perfect logic of a race card strategy whereby a natural winning issue for the party could not be ignored or sidelined by vote-maximising party strategists. Realigning the official position of the party to coincide with optimality in the structure of public opinion might have been seen to some as a small matter of detail within this framework. A slightly different perspective would tend to see the party's strategic choices as a whole and explain its repositioning across a range of political issues of which race and immigration was just one limited example. This view would also note that revising policy commitments is never easy for political parties not least because of the involvement of party activists, albeit activists with rather less genuine influence than their counterparts in the Labour Party. The ironic aspect to both of these interpretations is that the Conservatives' strong line on immigration in 1979 may have been successful in the short term but in the longer term only served to expose the diminishing importance of the issue. Mainly as a result of the successful enactment on the 1981 British Nationality Act, there is little doubt that the heat began to be turned down on the issue of Commonwealth immigration as a mass political concern.

The third distinct phase can be traced from the point at which the Conservatives in government were obliged to respond to the effective end of the old immigration issues, defined as it was in terms of non-white settlers from the New Commonwealth. As already noted, legislation from the early 1980s had successfully tackled this point of public anxiety and meant that the Tories had in effect removed one of their most attractive issues from the agenda of British electoral politics. In addition, it was striking that the Conservatives' own rhetoric in opposition against race relations activists, including most notably the Commission for Racial Equality, came to little when in government and given an opportunity to address this bugbear type of issue (Rich, 1998; Saggar, 1998d). Indeed this potential onslaught against race relations activists was only one aspect of a wider series of implied promises made by a Conservative front bench that rapidly developed a reputation for shrillness on the subjects of race and immigration. There had been considerable doubts expressed by critics of this strategy, with many issuing warnings about the resurrection of the option of repatriation. Miles and Phizacklea (1984: 106–14) writing in the early 1980s argued that the underlying influence of the far right in Conservative thinking could not be underestimated. Indeed, they contended that the administration's own ability to manage a multiracial society would inevitably be driven by the search for a permanent solution to the 'problem' of 'alien' immigrant settlers and their offspring. These and other predictions turned out to be rather hollow even in the short to medium term, not least because such arguments mistook the interest of the far right within and just beyond the party on race questions to be reflections of official party policy. In fact, the most significant aspect of the period after the 1983 election was that, not only did the traditional immigration issue effectively disappear from the radar of party competition, but that this signalled the beginning of a new era of pragmatism in the approach of the Tories.

At least three core building blocks can be identified within this pragmatic trend, the sum of which undoubtedly began to take on the hallmarks of a strategy on race as opposed to a series of unco-ordinated instincts. First, the party's drift to the right on immigration during the late 1970s was paradoxically accompanied by the first systematic attempt to attract ethnic minority voters to the party cause. Inevitably this was a risky and experimental initiative but it is striking that this approach received widespread backing from right across the party. For instance, the party's Anglo-Asian Conservative Society, launched in 1976, succeeded in recruiting to serve as vice-presidents such high profile figures as William Whitelaw, Michael Heseltine and Lord Carrington from the front bench alone. Additionally, John Biggs-Davidson, well known as a stalwart campaigner for hard-line immigration policies, was also brought into the Society's circle, thereby ensuring that the party's One Nation and New Right wings were not easily alienated from one another on the issue.[2] Secondly, there were natural limitations placed on the ideological shift that the party had instigated on immigration. One of the most prominent of these limits was the reaction of conservative-minded critics of the strategy. For example, writing in the national press, the columnist Bernard Levin rounded on Margaret Thatcher's 1978 interview in which she had talked about Britain being 'swamped' by immigrants. For Levin (1978), the offence lay in trying to reconcile this tough talk with the on-going need to take responsibility for day to day integration policy: 'You cannot by promising to remove the cause of fear and resentment fail to increase both. If you talk and behave as if black men were some kind of virus that must be kept out of the body politic, then it is the shabbiest hypocrisy to preach racial harmony at the same time.'

Thirdly, it cannot be overlooked that the constraints of office had produced a number of disciplines upon radical thinking on race. At the top of the list was the party's sudden need to address itself to the causes and consequences of the urban disorders of 1980 and 1981. While these riots were not particularly racial in character, it was nevertheless clear that the management of the Conservative government's response would be seen as indicative of its general attitude to ethnic minorities in British society as well as its stance on more specific matters like increasing social mobility, tackling dislocated labour markets and boosting inner city social and physical investment. The strategy adopted in response to these problems could not have been more high profile, led as it was by the intervention of Michael Heseltine. His approach, and that of the Department of the Environment, sought to recognise the legitimacy of many of the social causes of the riots, and in particular the initiative opted not to shy away from the role of ethnic minorities in rebuilding urban Britain. Much of the micro-detail of this strategy was picked up by Sir George Young, the minister appointed at the Department of the Environment in charge of urban policy and more specifically having the task of involving minority groups. Much of this effort was only possible against the backdrop of the inquiry report produced by Lord Scarman in 1982, in which the themes of ethnic minority exclusion and alienation were calculatedly given prominence. A few years later, the 1985 disorders served to retrench this strategy with the Department of the Environment, the Home Office and other ministries apparently keen and adamant in their desire to tackle racial disadvantage within broader urban renewal efforts. In the sum, it is possible see how the factors that had propelled the party to the right on immigration overlooked government factors that prevented the One Nation wing of the party from influencing policy in integration matters. The third period from the mid-1980s onwards, therefore, not only marks the demise of the immigration issue but also constitutes the start of a range of efforts to appear more conciliatory and engaging on questions of race.

The upshot of these various phases from the 1960s onward is to remind us that it is not wise to think of the race card in an historic vacuum.

Moreover, it is evident that Conservative thinking on the potential to harness anti-immigrant feeling has been rather more selective, even sophisticated, than is widely assumed. Finally, to argue that the race card always and consistently amounted to a veto upon Labour strategy may possibly capture the spirit of Labour's position but misses the subtlety of that position. In 1968 Richard Crossman, then a member of the Labour cabinet, described in his Diaries the awkwardness of the position in which he – and arguably his party – found himself. He wrote that: 'Mainly because I am an MP for a constituency in the Midlands, where racialism is a powerful force, I was on the side of [Home Secretary] Jim Callaghan' (Crossman, 1977: 676). The Crossman line, however, only encapsulates one part of the argument, namely the instinctive electoral vulnerability the Labour Party felt itself subject to on the traditional immigration question. There is much that can be easily recognised from this picture and it can be thought of as the intuitive school. However, a more complex and systematic position can also be identified and described. This school, best associated with the work of Crewe (1983), suggests that immigrants and ethnic minorities not only faced limited political opportunity structures (a view that at best requires significant updating given the recent findings of Le Lohé (1998) and LGMB (1998) in relation to local government representation), but that this social group had been perceived as an electoral albatross around the neck of the Labour Party. 'There are no votes to be had in embracing blacks and Asians' is in essence the flavour of this sloganised argument. The 'white, anti-ethnic vote', as it was crudely dubbed, 'could well have delivered more seats to the Conservatives than blacks have delivered to the Labour Party', reported Crewe soberly. An exploration of the evidence surrounding the electoral liability thesis, therefore, forms a central part of the agenda in the next part of the chapter.

Anti-immigrant sentiment in the 1990s
Despite the decline of the traditional immigration issue, the underlying strength of anti-immigrant feeling is a factor that cannot be dismissed in haste. For one thing, it is clear that the rise in migratory flows from the European Union, as well as into the EU from non-member sources, has gradually occupied a larger share of national political attention. Additionally, a number of developments at EU cross-border level from the mid-1980s onwards have ensured that immigration has remained on the political agenda for British national governments and opposition parties.[3] Finally, the so-called 'new' immigration question has been significantly fuelled by concerns over the numbers of asylum-seekers both across western Europe generally and arriving in Britain specifically. In the six years up to 1994 for instance, close to a quarter of a million asylum-seekers made their way to Britain, part of a picture of three

million seeking asylum throughout western Europe. The last of these factors has played a large role in feeding both press and political interest in immigration, an interest that in turn has had some resonance in public opinion. In Table 7.1 below, recent Eurobarometer data is presented to show that British public concerns about immigration numbers are both quite significant as well as fairly characteristic of public attitudes across several EU states. Indeed, the EU average looks remarkably similar to the picture of public opinion in Britain, with sizeable outliers in countries such as Greece and Finland. The main point, however, is that the data confirm rapidly the claim that substantial proportions of the British public perceive that immigrant numbers are excessive. More than 2 in 5 subscribe to the excessive numbers position, presumably also believing this to be an unacceptable number as well. Equally, a similar proportion believe that numbers are large but that this remains acceptable, again presumably while these numbers do not risk any further growth, especially in the short run. As a rough point of comparison it worth pointing out that the BES survey in 1966 revealed that 83 per cent of the electorate at that time felt that 'there were too many immigrants being allowed into the country'; moreover, some 86 per cent of respondents reported that they felt either very or fairly strongly about the immigration issue (Butler and Stokes, 1969: 468).

These data comprise only part of the wider picture concerning the potential for race card politics to influence electoral outcomes. A second and equally crucial aspect of this potential lies in the underlying saliency of public attitudes towards and interest in immigration as defined in the more European context of the 1990s. However, our analysis needs also to factor in public concerns about and feelings towards a number of other surrounding issues to do with perceptions about the rights and benefits enjoyed by ethnic minorities. Some of these minorities might be conceived of as immigrants in the sense that they are either migrants themselves or else the sons and daughters (or possibly even grandchildren) of settlers. That said, with a growing proportion of ethnic minorities no longer closely associated with the chapter of mass immigration in the 1950s and 1960s, it is important to recognise that public attitudes toward them may indeed circumvent the question of immigration

Table 7.1 *Public anti-immigrant sentiment within the EU, 1997*

Country	Views on the number of foreigners in each state (%)		
	Too many	A lot, but not too many	Not many
High (Greece)	71	27	1
EU average	45	40	10
Britain	42	40	12
Low (Finland)	10	34	53

Source: Eurobarometer, No. 48, autumn 1997, p. 71.

altogether. In that sense, our analytical focus needs to be widened out to capture the subtlety of white relationships towards non-whites generally, and to do so in a way that can also incorporate the potential for voters to reward or punish parties for their associations with the putative interests of sectional or ethnic groups.

A third dimension of the analysis concerns the part played by the political parties themselves. Consideration of this factor is partly driven by the need to communicate to the electorate the policy positions they have adopted in relation to immigrants and minorities and partly in response to distortions in the way in which voters perceive them. This aspect of the analysis mainly revolves around two related questions: first, the degree to which the parties hold divergent positions in policy and stance towards these issues; and secondly, the extent to which inter-party differences are understood by voters. In is not easy to disentangle each of the questions from one another, not least because party policy itself can be thought of as an independent variable that attempts to influence public perceptions of the position taken by the party. That said, what we are really trying to flesh out is a very interesting relationship, namely the sense by which voters believe that one or another party has interests and an outlook that conflates with those of a particular group. Such party–group relationships, and their possible costs and benefits, has been an area that has been central to a number of recent debates over the electoral crisis faced by the Labour Party during the 1980s and early 1990s (Heath et al., 1991; Heath and Curtice, 1998).

In the next section we turn to examine this problem more carefully. In particular, we are concerned with how a political party's broad identity can be translated by electors into comparatively firm propositions regarding its defence of discrete groups and causes. We are, additionally, concerned with how such an association operates and, most importantly, the extent to which this can be challenged and possibly reversed. If immigrants and ethnic minorities are really to be thought of as a political albatross around the Labour Party's neck, how far has this relationship served to damage the Labour's political fortunes? Moreover, what, if anything, has the party been able to do to mitigate against the losses that it might potentially suffer as a result? Finally, what can be said reliably about the repositioning of political parties either to recapture lost support or more modestly to avoid giving needless offence to marginal voters? The case of Labour and the road it trod back to office in 1997 is certainly one that can provide a better understanding of each of these questions.

The electoral albatross debate revisited

The starting point for examining perceptions of Labour's relationship with ethnic minorities is itself an awkward point. Much of the public debate over this relationship can frequently descend into the superficial and naive, chiefly as a result of the self-perpetuating belief that Labour constitutes the 'ethnic minority-friendly party' in British politics. The reasoning behind and in evidence for this belief has been examined in earlier chapters and is something that is raised again in the final chapter. However, for the moment we must proceed with caution in accepting this argument at face value. Two reasons in particular underscore this wariness. First, on some of biggest policy decisions that can be imagined the evidence is counter-intuitive. The examples that are most frequently cited are, of course, those of Labour's hasty decision to pass legislation restricting the right of Kenyan Asians to enter Britain during the nationality crisis of 1968. Additionally, the Conservative administration's decision to do much the opposite in relation to Ugandan Asians in 1972 also represented a powerful symbol of a party 'doing the wrong thing'. It is naturally quite easy to make more of these illustrations that is warranted by the nature of short-term crisis circumstances faced by Labour and Tory governments a generation ago. However, these examples also hold considerable symbolic value in helping to set – or in this case question – the basic reputation of parties in the eyes of ethnic minorities. A further case in point might be Labour's reasonably high profile policies to repeal the 1971 Immigration Act and the 1981 British Nationality Act. Both commitments were eventually dropped, the former against the backdrop of the realism of holding office between 1974–79 and the latter merely withering on the back of successive revisions during the party's long spell in opposition after enactment of the 1981 law.[4]

Secondly, attempting to draw neat associations between Labour and Conservative policies and the interests of ethnic minorities must also take account of the problem of perception. That is to say, parties can sometimes benefit or lose out from reputations that are either ill-deserved or else outdated. It is not always easy to track voters' perceptions, not least because such perceptions may be founded on crucial events or symbolic turning points. A good illustration of this disjuncture is the Powell controversy in 1968. At least two commentators have succeeded in establishing a positive correlation between this episode and Tory electoral fortunes in 1970 (Miller, 1980; Studlar, 1978), in spite of the fact that the party's official position had been to repudiate Powell both in person and in policy.

With this important caveat aside, what can be said about the reputation of political parties in promoting or obstructing the interests of ethnic minorities? The evidence from 1997 is somewhat revealing here. Table 7.2 below describes the attitudinal responses of white and non-white groups on the question of how closely each of the three parties are perceived to be to blacks and Asians as a social group and political constituency.

Table 7.2 *Political parties' perceived concern for blacks and Asians, 1997*

	Ethnic group (%)	
	Whites	Blacks and Asians
(i) The Labour Party looks after the interests of black people and Asians (Percentage change in white opinion since 1987 shown in brackets)		
Very closely	13.6 (−15)	14.7
Fairly closely	61.5 (+15)	51.0
Not very closely	17.1 (+1)	20.4
Not at all closely	1.4 (+1)	4.3
Not answered/DK	6.4	9.6
Total N	2987	416
Total %	100.0	100.0
(ii) The Conservative Party looks after the interests of black people and Asians		
Very closely	5.2	1.9
Fairly closely	36.1	19.5
Not very closely	42.5	48.6
Not at all closely	10.1	22.1
Not answered/DK	6.6	8.0
Total N	2987	416
Total %	100.0	100.0

Source: See Table 4.1, p. 94.

The results summarised above have three main points of significance for the thesis that is under examination. To begin with, it would seem that there are some quite large differences between the perceptions of all respondents of each of the two parties. Homing in on whites for moment, we can see that more than twice as many felt that Labour rather than the Conservative Party very closely looked after minority interests. Equally, almost two-thirds believed that Labour was fairly closely allied to these interests as against just over one-third who felt likewise about the Conservatives. In terms of mapping comparisons between the parties where lack of close alignment was concerned the contrast opens up even more. Over half perceived the Tories as either not closely or not at all closely allied to these interests, whereas one-fifth took a similar view of Labour's stance. What this means is that, even at the level of white voters, the thesis of electoral vulnerability endured by Labour is driven not only by perceptions of its own closeness to minority interests but also by the relative distance from these interests that is perceived to be occupied by their opponents. In short, a very large proportion of whites are agreed that ethnic minority interests are an area that the Conservatives are either unwilling to champion (through a conscious effort), or else ineffective in their promotion (despite any conscious effort to do otherwise). Meanwhile, around three-quarters of whites think that this is territory that the Labour Party succeeds in making its own (because it wishes to support such interests), or is naturally more effective at representing (possibly through its historic concern for the disadvantaged and 'have nots'). Therefore, at first glance the data appear to support a sharp distinction in public perceptions on this matter.

However, some fine-tuning is needed and, as the bracketed figures for perceptions of Labour by white respondents show, the picture is far from static. Ten years previously in 1987 perceptions of the Labour Party were somewhat different. In essence, the party has succeeded in (if through deliberate action) or benefited from (through seepage from other issues and concerns) a reduced emphasis on its especially close concern with ethnic minorities. Indeed, the proportion of those who felt in 1987 that Labour was very close to these interests was almost one-third of all whites; this proportion had effectively halved by 1997, signifying an important turnaround. Equally, the reduced emphasis here appears to have been matched by a heightened emphasis on the party as being closely identified with minorities but not especially so (up 15 points between 1987–97). One view may be to highlight the fact that this figure is substantially greater than that applicable to the Conservative Party, an argument that places weight on the sharpness of cross-party distinctions. A rival interpretation might be to acknowledge that very great potential benefit is embodied in Labour being thought of as less dogged and more modest in its alignment with ethnic minorities. The benefit, of course, may have material relevance to party strategists through the avoidance of electoral harm, and this is a point to which we shall return later in the chapter.

Secondly, Table 7.2 also reports some interesting variations between the perceptions of white electors, on the one hand, and their black and Asian counterparts on the other. In very broad terms the structure of minority attitudes tends to follow the pattern seen among whites. Ethnic minorities broadly take a more appreciative, possibly charitable, view of Labour in comparison with the Tories. Something like two-thirds of blacks and Asians acknowledge some degree of closeness in Labour's concern for their interests as against just one-fifth taking a similar view of the Conservatives. The Tories, meanwhile, are thought in some way not to be identified with these interests by around 60 per cent of blacks and Asians; this figure is noticeably only a little greater than the proportion found among white respondents (53 per cent). The proportion of blacks and Asians believing that Labour was not concerned with these interests totalled just one-quarter of this group.

These are the obvious top-line differences in the way in which the parties are perceived. What should be added is some feel for any large variations found within the ethnic minority group as a whole. Here it is worth reporting that a tendency existed among Indians to rather understate the Conservatives' lack of concern with black and Asian interests. That is to say, whereas sizeable proportions of other minority groups appeared more condemnatory in their assessment (by endorsing the position that the Tories were not at all closely identified with black and Asian interests), Indian opinion by contrast was heavily concentrated in believing that the relationship was not close (62 per cent). Furthermore, in relation to attitudes towards Labour it is striking that the variable position of different minority groups was remarkably flat. In other words, whereas we might expect some minority groups to take a more upbeat view than others of Labour's closeness to their interests, the evidence showed that strong a similarity existed across all groups. This in turn might suggest that there is something of a greater maturity and stability in ethnic minority attitudes towards Labour in terms of benefits and dis-benefits than in relation to the Conservatives. For reasons to do with evolving notions of party identification and emerging partisanship, the reputation of the Conservatives, while less flattering, may be subject to greater change and development. Indians, as we have seen, already stray from the pack in aspects of their political outlook and voting behaviour. It is perhaps not surprising to discover that elements of this non-conformism are also reflected in a less harsh perception of the Conservatives' willingness or effectiveness (or both) in backing ethnic minority interests. We might speculate that any possible future loosening of Labour partisanship among Indians or indeed any other minority group might also be accompanied by a greater scepticism towards Labour on the grounds of its reputation in promoting sectional interests.

With this in mind, a note of caution might also be added because it may be entirely plausible and defensible for growing numbers of ethnic minorities to view the question of sectional interests as, at best, irrelevant to their perceptions of parties and voting decisions. At worst, they may consider this assessment of reputation as patronising, unhelpful and very possibly naive in its political correctness. In other words, strong Labour identifiers among ethnic minorities, enthusiastic in electoral support for Labour, could (and perhaps already do) opt to see any closeness in Labour's articulation of their interests as counter-productive. The chief reason for this is their approval for notions of Labour as successfully promoting other more attractive sectional and economic alignments, in which case ethnicity is seen as a distraction from the party central purpose. Another reason may of course arise from a desire to see Labour embrace an inclusionary, One Nation agenda by which sectional representation ideas and practices are openly challenged and repudiated. Under these circumstances, some minority Labour supports might be expected to frown upon the perception of the party as closely aligned with minority interests. This is not because of any unwillingness to reward the party for a policy reputation it no doubt largely deserves (for instance as the author of three separate Race Relations Acts). Instead, their discomfort stems directly from an hostility toward the notion of party politics as being about sectional representation at all. Sceptics might conclude that neither of the major parties ought to be in the business of promoting such interests, never mind that one of the parties has been rather better at this job than its rivals.

Thirdly, the relative perception of Labour as 'ethnic minority-friendly' in its ethos and substance needs to be explored a little further. Clearly one of Labour's core difficulties during the 1980s stemmed from its perception as a force for sectional groups. The task before it was to find a way in which to turn down the emphasis on such perceptions while at the same time ensuring that it did not appear too distant too rapidly from some of these traditional constituencies. According to Heath and Curtice (1998: 8): 'The upshot of all this is that New Labour was indeed seen to be concerned with all groups in society and not just the working class, the unions and the disadvantaged minorities. In this respect Blair does seem to have achieved his objective of making Labour represent the great majority of the public, not an assemblage of minorities.'

Heath and Curtice also report considerable declines between 1987 and 1997 in the extent to which Labour was viewed as very closely aligned with a number of other sectional interests: the working class (down 13 points), the unemployed (down 14 points) and trade unions (down a staggering 36 points). In other words, the perception of Labour's very close alignment with ethnic minorities must be viewed in the wider context of similar and sometimes larger trends in its perceived relationship with other groups in society.

Where, then, does this leave the claim of electoral vulnerability? The evidence reviewed here suggests that the Labour Party certainly continued to be marked by an altogether different perception of its main sectional concerns than its Tory rivals. There is no doubt that this constitutes a form of potential vulnerability in the sense that attitudes towards the Conservatives on this point are generally more circumspect. We can also reasonably conclude that the modernised Labour Party has reduced its exposure on this front by stepping back from an especially close identification with ethnic minorities and their interests. The danger may, therefore, have been curbed by steering away from close intimacy both in policy as well as in presentation. Moreover, the evidence indicates that the vast majority of whites saw the party as fairly close to ethnic minority concerns. This may prove to be a source of strength and advantage for Labour in the short to medium run for two reasons. First, this perception allows the party to present a credible case for its reformist, social agenda while dispelling the charge that it is in the lap of powerful sectional groups. To be sure, there is world of difference between presenting a case for modest reform in areas of social, urban and employment policy that is the product of proactive effort on the one hand, and delivering identical policy commitments that are thought to be the outcome of a form of political ransom on the other. Secondly, by succeeding in gaining greater acceptance for the party as a moderate supporter of minorities, it is in a strong position to capitalise on elements of liberal and progressive opinion towards ethnic minorities among the majority white electorate. In the previous chapter we explored those areas in which such progressive opinion existed or might emerge as well as those in which it could be ruled out for the foreseeable future. Labour's strategic advantage, therefore, is to present itself and be seen as sufficiently responsive to black and Asian concerns without, crucially, being accused of being a puppet of such interests. It is arguably a fine balancing act to have to pull off, but it is plainly a trade-off that takes off a lot of the heavy pressure of the traditional school that saw Labour as permanently trumped by race card electoral politics. It also, incidentally, creates one or two fresh possibilities in terms of public policy.

Racial attitudes and questions of trust, veracity and credibility

Having examined some of the evidence about the reputation of parties in looking after minority interests, it is important to develop this knowledge into a wider argument about public attitudes towards ethnic and racial pluralism. The conventional wisdom in this field has been that non-white immigration and ethnic minorities are deeply unpopular in the hearts and minds of a white-dominated electorate. One commentator, Crewe (1983: 263) laboured the point that 'race and immigration offered easy electoral pickings [by] fanning the flames of racial resentment.' He concluded that 'unfortunately there are few extra votes to be won by dousing the flames.' His perception was undoubtedly heavily flavoured by the tense stand-offs on race that had become an almost routine feature of the political landscape at that time. Extending this basic point, Crewe cited BES evidence from the 1970s to show that a decisive white majority not only resented the black and Asian presence through immigration but also acted as a firm veto on any attempt to improve conditions or opportunities for these groups. Fully 30 per cent of respondents in 1979 felt that 'recent attempts to ensure equality for coloured people had gone too far' (quoted in Sarlvik and Crewe, 1983). Britain, in other words, was painted as a society in which deep pools of racism existed among large segments of the dominant white population. Political parties, it was implied, not only took note of the environment but went so far as to campaign and even govern on this basis. Those parties or individual politicians who did not, did so at enormous potential self-cost. These, it was stressed, were the brutal electoral truths of the matter and to isolate the possibility of playing tactical race cards was in effect to state the obvious. Such a perspective, it must be said, might be rather more likely to be questioned in the late-1990s or early twenty-first century, not least because of its bleakness and understatement of the possibilities of inter-generational change.

In this final part of the chapter we aim to revisit this orthodox account and to address ourselves to two related questions. First, we are interested in the extent to which this picture continues to characterise British society. The structure of public attitudes on matters of race and ethnicity can often be a terribly mercurial phenomenon and our task is to isolate those areas in which the evidence supports the race card veto position. In many respects the answer to this type of question is far from categorical and it is often the case that issues of context can have enormous influence upon the degree to which traditional or conservative hard-line views give way to more open and relaxed sentiment. Secondly, we must ask how far public attitudes on race are factors that operate electorally in isolation. That is to say, Labour's historic vulnerability in this area has often by tied in with one or two other weak flanks on issues as diverse as economic management and criminal justice. Our task is explore further the basis by which parties establish, retain or deplete relationships of trust and credibility with voters using lessons from racial and ethnic politics. A more integrated approach to this question is thus required.

The bleakness of racial attitudes?
In the previous chapter an attempt was made to re-examine some core public attitudes on race. In particular 1997 BES evidence was reviewed on areas such as the support for the value of non-white immigration, the retention of ethnic minority customs and traditions and the legitimacy of positive discrimination doctrines. These revealed that public attitudes are arguably more complex that the casual reader might suspect from inspecting the argument pursued in Crewe's (1983) now rather dated essay. For one thing, it was demonstrably the case that, while white opinion was less enthused than non-white opinion about the value of immigration to British society, it was by no means the case that whites differed fundamentally from non-whites on this point. Indeed, it worth repeating and stressing that a massive 41 per cent of whites opted to remain on the fence, stating that immigration had been neither good nor bad for Britain (see Chapter 6, Table 6.4). Although this was around twice the rate found among blacks and Asians, it does suggest that, coupled with those who believed it had been good for society, a considerable proportion could easily be separated out from the hostile camp that in Crewe's analysis might have been described as the resentful opponents of multiracial Britain. In fact, those not obviously resentful of immigration amounted to a clear majority among white opinion. At the very least this must imply that the capacity of parties and politicians to whip up old-style rows over the legitimacy of immigration and immigrants is rather constrained today than it was in the 1970s and 1980s.

The most basic ingredient in this picture must presumably be the role of younger generations of white voters who at the minimum have not experienced any major political debates over immigration within their formative years. At most, this generation can also lay claim to having been raised in a substantially more multiracial, multicultural society than their parents and it is not surprising to learn that they take a less bald line on the worth of immigration and immigrants. Of course this is not to say that these younger members of the white population are entirely indifferent or even supportive of the value of immigration, and it is likely that their position remains conditional on the pace and nature of contemporary immigration patterns and pressures. In this sense they are not be substantially different in their attitudinal outlook than the previous generation but the trend uncovered in Table 7.3 is unmistakable and significant for our purposes. It reveals that a generation effect does serve to shape attitudes among the white community on this basic question, but only to a degree. That is to say, there is virtually no impact made by generation when looking at the structure of white opinion among those who are broadly supportive of the view that immigration has been valuable to Britain. Younger whites are more or less as likely as older whites to take this supportive position. However, in the case of fence sitters on this question it is clear that age does influence opinion, with younger whites somewhat more likely to take an agnostic stance than their older peers. Finally, the real impact of generation can be seen when homing in upon the sceptics. Just over 45 per cent of the oldest cohort of white respondents took the view that immigration had been fairly or very bad for the country; in contrast, this line was found among fewer than 30 per cent of the youngest cohort. Throughout all age groups, the table indicates clearly that scepticism and hostility to non-white immigration is partially driven by generation. This finding should not be terribly surprising if we surmise that it is the younger groups of whites who have had greatest proportionate – and possibly substantive – exposure to ethnic minorities as friends, neighbours, colleagues and even relations. These younger whites are, therefore, by extension that much more familiar with and less likely to show hostile towards the doctrine and practice of a multicultural, multiracial society.

Our discussion in the previous chapter also contained some powerful lessons in relation to integration strategies for immigrants and doctrines of racial preference (see also Tables 6.5 and 6.6). In particular, while a strong majority of whites backed the proposal that immigrants should follow a path of 'adapting and blending', it would be hard to conclude that this position was not open to some element of tolerance and sensitivity to minority cultures and lifestyles. Certainly this should not be construed as support for forcing immigrants to break with traditional practices or the idea of compulsion in securing better racial integration.

Table 7.3 *Value of immigration among whites by generation, 1997*

	Age cohort (%)						
	18-24	25-34	35-44	45-54	55-9	60-4	
Do you believe immigration by blacks and Asians has been good or bad for GB?							
Very good	1.5	3.4	2.8	3.5	1.8	1.2	
Fairly good	16.5	14.9	18.1	17.4	16.8	16.8	
Neither good nor bad	51.1	50.4	42.8	39.7	38.2	33.2	
Fairly bad	22.4	20.0	25.0	26.6	26.8	28.1	
Very bad	5.9	8.2	9.5	10.8	15.0	17.2	
DK/not answered	2.6	3.0	1.8	2.1	1.4	3.5	
Total *N*	272	669	652	575	220	256	[2644]
Total	100.0	100.0	100.0	100.0	100.0	100.0	

Source: See Table 4.1, p. 94.

Furthermore, over one-quarter of whites were happy to ally themselves with a position of allowing, possibly encouraging, immigrants to retain their customs and traditions or remained on the fence in respect of the two paths offered. The point being pursued is that, although minority opinion differed from that of whites, it is nevertheless striking to note that well over a half of the latter also sided with the 'adapting and blending' option. To describe whites as occupying substantially different territory on this question would, therefore, be a crude distortion. Finally, and most significantly of all, the evidence on group support for racial preferences in employment was the most decisive of all. In a nutshell, our evidence firmly dispelled the myth that noticeable inter-ethnic group variations in attitude existed. It is certainly true that virtually all white respondents in the 1997 BES reported their clear rejection of the notion that blacks and Asians should be given priority in jobs and should therefore have to compete alongside the white counterparts. However, to label this as in any way unsympathetic to ethnic minorities would be to miss the central point that the vast bulk of blacks and Asians also shared this sentiment. In the case of Indians and black Caribbeans, Table 6.6 showed that there was nothing to distinguish them from attitudes among whites (89 and 91 per cent rejecting positive discrimination as against 97 per cent of whites). Even the waverers (Pakistanis, Bangladeshis and black Caribbeans) were characterised by at least 3 in 4 backing a similar position. In short, no significant differences are apparent between white and non-white opinion and evidence existed to support an unusually high degree of cross-group consensus on this often sensitive issue. Returning to our purpose of looking at recent evidence in order to assess the validity of the earlier bleak picture, it seems reasonable to conclude that on this issue whites are not especially opposed the rights of ethnic minorities. The former may continue to be harsh in their assessment of racial preferences but this is a very long way from being condemnatory toward minorities in general.

This much may be true for the evidence reviewed thus far, but what can be added to our description of contemporary white attitudes? In particular, in what respects, if any, can aspects of white opinion be distinguished from non-white opinion in a way that might potentially allow political exploitation by a vote hungry, principle-poor political party? What, if any, life can be breathed back into the characterisation offered by Crewe in the early 1980s?

A number of different possibilities suggest themselves here. One prospect would be to return to the theme of immigration, its regulation and its associated problems. In the 1960s the sole issue of consequence in this area appeared to be the question of the number of immigrants that had entered and settled in Britain. The principal reason for focusing on this sole dimension was the fear that governments had 'lost control' or possibly had underestimated the influx. In that respect, voters saw the immigration issue as being about a narrow terrain in which their attitudes towards complex aspects of ethnic pluralism could be detected by the response to raw immigrant numbers. For instance, the BES tracked through the 1960s and 1970s attitudes not just to the level of immigrant settlement but did so using the simple yet effective yardstick of whether 'too many' as opposed to 'not too many' immigrants had been let in the country. This evidence was then qualified by examining just those who belonged to the hostile, 'too many' camp and measuring the intensity of their feeling. Thus, in each election between 1964 and 79 no less than 40 per cent (and no more than 45 per cent) within this hostile group said that they felt very strongly about the matter (quoted in Butler and Stokes, 1974: 461). A further third or so reported that they were fairly strong in their views. Combined, these data showed that immigration was about as uni-dimensional a public issue as could be imagined and that the strength and intensity of public feeling was about as unambiguous as could be imagined.

It is questionable whether this description would suffice today. Evidence reported in the 15th British Social Attitudes survey (1998) for example suggests that the issue of immigration has moved on from the analysis pursued in the earlier BES surveys and that it has developed in a number of ways (see Jowell et al., 1998). For one thing, there is a much stronger emphasis in research on contemporary attitudes towards immigration placing the British case into comparative context. The 15th BSA Report shows that the British are rather less likely than the Germans, Spanish or Swedes to value the cultural input of immigrants to the society. This might imply that the British see any contribution of immigrants as lying in other fields such as the economy or possibly even in narrow aspects of commerce (stereotypically in corner shop opening hours or perhaps entertainment and sport). Alternatively, there may be no greater tendency among the British to value immigration in all respects.

That said, the BSA survey did note that around one-third of British respondents blamed rising levels of crime on immigrants; by contrast, in Germany and Sweden this was true of over 50 per cent of respondents, suggesting that, by international standards, there is possibly a greater willingness on the part of the British to see immigration in cross-cutting, multi-dimensional terms. A generation ago it would undoubtedly have been commonplace and uncontroversial to debate immigration publicly on the basis of crime and specifically criminality among minority groups. Today, this would be far from the norm and would probably be the basis of a fairly spirited campaign to tackle pejorative immigrant and ethnic minority stereotypes. Lastly, the 15th BSA survey also shows that, in comparison with a selection of continental European countries, British opinion is least likely to endorse the idea that government should assist in ethnic minority cultural preservation. How this finding should be interpreted is far from clear. On the one hand, it is fair to suggest that British objections may only be restricted to the matter of government involvement, implying that this might be an inappropriate or even ineffective tool in an otherwise worthy task. Such an interpretation would see support for minority cultures as something best left to private, group-based arrangements. A rather different reading would be that neither the objective nor the means for securing cultural preservation were felt to be legitimate by members of British society. In this case, a more robust conclusion might be reached on the basis of this evidence, suggesting that acceptance, let alone celebration, of cultural pluralism was far from the mainstream. Both interpretations, however, can be united in terms of the fundamental questions they raise concerning the preservation of minority cultures as well as the nature of underlying sentiment toward cultural pluralism. Aspects of this deeper question are picked up below in the discussion of voter sentiment on political credibility.

Ethnic pluralism and political credibility
Another approach that is different to revisiting the immigration issue would be to test public opinion on rather more specific or detailed aspects of the kinds of trade-offs that regularly feature in a mature multicultural society. The 1997 BES cross-section survey contains only a limited number of items that permit direct comparison of white and non-white attitudes on these types of trade-offs and on related questions to do with feelings about British national identity and character. For the most part, however, BES data in this broad area extends only to ethnic minority respondents who were the subjects of a distinct module of questions on such themes.

In Table 7.4, BES evidence is used to describe attitudes on the extent to which different ethnic groups felt that Britain as a nation had much to learn from other countries. This type of question is essentially

Table 7.4 *Britain learning from other countries, 1997*

	Ethnic group (%)	
	White	Black + Asian
Britain has a lot to learn from other countries		
Strongly agree	7.9	14.5
Agree	33.3	44.5
Neither agree/disagree	23.9	20.6
Disagree	28.2	12.7
Strongly disagree	4.8	2.0
DK	2.0	5.7
Total N	3471	733
Total %	100.0	100.0

Source: See Table 4.1, p. 94.

concerned with probing into sentiment and understanding that is notoriously difficult to pin down accurately. At a minimum it seems reasonable to think that the question successfully embodies opinion about the strength of confidence that respondents have in existing national characteristics and in patterns of current social relationships. Pushing a little more deeply, it is likely that it also describes approximately the awareness of respondents to external influences, most notably through trade and commerce, entertainment and 'ambassadorial' relationships found in areas such as sport. To that extent, the question probably conveys some useful insight into British feelings in these contexts. However, the difficulty arises in usefully interpreting the results. The most immediate and tangible use that can be made of this table is in its ability to say something about general openness to cross-national and international influences. That is to say, it seems reasonable to suggest that it is about testing, albeit a bit roughly, cosmopolitan outlooks and values among the British. We might safely surmise that those who believe that there is much to learn (and implicitly to be gained, both materially and otherwise, through such learning) are in essence those who perceive the least threat or anxiety from multicultural principles and practice. Naturally, care has to be taken not to interpret this angle too deeply, but the question does nevertheless begin the process of charting and measuring attitudes towards some of the types of social change brought about by and associated with non-white immigration. It may not directly test attitudes towards multiculturalism in Britain, but it does usefully touch on a closely related theme.

The findings shown in this table are largely as might be expected. White opinion is usually thought to be somewhat guarded toward the importance and value placed on foreign influences, and Table 7.4 tends to support this common perception but only to a degree. However, it is striking that the extent of the guardedness is perhaps less overwhelming than imagined. Certainly, more than 2 in 5 whites happily accepted or at least conceded that there was something to be learnt from others; in comparison, the opponents of this viewpoint number in total around one-third of all whites. Moving on, it might also be thought that ethnic minorities would be more supportive than whites of this general proposition, and again this is clearly confirmed. Well over half backed the 'a lot to be learnt' school of thought, with just 1 in 7 taking the opposite position. Given that the numbers of fence sitters were about the same among both groups analysed, it is fair to conclude that ethnicity overall does play a part in accounting for the shape of public attitudes on this question.

The interpretation put on the distinction that is contained in this table needs to be cautious, however. The most obvious reason for this is that white opinion is rather more evenly spread than concentrated. Any thesis of improving attitudes towards ethnic pluralism would undoubtedly maintain that the proportion of white 'supporters' would have been smaller a generation ago. Furthermore, this argument would also anticipate that much of the growth in this supportive opinion would have come from younger members of the white group, chiefly as a result of their greater exposure to different cultures, lifestyles, values and also direct experience of travel and residence abroad. Additionally, an element of this rise in support may also have been registered among whites across the board who, irrespective of age, had also experienced (and reacted to) change. However, among whites as a whole, there is no obvious reason to think that greater experience and awareness of foreign influences had not led to growth in its rejection or resistance at the least. That is to say, there is no basis to the argument that the rise of foreign or cosmopolitan influences in a country will directly result in growing warmth to them. Quite the opposite may result and this point may partially explain the quite sharp variations in white attitudes.

The key aspect of white comparisons with blacks and Asians appears to lie among those who moderately support the proposition that British has much to learn. This group of supporters does not vary enormously between whites and non-whites but it does vary nevertheless. Fully one-third of all whites back this position, but, crucially, almost half as many again of blacks and Asians also give their support to this proposition. For the latter, this proportion does not appear all that surprising and we may expect that many of them have chosen to interpret the question as a reference to the kind of foreign influence symbolised by immigration including their own or that of their families or communities. In the case of the white moderate supporters, there is little direct connection between their own positions and the meaning placed on the question. In that respect, supportive opinion, whether very or moderately strong, is driven almost entirely by external factors unconnected with individual circumstances or background. It is, in effect, driven by attitudes, possibly linked to experience, whereas among ethnic minorities it is largely propelled by experience that has gone on to shape attitudes. The causal underpinning of white and non-white opinion is substantially different and yet the extent of support among both groups remains fairly comparable. The interesting point to conclude might then be that the level of support among white respondents was as high as it was, given that this group's feelings on such a proposition are largely driven by factors other than immigration itself. With possibly growing levels of cross-European migration among all groups in the future, we might suppose that the influence of migration, however temporary and itinerant, will come to play a bigger part in public attitudes, including those on Britain's need to learn from others. For the time being, however, it is a factor that only plays a noticeable part among ethnic minorities rather than whites.

Exploring ethnic minority attitudes toward political motives

The shape of minority attitudes was also examined in the 1997 BES in isolation from white opinion in relation to the following themes: the extent of racial prejudice; the effectiveness of laws to tackle racial discrimination; and support for different dress codes for ethnic minorities. These findings were reviewed and commented upon earlier in Chapter 6. In the context of our discussion of the sources and consequences of political trust and credibility, it is worth reviewing the general remark made in that chapter that the extent of inter-ethnic differences in public opinion was fairly small. All ethnic groups, whether white or non-white, exhibited large variations in attitudes and it was difficult as a consequence to support the claim that a strong and influential racial agenda ran through the outlook of minorities in Britain. In this section, we shall focus on minority opinion alone in three areas relating to how the political system and the motives of component institutions of that system are perceived. The task is essentially twofold: first, to assess how far ethnic minorities feel that cynicism based on racial factors is present in the mainstream system; and secondly, to measure the degree to which minorities perceive that there is a party distinction at play in their wider understanding of political cynicism.

To start with, Table 7.5 begins by reviewing the broad shape of black and Asian opinion on the underlying issue of racial prejudice. It shows clearly that large and significant proportions of both minority groups believe that such prejudice exists in British society, though, interestingly it also reveals that there is a clear distinction between blacks and Asians in the extent to which they believe that prejudice is found. The former contains a majority for whom the problem is measured on a large scale, whereas among the latter a comparable majority reported that the problem was on a smaller scale. Beyond that, minority opinion is fairly united in the proportions thinking that prejudice was of either little or no concern.

Table 7.5 *Extent of racial prejudice, blacks and Asians, 1997*

	Ethnic group (%)	
	Black	Asian
How much racial prejudice do you think exists in Great Britain?		
A lot	38.3	54.5
A little	51.2	38.5
Hardly any	7.9	4.4
DK	2.6	2.2
Total N	457	275
Total %	100.0	100.0

Source: See Table 4.1, p. 94.

These results seem to suggest that fairly large proportions of ethnic minorities do not dismiss racial prejudice in contemporary Britain. The prevalence of such prejudice, presumably, is an important pre-condition for the possibility that political parties and others might prey on such anti-minority feeling and exploit it for electoral gain. These figures, therefore, remind us that among minorities this scenario is quite prominent in that the prerequisite of political exploitation, namely widespread prejudice, is widely perceived to exist.

The evidence that supports such a scenario can developed further. The BES cross-section survey looked at background attitudes towards each of the major parties' positions on equal opportunities. Of course, it almost goes without saying that responses to this type of question can be coloured by the fact that some ethnic minorities may themselves take a dim or low priority view of equal opportunities for blacks and Asians. These 'equal opportunities conservatives', so to speak, may conceivably treat less favourably those parties they believe to be more closely aligned to promoting such opportunities than others. That said, Table 7.6 shows that blacks and Asians make a clear distinction between the closeness of the Conservative Party and the Labour Party to this policy agenda.

The findings in the above table could not be starker in terms of painting a picture of party differentiation in the minds of minority voters. We can immediately see that around twice as many ethnic minorities felt that the Labour Party's position on this issue was encapsulated by point A on the scale (i.e. wholesale backing for the view that government intervention and responsibility is desirable to improve equal opportunities for ethnic minorities) than those who believed this to be the position of the Conservative Party. Equally, those just behind (B–D on the scale) who felt that Labour was closer or more sympathetic to the promotion of such a strategy were greatly larger than comparable opinion of the Tories. Finally, the 2:1 ratio was roughly reversed when it came to those minorities who believed that the political parties views were quite luke warm on

Table 7.6 *Views of the Conservative and Labour Parties' positions on equal opportunities, blacks and Asians, 1997*

	Ethnic group (%)	
	Black	Asian
What do you think is the Conservative Party (Labour Party) view on equal opportunities for blacks and Asians? (Ranked on scale, A–K below)[a]		
A (government should improve equal opportunities)	18.4 (27.1)	15.3 (32.4)
B–D inclusive (moderates: veering towards A)	21.0 (36.9)	16.0 (37.4)
E–I inclusive (moderates: veering towards J)	37.6 (21.2)	41.0 (22.9)
J (no need for government action)	6.1 (1.5)	13.1 (1.5)
DK/not answered	5.0 (4.6)	3.3 (2.9)
Total *N*	457	275
Total %	100.0	100.0

Note: [a] Labour Party position in brackets.
Source: See Table 4.1, p. 94.

equal opportunities for blacks and Asians. This impression is reinforced by almost one-tenth of all blacks and Asians who thought that Conservative policy here was to stand up for no action at all by government; conversely, hardly any thought that Labour stood for such a minimalist approach.

Inter-party distinctions among ethnic minorities on matters of general party policy or philosophical stance is one thing, but direct evidence to support the notion that the parties are seen differently in terms campaigning strategy is another. In Table 7.7 this argument is refined down to a crude, but none the less helpful, assessment of how far minorities believe that parties themselves will move to capitalise on white voters who are racially prejudiced against blacks and Asians. The findings are quite abrupt in their core message, confirming that ethnic minorities are pretty clear about the latent motives of the Conservatives.

The table's findings show that around one-third of blacks, along with one-quarter of Asians, plainly felt that such an election campaign strategy did not characterise the Labour Party. Such generosity of spirit could not have been more in absence in the case of ethnic minorities' assessment of the Conservative Party. In this case, around one-tenth of all blacks and Asians thought that the Tories had engaged in such a campaign, with black feeling running rather ahead of that of Asians. Nevertheless, similar sentiment among minorities was simply not picked up in any appreciable way in relation to Labour. This represents a powerful inter-party distinction in ethnic minority perceptions. The charge of cynicism against the Tories is, therefore, quite potent among minorities, not merely in terms of measuring the record of the party but also through

Table 7.7 *Perceptions of party campaigns to attract racially prejudiced voters, blacks and Asians, 1997*

	Ethnic group (%)	
	Black	Asian
Do you think that the Conservative Party (Labour Party) campaigned to win votes from whites prejudiced against blacks and Asians?[a]		
No perception of either party campaign aimed at whites only	57.3	51.6
Yes	7.4 (1.8)	12.7 (1.5)
No	17.9 (23.6)	21.5 (32.7)
DK/not answered	17.3	14.2
Total *N*	457	275
Total %	100.0	100.0

Note: [a] Labour Party in brackets.
Source: See Table 4.1, p. 94.

comparison with Labour and in particular the strength of feeling that believes that such a campaign did not represent Labour's record. One point of context that might lessen the depth of the indictment against the Tories appears to be the fact that, when examined as a party in isolation, around twice as many blacks and Asians had rejected the charge as had endorsed it. This suggests that, perhaps as expected, ethnic minority opinion of the Conservatives is divided on this point, and that to an extent the party's record and reputation must always be viewed in relation to that of the Labour Party. There seems little point in condemning one party on charges of pandering to voter prejudice when in fact its track record is seen merely as a case in point of a much wider contextual pattern among political parties generally.

Notes

1. The official opposition agreed not to oppose the 1976 Bill. Despite this position, a small number of Tory back benchers defied their front bench and cast their votes against the Bill at its second reading stage. Significantly, none were subject to disciplinary action or even the threat of such action.
2. Other then right-wingers such as Julian Amery and Winston Churchill were also prominent members of the Society.
3. Most notably the Schengen Agreement (1985), the Dublin Convention (1990), the Treaty on European Union (1992) and the Treaty of Amsterdam (1997).
4. An exception to this argument would be the Labour administration's rapid decision to scrap the controversial 'primary purpose' immigration rules shortly after taking office in spring 1997.

8

Candidates and representatives

Introduction

Debates and disagreements about the social background of those that are selected by parties and voted into elective office frequently underscore representative politics in Britain. That is to say, the representative standing of national and local elected bodies is not merely evaluated on the strength of the substantive ideological or party-based representation that they perform. Rather, assessments and conclusions are commonly drawn on the basis of how far these institutions and their members reflect – and thus represent – the social character of Britain. In shorthand terms, we often think of the notion of microcosm politics as encapsulating the pressure to make public institutions – not merely legislatures – more socially representative or reflective of the societies and communities that they serve. This notion of social representation has been common in debates over ethnic minority political participation, but, equally, has been influential in arenas concerned with women in politics and, to a lesser extent, generational and regional groups in public life. Moreover, this kind of assessment can operate not only at national level, whereby large generalisations about society at large are influential, but may also be especially influential at local level in seeking to tie would-be representatives more closely to their immediate would-be constituents. In any case, representative politics today embodies a large measure of essentially symbolic politics. This symbolism may often be seen as an end in itself. However, it is worth recalling that advocates of this kind of representative politics have argued that serious quality and performance issues also underlie the capacity of representation bodies to gauge accurately the needs and priorities of increasingly diverse groups within society. It is in this context, then, that supporters of descriptive representation principles have conceptualised, and then criticised the under-representation of ethnic minorities in both national and local elected politics.

The main task of this chapter is to take a closer look at attitudes and behaviour surrounding the debate over social and symbolic representation and ethnicity. Three central questions suggest themselves. First, to what extent is support for same ethnicity representation driven by those ethnic groups who have been traditionally under-represented? In this regard, the chapter aims to address the evidence surrounding the frequently repeated assumption that ethnic minorities provide some sort of natural constituency of support for greater same ethnicity representation. Secondly, what does the available evidence tell us about the representation of ethnic minorities as a coherent, discrete political group? Much has been said and noted about the so-called political interests of ethnic minorities throughout this volume, and the opportunity now exists to delve further into the logical, empirical and conceptual underpinnings of such arguments. Finally, which, if any, aspects of greater representation by social microcosm distinguish attitudes among different ethnic groups? That is to say, with so much concern about possible political alienation among ethnic minorities, does the evidence point to areas of particular concern that result in some, if not all, groups of ethnic minorities being detached and wary of the political process? This, in turn, might provide some useful insights into the potential roles, either complementary or competitive, of community and autonomous, self-help politics among ethnic minorities.

The chapter is structured around these main questions and begins with an overview of existing theorisation and evidence surrounding political under-representation of ethnic minorities. This opening section draws the distinction between traditional supply-side factors that have been cited and researched, on the one hand (factors that characterise particular groups' reluctance to get involved in politics), against demand-side factors, on the other hand (relating to possible discrimination against minority groups based on attitudes among political insiders or gatekeepers). Of course, many things can influence either side of this demand and supply type model, but it remains the case that overwhelming interest is focused on the proposition that minority candidates are political liabilities for mainstream parties. In fact, this kind of thinking has become increasingly flawed as we shall observe. The following section takes up the question of who precisely stands behind the idea that representative politics is socially and symbolically inadequate. It is clear from the evidence and discussion provided in this section that few satisfactory generalisations are available. Indeed, support for such a proposition is concentrated in some areas rather than others, but it remains doubtful whether this reflects a systematic pattern that can be capitalised upon from the perspective of building a coherent political strategy. At an extreme, same ethnicity political parties attract very patchy support, suggesting that the motives of supporters are somewhat more selective and tactical than is often thought. Thereafter, the third section is devoted to examining the notion of ethnic minority political interests. Not only does this idea-cum-doctrine contain enormous diversity, but, crucially, it can also comprise mutually conflicting interpretations. This dimension of the debate over minority political representation cannot be dismissed lightly. Finally, we shall turn to look at the claim that current political and electoral processes are more in tune with the needs and outlooks of some ethnic groups rather than others. If political alienation is one possible outcome, our discussion explores the attitudes of some of these groups and asks what, if anything, especially underscores their sense of estrangement. We shall also ask whether the evidence points to the limits of mainstream party-based channels of representation and, additionally, whether interesting variations in outlook on this point exist from one ethnic group to another?

Under-representation debates

The most common way in which ethnic minority political under-representation has been modelled has been to see it in terms of the social and other costs incurred by those seeking selection or appointment among the rare vacancies that occur. Therefore, researchers have been sensitive to what are usually described as the resources of participation as would-be candidates and political elites. These resources typically are time and money, as well as the availability of and access to things such as social networks and education. Those who are at the fringes of society – measured in terms of the lack of jobs, earnings, education and generous amounts of free time – are precisely those that resources-based models of participation would consider unlikely to gain advancement in areas such as securing political nomination (Norris and Lovenduski, 1993). Of course, additional impediments may also exist that disproportionately shape the opportunities and points of access that ethnic minorities might potentially enjoy. For instance, language barriers have long been thought to curb the participation in politics and public life of certain groups of minorities. Additionally, some of these minorities are also characterised by higher proportions of women who are not working (than in society generally) and who are thus unlikely to have access to discretionary funds or spare time. (The reverse may be true for the position of men in those parts of the country – typically many northern industrial towns and cities – where structural unemployment has placed high proportions of women in the traditional household, breadwinner role.) The cumulative impact of a series of barriers cannot be understated, not least because for so much of the time the political process may take for granted that the pool of possible candidates are equally endowed in terms of access to resources. This description, in effect, is the hub of the resource-based model. On the one hand, it notes that the candidate selection process is based on the notional open competition between different individuals judged in terms of their specific individual merits by party selectors. However, at the same time, the model draws attention to the wide disparities in resources enjoyed by different individual would-be candidates. Furthermore, if these disparities are more than *ad hoc*, that is, they are reflective of structural inequalities, then it is fairly easy to see that the whole system of political recruitment can be affected. Indeed, the worry for liberal supporters of the selection system is that the formal procedures in themselves may be largely free of discrimination while at the same time be guilty of only drawing a limiting cross-section of society into the pool of talent for consideration (Geddes, 1998). Before long, both the pool of hopefuls and the community of elected politicians appears to be alarmingly homogeneous in its social background and descriptive character. Elective politics, in short, is easily divorced from the descriptive representation of society.

The available evidence that can be used to flesh out this school of thought is limited. For one thing, it is almost meaningless to try to assess the impediments born of structural inequality that are faced by individual ethnic minority political hopefuls. The most obvious reason for this is that in many ways this group is far from reflective of the levels of income or education found among the minority population as a whole. Almost by definition these are individuals who have more than their typical share of such resources and in this sense they are not really all that different from the unrepresentative pool of white hopefuls and selected candidates for the major parties. To be sure, the interesting feature about ethnic minority parliamentary candidates over the years has been the degree to which they are not generally reflective of the constituencies they represent or ethnic minority communities from which they are drawn. In essence they have been uncharacteristic of both, but then again the same is largely true of white political elites. White-collar employment, perhaps in trades unions or the public services, with relatively ample supplies of spare time to devote to party or nomination purposes has been the typical profile of many of those who have succeeded (Nixon, 1998). A number have also held professional backgrounds in legal work, further concentrating their cross-over with the social and employment profiles of existing MPs. Given that most have been in Labour's ranks, such profiles hardly come as a surprise. On the Tory side, the background has been equally stereotypical with heavy reliance on would-be candidates drawn from the professions and the business community.

The evidence that has proven to be most useful in this area has been that relating to the membership structures and activist roles of the main political parties. The work of Seyd and Whiteley (1992) and Whiteley *et al.* (1994) mapped out the basic nature of the participation problem. They reported that just 1 per cent of the Tory membership was made up of Asian party members, with the numbers of blacks too few to even register in their survey. By contrast, the figure for all ethnic minorities among the Labour Party's membership came to a mere 3 per cent when surveyed in the early 1990s. Proponents of resource-based models would note from these surveys that ethnic minority participation at the level of basic party membership was about as high as might have been optimistically expected. This was because even membership imposed costs upon individuals and these in turn required resources in time and money if they were to be overcome. Comparatively few ethnic minorities were resource-rich in this sense as a result of their overall poor socio-economic position. To expect substantially higher levels of participation as members would be to imply that these groups had been unusually successful in either achieving rapid socio-economic mobility or overcoming these barriers through other resources.

With steadily improving rates of ethnic minority participation as party members, candidates and representatives it is probable that some minorities are succeeding in tackling the types of resource famine that would have been experienced by their predecessors. Job and social mobility will have been one important aspect of this slow turnaround, though such a factor will have impacted on some minority groups far more than on others. However, the evidence showing the types of barriers that unequal resources can result in has been hard to pinpoint. In the main, this has been because it is obviously difficult to map, let alone firmly quantify, the selection impact of any given resource in itself. The point of the model has been that it seeks to identify the knock-on, indirect consequences for selection chances among those who generally lack a range of intersecting resources (Parry *et al.*, 1992). Evidence stemming from candidates' attitudes in this area must, of course, be treated with caution, not least because of the difficulty of isolating diminished prospects that arise from lack of time and money on one hand from those that result from discrimination on the other.

Labour's specific problems: unexpected twists
Under-representation worries persist nevertheless. In their work based on the 1992 British Candidate Study, Norris *et al.* (1992) describe graphically the under-representation problem and rightly set it in its correct context. In short, they contended that ethnic minority under-representation amounted to a central political problem faced by the Labour Party. This group of voters, it was estimated, had provided Labour with about 8 per cent of its total vote; in return, ethnic minorities comprised just 1.4 per cent of the party's candidates and 1.8 per cent of its MPs. The issue at stake, therefore, was not merely about the sort of political resources that this group of would-be candidates lacked in general terms in order to get on in party selection battles. Certainly, the issue was a sensitive matter in the Conservative Party, but experiences such as that of John Taylor's candidacy in 1992 in Cheltenham meant that the spotlight was placed on party members' attitudes and behaviour rather than resource questions. In Labour's case, attention has been placed on both dimensions

and many have accepted that the socio-economic profile of its minority voters has created an uphill task in removing resource barriers to greater involvement. However, the underlying tension has been driven by the gross disparity between perceptions of that which the group could provide for the party, on the one hand, and that which the party delivered in return on the other. 'A poor and shameful deal' has been the cry of critics of this imbalance, and this, in turn, has undoubtedly affected minority perceptions of political under-representation more widely. The 1992 British Candidate Survey reported that in Labour's case, the bulk of opinion among the party's parliamentary candidates sided with the view that unfair and unequal opportunities stood in the way of higher levels of representation by black and Asian politicians (Geddes, 1998). Many of these elites were also willing to cite traditional supply-side factors as lying behind the low levels of minority representatives, but this type of sentiment hardly distinguished the party from its Tory rivals. In the case of the Conservatives, it was clear that elite opinion was agreed in thinking that blacks and Asians were held back chiefly as a result of their own actions or inactions. Strong support existed for the view that such candidates experienced problems of 'fitting in' or, more worryingly, came from ethnic groups who were not as interested in politics as their white counterparts. Myths or otherwise, Conservative parliamentary candidates were generally reluctant to see the opportunity structures within the party as the prime source of difficulty. Labour hopefuls, by contrast, were much more ready to ask awkward questions about the discriminatory impact of the party and its rules and procedures.

In highlighting the opportunity structure of the party itself, it is likely that many Labour activists and representatives saw this drawback in the context of wider prejudice against ethnic minorities in society. One of the traditional pleas in mitigation by party selectors (in all parties) has frequently been that rational, vote maximising parties have to be careful to avoid attracting anti-minority voters through the outcome of their selection procedures. In a nutshell, the spectacle of the poor or indifferent performance of many minority candidates over the years has, somewhat predictably, rendered selectors more risk averse than they were to begin with. This may be dubbed the doctrine of imputed racism, whereby selectors effectively go along with discrimination under the cover of best protecting the party's interests at the hands of those who are genuinely discriminatory. Of course, such a risk management argument hangs ultimately on the extent to which minority candidates have been vote losers for their respective parties. In the absence of firm and compelling evidence that can be used to generalise about this danger, one of the results has been that party selectors have erred on the side of caution (Le Lohé, 1983). Certainly they may have been mistaken in taking such a position, but the salient point has been that they may possibly have been wise to do so. Moreover, infamous individual cases: notably Taylor in Cheltenham (1992); Boateng in Hertfordshire West (1983); and, of course, Pitt in Clapham (1970) have regularly fuelled the anxiety felt by selectors. Le Lohé's original work on this question (1983) suggested that on average around 3 per cent of a party's share of the total vote was eroded by black or Asian candidates, though, of course, such a figure concealed enormous variation. Parties might thus reasonably conclude that the incentives involved in backing such candidates were far from attractive and respond accordingly. The upshot was that a less tangible set of barriers against minorities was given an effective platform from which to operate. The result, according to Geddes (1998: 155) is 'more insidious forms of indirect discrimination where selectors absolve themselves of prejudice and impute prejudice, instead, to the electorate. The end result of both explicit and implicit prejudice is the same: people from ethnic minorities find it hard to get selected.'

There is a real worry that this logic and practice is perhaps more widespread than most models of the selection process can easily reveal. In essence, the line of thinking that holds influence among selectors is really not about their own actions or position. It is, rather, about how their role responds to external realities such as presumed voter discrimination. The defence of selectors' behaviour is centred on the idea that it is the discrimination of others that needs to be tackled. Pinning down responsibility, let alone strategies for reform, is consequently much more difficult in this setting.

Measuring support for descriptive representation

The problems of indirect or displaced discrimination in the selection processes of political parties is just one of the factors thought to underpin growing interest in reforming the systems and procedures for representative selection. An additional argument has been that despite the shortcoming of existing arrangements (and these have been overhauled considerably by all parties in recent years), there remain doubts about the representative capacity of those selected to contest seats for the major parties. This criticism extends to both white and ethnic minority candidates in principle, though in practice much of this type of argument is levelled at party-based systems of representation which are white-dominated. In other words, greater descriptive representation may be valued as a political end by those – especially ethnic minorities – who are concerned about the poor prospects faced by blacks and Asians as would-be candidates within the parties. This observation, crudely based on the under-representation paradigm, itself originates from the perception of selection bias in the existing process. Our second factor is to this extent linked to the first explanation outlined in the previous section.

However, perceiving that black and Asian hopefuls faced poor opportunities is one thing; believing that the whole political system, and party managers in particular, are arraigned against ethnic minorities is another. These are in effect two ends of the spectrum of belief about the role of ethnic minorities in the mainstream political system. One of the study's underlying purposes has been to shed new light on the extent to which ethnic minorities enjoy political integration into the British democratic system. In this section of the chapter we set out to examine this broad thesis by homing in on attitudes about different aspects of the political system. These attitudes range from the extent of support found for entire political parties based on ethnic group membership through to rather narrower sentiment about the reasons for wooing ethnic minorities. This is, indeed, a broad range but it is important to try to set opinion about expanded descriptive representation into context. In particular, we are interested to find out if support for ideas of descriptive, ethnic-based representation is seen as a desirable and defensible end in itself. If not, the rival explanation for such support comes into play, namely that it is much more conditional on shortcomings and frustrations with extant arrangements. If this is the case, then support for descriptive representation is essentially circumstantial and, we might surmise, easily dislodged by advances made (and to be made) by ethnic minority candidates and representatives.

The question of same ethnicity representation
A further extension of this debate is located in the question of ethnic minority backing for same ethnicity or same group representatives. This question has become something of an old chestnut in the wider debates over the interpretation of ethnic minority (and white) political attitudes. Moreover, a key element of this controversy cannot be separated from empirical evaluations of the performance of minority candidates and would-be candidates, the subject of a separate analysis found elsewhere (Saggar and Geddes, 2000). However, it remains useful to examine the extent to which minority and white attitudes differ on the underlying question of the desirability – whether philosophically or pragmatically perceived – of ethnically-specific political representation. Debates over desirability matters and questions about the tactical attractiveness of such candidates have been in circulation for many years, and for a long period were underscored by the assumption about the electoral liability thought to accompany their fortunes. David (later Lord) Pitt's early experiences in the 1970s informed thinking on a range of tactical questions for a number of years. In more recent years, however, the question has been redefined, not just by the progress made by minority candidates in real electoral contests (Le Lohé, 1998), but also by the exposure given to the parallel question of the purpose of discrete representation of ethnic

minorities by ethnic minorities (Marable, 1995: 189). This, in turn, has provided a powerful additional literature and source through which to analyse the racial agenda school.

The Harris survey quoted earlier in Chapter 6 was one of the first pieces of empirical evidence to question traditional thinking about the supposed attractiveness of same- ethnicity candidates (Harris Research Centre, 1991). Just 17 per cent of Asian respondents reported that they would have been more likely to vote for a candidate from 'the same ethnic group' (as themselves) as compared with a candidate from another ethnic group. More recently, a MORI survey during 1997 election campaign showed that 27 per cent of Asians were either certain, very or quite likely to switch their vote on this basis (MORI, 1997). This kind of evidence suggests that, although there is clearly support for the proposition of same ethnicity representation it remains fairly modest. It might be inferred that the levels of support for such a proposition are understated by these survey questions since they only test the broad, generalised concept and do not seek to link any of this to specific context. For instance, same ethnicity representation might take on a different tone and appeal if assessed in relation to the articulation of some core issues such as combating racial attacks or possibly religious intolerance. However, although this line of thinking may be correct, its weakness in analytical terms is that it does not release us from the need to treat ethnic minority political opinion and attitudes in homogeneous terms. If, as the evidence suggests, there is doubt surrounding the existence of a universal and corporate set of ethnic minority political interests, it becomes extremely difficult to assess question of articulation let alone corporate representation.

A similar problem arises in relation the role occupied by politicians and leaders. Claims that ethnic minority politicians taking up fixed and anticipated positions enhance the representation of discrete issues are often far from accurate. Indeed, the experience here is patchy and even shows that minority voters are ultimately able and willing to assess individual contributions on their own merits. While expectations may surround the position taken by minority politicians, the line adopted is subject to a number of additional influences, not least of all the role of party loyalty and discipline. The distinction between the strict grounds of same ethnicity issue responsiveness, on the one hand, and the areas of party-led ideological discipline on the other, is very easy to confuse in the minds of voters. One reason undoubtedly is the perpetuation of a traditional assumption (in British politics) about the supposed discretion of party politicians on matters of conscience. Such leeway, so the argument runs, might also apply to areas in which representatives believe themselves to be directly accountable to constituency interests. Such a doctrine clearly is said to apply to representatives in any case, though its observance can be cause for tension and dispute. In the case of ethnic minority representatives, however, the line of accountability may certainly be with constituency forces, but in fact involves a much deeper link with group interest. The latter may possibly be organised geographically at constituency-level but can equally have little to do with this level. Instead, such representatives are typically subject to claims made at group level by which their responsiveness on certain issues is judged by the apparent or putative priorities of members of the ethnic group. In other words, the doctrine of individual discretion, usually thought to relate to fairly specific conscience matters such as the death penalty, has been extended on a fairly substantial scale. The nearest parallels that come to mind involve the historic relationship between Labour MPs and the corporate representation of working-class interests.

The debate over leadership and representation has a strong normative component but equally cannot avoid confronting the pattern of experience of leaders. After all, the evidence indicates that the ethnic background of political leaders is not a particularly precise predictor either of position or indeed definition of so-called 'ethnic minority issues'. A great deal is often asserted to the effect that ethnic background can begin to change the agenda of political issues and, as our discussion in this chapter has shown, there are elements of evidence that can support this line. However, the position taken by leaders on set issues, whether mainstream or not, does not appear to be especially influenced by ethnic background. Take for example the positions adopted by two Labour MPs, Max Madden and Keith Vaz, at the height of the Salman Rushdie dispute in the very early 1990s. Both MPs were comparatively quick to embrace a position that was highly critical of the author's behaviour, coming close to denouncing his motives at the same time. Plainly, constituency interests in taking this line heavily influenced both politicians, though in the case of Madden there was arguably a stronger need to address an organised Muslim community leadership (mainly in his constituency). The line taken by both did not, however, seem to be affected by the fact that one of them was a member of the Asian community while the other was not. Neither were Muslims, though it is doubtful that membership of the Muslim community would have brought about a different outcome on their response to the controversy. Furthermore, both MPs spoke freely of the interests of both Asians and Muslims in defending their positions, with little real regard to how far these personal credentials were based on group membership. This comparative freedom to experiment with the terms of corporate interests and their representation is a factor this is perhaps not fully appreciated in the debate.

The evidence drawn from the 1997 general election contains a little more detail and also dispels one or two myths about minority attitudes in this area. Table 8.1 tests attitudes on the basic proposition that links the

Table 8.1 *Attitudes toward increased ethnic minority parliamentary representation, 1997*

	Ethnic group (%)					
	Indian	Pakistani	Bangladeshi	Black African	Black Caribbean	Miscellaneous
Getting more black and Asian MPs would improve representation for blacks and Asians						
Strongly agree	19.2	43.3	15.5	29.4	29.5	26.9
Agree	48.3	37.3	46.6	41.3	42.2	42.9
Neither agree or disagree	16.6	11.2	19.0	14.7	15.1	15.6
Disagree	10.2	4.5	6.9	11.9	9.6	6.5
Strongly disagree	1.5	0.7	5.2	0.9	1.8	1.3
DK/not answered	4.2	3.0	6.9	1.8	1.8	7.8
Total N	265	134	58	109	166	77 [809]
Total %	100.0	100.0	100.0	100.0	100.0	100.0

Notes: See Table 4.1, p. 94. Includes 'don't knows'.
Source: See Table 4.1, p. 94.

'more is good' slogan with the representational aspirations of the main ethnic minority groups (the question was not asked of white respondents in the BES cross-section).

The headline findings within the table are fairly clear. First, we can see that Pakistanis are the only constituency of electors that is strongly behind this proposition. While opinion varies from one group to another, it is noticeable that getting on for a half of this group are supporters of the 'more is good' position. Interestingly, there is clear majority support for greater black and Asian parliamentary representation among all minority groups but the character of this support is rather more tempered among them with the exception of Pakistanis. By looking at the combined levels of support across those who strongly agree and those who agree with the proposition, the rather unusual position of Pakistanis is further reinforced: less than 1 in 5 of all members of this group fail to subscribe to this position. Secondly, rather in tune with common belief, the opponents of this proposition are fairly scarce. Among Bangladeshis and black Africans these opponents exceed 12 per cent of these respective groups, with similar modest proportions found among the remaining groups. The exception, again, are the Pakistanis, among whom dissent from the prevailing line stands at the 1 in 20 mark. Thirdly, the results also highlight possibly the most interest finding of all, namely the remarkably similar and modest levels of fence sitting among all the different ethnic minority groups examined. This pattern varies at the margin and only ever applies to a small fraction of any single group and to ethnic minorities as a whole. The implication is that the proposition is one that yields fairly clear responses among minorities and that, even when the non-committed are added to the ranks of the opponents, it is clear that support for the proposition prevails right across the ethnic minorities. Indeed, with such support levels confirmed, it is only the differential make up of this opinion among Pakistanis, on the one hand, and among remaining minorities on the other that is worthy of comment. The dynamics of group cohesion and solidarity may play a part in the rather distinctive character of Pakistani opinion but it is striking that no parallel pattern is found among other comparable groups. In all events, the results make clear that the frequently espoused slogan of 'more is better' carries clear weight within ethnic minority political opinion.

The suggestion that greater levels of black and Asian representation might be an end in itself has also been questioned. As previously mentioned, the suggestion has also been linked, rather unsurprisingly, to the tactical calculus of whether enhanced candidate opportunities are electorally appealing, at least for ethnic minority voters. A survey conducted in 1998 for the magazine, *Time Out*, reported that among younger blacks between 18 and 35 years of age, a staggering 45 per cent reported that 'more black candidates' was the single strongest factor that might raise their likelihood to vote (quoted in Ramesh, 1998: 51). This may be quite telling and also come as a surprise to party officials, many of whom have witnessed a mushrooming in local and national minority candidacies in recent years. However, it does not immediately tell us if there is any party advantage to be gained among minority voters. That is, how far is the Conservative's only modest track record in adopting such candidates a reason to think that its voting support would be boosted through raised candidate participation? Or is Labour's undisputed lead in this area a factor that might ironically dampen the electoral benefits of more candidate opportunities?

Ethnic enclave political parties
A further refinement of this debate is the question of how satisfied ethnic minorities are within traditional parties, on the one hand, and the extent of support for ethnic enclave political parties on the other. In part, the idea of such a political party stems from negative conclusions drawn by minority voters about the scope provided by mainstream parties for both their participation and also for the representation of their supposedly discrete political interests. However, the negative agenda is not all there as to the debate surrounding such parties. Additionally, a more positive set of arguments have been advanced in favour of such a move in British politics, not least in order to re-open the question of whether and how far British parties (excluding Northern Ireland) can be based on ethnically affiliations and loyalties. There have been numerous attempts to organise new ethnically-based political parties aimed at attracting votes from Britain's ethnic minorities. Some have tended to be single issue protest vehicles that have deliberately avoided the need to develop a comprehensive political philosophy or policy agenda. Others have been reactive

forces that have set out to defend the rights and space of minorities but again have tended not to exert much initiative even in relation to their sworn enemies on the far right. Examples of enclave parties that have sought a genuine and broad-based constituency have been scarce to say the least. Illustrations of successful ones have been scarcer yet.

One of the major stumbling blocks facing most of these efforts has been the question of the political interests that such parties might seek to defend or promote. Glazer and Moynihan (1975) dwelt on this basic problem a generation ago, arguing that the ethnic group must first possess a distinctive set of interests around which collective action might be mobilised. Recently, Shukra (1998b: 52) has commented that the history of ethnic minority political mobilisation has been at least partially driven by notions of ethnic allegiance. In effect, it is suggested that there are (at least) two sets of factors that lie behind the potential to politically mobilise ethnic minorities, one based on defining the limits of collective, shared interests, the other more loosely on the basis of common ethnic identity and kinship. For our purposes it is important to try to throw additional light in both of these directions, even though there is likely to be relationship between them. The most notable illustration of an attempt to organise a coherent party based on a religious aspect of south Asian ethnicity can be seen in the establishment of the Islamic Party of Great Britain. Founded originally to contest the Bradford North by-election in November 1990, the party was led by Daud Pidcock, a white convert to Islam, whose purpose was to put forward a wide-ranging policy programme based on core Islamic principles. The party, rather as predicted, floundered in that contest but nevertheless continued to be a potent force in local electoral politics in northern England for some time thereafter. More recently, the Fourth Party was launched during the 1997 general election campaign, submitting a batch of formal parliamentary candidate nominations in the West Midlands. Again, its tenor was familiar in claiming to promote policy ideas and pledges that would be of benefit to ethnic minorities (and Asians especially) in a range of spheres. The party's candidates could not escape being routed in the election but the media exposure it received suggested that the idea of separate political parties based chiefly, though not exclusively, on ethnic group membership was perceived in a novel way.

Table 8.2 describes evidence from 1997 testing attitudes among ethnic minorities toward a dedicated political party. It reveals a picture that is probably quite familiar and expected. Three findings are worth commenting upon here. First, with fairly even patterns of support and opposition across the different groups, it is significant that a separate party attracts backing from only about one-third of all ethnic minorities. This compares with over 40 per cent who do not accept the proposition overall. Secondly, the pattern of opinion found among Indians does not stand out

Table 8.2 *Attitudes toward a separate political party, 1997*

	Ethnic group (%)					
	Indian	Pakistani	Bangladeshi	Black African	Black Caribbean	Miscellaneous
There is a need for a black and Asian political party to deal with black and Asian problems						
Strongly agree	4.4	13.0	10.9	5.9	13.6	5.1
Agree	24.7	29.3	26.1	24.8	21.8	28.8
Neither agree or disagree	24.2	17.1	15.2	18.8	17.0	18.6
Disagree	28.2	29.3	32.6	35.6	34.7	32.2
Strongly disagree	9.3	4.9	10.9	9.9	10.9	11.9
DK/not answered	9.3	6.5	4.3	5.0	2.0	3.4
Total N	227	123	46	101	147	59 [704]
Total %	100.0	100.0	100.0	100.0	100.0	100.0

Notes: See Table 4.1, p. 94. Includes 'don't knows'.
Source: See Table 4.1, p. 94.

in any noticeable way. This group may contain very small numbers who strongly endorse such a party but this is also true of black Africans. Attitudes on this question at least do not allow us to isolate any particular minority group. Finally, levels and patterns of fence sitting appear to follow those found in relation to the need for more black and Asian MPs previously. This suggests that, even though the two propositions are radically different from one another, many minorities continue to see the concept of a separate party as an extension of the need for enhanced representation within mainstream parties. In this respect there is obviously a link between these two propositions and it is likely that the common thread seen by minority respondents is the on-going need to give a representative voice to a distinctive set of political interests – at either the party or individual level or both. This provides a further opportunity to return to the question of the distinctiveness of such a political agenda. Let us, therefore, turn to consider additional attitudinal evidence from the 1997 general election.

It is rarely apparent how far greater descriptive representation, typically through separate political parties, can allow specific ethnic minority groups direct accountability over representatives. This, arguably, has been one of the most enduring difficulties faced by those attempting to establish political parties on the basis of ethnic group membership. At one level, the notion of racial identity and allegiance is said to overcome other potential forms of political loyalty. At another, it is often the case that such essentialist racial politics fails to capture the full span and depth of ethnic minorities' political orientation. As a group, it is possible to think of Asians or blacks as increasing their representation in the political system by harnessing and backing discrete political parties. This, however, is a long way from demonstrating that symbolic, group-based representation is more likely to deliver political and other benefits to members of a traditionally under-represented group. Indeed, it is this kind of concept of differential probability that appears to settle most outstanding questions in the area of ethnic minority representation. It is a core theme taken up again in the final chapter of the study. For the time being, however, it is important to recognise some of the limitations of the lobby for enhanced descriptive representation. Writing of racial politics in the United States in the mid-1990s, Marable (1995: 188-9) observed:

> Any increase in the number of blacks as mayors, members of federal courts, and on boards of education, was championed as a victory for all black people. The development of a black-owned shopping plaza, supermarket or private school was widely interpreted as black social and economic empowerment for the group as a whole. The problem with 'symbolic representation' is that it presumes structures of accountability and allegiance between those blacks who are elevated into powerful positions of authority ... and millions of [blacks] clinging to margins of social and economic existence.

This, indeed, is the central dilemma encountered repeatedly in the descriptive representation debate. It seamlessly raises the wider question of the political interests of ethnic minorities and, how, if at all, these might be understood and promoted.

Revisiting ethnic minority political interests

Any theory of ethnic minority political integration would need to be based not only on political behaviour (such as voting choice), but also on the expectations placed on elected representatives (cited briefly in the previous section dealing with attitudes towards candidates and parties). Political integration is, therefore, understood not only in narrow terms to do with mapping and explaining differential party choice (beyond circumstantial factors if necessary), but also in terms of the roles and duties placed on those returned to represent the wider society. Elements of the wider representative task can be interpreted as, for example, the capacity and willingness of MPs to take on board the interests of their constituents as a whole. Rival interpretations, while not bogged down in MPs trying to represent ethnic minority groups exclusively, might reasonably seek to test the extent to which representatives are able to gather and utilise insights about those minority groups.

Of course, membership of such a group is one obvious and presumably (though not necessarily) reliable way in which such insight may be gained. Another route to much the same end could conceivably be a systematic attempt to identify with and show allegiance to certain political issues. A further option that is not incompatible with the former position, might be to go beyond merely dwelling on particular issues and to promote specific positions on these issues. Finally, there is the path of many mainstreamers who have argued that distinctive interests can be defended across a number of issues that have no immediate racial or ethnic dimension. It is not our task to review this debate here, but instead to point out that the responses taken by, and anticipated of, elected politicians are frequently driven by distinctive, and sometimes rival, understandings of ethnic minority political interests. In Chapter 3 we introduced the notion of ethnic minorities as a coherent political constituency. In this section, we explore the suggestion that imposition of the test of coherence is not only unrealistically tough but that it needlessly distorts the relationship between electors and representatives. This relationship encompasses a variety of subtle variations on how and where ethnicity has a bearing on the representative function. Measures of political integration, it is suggested, ought not to be dismissed on the grounds that ethnic minorities often fail to share a coherent political agenda.

In her study of black and Asian MPs, Nixon (1998) draws out the range of positions taken by the post-1992 crop of minority MPs in relation to race and ethnic issues and the representation of ethnic minorities. She rightly emphasises the unusual degree of similarity between the formal descriptions given by an Asian Tory MP and an Asian Labour MP. It was worth revisiting these short extracts from their respect parliamentary maiden speeches:

> My constituents will not tolerate racism of any kind ... [They are] united in their determination not to let the National Front or any other racists enter the constituency. We have the strength to resist racism; my constituency is proud of being multi-racial. I stand for secularism and democracy. (Khabra quoted in *Hansard*, 1992a)

> Mine is a multi-racial and cosmopolitan constituency in which all communities live side by side in harmony. We are an example to the rest of the country. We must work to build a sustainable partnership that will last for generations to come ... based on talent, merit and opportunity and in which class, colour and religion will have no part. (Deva quoted in *Hansard*, 1992b)

Both, it was observed, chose to play on philosophical values that actively intertwined the reputed strongly tolerant and anti-prejudicial views of their constituents. Although both represented noted multiracial constituencies, the purpose behind these MPs' declarations was to cite the local as a microcosm for the values of the public at large. Combating racism and discrimination, while fostering understanding and respect across ethnic boundaries, was thought to be manifesto for British society writ large.

In this respect, two obvious questions arise for the job of representation and representatives in an ethnically plural, democratic society. First, there is the point that is so often lost in the literature on the politics of race, namely that the agenda of curbing discrimination and hostility towards ethnic minorities can, and frequently is, shared across ethnic boundaries. More crudely, it is a call to arms that is backed by many white voters in British politics, though, inevitably, the bulk of white opinion has been historically characterised in rather less flattering terms. Ethnic minorities can be thought of as having a special stake in this agenda of basic values brought about by their proximity to the experience of prejudice, discrimination and hatred on racial grounds. However, the point about their relationship with such an agenda is that not all commentators are agreed that membership of an ethnic minority group itself determines the affinity and bond between voter and value. It is, rather, more a matter of degree by which members of different ethnic groups have a greater or lesser regard for these kinds of values. White voters can and do demonstrate backing for political values that uphold racial tolerance and most usually are thought to do so on the basis of wider ideological positions on questions of human rights, socio-cultural pluralism, social justice and possibly cosmopolitanism and internationalism. In other words, while these wider values and ideas are given mileage within the context of a multiracial society, there is precious little that links this agenda directly to race relations or racial politics. Links certainly do exist and occasionally these may be of a direct nature, whereby white opinion is tested on historic core race relations issues. However, for the most part, white political support for values and issues that are linked to the position of ethnic minorities in British society can be accounted for in terms that are largely disjointed from white and non-white ethnic categories. Similarly, it may be argued that the relationship between black and Asian minorities and the agenda of liberal race relations is in fact rather more tenuous and less determinist than is commonly thought. For one thing, even if empirical data demonstrate that these minorities perceive race relations issues to be more salient than their white counterparts (which is usually the case though far less emphatically than assumed), it remains the case that the bulk of this opinion may be driven by the immigrant and resettlement experience. Such a distinctive background will not usually be found among their white counterparts (though growing levels of intra-EU labour mobility may alter that in the future). Equally, any signs of reduced interest in or support for this broad agenda among younger cohorts of black and Asian Britons would further support the idea that the relationship is essentially conditional. As the first generation immigrant legacy wanes and eventually disappears, according to this perspective, it will be possible to identify greater levels of convergence in attitudes towards ethnic pluralism among whites and non-whites. The cross-ethnic group platform of support for liberal multicultural values outlined by the two quoted MPs is thus understood in less categorical terms. The support for – or indeed dissent from – this platform is consequently best thought of not in terms of an Asian, black or white constituency, but instead as a single body of opinion containing similar, differing and conflicting components.

Secondly, there is the old chestnut of how far, if at all, the kind of agenda quoted previously can only be advanced and articulated by members of ethnic minorities. The hard-line position of radical opinion on this question over the years has been that only minorities can successfully occupy such positions of representative authenticity. That is not to say that all minorities placed in or aspiring to this role will be successful, and indeed many mature commentators have been at pains to point to and concede the many examples of failure or dashed promise. However, supporters of this perspective nevertheless insist that genuinely successful examples are limited to ethnic minority representatives. This insistence is partly, though significantly, argued on the grounds of the supposed empathy that is felt between electors and representatives of the same ethnic background. Additionally, the argument is centred on an intergroup understanding of racial inequality and exclusion that is said to apply to members of different ethnic minority groups (i.e. black support for Asians in this role and vice versa). A more moderate interpretation of this stance has been to suggest that, although there is little that can or must be represented exclusively by ethnic minorities for ethnic minorities, there remains an underlying racial or ethnic twist to all or most political issues that requires unique insight and empathy. This perspective was explored extensively in Chapter 2 of this study, and it was noted that the argument could be successfully operationalised in a wide range of issue settings. Typical and robust examples might include many areas of criminal justice, education and welfare policy. We need not rehearse that debate again, though it is worth repeating the point that such issue agendas have not only involved an easily overlooked ethnic minority dimension, but one which many white representatives hold good track records in identifying and seeking to represent. Of course, the argument may ultimately revolve on the differential likelihood of white against non-white representatives to take up these ethnic minority dimensions. However, there is little to convince us that incisive representatives, irrespective of ethnic origin, cannot successfully articulate this domain.

9

British racial and electoral politics in transformation

Introduction

This study has been chiefly been concerned with two inter-related questions. To begin with, it is clear from the existing volume of research that there has been a pressing need to establish a viable, long-term framework for the study of ethnic minority political participation, especially in the realm of electoral politics, that enabled meaningful comparison with the white community. The research upon which this study is based, therefore, had to ensure that this ground was covered. The objective was reflected in the incorporation of an ethnic minority booster within the larger BES cross-section. On this basis, this research has been able to put forward results that have hitherto been difficult to obtain. Furthermore, it has set in place a framework that should prove to be both viable and effective for further, follow-up work on questions of ethnic minority political behaviour. Putting this methodological issue to one side for a moment, the core intellectual rationale of study has been devoted to throwing light on the degree to which Britain's ethnic minorities are influenced in their political attitudes and behaviour by considerations that distinguish them from their white counterparts. This focus, in other words, is the theory of political integration and stems from a long-standing debate among political and social scientists concerning political difference and its sources and consequences. The research featured in this study has sought to take this debate further both through the presentation of fresh empirical material, as well as through extending our theoretical understanding of how ethnicity impacts upon political outlook and action.

At the centre of this study has been the theme of how far the voting behaviour and political attitudes of ethnic minorities can be adequately described in terms that are fundamentally distinct from and potentially at odds with their more numerous white counterparts. In other words, we have been concerned with how far and in what sense does ethnicity shape and possibly divide the political behaviour of white and non-white Britons. To be sure, this has been a recurring point of contention over the years among academic researchers, political actors and others. The absence of reliable data that examined ethnic minority and white behaviour and outlook in an integrated way has undoubtedly hampered the underlying productivity of this debate, and the empirical evidence contained in this volume should serve to rectify this difficulty. Notwithstanding this constraint, controversy and disagreement have raged on the issue of the role and reputation of ethnicity in shaping political outcome. One especially vocal school of thought has, on a range of indicators, argued that any claims to distinctiveness among ethnic minorities are generally not driven by their ethnic origins but rather are largely circumstantial and linked to the underlying socio-economic position of these groups of voters. In particular, proponents of this school point to the social class composition (and related educational, housing and other features) of minorities as the basis for explaining superficial differences in voting participation and party choice. A contrasting school of thought takes a very different tenor and has challenged this line by emphasising two related points. First, it suggests that the so-called conventional view has underplayed the capacity or potential for ethnicity and lines of ethnic loyalty to exert influence upon both political thinking and political behaviour. This is a powerful theoretical claim and one that this study has sought to test from several different angles. Secondly, the counter school has drawn inspiration and evidence from the role of ethnicity in moulding public attitudes to democratic norms in Britain. It has also tried to draw a link between the political influence of ethnicity and minorities' association with and involvement in autonomous ethnic minority community organisations. This research was not designed to explore, let alone test, these relationships in any direct way. None the less, the research has provided some fresh evidence and insight to help clarify these kinds of theoretical claims made by the so-called 'ethnicity matters' school of thought. To be fair, this school may command growing influence and exposure in both academic and non-academic circles, but it has also been characterised by a long list of under-evidenced and poorly understood theoretical assumptions. The research contained in this study helps to unpack this powerful viewpoint by subjecting it to fairly rigorous examination and putting forward a framework through which further bench testing can be usefully designed and conducted. The upshot in the short run has been that in some specific areas the research is able to point to some real grounds for support for the counter school, though almost certainly not on scale that may have been thought (or expected) by sympathetic commentators.

Our aim throughout the study has been to find out more about the extent to which black and Asian ethnic minorities are integrated into or excluded from the mainstream democratic process in Britain. At this level, there can be no doubt that the study has pointed to some clear and sustained signs of minority integration, particularly in core areas such as electoral registration and turn out. That said, not all our results could be safely generalised to ethnic minorities across the board and, therefore, the signposts to political integration remain somewhat conditional. Rather more importantly, the study put forward an interpretation of the role played by social class in shaping voting behaviour that is rather different – and perhaps more muted and complex – among minorities than their white peers. The starting point of this line of inquiry was to see whether minorities were more likely to be characterised by a subliminal, less direct relationship between class membership and voting choice. In short, the evidence supported this general perspective. This insight allowed us to argue that black and Asian voting patterns contain clear elements of a class-based relationship and, therefore, these voters could not be thought of as entirely distinct from the majority white electorate. Certainly the overall pattern of ethnic minority party support tended to paint a vivid picture of a stand-alone group of voters, sharply contrasting with the rest of the electorate. However, this immediate picture also served to obscure the evidence for an underlying class effect that, despite continuing differences with class influences found among whites, stands at the heart of the study's interest in political integration.

The study also made progress in uncovering substantial grounds of political differentiation among the ethnic minorities themselves. This, arguably, is one of the most important lessons of the work because of the habit of studying ethnic minorities in homogeneous terms. The most striking pieces of evidence here related to the rate of Conservative support found among Indians, also, incidentally, the largest minority group studied (*The Times*, 1998). This pattern of support clearly allows meaningful comparisons to be made between this numerically large group, on the one hand and other minority groups, on the other. More significantly, it also permits comparison with white voters, not least because of the possibility of strong lines of Conservative partisanship operating against the grain of, and for different reasons than, those found among white Conservative supporters. This raises the question of which aspects of the sources of political difference vary between Indians and whites and which are applicable to both groups. Our results give illustrations of both aspects, while noting that issues of convergence and divergence underpin this assessment more generally. Levels and characteristics of inter-ethnic minority variance are undoubtedly of great academic importance. Such variations, and the trends that it may embody, are also of pressing interest for those concerned with mapping and implementing political strategy.

This final chapter of the study seeks to synthesise the understanding of ethnicity and political difference advanced in the study. Existing research in this field contains an on-going and largely inconclusive debate over the relative distinctiveness of Asian voters in Britain's democratic process and is concerned in particular with factors fuelling their dealignment from support for Labour. It is this topic that is featured in the next section of this final chapter. The theory of political integration is at the heart of this study and is taken up again in the second section devoted to the implication for British democratic institutions, political culture and the democratic tradition. The involvement of ethnic minorities in electoral politics has both shaped and been shaped by political behaviour in Britain more generally. This interface has been widely written about but has rarely benefited from an examination of these relationship based on genuine inter-ethnic comparison. This is a significant lacuna that is addressed in this closing discussion on the dilemmas and opportunities facing Britain's political parties.

South Asians, electoral alignment and political maturity

Several related aspects of the research have tended to concentrate on the long-standing interest among researchers and others in Asian voter alignment. As already mentioned, this theme has been a continuing feature of a lot of writing on ethnic minority political participation, with much of it centred on the strategic choices and calculations of parties. The research has been able to advance this debate somewhat, partly by the addition of fresh evidence on voting behaviour and partly through the breakdown of the group sources of the parties' respective support levels from ethnic minorities.

This approach to the general question of longer-term alignment is a matter that has been neglected in terms of empirical evidence. Having presented and discussed the BES evidence on this front, the study explored different aspects of the debate relating to first, the capacity to lead and influence played by Asian political (and economic) elites and, secondly, the so-called 'cultural thesis'. The research points to three broad lessons. First, it is reasonably clear that a model ethnic beachhead does exist for Labour's rivals – principally the Conservatives – among the numerically large Indian electorate. The opportunity cost of this development remains an open question from the perspective of Tory strategy, putting aside the question of how far, if at all, it is the product of conscious effort. Secondly, it is likely that Asian elites can and do have an influential role to play in advancing any dealignment with the Labour Party. However, this is compromised first, by the short-term success of Labour in winning (or retaining) a great deal of elite loyalty, and secondly, by the tendency to overstate the basic leverage capacity of elite activity. Certainly, this has been a continuing feature of Tory strategy, which has been led and often limited by over-reliance on elite initiatives. Finally, the 'cultural thesis' is probably a red herring in explaining, let alone predicting, the possibility for Asian dealignment. For one thing, this school of thought pays virtually no attention to the rather more illuminating evidence for class-based factors in possible dealignment, an approach that the research has rightly devoted a lot of emphasis. Additionally, the argument over Tory cultural campaign themes in 1997 was eclipsed by two undeniable factors: first, Labour's success in mobilising basic bourgeois themes for its own partisan benefit; and secondly, a tendency for the Tory campaign to get bogged down in sloganeering alone on various unproven cultural generalisations.

Asian political maturity: conflicting signals

In the future the question of Asian electoral mobilisation is only likely receive greater prominence from political parties, analysts and other commentators. The mobilisation of this group of voters has already been noted by writers such as Le Lohé (1998) and Shukra (1998a) who have stressed the extent to which local politics in many urban industrial districts have been transformed in the course of a generation or two. Three central factors appear to stand out in pressing home the centrality of Asians to British electoral politics in the future.

First, there is the matter of sheer population numbers and their patterns of expansion and potential reconfiguration. Now dated Census returns from the early 1990s place the total Asian population (from south, east and southeast Asian sources) at a little under two million or 3.5 per cent of the greater UK population. These numbers constitute almost two-thirds of all ethnic minorities, with south Asians alone making up 1 in 2 of all minorities. However, it is clear that some striking patterns of integration, socio-economic mobility and participation characterise the experience of some Asians as opposed to others (Brown and Foot, 1994). At the risk of slight over-generalisation, it is now permissible to speak of Indians as following a rather distinctive path from other south Asians. Certainly this perspective commands weight in areas such as employment and education, though, rather less so in the area of party political choice. In general, it is likely that these are the beginnings of class differentiation taking hold from within the Asian communities, thus rendering the notion of collective Asian interests as ever more improbable as well as implausible. That is not to say that there is no further steam in the idea of Asian politics as a major feature of the political landscape (Saggar, 2000a). Rather, it is likely that, where they can, Asians will take a more selective approach to the relevance of their ethnic origins in matters of attitudes and behaviour. Public policy-makers and political actors might therefore conclude that a form of a la carte Asian ethnicity is at play in framing political opportunity and choice. More seriously, this framework represents the best hope in preparing for cross-Asian responses in some areas alongside more targeted efforts in others.

Secondly, analysts and practitioners have already begun to make necessary allowance for the capacity for self-help and self-determination among some sections of the Asian population. This is not a trivial thing to speak of, not least because of the continuing criticisms of paternalism that have been levelled by many grassroots activists against liberal-inspired public policy programmes and strategies to mobilise minority voters. In this respect, policy-makers have been sensitive to the charge that possibly not all policy measures ought to be driven solely by the need to root out discrimination in the delivery of public services. The area of healthcare is a good case in point. While a wealth of evidence exists to show that Asians do not necessarily receive a full or even reasonable share of publicly funded healthcare services, it is also striking that many of these groups' demands have been focused on their particular health needs. Issues of ethnic genetics and epimediology have played a part in this agenda, though the basic driving force of poverty has remained central to the debate (*The Times*, 1997d). At the same time there has been a growing chorus calling for the focus and parameters of established health and social services to be recalibrated to better meet the needs of some Asian groups who traditionally are reluctant to search for external forms of assistance. Plainly there is the possibility that certain traditional values contribute to this reluctance. However, it is far from clear as to how much public services can be redrawn in order to cope with assumptions about ethnic groups which, in reality, may not operate at a group level (Atkin and Rollings, 1996). The challenge for public policy and the political system generally is to anticipate this possibility while avoiding a position of relying on assumptions that will often fail or disappoint or both (Anionwu, 1996).

Finally, we must consider what role, if any, is to be played by Asian politics in shaping the political landscape of Britain itself. Casting an eye upon racial politics in Britain at the end of the 1990s, it would appear that Asian participation in political life has developed, from a slow start, to relative maturity and strength. Electoral data confirms that in 1997 the registration and turn-out rate of this large and varied group ranked alongside or even exceeded their white (and black) counterparts. Five Asians were elected in that year's general election, all but one representing seats in which large numbers of Asian voters were concentrated.[1] In local government, estimates from the mid-1990s revealed that over 100 Asians had been elected outside London, achieving a position very close to parity. A similar picture emerged in several inner London boroughs. Lastly, due to the strong electoral alignment between Asians and the Labour Party, many independent commentators had begun by the mid-1990s speculating openly, perhaps naively, about the potential benefits that might accrue from this relationship (Messina, 1998). Half a generation previously, Asians had been few in number in electoral politics, rarely successful as candidates, often confined to the terrain of single issue homeland politics, and generally undervalued by mainstream parties (Bald, 1989).

With such a picture of political maturation, the question of strong Asian mobilisation rates and patterns cannot go without further comment. The research pushed home the point that aspects of Asian participation – in comparison with other ethnic groups – appeared to look quite robust. Although it is likely that the circumstantial factors that were associated with distinctions in Asian party choice are also behind this pattern, it has also been suggested Asians might also be part of and responsible for a special commitment to the democratic process. Certainly the earliest surveys of local grassroots Asian mobilisation (by Le Lohé in Bradford in the early and mid-1960s) revealed a tendency among even relatively impoverished Asians to lend their weight to the democratic wheel. These early snapshots in several northern cities by and large picked up large proportions of Asians of Pakistani ethnic origin, and it is interesting that our own findings in this study do not especially single out this sub-group for its strong participation rate. In fact, such attention has fallen on the Indian community, partly, as already mentioned, because of its increasingly distinctive class profile, but also because of the *prima facie* suggestion that communal, group-based values and processes may play a part in galvanising this group's involvement. Such factors are arguably at work among non-Indian Asians but have thus far generally failed to raise overall participation rates to equal, let alone exceed, those of the numerically large white population. A transformation of this scale cannot be ruled out in the near future, especially if it appears that group-based, collectivist identity has a role to play in fuelling democratic participation both electoral and non-electoral.

Asian politics and democratic norms

These distinctions within the Asian population may also carry some weight in terms of the traditions of and familiarity with democratic politics among their members. For instance, it is frequently noted in passing that for over half a century India has been the world's largest democracy subject to relatively limited forms of instability.[2] The magnitude of this democratic system can be easily underestimated, not least in terms of the continuing pressures that are placed on core democratic institutions by a variety of regional, sectional, religious and other factors. Moreover, Indians' 'home country' experiences of democracy are based on a Westminster model that has many derivative features based on British parliamentary democracy. At the very minimum, this influence must permit a greater degree of casual and superficial familiarity among Indians than might otherwise be the case. It is also a line of cross-cultural commonness that might be expected to have some effect among those black Caribbeans originating from comparable situations. It is worth noting that a similar point is not readily applicable to either the Pakistani or Bangladeshi cases. Both have endured extensive disruption and destabilisation to their democratic arrangements, cumulatively far in excess of the turmoil associated with Emergency Rule in India in the mid-1970s, and indeed British Asians from these national origins are rather more likely to be familiar with the politics of military dictatorships. However, it is not uncommon for politicians and commentators in both these communities (in Britain) to make the point that this absence of democratic politics has not in any way extinguished their public commitment to democratic norms and values. It might even be suggested, according to this argument, that a democratic yearning has been one of the more unexpected by-products of this superficially incompatible background. Ballot box democracy can be treasured and transmitted as a shared set of values according to a variety of means and in some surprising environments. The point that matters, however, is the extent to which Asians in this sense can boast national and ethnic backgrounds in which a political culture centred on democratic ideals can be identified. To the extent that this is the case (irrespective of actual political circumstances in these countries at any particular moment), then it is a potentially important factor that ought not to be sidelined in the analysis. Placing a weight on its influence is a rather less straightforward matter, however.

The Indian presence among the highly participative sections of the electorate is no doubt further accentuated by the small but important East African Asian component. Largely Indian in their national origins, this group could additionally claim a background in which a strong civic culture, loosely modelled on British institutions, played a central role in the post-war societies of Kenya, Uganda and Tanzania (Mangat, 1969; Gregory, 1993). The importance of a well-developed series of public institutions in these countries (in areas such as education, administration and even transportation) is another factor that lends weight to the idea of a cross-ethnic, shared political culture. Lastly, few would wish to overlook the influence of the English language as the *lingua franca* of public life in several East African societies. The ability to communicate at a comparatively high level of sophistication has been identified by many researchers as of importance in terms of a range of non-political opportunities (education and employment to name just two obvious areas) – (see, for instance, Blackaby *et al.*, 1998a, 1998b: 81–5; Clarke, 1998; Clark and Drinkwater, 1998: 148–9; Drinkwater, 1998). Not only were these structural advantages rather less widely found among other Asian and black immigrant groups, it is also fairly easy to imagine the likely political opportunities to which this background may have also contributed. For the most part, commitment to a political process in which a group can communicate and gain an appreciation of the issues that matter in the political system of their adoption, is rather more plausible than a picture in which this relationship is extensively disrupted by linguistic barriers.

Whether this process in anchored in internal community-based dynamics is not always easy to gauge at the aggregate level. A number of smaller-scale investigations have pursued this possibility and several have reported that the notion of an 'ethnic community', both reactive and proactive in character appears to be important in accounting for the group dynamics and mobilisation of its members. The crucial thing that many researchers have pointed to has been the idea that ethnicity in this sense clearly does matter a great deal in shaping the participation of group members in a range of fields and not merely in the political realm. Indeed, some have specifically made the point that mainstream political participation is often best conceptualised and thus understood in terms of its relationship with ethnically-based involvement in other, adjacent spheres of activity. Some of these, in fact, centre on informal, community-based political and quasi-political institutions, processes and even issues. Furthermore, it is by no means unreasonable to assume that various linkages, most often at the informal level, exist across these boundaries. With this in mind, the idea that characteristics of so-called 'ethnic politics' can be deployed within the mainstream political process is one that takes on a new and tangible credibility. Electoral politics, in short, are far from a stand-alone set of activities and relationships. To understand Asian electoral participation, therefore, requires a greater understanding of Asian communities.

Three central factors underscore this story of relative political maturation. First, Britain's electoral arrangements have placed weight on electoral strength derived from sheer numbers of voters. For Asians, this has been an opportunity in the sense that the combined size of the three largest Asian groups – Indians, Pakistanis and Bangladeshis – had reached 1.5 million (according to the General Census and thus clearly a gross understatement of the true size). One Asian media outlet in the 1997 election campaign boasted of the possibility of some 36 'Asian marginals', where notional Asian voter numbers were greater than the size of the majorities being defended (Zee TV, 1997). While this estimate may have talked up the actual figure, a number of candidates saw the importance of this potential voting bloc. Secondly, the constellation of issues and interests that comprise mainstream parties' interest in Asian affairs has gradually shifted away from immigrant matters and toward the aspirations of British-born younger Asians, now a majority within the community (Ballard, 1994). The upshot of this has been that interest has gravitated to mainstream educational, employment and related policies in which it is increasingly conceded there is a legitimate Asian dimension. For instance, distinctive, though complementary, arrangements aimed at trying to boost recruitment in areas such as policing, civil service employment and higher education are now commonplace. Lastly, the face of Asian political involvement cannot be divorced from the group's participation in British economic life. In this regard, recent Labour Force Survey evidence has shown wide divergence in the economic patterns of some groups of Asians as compared with others. In education, employment and business start-ups decisive headway has been achieved among Indians, in particular. As part of a wider picture of advancement, such economic progress has been described by many as heralding a new era of weakening partisanship with the Labour Party. One of the most conspicuous barkless dogs, therefore, has been the singular failure of Labour's opponents to build a sizeable following among Asians. Evidence from the 1997 election indicated that the problem has not stemmed from lack of effort (there has been plenty), but rather from a failure to exploit a growing social class division in the political outlook of middle-class Asians as compared with their more numerous working-class peers. The secret of Asian politics may thus lie in first understanding traditional British class politics.

The theory of political integration revisited

The general thematic cutting edge of this study has been to do with mapping the basis and significance of ethnicity in British electoral politics. This is a theme that has been the focus of an enormous amount of interest and inquiry over several decades (Sagger *et al.*, forthcoming). In the very early period of post-war black and Asian immigration it was at best widely assumed, though rarely said, that the political interests and behaviour of these new groups of citizens-voters would come to resemble those of the larger white community. No great thought was given to the implications that this assumption involved, namely the importance of British class-based politics and its fusion into the political thought and actions of these new Britons. Another early response to the non-white settlement was, of course, that race and ethnicity would undoubtedly impact upon British electoral politics but in a way that was only concerned with anti-immigrant sentiment and its transmission into the policies and positions of the major parties. In fact, it was only after the early studies of ethnic minority voting choice revealed that patterns were dramatically at variance with white voters that attention began to focus on the question of factors that propelled such behaviour. In the period thereafter there has been a more or less continuous fascination with the role of ethnicity in shaping electoral behaviour and political action more generally.

This study is, therefore, very much about the job of pinning down in specific evidence the large volume of sometimes loose theorising on this subject. A number of theoretical interpretations (reviewed generally throughout the study) have been put forward of broader themes of the relationship between ethnic and racial identity and political choice. However, by and large these accounts have been bereft of suitable empirical specifics that allow us to sketch patterns of behaviour, let alone draw generalisations about the attitudes and behaviour of ethnic minorities and whites in relation to one another. Most pressing of all has been the need for empirically-based research to say something generalisable as to whether ethnicity acts as a separate, discrete force upon minority electoral behaviour and, if so, whether this tendency can be adequately reconciled with the factors that mould white electoral behaviour. This study has sought to provide a theoretically grounded, empirical response to this basic question. The responses that are advanced in the study rely on evidence that is not only rigorously assembled but also genuinely like for like in its comparative suitability. There are, inevitably, limitations in the extent to which the data contained in this study can fill this yawning gap but a start has none the less been made that points theoretical debates on ethnicity and politics in Britain in the right direction.

One of the hallmarks of the debate over the importance of ethnicity and political behaviour in Britain has been the relatively polarised nature of the argument. The responses have either been very difficult to reconcile or some cases have served to conceptualise the nature of the research problem in rather starker and possibly misleading terms than is probably required. Indeed, the shrillness of the exchanges cannot have been lost on many dispassionate readers. One of the chief contributing causes for this has been a ready acceptance of caricatures of ethnic minority voting that are often based on very limited evidence or possibly on no evidence of worth at all. This has tended to lead to a contrast of theoretical positions that are either inordinately difficult to test empirically or, worse still, little interested in evaluation across different ethnic groups. The upshot has been that even the most flimsy pieces of evidence on voting have been seized on by proponents of the two schools of thought, and have quickly been interpreted in skewed and shallow terms. This position has been far from satisfactory, not least because of the virtual silence among race and ethnicity specialists on the question of how far behavioural changes among the white electorate have resonance among black and Asian electors. Not only has the debate been about the effects and nature of a presumed stand-alone cleavage on ethnicity, but it has often seemed that this debate has been conducted in stand-alone terms that have been out of touch with mainstream electoral research. Any serious attempts to investigate or comment on ethnic minority political integration have consequently been lost in a specialist literature that has not easily been able to distinguish the wood from the trees.

The theory of ethnic minority political integration has tended to emerge from the conventional school of thought that sees ethnically-based differences in political attitudes and behaviour as masking other more critical

232 · Race and representation

relationships in British electoral politics. By this is meant that the theory supposes that there are solid grounds for thinking that differences across ethnic groups are associated with and can be explained by the nature of differential experience in areas such as employment, education and housing markets. Other lines of differential background and experience can also been drawn into the theory because of the interest it shows in the idea that political attitudes and forms of behaviour are driven by a range of basically circumstantial factors. Of course, the biggest drawback for this type of approach is that it may not necessarily be able to cope with accounting for very wide political differences on the basis of such independent variables alone. For instance, the phenomenal rate of Labour support among ethnic minorities does not at first glance appear to be explained in terms of a differential social class profile among whites and non-whites. Indeed, as the research showed, it is not attributable to this background factor alone when seen in terms of its absolute level of party support. Rather, political integration is a thesis that seeks to look for the voting variations that are linked with class and then to assess how far these relationships are common to voters across ethnic groups. The study here showed that inter-ethnic commonality was in evidence but that the relative weight and impact of this relationship was more profound for some ethnic groups than others.

The implications for the theory of political integration are essentially twofold. On the one hand, ethnic minorities and their white counterparts would appear to share a relationship based on social class as a conditioner of their votes. This is an important result chiefly because it brings home a relationship that is frequently overlooked by researchers in their own data. It may also have been skipped over in the data presented in this study but for the insistence on examining class-based voting at a deeper level. By auditing the class relationship more rigorously using the idea of relative class voting, the study pointed to the presence of an influence that operates across ethnic boundaries. Ethnic minorities, it can be said, are integrated into a core aspect of British electoral choice. Caveats always raise their heads with such conclusions and two in particular must be appended here. First, it is not clear from the research featured in this study whether these minorities are being integrated more or less than was the case in the past. This exclusion stems inevitably from the first use made of the research design in this study and future work that follows up this question using comparable data can hope to tell us more about integration trends. Secondly, the cross-ethnic line of political commonness failed to isolate those minority communities in which this generalisation had most accuracy and thus meaning. Of course, surrounding evidence about the political behaviour of Indians in particular served to give the study more than half a clue as to where the greatest class impacts were expected to be found. If Indians exhibit attitudinal and behavioural

British racial and electoral politics in transformation · 233

patterns that systematically imply that they have at least as much in common with white voters as with other ethnic minorities, then it is not unreasonable to think that larger data sets will confirm this tendency in the area of the class–voting nexus. For the time being we are left with a presumption that Indian exceptionalism, while not demonstrated over time, may have more substance than even our data is able to show.

On the other hand, however much the evidence pointed to cross-ethnic commonality, the independent variables cannot be described as successfully accounting for inter-ethnic differences in total. Indeed, the fact remains that the evidence in this study continued to point a remarkable degree of political difference across ethnic groups (principally white against non-white) that could not be traced to familiar sources. In this respect, ethnicity divides the politics of whites as compared with their black and Asian fellow-citizens. It remains a powerful conditioner of attitudes and votes in its own right; it cannot be easily dismissed as a reflection of external structural divisions in the condition of whites as compared with ethnic minorities. In sloganised terms, race does indeed trump class in British electoral behaviour, even though an element of the headline discrepancy it yields is attributable to other factors. For our purposes, there is a pressing need to re-examine why this is the case and to map out the mechanisms through which collective ethnic loyalty can serve to influence political attitudes and behaviour.

One significant response to this conundrum was first raised in Chapter 2 in which inter-ethnic voting variations were conceptualised in four distinct ways. These accounts need not be rehearsed again here, but it is useful to recall that the debate pivoted on the ideological and historical bases for presenting race as a fundamental source of division and conflict. At one end of the spectrum there were those who spoke in terms of a formal race agenda whereby all public matters and political issues could be reduced to the question of race. A racial prism operated through which the world was observed and understood politically. At the other end of the spectrum others contended that ethnic minorities overwhelmingly shared the political outlook, values and motives of their white counterparts. Race and ethnicity, put bluntly, simply failed to affect minority groups' political interests or perceptions. It amounted, therefore, to a hollow thesis that spuriously divided citizens and voters on the basis of superficial, though not fundamental, differences. Within these polarised views, there has been an attempt to grapple with the question in rather more sober and realistic terms. If ethnicity can be shown to have an influence upon electoral behaviour (it can), it is also clear that this is often a factor associated with a partial and sporadic impact. This means that it accounts for some, though all, the variance that is often found in empirical research, and that it typically serves as a bigger influence in certain areas of political life than perhaps others. One particularly appealing approach to mapping this tendency is to suggest that many, possibly even all, political issues and interests involve a latent racial or ethnic dimension. Accordingly, the political participation of ethnic minorities can be described as a process that has few fixed ethnic distinctions or boundaries. Pinning down which issues can be thought of as racial or ethnic issues is far from straightforward as a consequence.

It soon becomes apparent that this interpretation sees just about all issues and concerns as racial issues and non-racial issues simultaneously. Distinctions that purport to separate out so-called mainstream political issues from racial ones have little meaning, therefore. This is because ethnic minorities – and in some cases their white peers – will often see political issues as comprising a number of racial and ethnic elements alongside other ostensibly non-racial or ethnic aspects. The Stephen Lawrence affair, followed by the Macpherson Report and debate, graphically illustrated the complex and hidden interplay between the racial and non-racial faces of the criminal justice system. As a political issue, it is unlikely that this complexity and subtlety was lost on many sections of the black, Asian and white population. Such an a la carte ethnicity in politics is not merely a description of the political thinking found among Britain's ethnic minorities. It also appears to be a useful way of credibly describing large areas of political life in a mature, multicultural society such as Britain. One simplistic view would be to equate politics as inevitably being about race and ethnicity, and that to observe aspects of political behaviour being shaped by these factors is hardly surprising. This would be a crude distortion. Rather, it might be better to think of many aspects of politics involving an element of racial and ethnic influences. This element accords with the findings of this study and also presents us with a convincing ethnically related theory of political thinking and behaviour.

British party politics: dilemmas and opportunities

A lot of attention has been devoted to the narrow party political implications of this study thus far. In this closing section it is worth giving some space to the interface between party strategy and voter mobilisation. A word or two should also be added about the positioning of parties on policy questions in the face of a turbulent debate over the relative influence of ethnicity in shaping political choice. In particular, we need to respond to the question, often put, about how far and in which ways should political parties trim and adapt their roles to accommodate the influence of ethnicity upon ethnic minority voters. This sort of question matters precisely because it relates to the overall role of ethnicity within the British political tradition. This tradition can be said to be partly the product of the attitudes and behaviour of citizen-voters and partly a reflection of the instincts and operation of major political institutions. Rhetorically, institutions such parties certainly embrace many elements of the doctrine of political and policy colourbliness, but is this necessarily an accurate portrayal of their deeds as well?

The first thing to note in this regard is that the evidence undoubtedly questions the general claim that 'race trumps class' in British voting behaviour. This does not mean that ethnic loyalties and affiliations count for little or nothing, because in fact a large slice of the political behaviour of Britain's ethnic minorities continues to be shaped by a set of collective, group-based identities and concerns. However, whether these can be modelled as a coherent set of political interests is surely questionable, according to the picture painted by this study. A political constituency of sorts plainly does exist in the sense that ethnic minorities are located within a political culture that is not entirely shared by their white counterparts. In essence, 'ethnic politics' counts because it partially distinguishes the political inputs and outputs found among some sections of the electorate rather than others. Ethnicity, therefore, counts though without any serious suggestion that it does so in any fundamental way. The real point of debate, then, is the question of how far political institutions respond to this picture by attempting to aggregate and then articulate the political interests of ethnic minorities.

There is constant evidence to suggest that political parties do little more than dabble and churn over this task. In other words, lacking any real conviction that ethnicity is a stand-alone cleavage in British politics, let a major one, the instinctive response has tended to assume that it cannot be overlooked (safety first) or, less flatteringly, to embrace it as a vote mobiliser when strictly needed (self-interest). The Labour Party has tended to have to grapple with this 'on-off' relationship with ethnicity as a political tool. The mantle and reputation of Britain's 'ethnic minority friendly' party has made this dilemma unavoidable. Its priorities in fighting for (or rather mainly trying to hold on to) minorities votes have often been determined by tactical considerations. This does not mean that it has been strictly mercenary in its approach (it has not), but the party has undoubtedly had to face up the issue of the wider electoral consequences of pursuing a nakedly ethnically- or racially-centred strategy in appealing to its black and Asian constituency. For one thing, the evidence since 1975 has not especially suggested that the party stands to lose this group's electoral support. Indeed, the Labour Party's grip here has only become more vice-like over the years rather than less.

More importantly, it is fairly clear that the party deserves its reputation for essentially being on the side of minority voters for a combination of two basic reasons. First, the Conservatives, starting from a poor and turbulent base, have failed to achieve any sustained results from their lengthy efforts to attract black and Asian voters. Labour, in other words, has often triumphed by default. It has been common for analysts to lay the blame for this aborted strategy at the feet of the Little Englanders and Powellites in the party's ranks. Secondly, there is the matter of the pitch that the Labour Party has managed to adopt and project in relation to ethnic minorities. Its friendliness to the cause, so to speak, has generally been hallmarked by sympathy but singularly without the need to embrace explicitly racialised policies. A dictum of sensitivity while avoiding targeting has tended to be at the heart of Labour's orientation to this task. For instance, significantly Labour has never been obliged or bound by a need to stand up for US-style affirmative action, either in principle or in practical terms. That there have been demands for it to do so (most notably from its own black and Asian activists) is not in doubt. However, the party (like British parties in general) has historically always contained a powerful counter-balance among its leadership and rank and file that have been deeply sceptical of any moves in this direction. Our evidence indicates that their resistance to doctrines of so-called positive discrimination not only has strong grounds in the electorate at large but probably among ethnic minorities as well. This finding would appear to tell us more about British political culture more generally than about the instincts of specific parties.

Significantly, the Labour Party continues to perceive itself as representative – though more plausibly as representing – of ethnic minority interests in a broad sense. This understanding is on the basis of a series of indirect policy commitments and obligations that aim to promote traditional left or centre-left interests and communities. Thus, by adopting policy obligations in areas such as employment and training policy, education, housing, urban regeneration, and so on, Labour is in position to make a number of credible claims about the differential impact of its policies upon various groups in society. These policy commitments, particularly if honoured and effective in practice, serve to protect and promote ethnic minority interests en passant. Critics, radical and otherwise, can and have attacked this approach, not least because of its inherent tendency to lead to what may be dubbed as the 'trickle down' politics. Policy benefits accrue for minorities as a consequence of indirect spillover at best. Supporters, meanwhile, have generally made the point that such an approach need not be *ad hoc* or defeatist by nature. Indeed, enthusiasts might counter by suggesting that this approach contains all the vital ingredients for a coherent political strategy to mobilise and reward ethnic minorities on the grounds that these voters stand to be the disproportionate winners from such policies. It is a moot point as to whether this line is likely to be enough to convince minority voters over the longer run. In any case, it remains the case that from time to time parties have to stick their necks out and tackle racial politics and integration policy directly. The Race Relations (Amendment) Bill, 1999 is a powerful case in point. Whatever else may be concluded from this episode, it is clear that ethnically discrete politics could not be sidelined when dealing with such ethnically specific public policy. What this study has shown, however, is that it is an open question as to whether such an outcome resulted from any prior belief that ethnicity *alone* drove political interest and action. Indeed, the late yet influential intervention of black and Asian peers, along with the concessions provided by the Home Secretary, indicate that powerful cross-ethnic alliances are found at the heart of British politics and government. British electoral politics also contains comparable alliances and sources of commonness. Ethnicity may be an important influence in the democratic process, but these patterns seem to indicate that it is the interaction between ethnicity and ideology, notably liberalism, that best captures the essence of racial and electoral politics in Britain.

It is worth inspecting the notion of differential impact a little closer. As already said, this principle has been of central importance in accounting for the strategic calculus of Labour in facing its ethnic minority constituency. The idea has basically hung on the importance of this broad group of voters tempered by the need to steer away from explicit policy targeting. Ethnic minorities have emerged as indirect beneficiaries of a public policy that is ostensibly not racially defined in any overt sense. The realm of electoral participation appears to contain a number of extensions to this argument. To begin with, this study has demonstrated quite firmly that the doctrine of ethnic minorities as a political constituency persists largely in spite of rather than because of the evidence for ethnic minorities sharing a coherent set of political interests. Indeed, in a number of diverse policy areas we can see that such interest are certainly shared among minorities but, crucially, are also firmly lodged among white voters as well. Ethnicity serves to provide comparatively little basis for political distinctiveness on any significant scale. It is in the domain of voting choice that such distinctiveness comes into its own. One obvious response to this picture, therefore, is to raise the possibility that differential impact of various public policies is a factor that is not just observed by political parties but is also a conditioner of black and Asian electoral behaviour. Put simply, ethnic minorities do not merely consume Labour's (or indeed any party's) stance of sensitivity over targeting. This group of voters additionally display evidence of self-awareness of such differential ethnic group impact and tailor their issue saliency and responsiveness accordingly. In analytical terms, this argument is about treating dominant styles of electoral campaigning for minority votes as both a dependent and an independent variable.

While it is the case that our analysis of ethnicity as social and political cleavage produced mixed results, in some respects the outcome was rather clearer cut. For instance, there are several powerful examples –

from both the 1997 general election and earlier – to show that race divided voters in an unusual and extreme way. The performance of a handful of ethnic minority candidates in exceptional local contests involving cross-cutting ethnic loyalties in 1997, reminded us of the latent potential of ethnic politics to produce dramatic results. In Bethnal Green and Bow and in Bradford West there is strong evidence to show that Asian minority voters were able to side with the candidates from the 'right' ethnic background though the 'wrong' political party. This, surely, must be confirmation of the triumph of ethnic label over that of ideology, albeit on a limited scale.

However, in order to get a fuller approximation of the influence of ethnic loyalties in shaping electoral behaviour it is necessary to look toward local politics and elections. For the most part this study has not been concerned with formally measuring patterns of electoral behaviour beyond general elections. This orientation has meant that the underlying influence of party label upon political behaviour has probably been distorted somewhat. General election participation involves a far greater degree of constraint imposed by parties than is found at the level of local politics. The latter also implies heavy party influence as well but, crucially, has also been characterised by structural conditions that have lent themselves more to the potential of ethnicity as a political force. Smaller electoral constituencies, more closely associated with 'ethnic neighbourhoods', have undoubtedly encouraged a number of genuine cases of minority electoral leverage. Additionally, voting in small, multi member electoral contests has created a number of rare opportunities for distinctive and well organised ethnic minority groups to mobilise their ranks to the benefit of specific candidacies.

Finally, it has been at the local level *per force* in which the bulk of critical issues related to specific ethnic minority communities have been fought. It is no casual accident that, while organised Muslim electoral mobilisation has had barely any impact on Westminster elections, the realm of local politics is littered with examples of Muslim electoral leverage. Moreover, these illustrations involve a very wide range of issues and concerns. In some cases the local electoral strength of the group has been targeted at what may be described as the ethnic or religious twist of mainstream political issues. Typically, British local politics, particularly in urban areas, boasts countless cases of such minority groups seeking to gain influence through the ballot box on matters such as the local aspects of education, housing, social welfare, and so on. Indeed, the bulk of the conflicts over race and ethnicity in British politics have been contested at this level in which new and traditional groups have collided on substantive questions, such as religious dietary provision in local schools, the availability of religious burial grounds, the supply of multi-occupancy public housing suitable for extended families, and so on. It is against this backdrop that various ethnic minority groups have mobilised to gain access to decision-making processes. However, more importantly, many such groups have done so because of the comparatively greater points of access into local electoral politics. In this respect, many groups have quickly understood and internalised the lessons of concentrating at some levels, and through certain channels, of democratic politics than others.

The world of local politics in urban areas of relatively high minority concentration has tended to be seen as a beacon of opportunity in which to get across core political messages and to gain substantive group-wide benefits. Additionally, the impact of race in dividing local electorates has been profound in some cases featuring overt anti-minority and anti-immigrant forces. The 1993 Isle of Dogs local by-election is widely thought of as a modern exemplification of overt race card politics, sucking in not merely extreme parties but also the reputation of mainstream parties. What is less appreciated, however, is the point that this symbolic breakthrough for racial extremism perhaps could only have occurred in a local contest. Such extremism has been conspicuous by its long-term negligible presence in national electoral competition. Local politics, therefore, is of importance but, paradoxically, it may serve to distort the picture of ethnically-based political thinking and behaviour. This is because rationally minded minority groups will respond to the structural context in which they find themselves and utilise ethnically-based political strategy where it works and is seen to deliver. In other words, ethnicity counts in this context but the perhaps untypical environment distorts analytical questions about its impact. Local politics, therefore, may serve to reveal the potential behind ethnicity as a political influence but it is not necessarily a reliable guide to the wider picture found in national electoral politics.

Finally, the importance of the study is arguably best seen in terms of the conclusions that can be drawn about the relationship between voters and parties. The study has not sought to extend to non-electoral-based forms of democratic politics, and nor has it been primarily concerned with informal and non-traditional channels of community-based politics. These dimensions are undoubtedly of importance in mapping the politics of race and ethnicity in Britain. However, their links with the formal democratic process centred on mainstream political parties have been extremely limited in the British case. Parties have at best been slow and reluctant to embrace informal political organisations and ethnic group-based forms of allegiance, whether overtly political or otherwise. At worst, or at a minimum (depending on whether or not parties' limited track record in harnessing ethnic community politics is viewed in pejorative terms), there has been a tendency to assume that minority groups can always and easily translate the energy found in their communal activities into the realm of formal party politics. This assumption has been widely criticised for inevitable naivety in failing to see, let alone give weight to, the heavy cultural biases and restrictions that may be faced by community organisations aspiring to party-based political representation. However, the larger problem with this conventional understanding of parties as open, welcoming political institutions is that it relies very heavily on a pluralist conception of access to the democratic process. In other words, it severely negates the possibility that community-based social and cultural institutions may also play a role as a quasi-political alternative to party politics. Evidence in support of this conception would be deeply damaging to the reputation of mainstream party politics. Although this study has not been geared to gathering evidence about the role and operation of so-called alternative politics and participation, it is certainly worth bearing this link in mind when tying together the threads of our analysis.

The generalisations that we have arrived at have been concerned with charting and promoting understand of those lines of inter-ethnic group variance that are recurring features of black and Asian electoral behaviour. These questions have started with mainstream party-centred democracy and our generalisations have inevitably been restricted to this arena. We can, therefore, purport to characterise the processes and institutions that underpin the essential relationships that the study has focused upon. In doing so, one or two things may be usefully added about the implications for the British democratic tradition. The primary concluding thought of the study is that mainstream political engagement itself appears to be something in which Britons – white, black and Asian – continue to have a large stake. Of course, there remain some fundamental doubts as to whether the participative culture is driven by largely symbolic or substantive grounds. Electoral politics provides opportunities to try to leverage influence and benefit alongside opportunities to register discord, dissent and even alienation. Across a range of inter-related indicators, the study appears to point to the British system of electoral representation operating to fulfil these requirements in large measure. Ethnic minority voters' singular pattern, habit even, of turning their backs on the Conservative Party is surely a measure of a tangible piece of political communication. It is a pattern of electoral behaviour that is profoundly telling and, thus, of value in explaining voting choice among black and Asian Britons.

The final, and related, thought concerns ideology. The study has mainly been geared to unpacking the role played by ethnic label in voting behaviour. The assumption that has run throughout the investigation has been that ethnicity and party ideology are necessarily in tension with one another. Certainly there is a large volume of historic evidence to indicate that such an assumption has been safe. However, it is worth considering the idea that these two variables may embody elements of inter-connection and, therefore, reveals important new insights into the electoral politics against the backdrop of ethnic pluralism. As mentioned above,

British politics today contains some impressive illustrations of both expectation and achievement through cross-ethnic political alliances. Not all of these examples are grounded in the formal electoral system, but the dictum of 'racial sensitivity, not targeting' ensures that this thought is rarely far from the agenda of rational party strategists. This may not stop vital issues and concerns for ethnic minorities from being consigned to the backburner of British politics. However, the evidence implies that the effects of long-term depoliticisation have often been counter-productive. Moreover, racial and ethnic concerns, as we can perhaps all agree, are often of profound importance to both ethnic minority and white groups and for largely similar reasons. Britain liberal traditions and instincts in race relations have left an important residue in terms of integration policy. It is not so unusual then to point out that important aspects of this tradition have been felt and reflected within Britain's democratic process. The interesting point is that this process could not be described as having set out to fulfil any serious integration goals. And yet, the idea of ethnic minority political integration is surely of enormous significance as part of the wider assessment of British ethnic pluralism.

Notes

1 Ashok Kumar, mentioned previously, was successfully elected to the northeast constituency of Middlesborough South and Cleveland East (containing less than 2 per cent who were ethnic minorities). Additionally, Shailesh Vara, a defeated Tory candidate in 1997, was successfully adopted as the Conservative PPC in Northampton South in late 1999. Given the highly marginal nature of this seat, his prospects for victory in next general election must appear quite encouraging. The non-white ethnic minority population of this constituency (based on 1991 Census figures) was notionally estimated in 1996 to be 4.1 per cent – or a little under the national average of 5.5 per cent.
2 The country's official State of Emergency between 1975–77 must rank as the most serious interruption to its long democratic tradition, at least measured by the standards of the region.

Methodological appendix

Background

The original research ESRC application proposed to administer the British Election Study cross-section questionnaire to a booster sample of 650–700 ethnic minority respondents. The booster would involve a small number of additional items constituting up to an additional 10 minutes of interview time. By adding the boosted cases to the expected number of ethnic minority cases from the main cross-section (anticipated to be 150 cases), the aim was to be able to create an enlarged target sample of around 800 cases. The absence of a suitable sampling frame for ethnic minority respondents meant that a random sample of the general population would be used to screen for potential cases for the booster sample. However, this approach would be compromised on grounds of time and expense unless constraints were applied. By recognising the highly geographically concentrated nature of the minority population, the research design and fieldwork strategy then resolved to restrict sampling to areas of relatively high ethnic minority density. A similar approach was previously used by Social and Community Planning Research (renamed the National Centre for Social Research) in the British Crime Survey involving a large-scale sample in which 2,500 minority cases were generated.

Technical description of sample and commentary

This section provides a description of the actual method of data collection deployed in the project and includes a commentary on issues of practical fieldwork, response rates and numbers of achieved cases.

Context and terms

The ethnic minority study covered England and Wales and comprised an ethnic minority boost sample generated via focused enumeration (see following section), giving a total sample of 705 ethnic minority respondents (106 from the main sample and 599 from the boost sample). Ethnic minority respondents were asked a module of approximately ten minutes of extra questions.

In this Appendix:

- the 'ethnic sample' refers to the 705 ethnic minority respondents identified by any of the various sampling methods;
- the 'ethnic boost' refers to the 599 ethnic respondents identified via focussed enumeration (and hence who are not part of the main cross-section sample).

The ethnic minority boost

The ethnic minority sample covers England and Wales only. The survey definition of 'ethnic' was 'black or of Indian, Pakistani or Bangladeshi origin'. Other ethnic minority groups were excluded on the grounds that there would be insufficient numbers for separate analysis. (This exclusion probably has greatest relevance for Chinese and Indo-Chinese groups.)

The ethnic minority sample was drawn from three different sources:

- ethnic minority respondents in England and Wales who were generated as part of the main study (samples A and B);
- a large-scale screening exercise in areas of high ethnic minority concentration (sample C); and
- next-door screening at main study sample B points – these being sample points with high ethnic minority concentrations (sample D).

The latter two are referred to as the 'ethnic boost'.

Large-scale screening exercise (sample C)

The sample was selected by the following multi-stage procedure:

1. From the complete list of England and Welsh (grouped) postal sectors, the 164 already selected were excluded.
2. Then all with a proportion of the total population categorised as 'ethnic minority'[1] below 9 per cent were removed.
3. The list of (grouped) sectors was stratified according to sub-region (see above) and population density.
4. Postal sectors were selected with probability proportional to delivery point (DP) count. 137 DPs were sampled systematically from throughout each sector, giving 3425 issued addresses.
5. The interviewer established whether there were any eligible dwelling units (DUs) at the address, i.e. DUs containing member(s) of the ethnic minorities covered by the survey definition. If there were several eligible households, they selected one DU at random (using a Kish grid and random numbers generated separately for each serial number).
6. At each (selected) DU, the interviewer established the number of

eligible adults, i.e. person aged 18+ normally resident there who were members of the ethnic minorities covered by the survey definition. If there were several eligible adults, they selected one at random (using the same procedure as for selecting a DU).

The unequal selection probabilities arising from steps 5 and 6 are taken into account by the weighting.

Next-door screening exercise (sample D)
In main study sample points (in England and Wales) with high ethnic minority concentrations (referred to as sample B), interviewers conducted a next-door screening exercise. They listed the two addresses to the left and the two addresses to the right of the issued address using strict predetermined procedures.

At the end of the contact with the issued address, the contact person was asked:

Is there anyone living at these addresses who is black or of Asian origin? By someone of Asian origin I mean someone whose family came originally from India, Pakistan or Bangladesh.

If the contact person at the issued address said 'yes', or was in any doubt, the screening address was contacted. On contact, steps 5 and 6 of the procedures described above for sample C were used. The unequal selection probabilities arising from this are taking into account by the weighting.

Main stage fieldwork

Interviewing began on 2 May immediately after the general election; 74 per cent of the main cross-section (including the Scottish boost) was complete by the end of May and 96 per cent by the end of June; the remainder was completed by 1 August 1997 – mainly involving recalls on respondents who were unable or unwilling to be interviewed earlier. The corresponding figures for Scotland were 68 per cent and 95 per cent and for the ethnic minority sample were 56 per cent and 89 per cent. All interviewing in Scotland was complete by 19 July and for the ethnic minority sample by 1 August.

The names of some potential respondents, who had been difficult to find at home or who had refused or broken appointments, were re-issued to interviewers (in most cases interviewers who had not made the initial call) during the later phases of fieldwork.

An advance letter was sent to 'the resident' at all selected addresses in the main cross-section sample. It briefly described the purpose of the survey and the coverage of the questionnaire, and asked for co-operation when the interviewer called. Advance letters were not sent to addresses to be screened for the ethnic boost, but an explanatory letter was available for interviewers to use once an ethnic minority household had been identified.

The face-to-face interview lasted on average 60 minutes for respondents who did not complete the ethnic minority questions and 72 minutes for ethnic minority respondents.

The self-completion supplement, either collected by the interviewer or returned by post, was completed by 86 per cent of main cross-section respondents and 75 per cent of ethnic minority respondents.[2] The self-completion supplement was first introduced on the 1987 election study, and has been used at each study since then; it substantially increases the number of questions that can be asked.

Interviewers drawn from SCPR's regular panel conducted the fieldwork. They attended one-day briefing conferences conducted by the researchers to familiarise them with the selection procedures and questionnaires. In all, 222 interviewers worked on the main cross-section survey, of which 52 were in Scotland. In addition, 38 interviewers worked on ethnic boost assignments in areas that were not part of the main cross-section sample (sample C).

Response

The response rates for the different parts of the sample are shown in the next table. In general, response rates, both for the main BES and for the ethnic minority boost in particular, were disappointingly low. There are several possible explanations for the low response rates:

- The main survey used the Post Office Address Files as the sampling frame rather than the electoral register. The denominator used in calculating the response rate is thus different from that used in previous BES surveys, and it might well be expected that people who did not register would also be less likely to participate in surveys.
- The election itself was characterised by low turn out and this may have affected willingness to participate in the election survey (or rather the factors that led to low turn out might also have led to low willingness to participate).
- On the ethnic minority boost it should be noted that there were relatively high non-contact rates (16 per cent in the large-scale screening exercise compared with only 4 per cent for the England and Wales cross-section). It could well be that some of these non-contacts were in fact out of scope and should therefore be limited in their inclusion in the calculations.

- Non-response due to inadequate English language proficiency was high (15–19 per cent on the boost sample). It was not possible within the financial constraints of the survey to translate the questionnaire into the main minority languages and assign interviewers speaking these languages to the relevant sample points. Nor was it thought desirable that the interview should be conducted wholly through an interpreter, as many questions were of the sort that are sensitive to minor changes in question wording. (Interviews were allowed where the respondent spoke some English, but occasionally called on the help of someone else present.)

Electoral registration check

An electoral registration check was conducted, though there were some unanticipated problems with this. Checking of the registration had to be continued beyond the initial deposit of the data in April 1998. Apart from weighting variables, these difficulties did not affect other variables.

Weighting

Weighting variables were added to the data in order to take account of:

- unequal selection probabilities at the household level;
- non-response (by using information about all sampled addresses collected by the interviewers); and
- the three separate sample types.

A note on statistical analysis

Given the high degree of clustering in our sample of ethnic minority respondents resulting from our sample design, it was appropriate to use a multilevel model in the statistical analysis that explicitly takes into account the clustering. This is both of methodological and substantive importance. Methodologically it is important because our booster sample of ethnic minority respondents was drawn from areas that were known to have concentrations of ethnic minorities living in them. There is, therefore, a risk that we have in this respect a biased sample. Substantively it is also of considerable interest to determine whether ethnic minority concentration has an effect in its own right on support for the political parties. Theories of assimilation, for example, might suggest that the voting patterns of ethnic minority members who live in predominantly white neighbourhoods might accord more with those of the white population.

The multilevel model in effect takes account of any contextual processes arising from the clustering of respondents, for example, into

Response rates attained at different stages of the ethnic minority booster sample, BES cross-section survey, 1997

	Main cross-section						Ethnic boost						
	England and Wales		Scotland		Total		Large-scale screening		Next-door screening		Total	
	N	(%)	N	(%)	N	(%)	N	(%)	N	(%)	N	(%)
Address issued	4920	100	1620	100	6540	100	3425		504		–	
Address out of scope	561		165		726		2495		74		–	
Total in scope	4359	100	1455	100	5814	100	930	100	430	100	1360	100
Interview obtained of which:	2733	63	882	61	3615	62	405	44	194	45	599	44
self completion	2337	54	756	52	3093	53	322	35	128	30	450	33
Interview not obtained of which:	1626	37	573	39	2199	38	525	56	236	55	761	56
Refusal	1206	28	378	26	1584	27	197	21	89	21	286	21
Non-contact	196	4	104	7	300	5	151	16	35	8	186	14
Inadequate English	58	1	3	a	61	1	139	15	82	19	221	16
Other	166	4	88	6	254	4	38	4	30	7	68	5

Notes: Out of scope – vacant, derelict, no private dwelling etc; Refused – refusal before or after the selection procedure, 'proxy' refusals (on the selected person's behalf), broken appointments after which the respondent could not be recontacted; Non-contacts – households where no one could be contacted and those where the selected person could not be contacted; Other interview not obtained – ill or away during survey period, selected person senile or incapacitated, 'partial unproductive' (a few question asked but interview not completed).

[a] Less than 0.5%.

areas of high ethnic minority concentration. It is also possible to include contextual variables, measured at the area level, explicitly in the model along with the usual individual-level variables. This is done in this study as well as in Saggar and Heath (1999), where census data on levels of ethnic minority concentration are merged with the individual-level data set, thus giving a two-level structure. The results of the multilevel logistic model show that there is indeed significant clustering (that is, level two variance) in the sample as a whole and that some of this variance can be explained by the variable ethnic concentration (measured from census data). The results at the individual-level are also to be preferred over those in the usual single-level model since they control for this contextual effect.

In effect, then, the use of the multilevel model takes account of any 'design effects' arising from the particular, highly clustered, sample design and also are of substantive importance in their own right.

Notes

1 Census categories: Black-Caribbean; Black-African; Black other; Indian; Pakistani; and Bangladeshi.
2 Ethnic minority respondents generated via the boost sample were given a slightly shorter version of the self-completion that did not include the CSES questions.

References

Abbott, D. and Davis, A. (1987), 'A revolution by other means', *New Statesman*, 14 August.
Adolino, J. (1998), 'Integration within the British political parties: perceptions of ethnic minority councillors', in S. Saggar (ed.), *Race and British Electoral Politics*, London: UCL Press.
Ageyman, J. and Spooner, R. (1997), 'Ethnicity and the rural environment', in P. Cloke and J. Little (eds), *Contested Countryside Cultures*, London: Routledge.
Alderman, G. (1983), *The Jewish Community in British Politics*, Oxford: Clarendon Press.
Ali, A. and Percival, G. (1993), *Race and Representation: Ethnic Minorities and the 1992 Elections*, London: Commission for Racial Equality.
Ali, Y. (1992), 'Muslim women and the politics of ethnicity', in G. Saghal and N. Yuval Davis (eds), *Refusing Holy Orders*, London: Virago.
Alibhai-Brown, Y. (1999), *True Colours: Public Attitudes to Multiculturalism and the Role of Government*, London: Institute for Public Policy Research.
Amin, K. and Richardson R. (1992), *Politics for All: Equality, Culture and the General Election 1992*, London: The Runnymede Trust.
Amin, K. and Richardson R. (1998), 'The public policy agenda: campaigning and politics for a multi-ethnic good society', in S. Saggar (ed.), *Race and British Electoral Politics*, London: UCL Press.
Anionwu, E. (1996), 'Sickle cell and thalassaemia: community experiences and official response', in W. Ahmed and K. Atkin (eds), *'Race' and Community Care*, Birmingham: Open University Press.
Anwar, M. (1986), *Race and Politics*, London: Tavistock.
Anwar, M. (1990), 'Ethnic minorities and the electoral process: some recent developments', in H. Gouldbourne (ed.), *Black British Politics*, Aldershot: Avebury.
Anwar, M. (1991), 'Ethnic minorities' representation: voting and electoral politics in Britain', in P. Werbner and M. Anwar (eds), *Black and Ethnic Leadership*, London: Routledge.
Anwar, M. (1994), *Race and Elections: The Participation of Ethnic Minorities in Politics*, Coventry: Centre for Research in Ethnic Relations, University of Warwick.
Anwar, M. (1998), 'Ethnic minorities and the British electoral system', working paper, Centre for Research in Ethnic Relations, University of Warwick and Operation Black Vote.
Atkin, K. and Rollings, R. (1996), 'Looking after their own: family care-giving among Asians and Afro-Caribbean communities', in W. Ahmed and K. Atkin (eds), *'Race' and Community Care*, Birmingham: Open University Press.
Azim, W. (1996), 'Ethnic socialisation and political behaviour: the case of south

Asians in Britain', *Social Science Occasional Papers 7,* Southampton: Southampton Institute.
Back, L. and Solomos, J. (1992), 'Who represents us? Racialised politics and candidate selection', Research Paper No. 4, Department of Politics and Sociology, Birkbeck College, University of London.
Bald, S. (1989), 'The south Asian presence in British electoral politics', *New Community,* 15(4): 537-48.
Ballard, R. (ed.) (1994), *Desh Pardesh: The South Asian Presence in Britain,* London: Hurst.
Ballard, R. and Khalra, V. S. (1994), *The Ethnic Dimensions of the 1991 Census,* Manchester: University of Manchester.
BBC (1995), 'East', broadcast on BBC2, 16 May.
BBC/Gallup (1979), 'General election exit poll', unpublished data set, University of Essex: ESRC Data Archive.
BBC/Gallup (1987), 'General election exit poll', unpublished data set, University of Essex: ESRC Data Archive.
Beer, S. (1982), *Britain Against Itself: The Contradictions of Collectivism,* London: Faber.
Behrens, R. and Edmonds, J. (1981), 'Kippers, kittens and kipper boxes: Conservative populists and race relations', *The Political Quarterly,* 52: 342-47.
Berthoud, R. (1999), *Young Caribbean Men and the Labour Market: Comparison with other Ethnic Groups,* York: Joseph Rowntree Foundation/York Publishing.
Berthoud, R. (2000), 'Family formation: three patterns of diversity', in S. Saggar, A. Heath and K. Thomson (eds), *Social Change and Minority Ethnic Groups in Britain,* London: The British Academy.
Bhachu, P. (1985), *Twice Migrants: East African Sikh Settlers in Britain,* London: Tavistock.
Billig, M. and Golding, P. (1992) 'Debates: did race tip the balance?', *New Community,* 19: 161-3.
Blackaby, D. *et al.* (1998a), 'Unemployment among Britain's ethnic minorities', in D. Leslie *et al.* (eds), *An Investigation of Racial Disadvantage,* Manchester: Manchester University Press.
Blackaby, D. *et al.* (1998b), 'The ethnic wage gap and the distribution of earnings', in D. Leslie *et al.* (eds), *An Investigation of Racial Disadvantage,* Manchester: Manchester University Press.
Blackstone, T., Parekh, B. and Sanders, P. (eds) (1998), *Race Relations in Britain: A Developing Agenda,* London: Routledge.
BNP (1997), *Britain Reborn: A Programme for the New Century* (BNP Election Manifesto), Sidcup: British National Party.
Bonnet, A. (1993), 'Contours of crisis: anti-racism and reflexivity', in P. Jackson and J. Penrose (eds), *Constructions of Race, Place and Nation,* London: UCL Press.
Brand, J., Mitchell, J. and Surridge, P. (1994), 'Social constituency and ideological profile: Scottish nationalism in the 1990s', *Political Studies,* 42: 616-29.
Braunhotlz, S. (1997), 'The black vote', letter to the *Guardian,* 15 January.
Brown, A., McCrone, D., Patterson, L. and Surridge, P. (1998), *The Scottish Electorate,* London: Macmillan.
Brown, J. and Foot, R. (eds) (1994), *Migration: The Asian Experience,* London: St Martins Press.
BSC (1999), *Count Us In,* London: The Broadcast Standards Commission.
Buscombe, P. (1999), Closing remarks made at the London Business School,

advisory group private dinner on Conservative Party policy strategy and Asian political concerns, 19 October.
Butler, D. and Stokes, D. (1969), *Political Change in Britain: Forces Shaping Electoral Choice*, 1st edn, London: Macmillan.
Butler, D. and Stokes, D. (1974), *Political Change in Britain*, 2nd edn, London: Macmillan.
Catt, H. (1999), 'Are demands for a "politics of presence" defeated by the Democratic Audit?', *Commonwealth and Comparative Politics*, 37(1): 56–70.
Cheng, Y. and Heath, A. (1993), 'Ethnic origins and class destinations', *Oxford Review of Education*, 19: 151–65.
Clarke, C. (1998), 'Education aims', *The Runnymede Bulletin*, No. 316, November–December.
Clarke, K. and Drinkwater, S. (1998), 'Self-employment and occupational choice', in D. Leslie *et al.* (eds), *An Investigation of Racial Disadvantage*, Manchester: Manchester University Press.
Coleman, D. (1998), 'Immigration as an election issue', letter to *The Times*, 28 April, p. 21.
Coleman, D. and Salt, J. (eds) (1996), *Ethnicity in the 1991 Census: Demographic Characteristics of the Ethnic Minority Population*, Vol. 1, London: Office for Population Censuses and Surveys.
CRC (1975), *Participation of Ethnic Minorities in the General Election of October 1974*, London: Community Relations Commission.
CRE (1980), *Votes and Policies: Ethnic Minorities and the General Election 1979*, London: Commission for Racial Equality.
CRE (1984), *Ethnic Minorities and the 1983 General Election: A Research Report*, London: Commission for Racial Equality.
CRE (1994), 'Don't take them for granted', *Connections*, No. 1, 5–8.
CRE (1998), 'Ethnic minorities and electoral politics: Lessons from the 1997 general election', published summary of CRE research report on the 1997 general election, London: CRE.
CRE (1999), 'Shadows of the future', *Connections*, autumn, p. 20.
Crewe, I. (1979), 'The black, brown and green votes', *New Society*, 12 April.
Crewe, I. (1983), 'Representation and the ethnic minorities in Britain', in N. Glazer and K. Young (eds), *Ethnic Pluralism and Public Policy: Achieving Equality in the United States and Britain*, London: Heinemann.
Crewe, I. and Sarlvik, B. (1980), 'Popular attitudes and election strategy', in Z. Layton-Henry (ed.), *Conservative Party Politics*, London: Macmillan.
Crossman, R. (1977), *Diaries of a Cabinet Minister, Vol. 3: Secretary of State for Social Services 1968–70*, London: Hamish Hamilton and Jonathan Cape.
Crowley, J. (1993), 'Paradoxes in the politicisation of race: a comparison of the UK and France', *New Community*, 19(4): 627–43.
Curtice, J. (1983), 'Proportional representation and Britain's ethnic minorities', *Contemporary Affairs Briefing*, 6 (2): 2–13.
Curtice, J. and Jowell, R. (1997), 'Trust in the political system', R. Jowell *et al.* (eds), *British Social Attitudes: The 14th Report*, Aldershot: Ashgate.
Dahya, B. (1974), 'The nature of Pakistani ethnicity in industrial cities in Britain', in A. Cohen (ed.), *Urban Ethnicity*, London: Tavistock.
Deakin, N. (1965), *Colour and the British Electorate*, London: Pall Mall.
Deakin, N. and Bourne, J. (1970), 'The minorities and the 1970 general election', *Race Today*, 2(7): 205–10.
Dean, D. (1987), 'Coping with colonial immigration, the Cold War and colonial

policy: the Labour Government and black communities in Great Britain, 1945-51', *Immigrants and Minorities*, 6(3) pp. 305-34.
Drinkwater, S. and Leslie, D. (1998), 'Staying-on rates in full-time education', in D. Leslie et al. (eds), *An Investigation of Racial Disadvantage*, Manchester: Manchester University Press.
Eade, J. (1989), *The Politics of Community*, Aldershot: Avebury.
Eade, J. (1993), 'The political articulation of community and the Islamisation of space in London', in R. Barot (ed.), *Religion and Ethnicity: Minorities and Social Change in the Metropolis*, Kamppere: Kuk Paros.
Eade, J. (1996), 'Ethnicity and the politics of cultural difference: an agenda for the 1990s?', in T. Ranger, Y. Samad and O. Stewart (eds), *Culture, Identity and Politics Ethnic Minorities in Britain*, Aldershot: Avebury.
Elmer, N. and L. Frazer (forthcoming), 'The education effect', *Oxford Review of Education*.
Espiritu, Y. L. and Omi, M. (2000), 'Shifting identity claims and racial classification: Asian Pacific Americans and the Census', in P. Ong, (ed.) (2000), *The State of Asian Pacific Americans: Race Relations*, Los Angeles, CA: UCLA Asian Pacific American Public Policy Institute.
Evans, G., Heath, A. and Payne, C. (1991), 'Modelling the class/party relationship 1964-87', *Electoral Studies*, 10: 99-117.
Evening Standard The (1997), Woolley, 8 January.
Field, S. (1984), *The Attitudes of Ethnic Minorities: Myth and Reality*, Home Office Research Study No. 80, London: HMSO.
FitzGerald, M. (1985a), 'Preliminary report on GLC sponsored survey of ethnic minority political attitudes in London', unpublished discussion paper, January.
FitzGerald, M. (1985b), 'Conceptual and methodological problems in political studies of Britain's black ethnic minorities', unpublished discussion paper, June.
FitzGerald, M. (1987), *Political Parties and Black People*, 2nd edn, London: The Runnymede Trust.
FitzGerald, M. (1988), 'There's no alternative: Black people and the Labour Party', *Social Studies Review*, 4(1): 20-3.
FitzGerald, M. (1990), 'The emergence of black councillors and MPs in Britain: some underlying questions', in H. Gouldbourne (ed.), *Black Politics in Britain*, Aldershot: Avebury.
Fletcher, W. and Newport, E. (1992), 'Race and economic development: the need for a black agenda', in J. Jennings (ed.), *Race, Politics and Economic Development*, London: Verso.
Foot, P. (1965), *Race and Immigration in British Politics*, London: Penguin.
Frasure, R. (1971), 'Constituency racial composition and the attitudes of British MPs', *Comparative Politics*, 3(1): 201-10.
Fritchie, R. (1999), Speech as Commissioner for Public Appointments on ethnic monitoring of non-executive appointments to NHS bodies, conference organised by the NHS Executive Equal Opportunities Unit on 'Black and minority ethnic non-executive directors in the NHS', London, 12 July.
Geddes, A. (1993), 'Asian and Afro-Caribbean representation in elected local government in England and Wales', *New Community*, 20(1): 43-57.
Geddes, A. (1998), 'Inequality, political opportunity and ethnic minority parliamentary candidacy', in S. Saggar (ed.), *Race and British Electoral Politics*, London: UCL Press.
Geddes, A. (2000), 'Political participation, candidate selection and patterns of representative politics', in S. Saggar, A. Heath and K. Thomson (eds), *Social*

Change and Minority Ethnic Groups in Britain, London: The British Academy.
Gillan, C. (1997), Published response of the Conservative Party to the 'Twelve questions for political parties on education and equality' presented by The Runnymede Trust and The International Centre for Intercultural Studies, *The Runnymede Bulletin*, No. 300, 2-3.
Gilroy, P. (1987), *There's No Black in the Union Jack*, London: Hutchinson.
Glazer, N. and Moynihan, D. P. (1975), *Ethnicity: Theory and Practice*, Cambridge, MA: Harvard University Press.
Gordon, P. (1989), *Citizenship for Some?* London: The Runnymede Trust.
Gordon, P. (1990), 'A dirty war: the New Right and local authority anti-racism', in W. Ball and J. Solomos (eds), *Race and Local Politics*, London: Macmillan.
Gouldbourne, H. (1998a), *Race Relations Since 1945*, Basingstoke: Macmillan.
Gouldbourne, H. (1998b), 'The participation of new minority ethnic groups in British politics', in T. Blackstone, B. Parekh and P. Sanders (eds), *The Politics of Race Relations*, London: Routledge.
Gregory, R. (1993), *The South Asians in East Africa*, Boulder, CO: Westview Press.
Guardian (1995), 'Most white Britons say prejudice lives on', 20 March, p. 1.
Guardian (1996a), 8 July, p. 10.
Guardian (1996b), 'Campaign will urge black people to use their vote', 2 December, p. 7.
Guardian (1997), Simon Braunholtz, letter, 'The black vote', 15 January.
Guardian (1998), 'The Tories' cultural revolution' (editorial), 17 February, p. 23.
Guardian (1999), 'A man for all women: Lib Dems may have started something' (editorial), 19 October, p. 19.
Gyford, J. (1985), *The Politics of Local Socialism*, London, George Allen and Unwin.
Hall, S. (1996), 'Politics of identity', in T. Ranger, Y. Samad and O. Stewart (eds), *Culture, Identity and Politics: Ethnic minorities in Britain*, Aldershot: Avebury.
Hansard (1992a), *Official Report. Parliamentary Debates. Commons*, Vol. 207, cols. 335-6.
Hansard (1992b), *Official Report. Parliamentary Debates. Commons*, Vol. 210, cols. 446-8.
Hardy, J. (1991), 'Playing the race card', *Guardian*, 23 November.
Hargreaves, A. and Leaman, J. (eds) (1995), *Racism, Ethnicity and Politics in Western Europe*, Aldershot: Edward Elgar.
Harris Research Centre (1983), 'National election issues – Asians and Afro-Caribbeans', survey conducted for London Weekend Television, unpublished data set JN49913.
Harris Research Centre (1987), 'Political attitudes among ethnic minorities', survey conducted for Hansib Publishing Group, unpublished data set JN98746.
Harris Research Centre (1991), 'Asian poll 1991', survey conducted for BBC Pebble Mill, unpublished data set JN99245.
Heath, A. et al. (1991), *Understanding Political Change: The British Voter 1964-87*, Oxford: Pergamon Press.
Heath, A. and Curtice, J. (1998), 'New Labour, New voters?', unpublished paper presented to the annual conference of the Political Studies Association.
Heath, A. and McMahon, D. (1997), 'Education and occupational attainments: the impact of ethnic origins', in V. Karn (ed.), *Ethnicity in the 1991 Census, Vol. 4*, London: HMSO.

Hewitt, P. and Mattinson, D. (1987), *Women's Votes: The Keys to Winning*, Fabian Pamphlet, London: Fabian Society.
Heywood, P. (1994), 'Britain's dominant party system', in L. Robbins, H. Blackmore and R. Pyper (eds), *Britain's Changing Party System*, Leicester: Leicester University Press.
Hill, M. and Issacharoff, R. (1971), *Community Action and Race Relations*, London: Oxford University Press, for the Institute of Race Relations.
Hofferbert, R. and Budge, I. (1994), *Parties, Policies and Democracy*, Boulder CO: Westview Press.
Holdaway, S. (1998), 'Incompetent or just racist?', *The Runnymede Bulletin*, No. 313, pp. 1-2.
Holmes, C. (1988), *John Bull's Island: Immigration and British Society, 1871-1971*, London: Macmillan.
Howe, D. (1988), *Black Sections and the Labour Party*, London: Race Today Publications.
Husbands, C. (1994), 'Following the "continental model"?: Implications of the recent electoral performance of the British National Party', *New Community*, 20(4): 563-79.
Ignatieff, M. (1998), 'Forget the race commissars, what we need now is justice', *The Daily Mail*, 25 March, p. 12.
Jacobs, B. (1982), 'Black minority participation in the USA and Britain', *Journal of Public Policy*, 2(3): 237-62.
Jacobs, B. (1986), *Black Politics and Urban Crisis in Britain*, Cambridge: Cambridge University Press.
James, S. (1997), *British Government: A Reader in Policy-making*, London: Routledge.
Jeffers, S. (1991), 'Black Sections in the Labour Party: the end of ethnicity and "Godfather" politics', in P. Werbner and M. Anwar (eds), *Black and Ethnic Leadership*, London: Routledge.
Jenkins, R. (1967), 'Racial equality in Britain', in A. Lester (ed.), *Essays and Speeches by Roy Jenkins*, London: Collins.
Johnson, P. (1991), *Daily Mail*, 8 July.
Jones, T. (1993), *Britain's Ethnic Minorities*, London: Policy Studies Institute.
Josephedes, S. (1990), 'Principles, strategies and anti-racist campaigns: the case of the Indian Workers Association', in H. Gouldbourne (ed.), *Black Politics in Britain*, Aldershot: Avebury.
Jowell, R. et al. (eds) (1998), *British Social Attitudes: How Britain Differs*, 15th Report, 1998-99 edn, Aldershot: Ashgate.
Kalka, I. (1991), 'Striking a bargain: political radicalism in a middle-clas borough', in P. Werbner and M. Anwar (eds), *Black and Ethnic Leaderships in Britain*, London: Routledge, pp. 203-25.
Katznelson, I. (1973), *Black Men, White Cities: Race Relations and Migration in the United States 1900-30 and Britain 1948-68*, London: Oxford University Press, for the Institute of Race Relations.
Keith, M. (1993), *Race, Riots and Policing: Lore and Disorder in a Multi-racist Society*, London: UCL Press.
Kellner, P. (1999), Closing remarks to the 1999/2000 CREST conference on Social Change and Minority Ethnic Groups in Britain (in association with the British Academy), London, 24 November.
Kellner, P. and Cohen, N. (1991), 'Racism: someone else to blame', *The Independent on Sunday*, 7 July.
Khamis, C. (1992), 'Community participation in Wolverhampton City Challenge',

unpublished paper presented to an OECD/CDF conference on 'The Challenge of Urban Regeneration', Birmingham, September.
Knowles, C. (1992), *Race, Discourse and Labourism*, London: Routledge.
KPMG/LWT (1998), *The Race Debate*, published in conjunction with the London Weekend Television series 'Countdown into the Millennium', London: KPMG/LWT.
Lansley, A. (1995), 'Accentuate the negative to win again', *Observer*, 3 September.
Lawler, G. (1984), 'The Asian Community', *Reformer*, spring issue, pp. 16-18.
Layton-Henry, Z. (1983), 'The importance of the black electorate', *Shakti*, 2(8): 13-16.
Layton-Henry, Z. (1986), 'Race and the Thatcher Government', in Z. Layton-Henry and P. Rich (eds), *Race, Government and Politics in Britain*, London: Macmillan .
Layton-Henry, Z. (ed.) (1990), *The Political Rights of Migrant Workers in Western Europe*, London: Sage.
Layton-Henry, Z. (1992), *The Politics of Immigration*, Oxford: Blackwell.
Layton-Henry, Z. (1993), 'Black electoral participation in Britain 1964-92: the myth of declining Labour Party support', unpublished paper presented to the ECPR joint sessions, University of Leiden, April.
Layton-Henry, Z. and Studlar D. (1985), 'The electoral participation of black and Asian Britons: integration or alienation?', *Parliamentary Affairs*, 38: 307-18.
Lee, P. and Murie, A. (1998), *Poverty, Housing Tenure and Social Exclusion*, London: Polity Press.
Le Lohé, M. (1975), 'Participation in elections by Asians in Bradford', in I. Crewe (ed.), *British Political Sociology Yearbook*, Vol. 2: *The Politics of Race*, London: Croom Helm.
Le Lohé, M. (1983), 'Voter discrimination against Asian and black candidates in the 1983 General Election', *New Community*, 11(1-2): 101-84.
Le Lohé, M. (1989), 'The performance of Asian and black candidates in the British General Election of 1987', *New Community*, 15(2): 159-70.
Le Lohé, M. (1990), 'The Asian vote in a northern city', in H. Gouldbourne (ed.), *Black British Politics*, Aldershot: Avebury.
Le Lohé, M. (1998), 'Ethnic minority participation and representation in the British electoral system', in S. Saggar (ed.), *Race and British Electoral Politics*, London: UCL Press.
Lentze, G. (1998), 'Racial thinking in the Labour Party between 1990 and 1997', unpublished manuscript.
Levin, B. (1978), *The Times*, 14 February.
LGMB (1998), *Survey of Local Authority Councillors in England and Wales*, London: Local Government Management Board.
Lipset, S. (1960), *Political Man: The Social Bases of Politics*, Garden City, NY: Doubleday.
LPRAG (1979), *Don't Take Black Votes for Granted*, London: Labour Party Race Action Group.
Lyon, M. and West, B. J. M. (1995) 'London Patels: caste and commerce', *New Community*, 21(3): 399-419.
McAllister, I. and Studlar, D. (1984), 'The electoral geography of immigrant groups in Britain', *Electoral Studies*, 3(2): 139-50.
Malik, K. (1995), 'Party colours', *New Statesman and Society*, 14 July, p.17.
Mangat, J. S. (1969), *A History of the Asians in East Africa*, Oxford: Clarendon Press.

Manzoor, Z. (1999), Unpublished speech given to a conference organised by the NHS Executive Equal Opportunities Unit on 'Black and minority ethnic non-executive directors in the NHS', London, 12 July.

Marable, M. (1995), *Beyond Black and White: Transforming African-American Politics*, London: Verso.

Messina, A. (1989), *Race and Party Competition in Britain*, Oxford: Clarendon Press.

Messina, A. (1998), 'Ethnic minorities and the British party system in the 1990s and beyond', in S. Saggar (ed.), *Race and British Electoral Politics*, London: UCL Press.

Miles, R. (1978), 'Racism, Marxism and British politics', *Economy and Society*, 17(3), 428–60.

Miles R. and Phizacklea, A. (1984), *White Man's Country: Racism in British Politics*, 1st edn, London: Pluto Press.

Miller, W. (1980), 'What was the profit of following the crowd? Aspects of the Conservative and Labour strategy since 1970', *British Journal of Political Science*, 10, 15–38.

Modood, T. (1990), 'British Asian Muslims and the Rushdie affair', *The Political Quarterly*, 61(2), 143–60.

Mowlam, M. (2000), Speech made to a conference on 'The Corporate Face in Europe', organised by The Runnymede Trust, The Migration Policy Group and The City of Amsterdam, London, 7 February.

MORI (1996), 'Black Britain', *British Public Opinion*, July.

MORI (1997), 'Asian poll: preliminary results', unpublished briefing notes, London: Market and Opinion Research International.

Morris, A. (1992), 'The future of black politics: substance versus process and formality', in L. Barker (ed.), *Ethnic Politics and Civil Liberties – National Political Science Review*, Vol. 3, New Brunswick, NJ: Transaction Publishers and the National Conference of Black Political Scientists.

Mullard, C. (1973), *Black Britain*, London: Allen and Unwin.

Mullard, C. (1985), *Race, Power and Resistance*, London: Routledge and Kegan Paul.

Nanton, P. (1989), 'The new orthodoxy: racial categories and equal opportunities', *New Community*, 15(4), 549–64.

Nazroo, J. (2000), 'Patterns of identity', in S. Saggar, A. Heath and K. Thomson (eds), *Social Change and Minority Ethnic Groups in Britain*, London: The British Academy.

NHS Executive (1999), 'Equal opportunities across the board', *Update*, London: NHS Confederation.

Nie, N. *et al.* (1976), *The Changing American Voter*, Cambridge, MA, Harvard University Press.

Nixon, J. (1982), 'The Home Office and race relations policy: co-ordination and initiation?', *Journal of Public Policy*, 2(4), 369–84.

Nixon, J. (1998), 'The role of black and Asian MPs at Westminster', in S. Saggar (ed.), *Race and British Electoral Politics*, London: UCL Press.

NOP (1978), 'Immigration and race relations', *Social and Economic Review*, 14, 6–8.

NOP (1991), 'Race issues opinion survey' (reported in Kellner, P. and Cohen, N, 'Racism: someone else to blame', *The Independent on Sunday*, 7 July).

Norris, P. (1997a), *Electoral Change in Britain Since 1945*, Oxford: Blackwell.

Norris, P. (1997b), 'British Parliamentary Constituencies 1992–97', unpublished briefing paper Cambridge MA: Harvard University Press.

Norris, P., Geddes, A. and Lovenduski, J. (1992), 'Race and parliamentary representation', in D. Broughton, I. Crewe, D. Denver and P. Norris (eds), *The British Elections and Parties Yearbook 1992*, Hemel Hempstead: Harvester Wheatsheaf.

Norris, P. and Lovenduski, J. (1993), '"If only more candidates came forward ...": supply-side explanations of candidate selection in Britain', *British Journal of Political Science*, 23, 373-408.

Norris, P. and Lovenduski, J. (1995), *Political Recruitment: Gender, Race and Class in the British Parliament*, Cambridge: Cambridge University Press.

Ong, P. (ed.) (2000), *The State of Asian Pacific Americans: Race Relations*, Los Angeles, CA: UCLA Asian Pacific American Public Policy Institute.

Owen, D. (1985), 'Britain's black communities', speech to mark the fourth anniversary of the Limehouse Declaration, London: Social Democratic Party, 24 January.

Owen, D. (1994), 'Black people in Britain: social and economic circumstances', 1991 Census Statistical Paper No. 6, University of Warwick, Centre for Research in Ethnic Relations/National Ethnic Minority Data Archive.

Owen, D. and Green, A. (1992), 'Labour market experience and change among ethnic groups in Great Britain', *New Community*, 19(1), 17-29.

Parekh, B. (1998), 'Integrating minorities', in T. Blackstone, B. Parekh and P. Sanders (eds) (1998), *Race Relations in Britain: A Developing Agenda*, London: Routledge.

Parekh, B. (1999a), 'Britain's Changing Ethnic Profile', The 1999 British Academy Lecture, London, 24 November.

Parekh, B. (1999b), 'From ethnic groups to new Britons', *Connections*, winter 1999/2000, 6-9.

Parmar, P. (1982), 'Gender, race and class: Asian women in resistance', in CCCS (eds), *The Empire Strikes Back*, London: Hutchinson.

Parry, G., Moyser, G. and Day, N. (1992), *Political Participation and Democracy in Britain*, Cambridge: Cambridge University Press.

Pattie, C. and Johnston, R. (1998), 'Voter turnout at the British general election of 1992: rational choice, social standing or political efficacy?', *European Journal of Political Research*, 33, 263-83 .

Peach, C. (1984), 'The force of West Indian island identity in Britain', in C. Clarke *et al.* (eds), *Geography and Ethnic Pluralism*, London: George Allen and Unwin.

Perrigo, S. (1996), 'Women and change in the Labour Party 1979-95', in J. Lovenduski and P. Norris (eds), *Women in Politics*, Oxford: Oxford University Press.

Perry, J. (1992), 'Portrait of the electorate', *Wall Street Journal*, 27 October.

Peston, R. (1994), 'The Tories need "killer facts" to stop electoral death', *The Financial Times*, 21 November.

Phillips, A. (1995), *The Politics of Presence*, Oxford: Oxford University Press.

Pinto-Duschinsky, M. (1997), 'Conservative Party membership', paper presented to the EPOP annual conference, University of Essex, 27 September.

Pitkin, H. (1967), *The Concept of Representation*, Berkely: University of California Press.

Platt, L. and Noble, M. (1999), *Race, Place and Poverty: Ethnic Groups and Low Income Distribution*, York: York Publishing Services/Joseph Rowntree Foundation.

Prashar, U. (1999), Opening remarks made to the 1999/2000 CREST conference on Social Change and Minority Ethnic Groups in Britain (in association with the British Academy), London, 24 November.

Price, S. and Sanders, D. (1993), 'Economic expectations and voting intentions in the UK: a pooled cross-section approach', *Political Studies*, 41(3): 451–71.
Pryce, E. (1990), 'Culture from below: politics, resistance and leadership in the Notting Hill Gate Carnival, 1976–78', in H. Gouldbourne (ed.), *Black Politics in Britain*, Aldershot: Avebury.
Pryce, K. (1979), *Endless Pressure*, Harmondsworth: Penguin.
Pulzer, P. (1967), *Political Representation and Elections in Britain*, London: Allen and Unwin.
Purdham, K. (1998), 'The political identities of Muslim local councillors in Britain', *Manchester Papers in Politics*, No. 3/98.
Pluzer, P. (1967), *Political Representation and Elections in Britain*, London: Allen and Unwin.
Purdham, K. (1999), 'Muslim experiences of democracy and local Labour Party politics in Britain', mimeo.
Race for the Election (1997), campaign statement (untitled), London: Churches Commission for Racial Justice.
Ramesh, R. (1998), 'Few black faces in corridors of power', *The Independent*, 26 March, p. 51.
Rankin, A. (1999), 'If Parliament is to be a mere statistical mirror, 19 per cent should be unable to read and we should recruit more Manchester United supporters', *The Times*, 30 November, p. 24.
Ranger, T., Y. Samad, and O. Stuart (eds) (1996), *Culture, Identity and Politics: Ethnic Minorities in Britain*, Aldershot: Ashgate.
Rath, J. and Saggar, S. (1992), 'Ethnicity as a political tool in Britain and the Netherlands', in A. Messina *et al.* (eds), *Ethnic and Racial Minorities in Advanced Industrial Societies*, New York, Greenwood Press.
Rex, J. and Moore, R. (1967), *Race, Community and Conflict: A Study of Sparkbrook*, Oxford: Oxford University Press.
Rich, P. (1986), 'Conservative ideology and race in modern British politics', in Z. Layton-Henry and P. Rich (eds), *Race, Government and Politics in Britain*, London: Macmillan .
Rich, P. (1998), 'Ethnic politics and the Conservatives in the post-Thatcher era', in S. Saggar (ed.), *Race and British Electoral Politics*, London: UCL Press.
Roach, P. and Morrison, M. (1998), *Public Libraries, Ethnic Diversity and Citizenship*, Coventry: Centre for Research in Ethnic Relations, University of Warwick.
Robertson, D. (1984), *Class and the British Electorate*, Oxford, Basil Blackwell.
Robinson, V. (1990), 'Roots to mobility: the social mobility of Britain's black population, 1971–87', *Ethnic and Racial Studies*, 13 (2), 274–86.
Rodriguez, G. (1999), *From Newcomers to Americans: The Successful Integration of Immigrants into American Society*, Washington DC: National Immigration Forum.
Runnymede Trust, The (1997), *The Runnymede Bulletin*, March, p. 5.
Sabucedo, J. and Cramer, D. (1991), 'Sociological and psychological predictors of voting in Great Britain', *Journal of Social Psychology*, 131: 647–54.
Saggar, S. (1984), 'Ethnic minorities and the 1983 parliamentary election', Department of Government, University of Essex, mimeo.
Saggar, S. (1997a), 'Racial politics', *Parliamentary Affairs*, 50(4): 693–707.
Saggar, S. (1997b), 'The dog that did not bark? Immigration, race and the election', in A. Geddes and J. Tongue (eds), *Labour's Landslide*, Manchester: Manchester University Press.
Saggar, S. (1997c), 'Pipeline politics', *India Today*, 31 March, p. 52.

Saggar, S. (1997d), 'Racial issues and the 1997 general election in Britain', paper presented to the EPOP annual conference, University of Essex, 27 September.
Saggar, S. (1998a), 'Piecing together the puzzle: ethnic and racial politics and the British electoral map', in S. Saggar (ed.), *Race and British Electoral Politics*, London: UCL Press.
Saggar, S. (1998b), 'Ethnic minority political mobilisation in Britain: competing claims and agendas', in M. Martiniello (ed.), *Reflections on Two European Multicultural Societies: Belgium and the United Kingdom*, Utrecht: ERCOMER.
Saggar, S. (ed.) (1998c), *Race and British Electoral Politics*, London: UCL Press.
Saggar, S. (1998d), 'A late, though not lost, opportunity: British ethnic minority electors and the Conservative Party', *The Political Quarterly*, 69(2): 148–59.
Saggar, S. (1998e), 'Smoking guns and magic bullets: The "race card" debate revisited in 1997', *Immigrants and Minorities*, 17(8): 1–21.
Saggar, S. (1998f), 'British south Asian elites and political participation: testing the cultural thesis', *Revue Européene des Migrations Internationales*, 14(2): 51–70.
Saggar, S. (1998g), *Ethnic Minorities and Electoral Politics: The 1997 General Election*, London: Commission for Racial Equality.
Saggar, S. (1999), 'Where the black vote goes', *Guardian*, 26 November, p. 20.
Saggar, S. (2000a), 'Asians and race relations in Britain', in P. Ong (ed.), *The State of Asian Pacific Americans: Race Relations*, Los Angeles CA: UCLA Asian Pacific American Public Policy Institute.
Saggar, S. (2000b), 'Asian politics in Britain', in J. Ramsden (ed.), *The Oxford Companion to Twentieth Century British Politics*, Oxford: Oxford University Press.
Saggar, S. (2000c), 'Testing claims about south Asian political leverage in the British political system', *The Indo-British Review*, forthcoming.
Saggar, S. and Heath, A. (1999), 'Race: towards a multicultural electorate?', in P. Norris and G. Evans (eds), *Critical Elections: British Parties and Voters in Long-term Perspective*, London: Sage.
Saggar, S., Thomson, K. and Heath, A. (eds) (2000), *Social Change and Minority Ethnic Groups in Britain*, London: The British Academy and Oxford University Press.
Saggar, S. and Geddes, A. (2000), 'Positive and negative racialisation: ethnic minority political representation in the UK', *Journal of Ethnic and Migration Studies,* 26(1): 1–20.
Samad, Y. (1993), 'Imagining a British Muslim identification', paper presented to a conference on 'Islam in Europe: Generation to Generation', St Catherine's College, Oxford.
Samad, Y. (1996), 'The politics of Islamic identity among Bangladeshi and Pakistanis in Britain', in T. Ranger, Y. Samad and O. Stewart (eds), *Culture, Identity and Politics Ethnic Minorities in Britain*, Aldershot: Avebury.
Sanders, D. (1999), 'The impact of left-right ideology' in P. Norris and G. Evans (eds), *Critical Elections: British Parties and Voters in Long-term Perspective*, London: Sage.
Sarlvik, B. and Crewe, I. (1983), *Decade of Dealignment*, Cambridge: Cambridge University Press.
Schaffer, S. (1981), 'A multivariate explanation of decreasing turnout in presidential elections, 1960–76', *American Journal of Political Science*, 25: 68–95.
Schiele, J. (1990), 'Organisational theory from an Afrocentric perspective', *Journal of Black Studies*, 21(2): 38–56.

Seyd, P. and Whiteley, P. (1992), *Labour's Grassroots: The Politics of Party Membership*, Oxford: Clarendon Press.
Sewell, T. (1993), *Black Tribunes: Black Political Participation in Britain*, London: Lawrence and Wishart.
Shaw, A. (1994), 'The Pakistani community in Oxford', in R. Ballard (ed.), *Desh Pardesh: The South Asian Presence in Britain*, London: Hurst.
Shukra, K. (1990), 'Black Sections in the Labour Party', in H. Gouldbourne (ed.), *Black Politics in Britain*, Aldershot: Avebury.
Shukra, K. (1998a), 'New Labour debates and dilemmas', in S. Saggar (ed.), *Race and British Electoral Politics*, London: UCL Press..
Shukra, K. (1998b), *The Changing Pattern of Black Politics in Britain*, London: Pluto.
Sia (1994), *Agenda 2000: The Black Perspective*, Conference Report, London: Sia.
Sivanandan, A. (1983), 'Challenging racism: strategies for the 1980s', *Race and Class*, 25(2).
Small, S. (1994), *Racialised Barriers*, London: Routledge.
Smith, M. and Spear, J. (eds) (1992), *The Changing Labour Party*, London: Routledge.
Sooben, P. (1990), *The Origins of the Race Relations Act*, Research Paper in Ethnic Relations No. 12, Coventry: Centre for Research in Ethnic Relations, University of Warwick.
Southall Rights/CARF (1981), *Southall: Birth of a Black Community*, London: Southall Rights and the Campaign Against Racism and Fascism.
Spencer, I. (1997), *British Immigration Policy Since 1939*, London: Routledge.
Statham, P. (1999), 'Political mobilisation by minorities in Britain: negative feedback of "race relations"?', *Journal of Ethnic and Migration Studies*, 25(4): 597–626.
Steele, S. (1990), *The Content of Our Character*, New York: St Martin's Press.
Studlar, D. (1974), 'British public opinion, colour issues and Enoch Powell: a longitudinal analysis', *British Journal of Political Science*, 4, 371–81.
Studlar, D. (1978), 'Policy voting in Britain: The coloured immigration issue in the 1964, 1966 and 1970 general elections', *American Political Science Review*, 72: 46–72.
Studlar, D. (1983), 'The ethnic vote 1983: problems of analysis and interpretation', *New Community*, 11: 92–100.
Studlar, D. (1985), 'Waiting for the catastrophe: race and the political agenda in Britain', *Patterns of Prejudice*, 19 (1): 3–15.
Studlar, D. (1986), 'Non-white policy preferences, political participation and the political agenda in Britain', in Z. Layton-Henry and P. Rich (eds), *Race, Government and Politics in Britain*, London: Macmillan.
Studlar, D. (1993), 'Ethnic minority groups, agenda setting and policy borrowing in Britain', in P. McClain (ed.), *Minority Group Influence: Agenda Setting, Formulation and Public Policy*, Greenwood, Conn.: Greenwood Press.
Studlar, D. and Layton-Henry, Z. (1990), 'Non-white access to the political agenda in Britain', *Policy Studies Review*, 9(2): 273–93.
Surridge, P. *et al.* (1999), 'Scotland: constitutional preferences and voting behaviour', in P. Norris and G. Evans (eds), *Critical Elections: British Parties and Voters in Long-term perspective*, London: Sage, pp. 223–39.
Swaddle, K. and Heath, A. (1989), 'Official and reported turnout in the British general election of 1987', *British Journal of Political Science*, 19: 537–70.
Swain, C. (1993), *Black Faces, Black Interests: The Representation of African-Americans in Congress*, Cambridge MA: Harvard University Press.

The Times (1995), 'Duck and weave: new laws for an election campaign that is well under way', 16 November.
The Times (1997a), 2 April, p. 14.
The Times (1997b), 'Election results 1997', 3 May.
The Times (1997c), 'Race to be modern' (editorial), 9 October, p. 21.
The Times (1997d), 'Ethnic minorities 50 per cent more likely to fall ill', 5 August, p. 7.
The Times (1998), 'Unhappy anniversary' (editorial), 19 June, p. 25.
The Times (1999), 'No token choice' (business news editorial), 27 April, p. 29.
Troyna, B. (1979), 'Differential commitment of ethnic identity by black youths in Britain', *New Community*, 7(3).
TUC (1999), *Black and Excluded*, London: Trades Union Congress.
UCAS (1998), *Applications to Universities and Colleges in the United Kingdom*, Cheltenham: Universities Central Admissions System.
UKACIA (1997), *Elections 1997 and British Muslims*, London: United Kingdom Action Committee on Islamic Affairs.
Verba, S. and Nie, N. (1972), *Participation in America: Political Democracy and Social Equality*, New York: Harper and Row.
Vertovec, S. (1996), 'On the reproduction and representation of Hinduism in Britain', in T. Ranger, Y. Samad and O. Stewart (eds), *Culture, Identity and Politics Ethnic Minorities in Britain*, Aldershot: Avebury.
Virdee, S. (2000), 'Explaining racial disadvantage in the labour market', in S. Saggar, K. Thomson and A. Heath (eds), *Social Change and Minority Ethnic Groups in Britain*, London: The British Academy.
Wald, K. (1983), *Crosses on the Ballot: Patterns of British Voter Alignment since 1885*, Princeton NJ: Princeton University Press.
Weakliem, D. and Heath, A. (1999), 'The secret life of class voting: Britain, France and the United States since the 1930s', in G. Evans (ed.), *The End of Class Politics? Class Voting in Comparative Context*, Oxford: Oxford University Press.
Weil, P. (1996), 'Nationalities and citizenships: the lessons of the French experience for Germany and Europe', in D. Cesarani and M. Fulbrook (eds), *Citizenship, Nationality and Migration in Europe*, London: Routledge.
Werbner, P. (1991a), 'Black and ethnic leaderships: a theoretical view', in P. Werbner and M. Anwar (eds), *Black and Ethnic Leaderships: The Cultural Dimensions of Political Action*, London: Routledge.
Werbner, P. (1991b), 'The fiction of unity in ethnic politics: aspects of representation and the state among Manchester Pakistanis', in P. Werbner and Anwar, M (eds), *Black and Ethnic Leaderships: The Cultural Dimensions of Political Action*, London: Routledge.
Werbner, P. and M. Anwar (eds) (1991), *Black and Ethnic Leaderships: The Cultural Dimensions of Political Action*, London: Routledge.
Whiteley, P., Seyd, P. and Richardson, J. (1994), *True Blues: The Politics of the Conservative Party*, Oxford: Oxford University Press.
Woolley, S. (1997), News report, *Evening Standard*, 8 January.
Wrench, J. *et al.* (1993), *Invisible Minorities: Racism in New Towns and New Contexts*, Coventry: ESRC Centre for Research in Ethnic Relations, University of Warwick.
Young, K. (1983), 'Ethnic pluralism and the policy agenda in Britain', in N. Glazer and K. Young (eds), *Ethnic Pluralism and Public Policy: Achieving Equality in the United States and Britain*, London: Heinemann.
Zee TV (1997), 'Asian poll', unpublished briefing notes, London: Zee Television.

Index

Note: first name initials only given for academic authors and journalists; full first names given for all others; 'fn' after a page reference indicates a note on that page.

Abbott, Diane 10, 71
abstention *see* electoral abstention
Adolino, J. 25fn
affirmative action 13, 236
African-Americans 4
Ageyman, J. 62
Alderman, G. 56
Ali, A. 20, 41-2, 122
Ali, Y. 18
Alibhai-Brown, Y. 11, 21, 39, 148, 158
alienation hypothesis 105-18
anti-discrimination laws, effectiveness of 163-4
American Political Science Association (APSA) 57fn
Amery, Julian 202
Amin, K. 17, 51-2, 72-3, 128
Anionwu, E. 226
Anwar, M. 2-3, 19, 86, 91, 95, 98-100, 102, 152
Asian-Americans 4
Asian conservatism 173-4
'Asian marginals' 93
Atkin, K. 226
Azim, W. 3, 6, 149, 152

Back, L. 26
Bald, S. 16, 227
Ballard, R. 93, 229
Beer, S. 14
Behrens, R. 80
Belgium 42
Berthoud, R. 50, 58fn, 62, 98, 112
Bethnal Green and Bow 6, 84, 238
Bhachu, P. 55

Biggs-Davidson, John 181
Billig, M. 178
Birmingham Small Heath 72
Blackaby, D. 228
black and Asian MPs, attitudes towards increased representation 213
Black Sections *see* Labour Party
Blackstone, Tessa (Baroness) 7, 148
Blair, Tony 158
Boateng, Paul 209
Bonnet, A. 62
Bourne, J. 61
Bradford xv, 227
Bradford North by-election, November 1990 215
Bradford West 25fn, 84, 238
Brand, J. 123
Braunholtz, Simon 118fn
Brentford and Isleworth 72
British Broadcasting Corporation (BBC) 21, 33, 41, 49, 67, 71, 121, 136
British Council 57fn
British Candidate Survey (BCS) (1992) 207-8
British Crime Survey 223
British Election Study (BES)
  1966 survey 184
  1960s and 1970s evidence on immigration 195
  cross-section survey xix-xx, 21-2, 24fn, 58fn, 77, 97, 126, 128, 147fn, 151, 161, 221, 223, 244
  ethnic minority boost 165, 221, 224, 245-6
  Scottish boost 244

British Ethnic Minority Election Study xix
British history 158-9
British national history 36
British Nationality Act (1981) 44, 79, 180, 186
British National Party (BNP) 95, 118fn, 178
British Social Attitudes (BSA), 15th Report 195-6
Brixton 36
Broadcasting Standards Commission (BSC) 10
Brook, L. xx
Brown, A. 25fn, 123
Brown, J. 225
Budge, I. 12
Buscombe, Peta (Baroness) xx, 55, 90
Butler, D. xix, 48, 134, 177, 184

Callaghan, James 183
Campaign Against Racism and Fascism (CARF) 33
Canada 42
Carrington, Peter (Lord) 181
Catt, H. 4, 12
Census
  1971 40, 62-3, 87fn
  1981 93
  1991 24fn, 50, 55, 62, 93-4, 141, 225, 229
  2001 58fn
Centre for Research in Ethnic Relations (CRER) 118fn
Centre for Research into Elections and Social Trends (CREST) xix
Cheltenham 46, 71, 207, 209
Cheng, Y. 21
Chinese xi, 24fn
  respondents, exclusion of 243
  voters 135, 147fn
Churchill, Winston (Jnr) 202
citizenship influences upon voting 94-8
Clapham 209
Clarke, K. 228
class *see* social class
Commission for Racial Equality (CRE) xii, xix, 10, 19, 20, 41-2, 44-5, 49-50, 57fn, 64, 66-7, 70, 78-9, 89, 91, 99, 122, 128, 181

Community Relations Commission (CRC) xv, 20, 39-40, 42, 57fn, 61-3, 66, 87fn, 122
Cohen, N. 30-1, 157
Coleman, D. 62, 150
Commonwealth citizenship 99
Commonwealth Immigrants Bill (1968) 74
comparative research xvii
community values 56
Conservative Party
  Anglo-Asian Conservative Society 39, 181
  Anglo-West Indian Society 39
  Community Affairs Department 65
  New Right wing 181
  One Nation Forum 46
  One Nation wing 181-2, 189
  perceived concern for blacks and Asians 187-91
  and Powellism/Powellites 80-4
  Shadow Home Secretary (1976) 82
  support among Indians 223
Crewe, I. 3-5, 25fn, 28, 34, 54, 65, 91, 138, 175, 177, 183, 191-2, 195
criminal sentencing policy 172
Crossman, Richard (Dick) 183
Crowley, J. xix, 95
cultural relativism 165-7
cultural thesis 55-7, 127, 173-4, 224
'culture of resistance' 53
Curtice, J. xix, 4, 12, 118fn, 137, 185, 190

Dahya, B. 27
Deakin, N. 17, 61, 152
Dean, D. 74
demographic influences upon voting 93-4
Deva, Nirj 218
Downsian, perspective of Tory strategy 180
dress codes, separate 163, 165-7
Drinkwater, S. 228
Dublin Convention (1990) 202fn
dual citizenship rates 96-7

Eade, J. 6, 18, 32, 102
East African Asians 55, 74, 228
East African nationality crises 96
East Asians groups 147fn

Economic and Social Research Council (ESRC) xii, xix
Edmonds, J. 80
educational qualifications and vote 142
electoral abstention, debates over 114–18
electoral register, age of 118fn
Elmer, N. 134
Environment, Department of the 182
'equal opportunities conservatives' 200
equal opportunities for blacks and Asians, ethnic minority views on party positions 200–1
'equal shares'/'fair shares' doctrine 13
Espiritu, Y. L. 4
'ethnic bloc' voting 3, 28, 63, 92, 138
ethnic enclave parties 214–17
'ethnicity counts'/'ethnicity matters' school of thought 5, 7, 86–7, 124, 222, 235
ethnicity as a variable 27–8
ethnic group sources of party support 130–4
'ethnic marginals' xiii, 20, 40, 57fn, 63, 91
ethnic minority political interests, debates over 217–20
ethnic monitoring (of electoral registration) 100
ethnic neighbourhood effect 142–4
'ethnic safe seats' 28, 85
Evans, G. 134
Evening Standard 37
Eurobarometer data 184
European Union (EU), anti-immigrant/foreigner sentiment within 184

'fair shares' *see* 'equal shares'
Field, S. 32
Finland 184
FitzGerald, M. 2, 21, 29, 41, 51, 61, 73, 80, 122, 152, 156
Fletcher, W. 29
Foot, P. 61
Foot, R. 225
Fourth Party 215
France 1
Frasure, R. 81
Frazer, L. 134
Fritchie, Rennie (Dame) 10

Gallup 33, 49, 67, 21, 136–7
gays 12
Guardian 36, 65, 75, 91, 100, 118fn
Geddes, A. xix, 6, 47, 91, 102, 123, 151, 206, 208–10
gender
  influences upon non-participation 111–12
  and vote 12, 19, 23
general election
  1964 178
  1970 177, 186
  1974 (February) 87fn
  1974 (October) 61–4, 87fn
  1979 64–6, 177
  1983 66–8, 181
  1987 68–70, 121
  1992 70–2, 121, 176–8
generation(al)
  and attitudes towards race 193–4
  influences on participation 106–8
  and voting 12, 19, 69–70
Germany 1, 95
Gillan, C. 38
Gilroy, P. 9
Glazer, N. 215
Golding, P. 178
Goldthorpe, J. 135
Gordon, P. 80, 118fn
Gordon-Walker, Patrick 178
Gouldbourne, H. 1, 3, 28, 149
graduate *see* 'overseas graduate effect'
Greater London 51
Greater London Council (GLC) 21
Greece 184
Green, A. 50
Gregory, R. 228
Groce, Cherry 35
Gyford, J. 42

Hackney North and Stoke Newington 71
Hall, S. 18
Hann, Colin xx
Hansard 218
Hansib Publishing Group 20
Hardy, J. 178
Hargreaves, A. 95
Harris Research Centre 20–1, 30–1, 34, 42, 49, 54, 67–9, 77, 83, 122, 159, 161, 211
Heseltine, Michael 181–2

Hattersley, Roy (Lord) 155-6
healthcare 37
Heath, A. xix, 5, 7, 21-3, 27-8, 49, 51, 58fn, 76, 84, 112, 137, 185, 190, 248
Heath, Sir Edward 53, 179
Hertfordshire West 209
Hewitt, Patricia 15
Heywood, P. 12
Hill, M. 18
higher education 146
Hofferbert, R. 12
Holmes, C. 176
Home Office 182
House of Lords 174fn
housing tenure and vote 142
Howe, D. 41
Husbands, C. 178

Iberia 42
Ignatieff, M. 150
immigrants
    attitudes towards customs and traditions of 168-9
    attitudes towards past immigration 167-8
Immigration Act (1971) 186
immigration issue 160-1
Indian Emergency Rule (1975-7) 228, 241fn
Indian Independence (1947) 74
indirect representation 59
Indo-Chinese respondents, exclusion of xi, 24fn, 243
Institute for Public Policy Research (IPPR) 21, 158-9
'institutional racism' 154
Irish xi
'iron law' of ethnic minority voting 120-1, 124-5, 128
Islamic Party of Great Britain 215
Isle of Dogs local by-election 1993 239
Issacharoff, R. 18
issue voting 51-4
Italy 95

Jacobs, B. 5, 65
James, S. 149
Jeffers, S. 61
Jenkins, Roy (Lord) 74
Jewish-Asian parallels 56

Jewish refugees 176
Johnson, P. 37
Johnston, R. 8
Jones, R. W. xix
Josephedes, S. 2
Jowell, R. xix, 12, 137, 195

Kalka, I. 18
Kalra V.S. 93
Katznelson, I. 18
Keith, M. 9
Kellner, P. xix, 12, 30-1, 90, 157
Kenya 228
Kenyan Asians 53, 186
Keynesian consensus 180
Khabra, Piara 71, 218
Khamis, C. 102
Knowles, C. 61
KPMG see KPMG/LWT
KPMG/LWT 89-91
Kumar, Ashok 241fn

Labour Force Survey (LFS) 24fn 34, 50, 58fn, 93
Labour Government (1964-70) 87fn
Labour Party
    affiliation with ethnic minorities, debates over 43-7, 72-80
    Black Sections 29, 46, 155-6
    ethnic minority bias towards 4
    'ethnic minority-friendly party' slogan 235
    Foreign Secretary-designate see Gordon-Walker, Patrick
    perceived concern for blacks and Asians 187-91
    Race Action Group (LPRAG) 20, 155
Lansley, Andrew 179
Lawler, S. 65
Lawrence, Stephen 150, 154-5, 234
Layton-Henry, Z. xix, 1, 3, 8-9, 18, 44, 62, 66, 71, 86, 94, 177
Leaman, A. 95
learning from other countries, British attitudes towards 196-9
Lee, P. 58fn
Leicester East 71
Lenze, G. 61
Le Lohé, M. 12-13, 16, 47, 87fn, 91-2, 100, 102, 119fn, 147fn, 183, 208, 210, 225, 227

Levin, Bernard 182
Liberal Democrats 38, 46
Liberal-SDP Alliance 68
linguistic groups 12
Lipset, S. 48
Little Englanders 236
Liverpool 147fn
Local Government Management Board (LGMB) 183
London Business School (LBS) xx
Lord Chancellor's Department (LCD) 118fn
Lovenduski, J. xix, 14, 47, 205
LWT *see* KPMG/LWT
Lyon, M. 6

McAllister, I. 3, 34
McMahon, D. 21, 23, 112
Macpherson Report 155, 234
Madden, M. 31, 212
mainstream issues 171–4
mandate representation, theories of 16
Mangat, J. S. 228
Manzoor, Z. 14
Malik, K. 26
Marable, M. 4, 13, 17, 211, 217
Martiniello, M. xix
Mediterranean groups xi
Merchant, K. xx
Messina, A. xix, 2, 5, 9, 17, 26, 61, 65, 71, 73, 78, 80–1, 86–7, 123, 152–3, 177, 226
Metropolitan Police Force 154
'microcosm politics' 89, 203
Middle Eastern groups xi
Middlesborough South and Cleveland East 241fn
Miles, R. 30, 157, 181
Miller, W. 23, 175, 177, 186
Modood, T. 152
Moore, R. 145
Market and Opinion Research International (MORI) 31, 33, 49–50, 58fn, 77–8, 83, 98, 118fn, 126, 147fn, 211
Morris, A. 32
Morrison, M. 58fn
Mowlam, Mo 80
Moynihan, P. 215
Mullard, C. 30, 152
Murie, A. 58fn
Muslim identity 152

Nanton, P. 42
National Centre for Social Research (NCSR) xx, 242
National Opinion Polls (NOP) 20, 30–1, 51, 83, 102, 128, 138, 157, 159
Nazroo, J. 27
Newcastle 147fn
New Commonwealth and Pakistan (NCWP) 40
New Commonwealth citizenship 94
New Labour 190
Newport, E. 29
Nie, J. 27
NHS Executive 10
Nixon, J. 9, 206, 218
Noble, M. 149
non-participation, reasons given for and attitudes towards 108–11
Norris, P. xix, 5, 14, 24fn, 47, 63, 205, 207
Northampton South 229fn
Northern Ireland 214

Omi, M. 4
Ong, P. 4
Operation Black Vote (OBV) 131
'overseas graduate effect' 146–7
Owen, D. 50, 118fn
Owen, David (Lord) 69

Pakistani Independence (1947) 74
parallel agendas 35–7
Parekh, B. (Lord) 24fn, 149, 173
Park, A. xx
Parmar, P. 29
Parry, G. 207
Pattie, C. 8
Peach, C. 70
pensions 37
Percival, G. 20, 41–2, 122
Perrigo, S. 14
Peston, R. 179
petty bourgeoise 142–3
Phillips, A. 12
Phizacklea, A. 181
Pidcock, Daud 215
Pinto-Duschinsky, M. 12, 75
Pitkin, H. 14
Pitt, David (Lord) 209–10
Platt, J. 149
political integration of ethnic

minorities, the theory of 7–10, 230–4
political motives of parties, views of ethnic minorities 199–202
'politics of presence' 12
positive discrimination, attitudes towards 169–70, 194
Post Office Address Files (PAF) 245
poverty, government spending to tackle 171
Powell, J. Enoch 80, 179, 186
Powellites 236
Prashar, Usha (Baroness) xix, 2
Price, S. 48
'primary purpose' immigration rules 45, 79, 202fn
prisons 37
Pryce, E. 29
Pryce, K. 9
public appointments 10
Pulzer, P. 48, 134
Purdham, K. 25fn, 151

'race agenda' 29–33, 153–60
'race trumps class' slogan 235
racial prejudice, extent of 162
Race for the Election 90
Race Relations Act
  1965 180, 189
  1968 180, 189
  1976 180, 189
Race Relations (Amendment) Bill (1999) 174fn, 236–7
Race Relations Bill 1976 81, 174fn, 202fn
racial attacks 30
racial attitudes, bleakness of 192–6
racism and housing 145
Ramesh, R. 214
Ranger, T. 6
Rankin, A. 12
Rath, J. 33
rational choice model 53
registration 98–101
relative class voting 139–41
religious groups 12
responsible party government, the theory of 12
'reverse Apartheid' 156
Rex, J. 145
Rich, P. 38–9, 177, 181
Richardson, R. 17, 51–2, 72–3, 128

Roach, P. 58fn
Robertson 48, 134
Robinson, V. 34, 97
Rodriquez, G. 32
Rollings, R. 226
'rotten borough' claims 120
Runnymede Trust, the 12, 71–2, 118fn
Rushdie affair 31, 149, 152, 212

'same ethnicity' representation 210–14
Salt, J. 62
Samad, Y. 6, 27
Sanders, D. xix, 48, 56
Sarlvik, B. 54, 177, 191
Scarman, Leslie (Lord) 182
Schaffer, B. 8
Schengen Agreement (1985) 202fn
Schiele, J. 29
Scottish electorate 25fn
Scottish nationalists 147fn
Sewell, T. 5
Seyd, P. 45, 206
Shaw, A. 70
Sheffield 147fn
Shukra, K. 2, 3, 8–10, 19, 23, 28–9, 41, 61, 73, 124, 179, 215, 225
Sikh 25fn
Sia 9
Sivanandan, A. 10
Small, S. 2
Smethwick 178–9
Smith, M. 14
Social and Community Planning (SCPR) 242, 245
social class 6–7, 12, 48–51, 68, 72, 75–6, 134–47
Sooben, P. 9
Spain 95
Spear, J. 14
Spencer, S. 96
Spooner, R. 62
South Asians and electoral alignment 224
Southall 33, 72
Southall Rights 33
southeast Asian groups xi, 24fn, 147fn
Southern Confederacy (US) 158
Statham, P. 148
Steele, S. 32
Stokes, D. 48, 134, 177, 184
Studlar, D. 29, 34, 51, 66, 86, 152, 175, 177, 186

Swaddle, K. 22

Tanzania 228
Taylor, John 46, 71, 207
terminology, convention on xi-xii
Thatcher, Margaret 81, 179, 182
Thomson, K. xx
Time Out 214
Times, The 75, 93, 150, 179, 223
Tower Hamlets 46
Trades Union Congress (TUC) 5
Treaty of Amsterdam (1997) 202fn
Treaty on European Union (1992) 202fn
Troyna, B. 30, 157
turn out 101-5

Universities Central Admissions System (UCAS) 173
Uganda 228
Uganda Asians 53, 81, 179, 186
UKACIA 90
under-representation debates 205-7
US racial politics 217

US voters 27

Vara, Shailesh 229fn
Vaz, K. 31, 71, 212
Verba, S. 27
Vertovec, S. 96
Virdee, S. xix, 50
Voice, The 119fn

Wald, K. 134
Weakliem, D. 76
Welsh nationalists 147fn
Werbner, P. 2, xx, 28, 74, 86, 152
white 'backlash' 42
Whitelaw, William (Lord) 181
Whiteley, P. 5, 45, 81, 206
women, equal opportunities for 173
Woolley, S. xx, 37
Wrench, J. 62

Young, Sir George 182
Young, K. xx, 9

Zee TV 93, 229

EU authorised representative for GPSR:
Easy Access System Europe, Mustamäe tee 50,
10621 Tallinn, Estonia
gpsr.requests@easproject.com

www.ingramcontent.com/pod-product-compliance
Ingram Content Group UK Ltd.
Pitfield, Milton Keynes, MK11 3LW, UK
UKHW021836140426
5217IPUK00021B/1485